BATMAN™

ARKHAM UNHINGED™

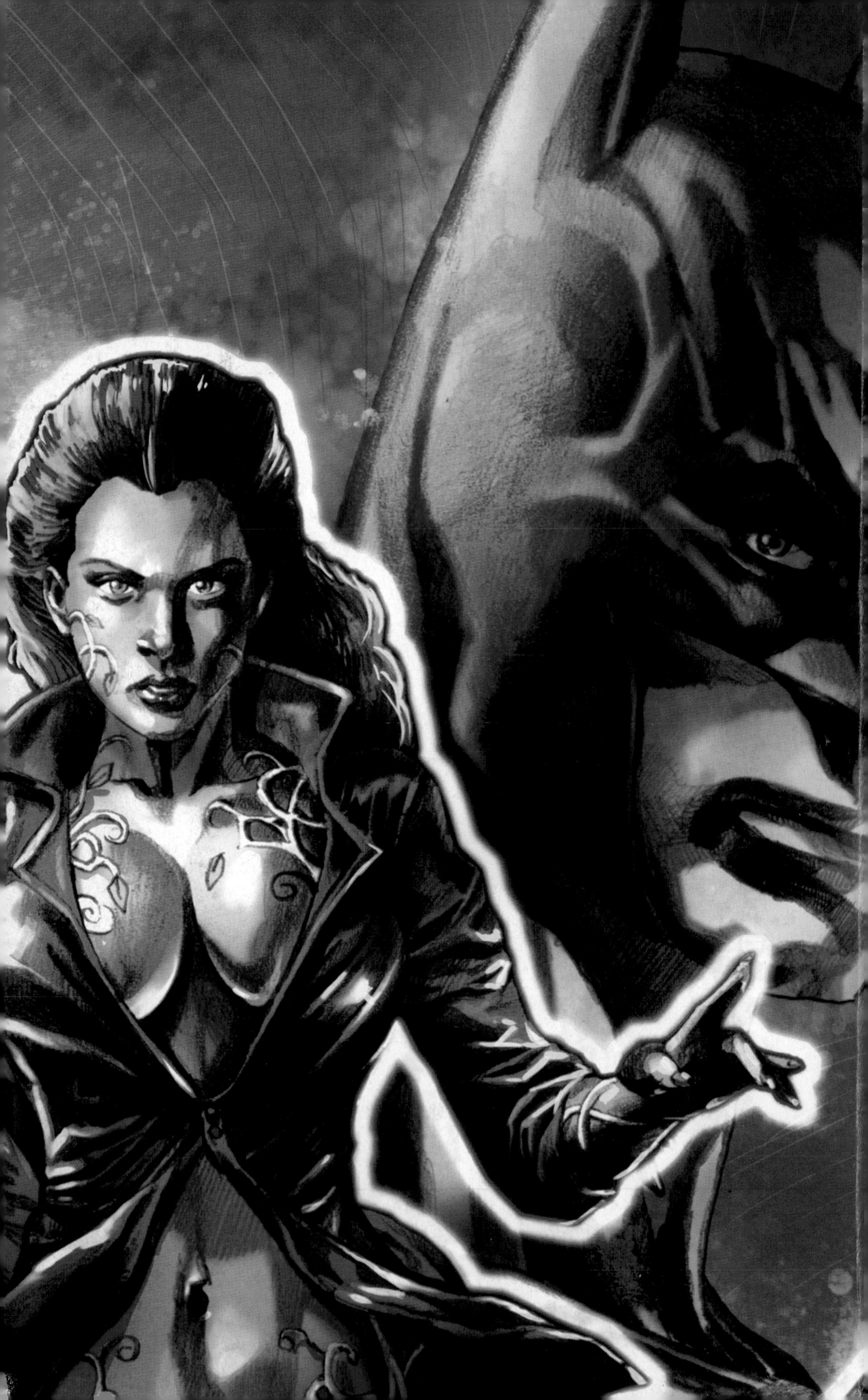

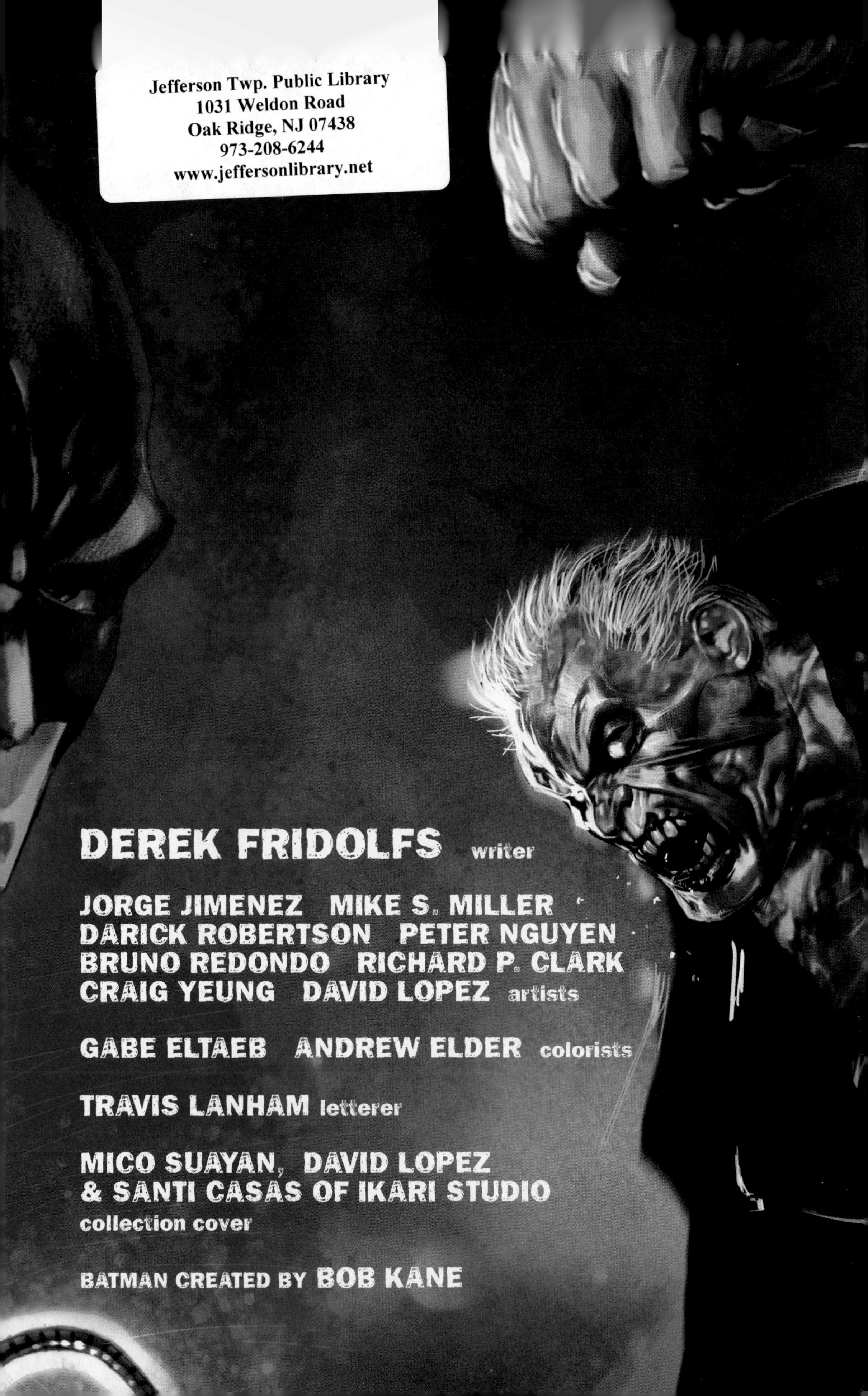

DEREK FRIDOLFS writer

**JORGE JIMENEZ MIKE S. MILLER
DARICK ROBERTSON PETER NGUYEN
BRUNO REDONDO RICHARD P. CLARK
CRAIG YEUNG DAVID LOPEZ** artists

GABE ELTAEB ANDREW ELDER colorists

TRAVIS LANHAM letterer

**MICO SUAYAN, DAVID LOPEZ
& SANTI CASAS OF IKARI STUDIO**
collection cover

BATMAN CREATED BY **BOB KANE**

Jim Chadwick Editor – Original Series
Sarah Gaydos Assistant Editor – Original Series
Robin Wildman Editor
Robbin Brosterman Design Director – Books
Louis Prandi Publication Design

Hank Kanalz Senior VP – Vertigo & Integrated Publishing

Diane Nelson President
Dan DiDio and Jim Lee Co-Publishers
Geoff Johns Chief Creative Officer
John Rood Executive VP – Sales, Marketing and Business Development
Amy Genkins Senior VP – Business and Legal Affairs
Nairi Gardiner Senior VP – Finance
Jeff Boison VP – Publishing Planning
Mark Chiarello VP – Art Direction and Design
John Cunningham VP – Marketing
Terri Cunningham VP – Editorial Administration
Alison Gill Senior VP – Manufacturing and Operations
Jay Kogan VP – Business and Legal Affairs, Publishing
Jack Mahan VP – Business Affairs, Talent
Nick Napolitano VP – Manufacturing Administration
Courtney Simmons Senior VP – Publicity
Bob Wayne Senior VP – Sales

BATMAN: ARKHAM UNHINGED VOLUME 2

Published by DC Comics. Compilation Copyright © 2013 DC Comics. All Rights Reserved.

Originally published in BATMAN: ARKHAM UNHINGED Digital Chapters 14-28 Copyright © 2012, 2013
DC Comics. All Rights Reserved. All characters, their distinctive likenesses and related elements
featured in this publication are trademarks of DC Comics. The stories, characters and incidents
featured in this publication are entirely fictional. DC Comics does not read or accept unsolicited
ideas, stories or artwork.

DC Comics, 1700 Broadway, New York, NY 10019
A Warner Bros. Entertainment Company.
Printed by RR Donnelley, Salem, VA, USA. 11/29/13. First Printing.
ISBN: 978-1-4012-4283-1

Library of Congress Cataloging-in-Publication Data

Fridolfs, Derek.
  Batman : Arkham unhinged. Volume 2 / Derek Fridolfs.
     pages cm. — (Batman: Arkham Unhinged)
  "Originally published in Batman: Arkham Unhinged, Digital Chapters 14-28."
  ISBN 978-1-4012-4019-6
  1. Graphic novels. I. Title.
  PN6728.B36F76 2013
  741.5'973—dc23
                    2013010706

SUSTAINABLE FORESTRY INITIATIVE
Certified Chain of Custody
At Least 20% Certified Forest Content
www.sfiprogram.org
SFI-01042
APPLIES TO TEXT STOCK ONLY

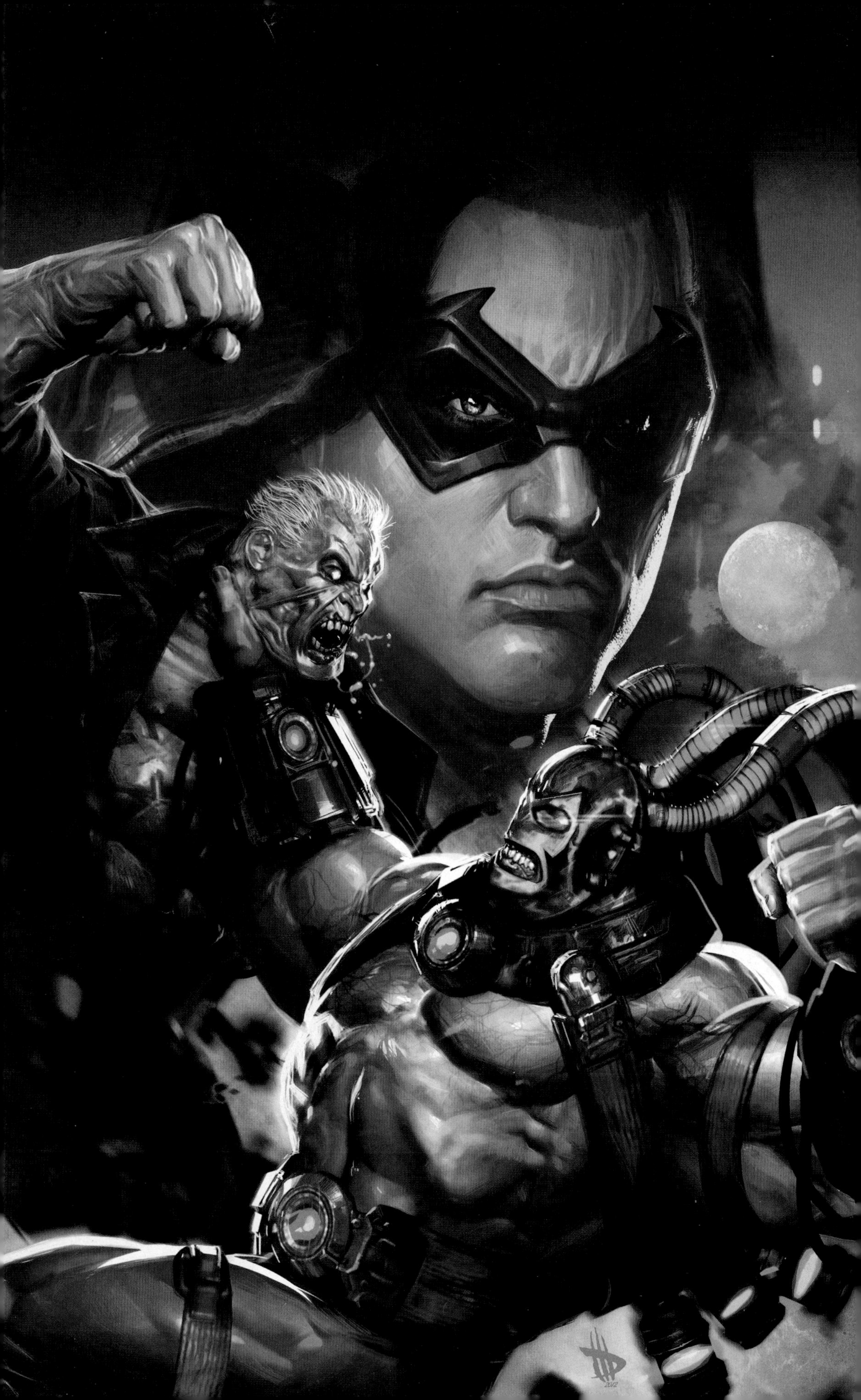

THEATRE OF VIOLENCE

WRITTEN BY: DEREK FRIDOLFS

ART BY: JORGE JIMENEZ

COLORS BY: GABE ELTAEB

LETTERS BY: TRAVIS LANHAM

COVER BY: DAVE WILKINS

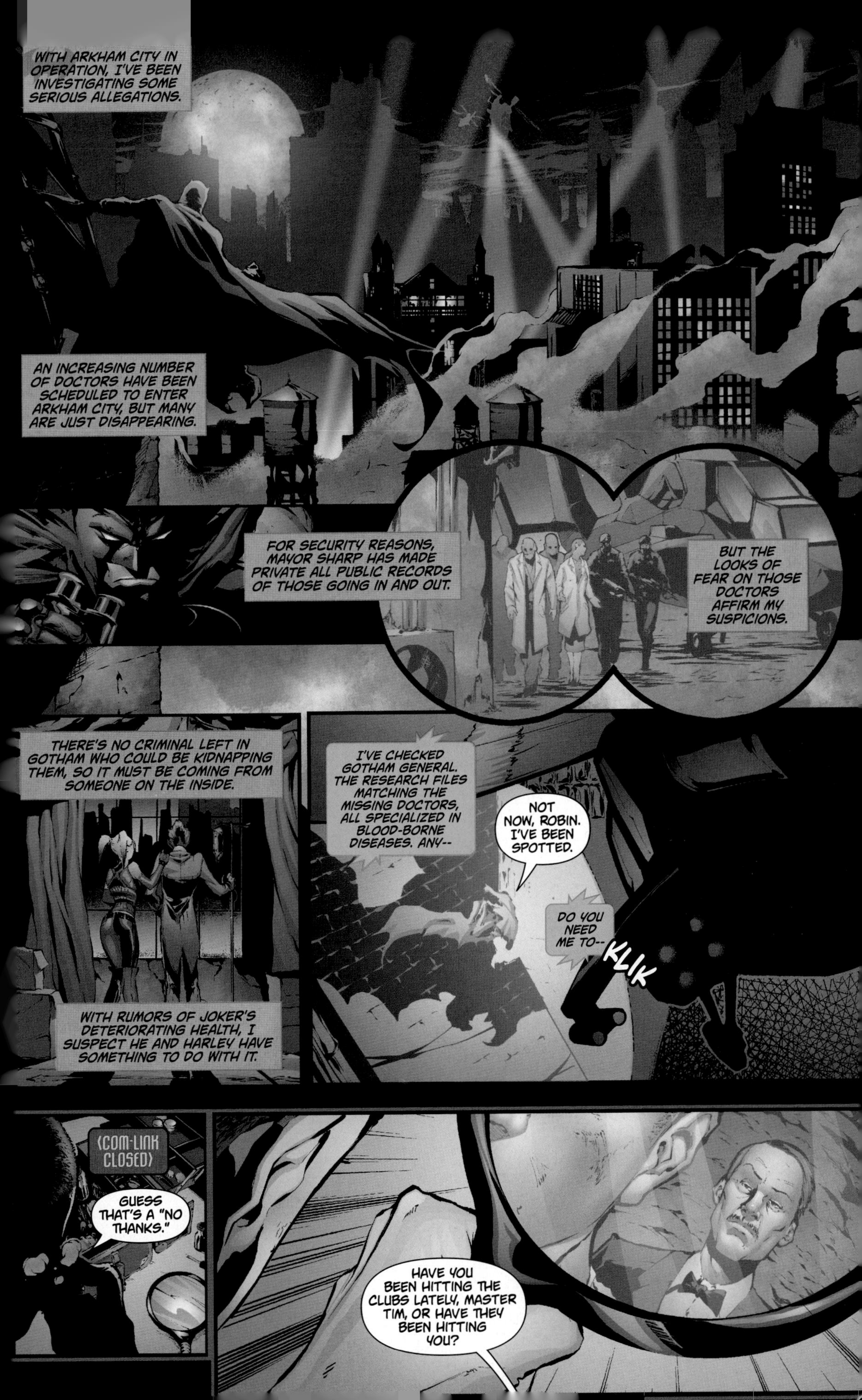
WITH ARKHAM CITY IN OPERATION, I'VE BEEN INVESTIGATING SOME SERIOUS ALLEGATIONS.
AN INCREASING NUMBER OF DOCTORS HAVE BEEN SCHEDULED TO ENTER ARKHAM CITY, BUT MANY ARE JUST DISAPPEARING.
FOR SECURITY REASONS, MAYOR SHARP HAS MADE PRIVATE ALL PUBLIC RECORDS OF THOSE GOING IN AND OUT.
BUT THE LOOKS OF FEAR ON THOSE DOCTORS AFFIRM MY SUSPICIONS.
THERE'S NO CRIMINAL LEFT IN GOTHAM WHO COULD BE KIDNAPPING THEM, SO IT MUST BE COMING FROM SOMEONE ON THE INSIDE.
WITH RUMORS OF JOKER'S DETERIORATING HEALTH, I SUSPECT HE AND HARLEY HAVE SOMETHING TO DO WITH IT.
I'VE CHECKED GOTHAM GENERAL. THE RESEARCH FILES MATCHING THE MISSING DOCTORS, ALL SPECIALIZED IN BLOOD-BORNE DISEASES. ANY--
NOT NOW, ROBIN. I'VE BEEN SPOTTED.
DO YOU NEED ME TO--
KLIK
(COM-LINK CLOSED)
GUESS THAT'S A "NO THANKS."
HAVE YOU BEEN HITTING THE CLUBS LATELY, MASTER TIM, OR HAVE THEY BEEN HITTING YOU?

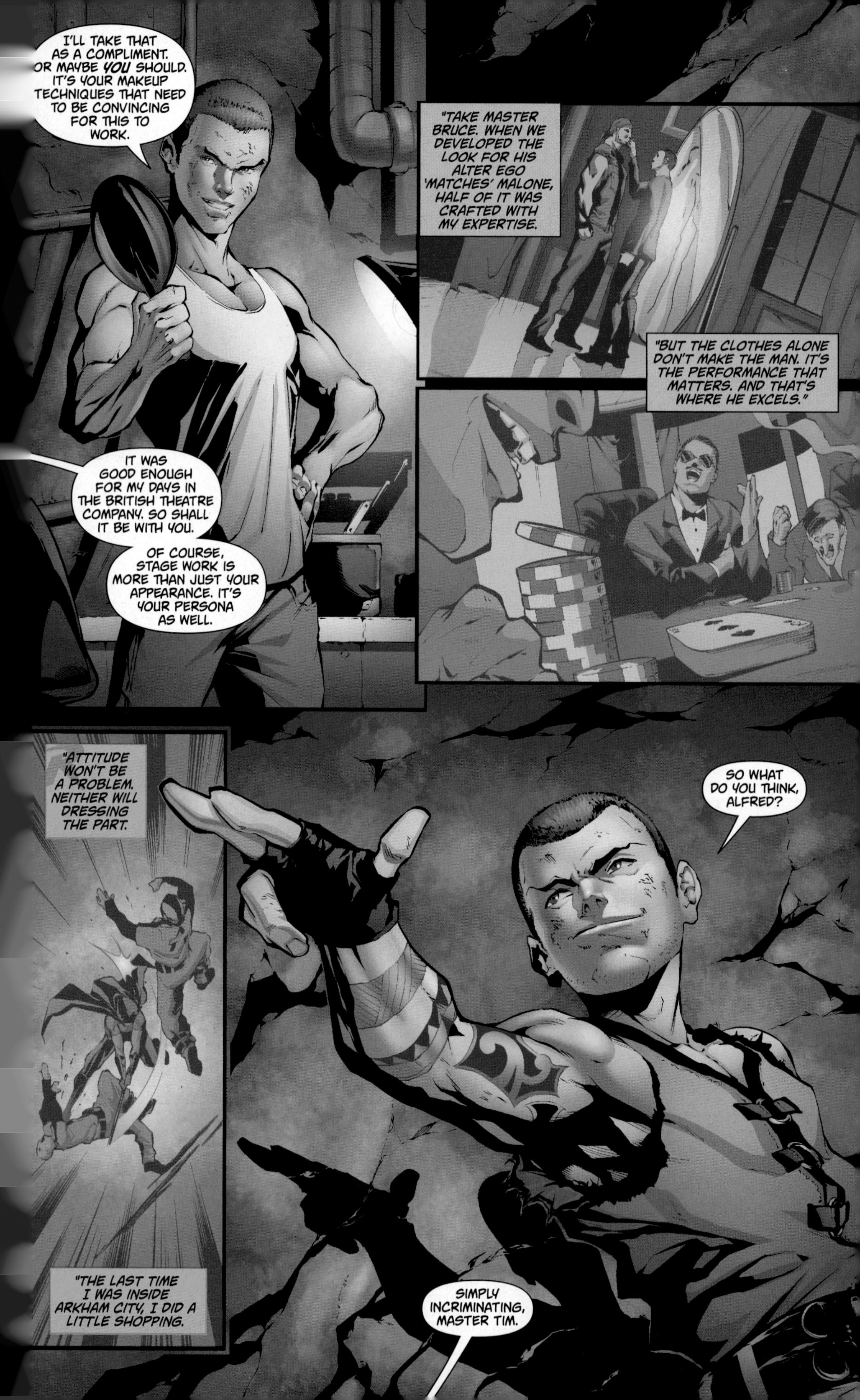
I'LL TAKE THAT AS A COMPLIMENT. OR MAYBE YOU SHOULD. IT'S YOUR MAKEUP TECHNIQUES THAT NEED TO BE CONVINCING FOR THIS TO WORK.
"TAKE MASTER BRUCE. WHEN WE DEVELOPED THE LOOK FOR HIS ALTER EGO 'MATCHES' MALONE, HALF OF IT WAS CRAFTED WITH MY EXPERTISE.
"BUT THE CLOTHES ALONE DON'T MAKE THE MAN. IT'S THE PERFORMANCE THAT MATTERS. AND THAT'S WHERE HE EXCELS."
IT WAS GOOD ENOUGH FOR MY DAYS IN THE BRITISH THEATRE COMPANY. SO SHALL IT BE WITH YOU.
OF COURSE, STAGE WORK IS MORE THAN JUST YOUR APPEARANCE. IT'S YOUR PERSONA AS WELL.
"ATTITUDE WON'T BE A PROBLEM. NEITHER WILL DRESSING THE PART.
SO WHAT DO YOU THINK, ALFRED?
"THE LAST TIME I WAS INSIDE ARKHAM CITY, I DID A LITTLE SHOPPING.
SIMPLY INCRIMINATING, MASTER TIM.

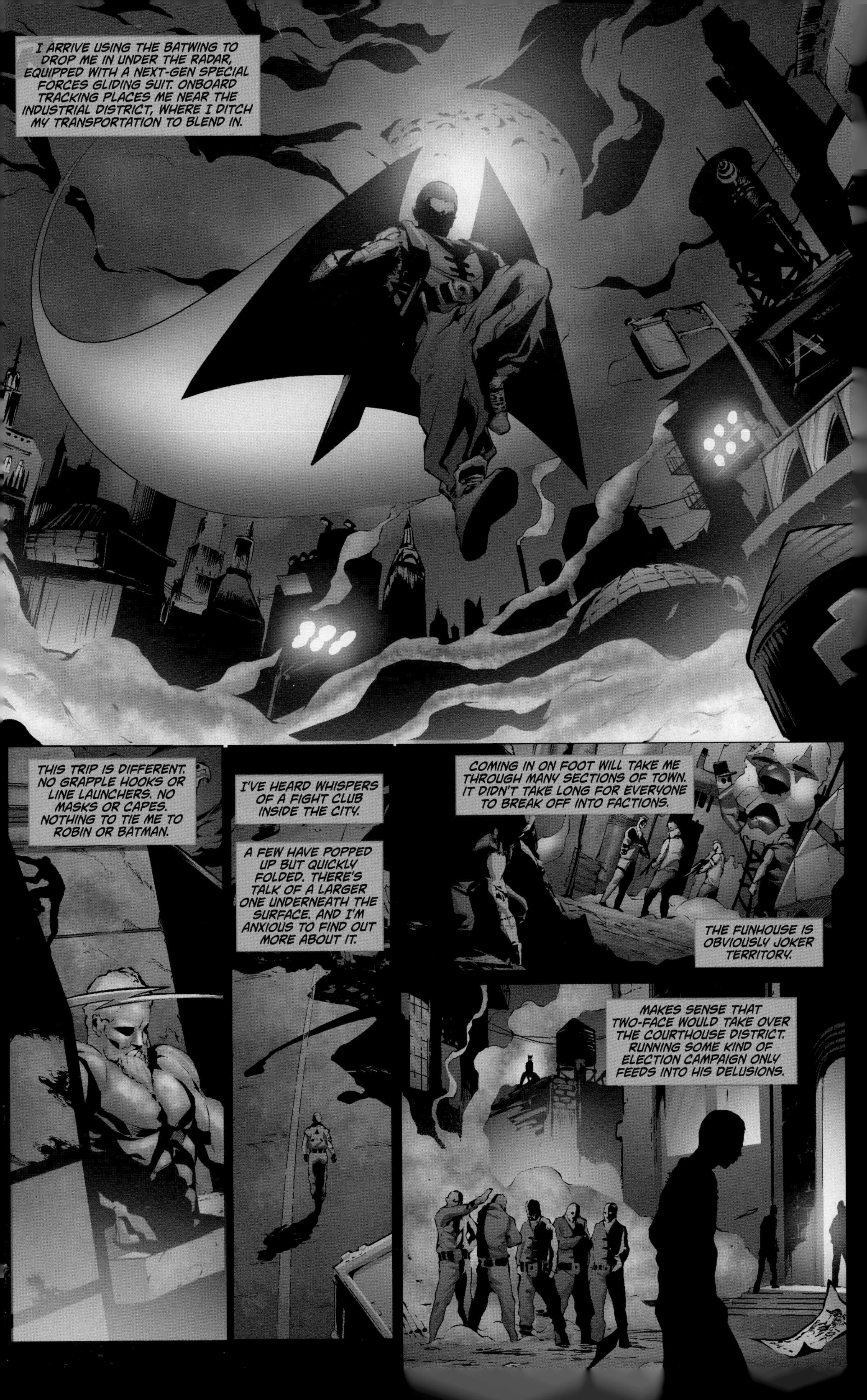

I ARRIVE USING THE BATWING TO DROP ME IN UNDER THE RADAR, EQUIPPED WITH A NEXT-GEN SPECIAL FORCES GLIDING SUIT. ONBOARD TRACKING PLACES ME NEAR THE INDUSTRIAL DISTRICT, WHERE I DITCH MY TRANSPORTATION TO BLEND IN.
THIS TRIP IS DIFFERENT. NO GRAPPLE HOOKS OR LINE LAUNCHERS. NO MASKS OR CAPES. NOTHING TO TIE ME TO ROBIN OR BATMAN.
I'VE HEARD WHISPERS OF A FIGHT CLUB INSIDE THE CITY.
A FEW HAVE POPPED UP BUT QUICKLY FOLDED. THERE'S TALK OF A LARGER ONE UNDERNEATH THE SURFACE. AND I'M ANXIOUS TO FIND OUT MORE ABOUT IT.
COMING IN ON FOOT WILL TAKE ME THROUGH MANY SECTIONS OF TOWN. IT DIDN'T TAKE LONG FOR EVERYONE TO BREAK OFF INTO FACTIONS.
THE FUNHOUSE IS OBVIOUSLY JOKER TERRITORY.
MAKES SENSE THAT TWO-FACE WOULD TAKE OVER THE COURTHOUSE DISTRICT. RUNNING SOME KIND OF ELECTION CAMPAIGN ONLY FEEDS INTO HIS DELUSIONS.

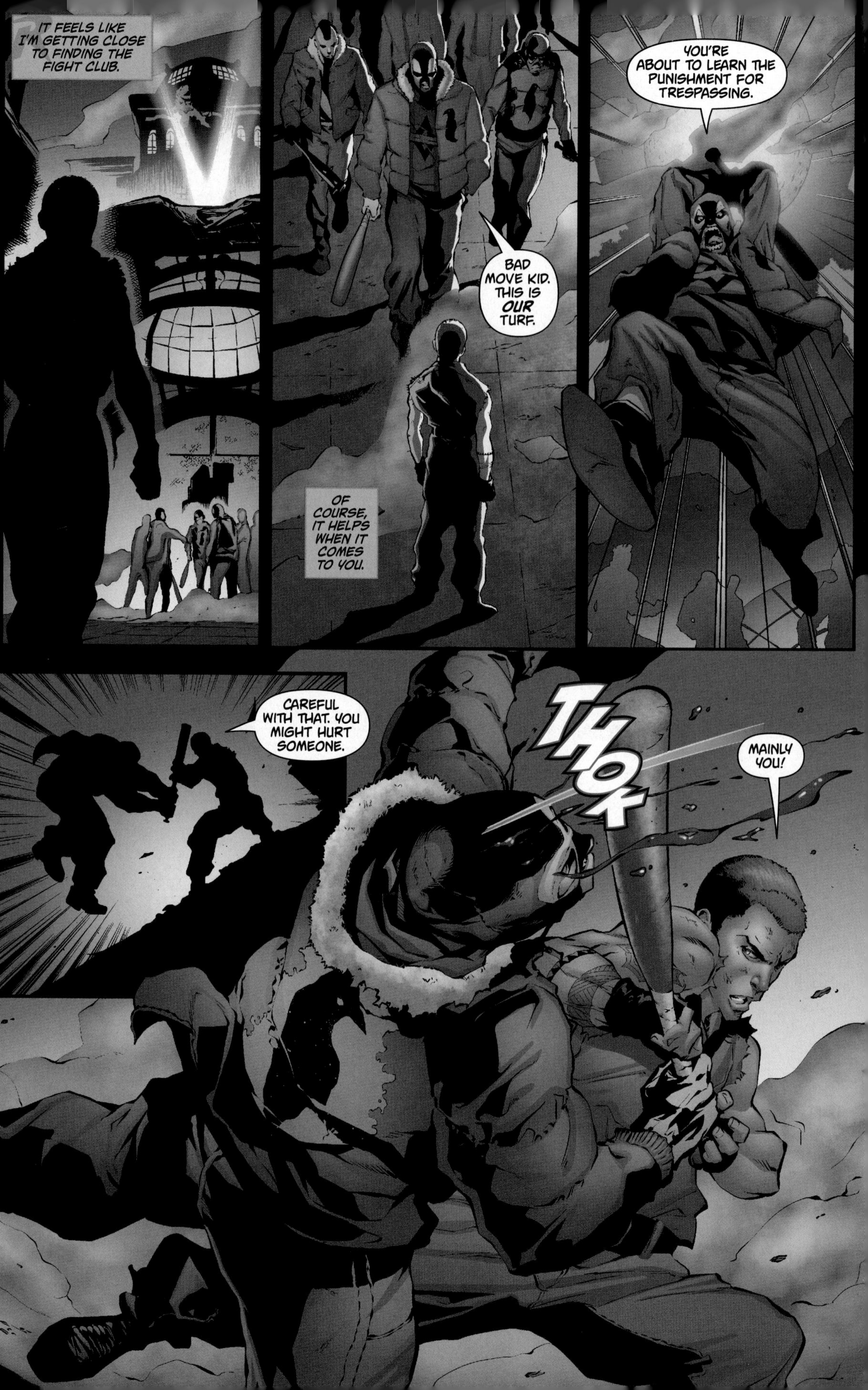
IT FEELS LIKE I'M GETTING CLOSE TO FINDING THE FIGHT CLUB.
BAD MOVE KID. THIS IS *OUR* TURF.
OF COURSE, IT HELPS WHEN IT COMES TO YOU.
YOU'RE ABOUT TO LEARN THE PUNISHMENT FOR TRESPASSING.
CAREFUL WITH THAT. YOU MIGHT HURT SOMEONE.
THOK
MAINLY YOU!

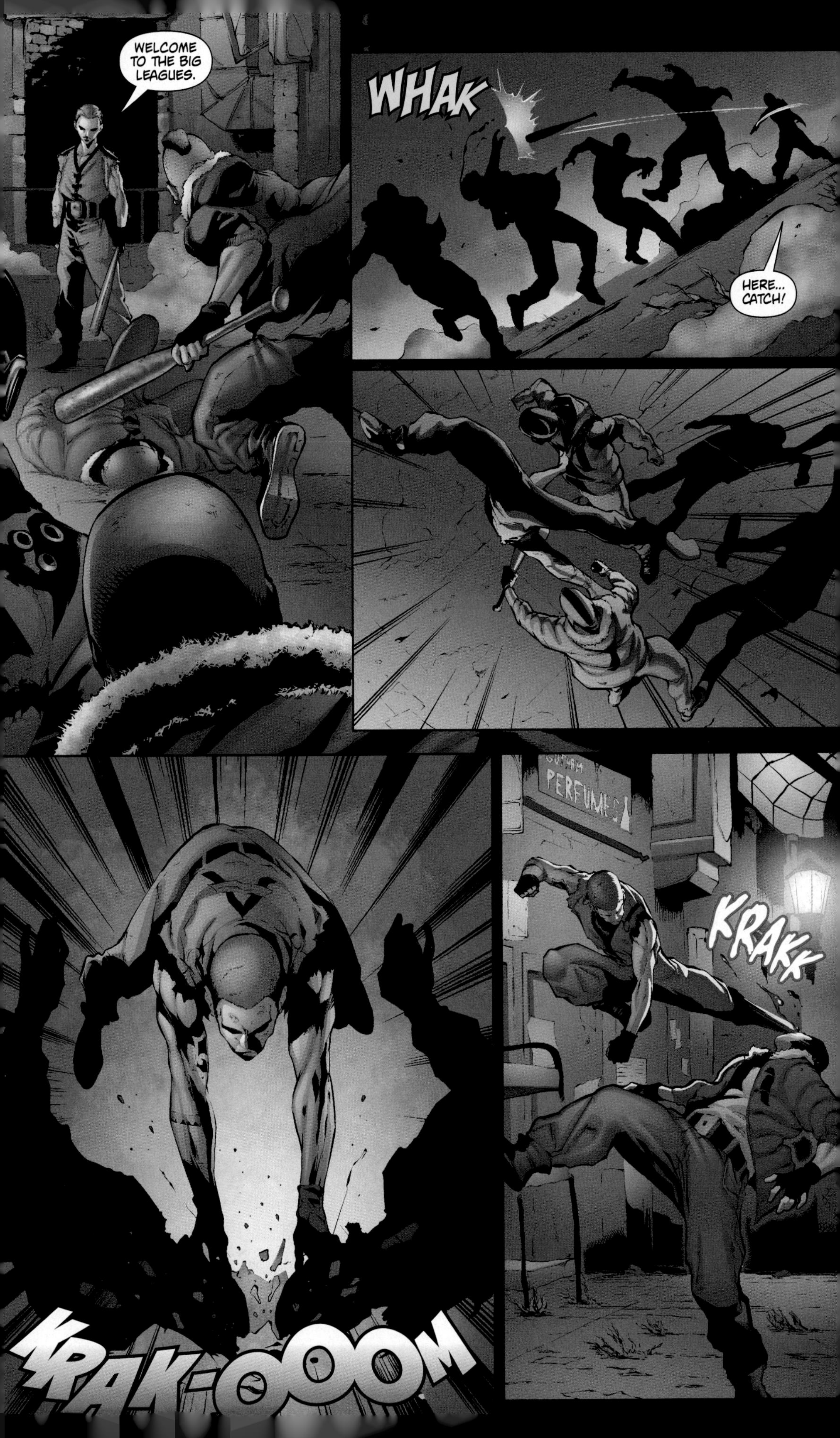
WELCOME TO THE BIG LEAGUES.
WHAK
HERE... CATCH!
KRAK-OOOM
PERFUMES
KRAKK

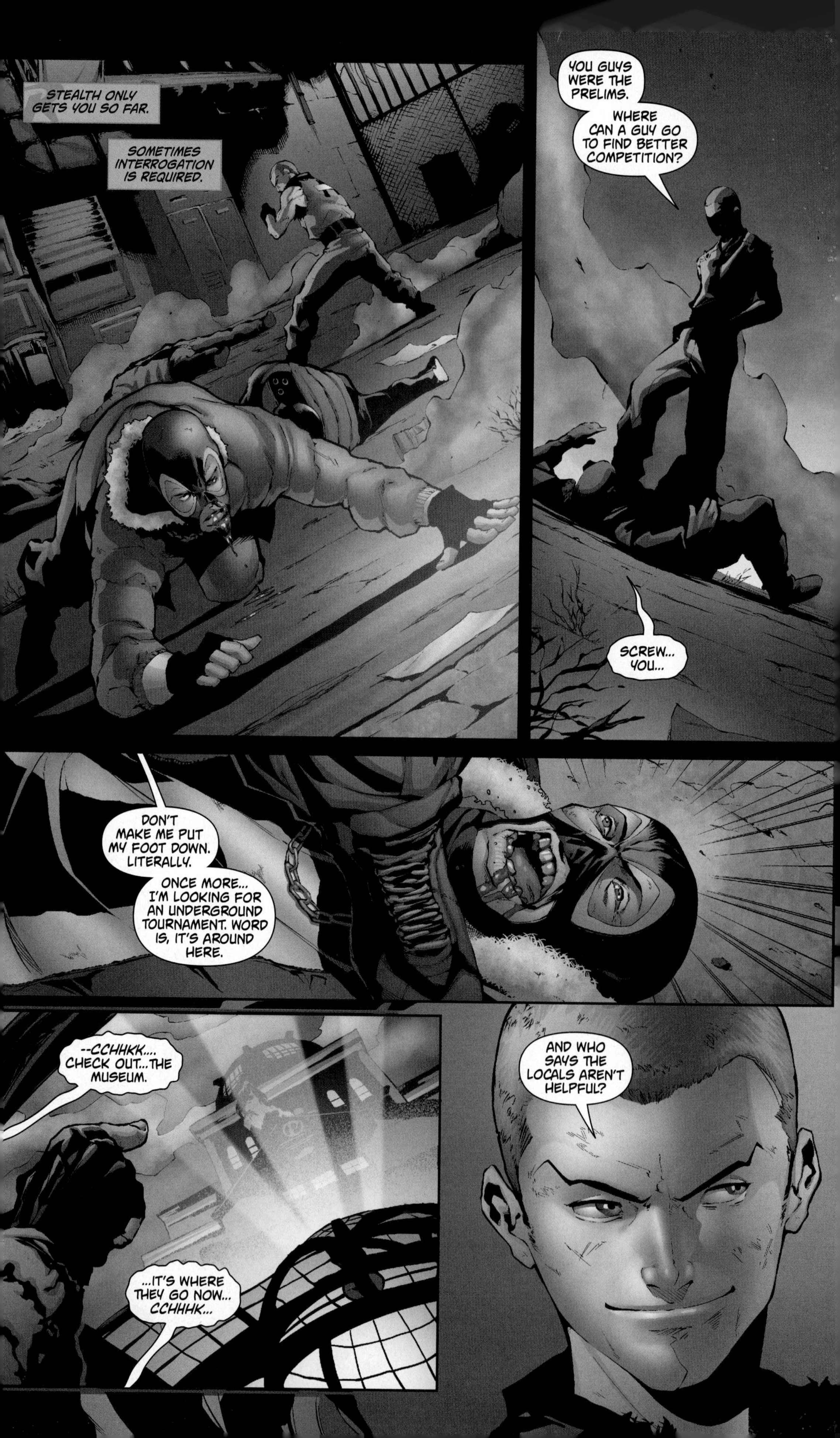
STEALTH ONLY GETS YOU SO FAR.
SOMETIMES INTERROGATION IS REQUIRED.
YOU GUYS WERE THE PRELIMS.
WHERE CAN A GUY GO TO FIND BETTER COMPETITION?
SCREW... YOU...
DON'T MAKE ME PUT MY FOOT DOWN. LITERALLY.
ONCE MORE... I'M LOOKING FOR AN UNDERGROUND TOURNAMENT. WORD IS, IT'S AROUND HERE.
--CCHHKK.... CHECK OUT...THE MUSEUM.
...IT'S WHERE THEY GO NOW... CCHHHK...
AND WHO SAYS THE LOCALS AREN'T HELPFUL?

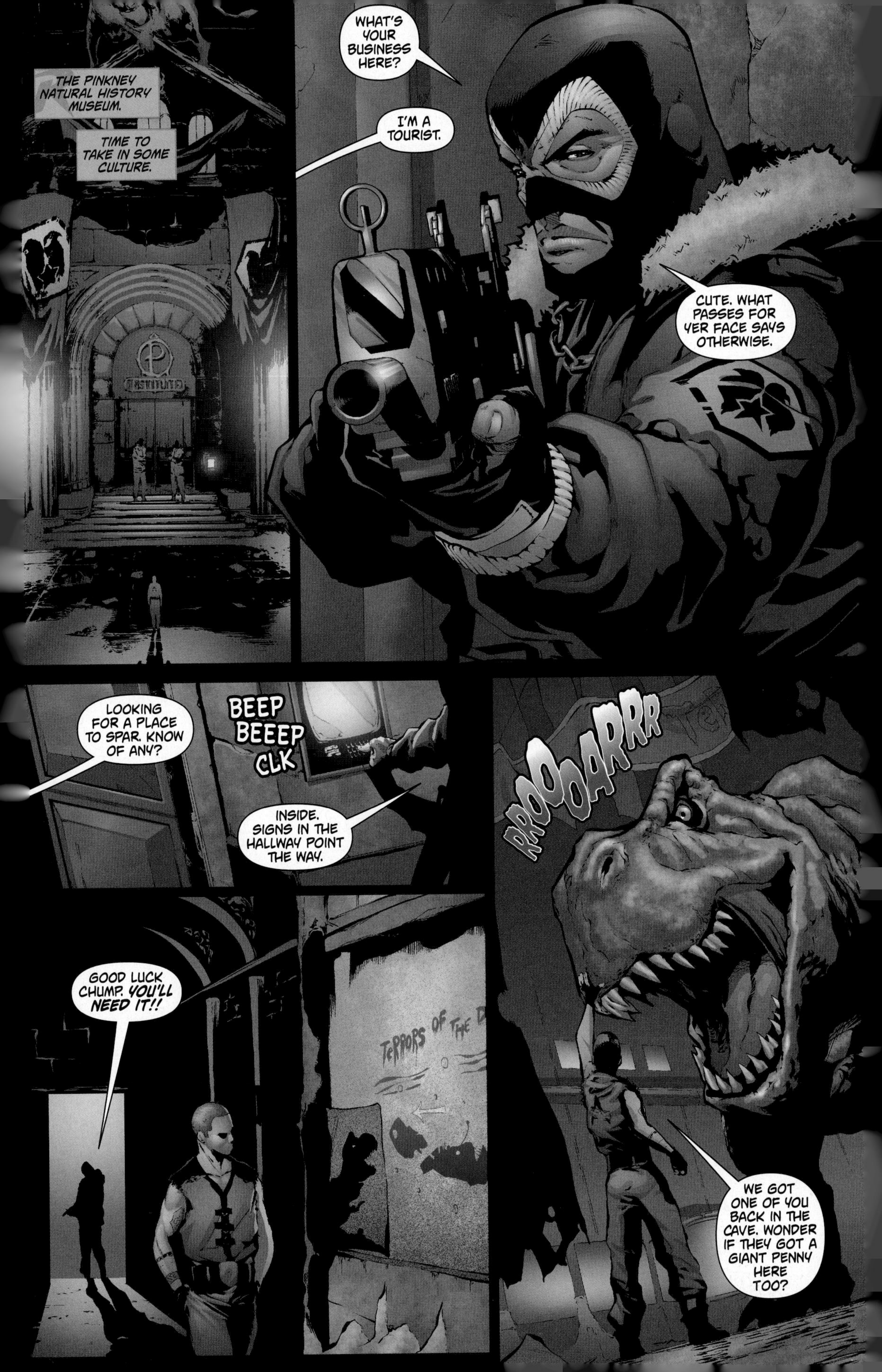
THE PINKNEY NATURAL HISTORY MUSEUM.
TIME TO TAKE IN SOME CULTURE.
INSTITUTE
WHAT'S YOUR BUSINESS HERE?
I'M A TOURIST.
CUTE. WHAT PASSES FOR YER FACE SAYS OTHERWISE.
LOOKING FOR A PLACE TO SPAR. KNOW OF ANY?
BEEP BEEEP CLK
INSIDE. SIGNS IN THE HALLWAY POINT THE WAY.
RROOOOARRRR
GOOD LUCK CHUMP. YOU'LL NEED IT!!
TERRORS OF THE D
WE GOT ONE OF YOU BACK IN THE CAVE. WONDER IF THEY GOT A GIANT PENNY HERE TOO?

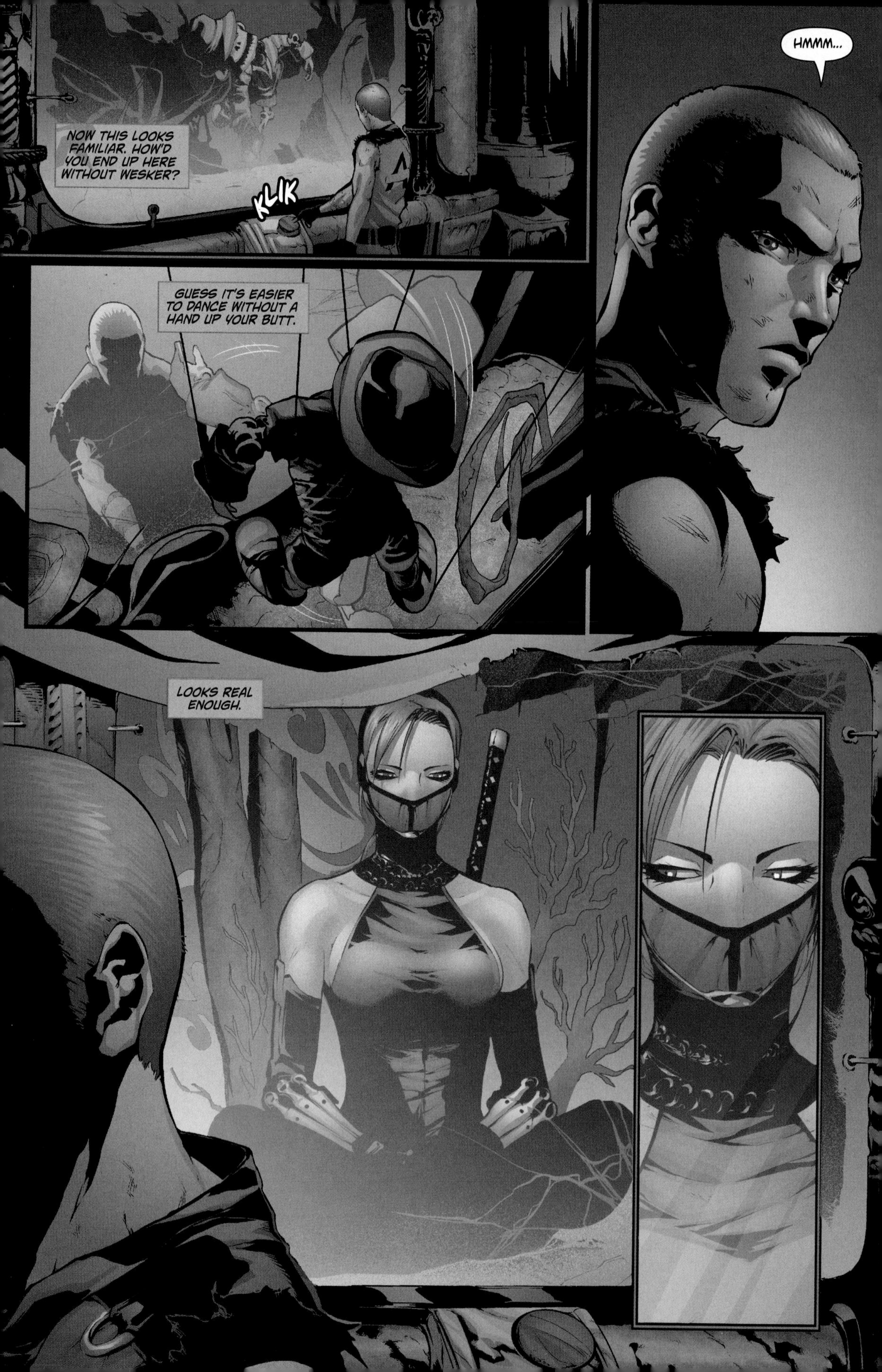
NOW THIS LOOKS FAMILIAR. HOW'D YOU END UP HERE WITHOUT WESKER?
KLIK
HMMM...
GUESS IT'S EASIER TO DANCE WITHOUT A HAND UP YOUR BUTT.
LOOKS REAL ENOUGH.

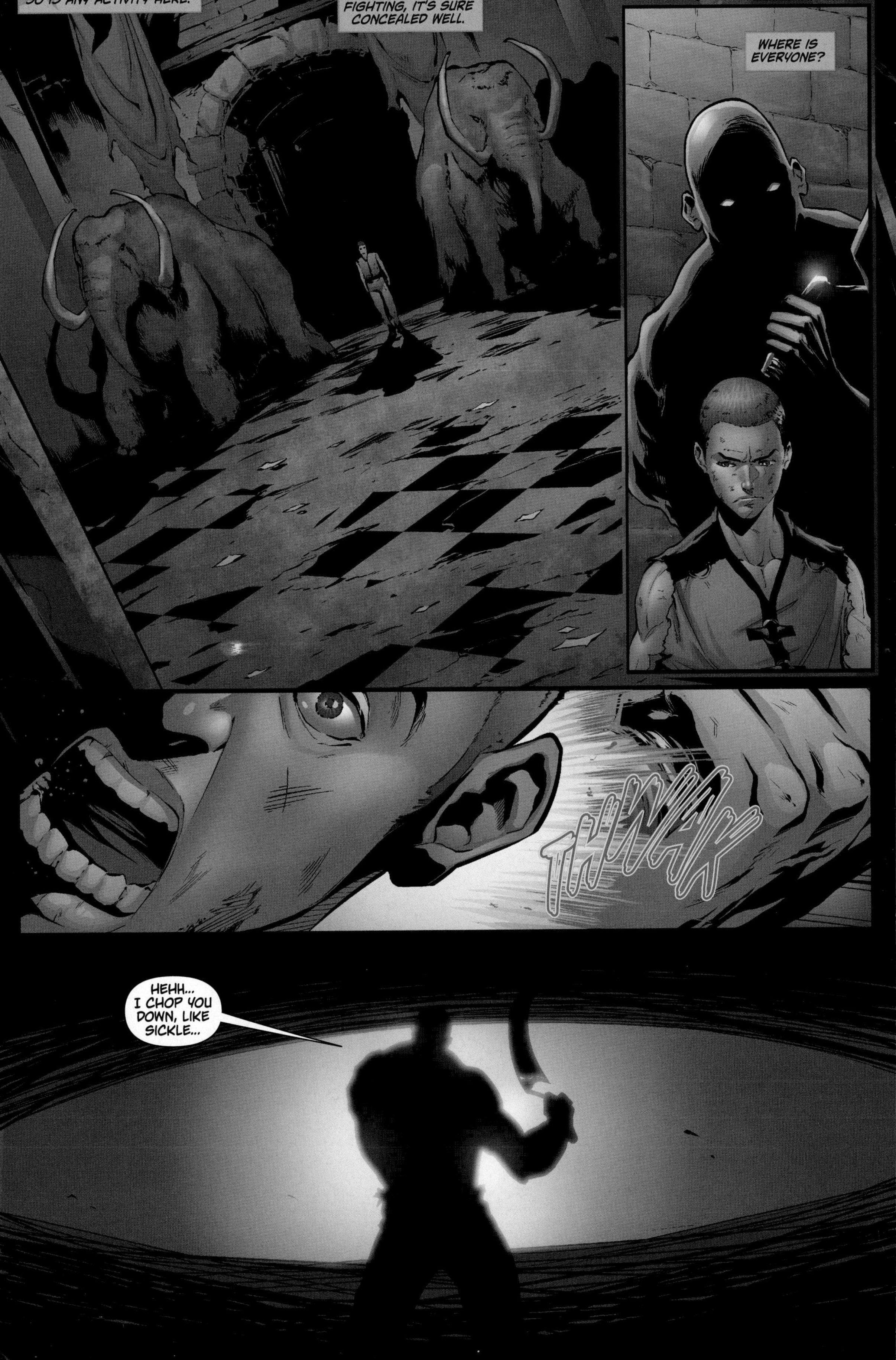
FIGHTING, IT'S SURE CONCEALED WELL.
WHERE IS EVERYONE?
HEHH... I CHOP YOU DOWN, LIKE SICKLE...

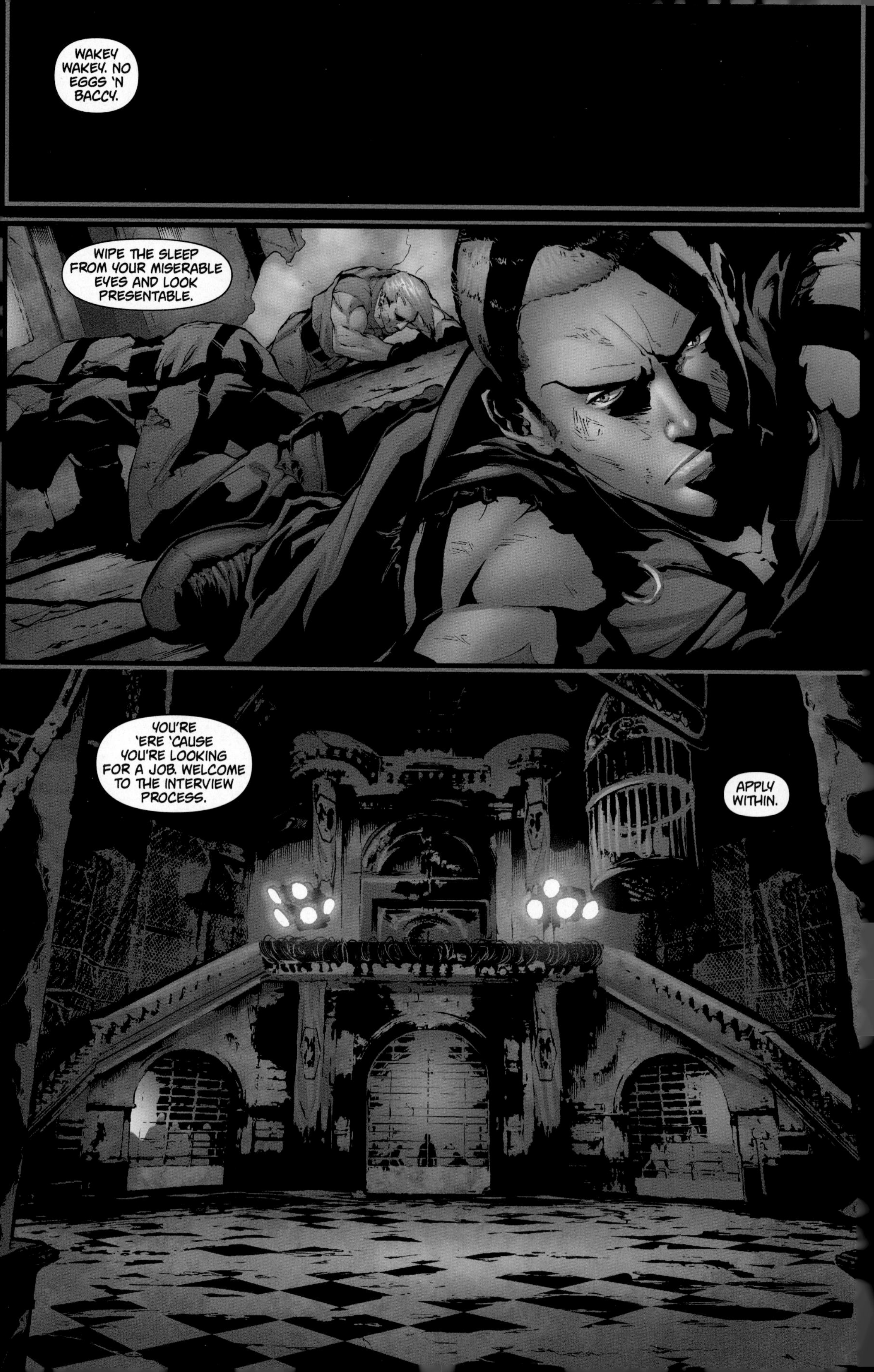
WAKEY WAKEY. NO EGGS 'N BACCY.
WIPE THE SLEEP FROM YOUR MISERABLE EYES AND LOOK PRESENTABLE.
YOU'RE 'ERE 'CAUSE YOU'RE LOOKING FOR A JOB. WELCOME TO THE INTERVIEW PROCESS.
APPLY WITHIN.

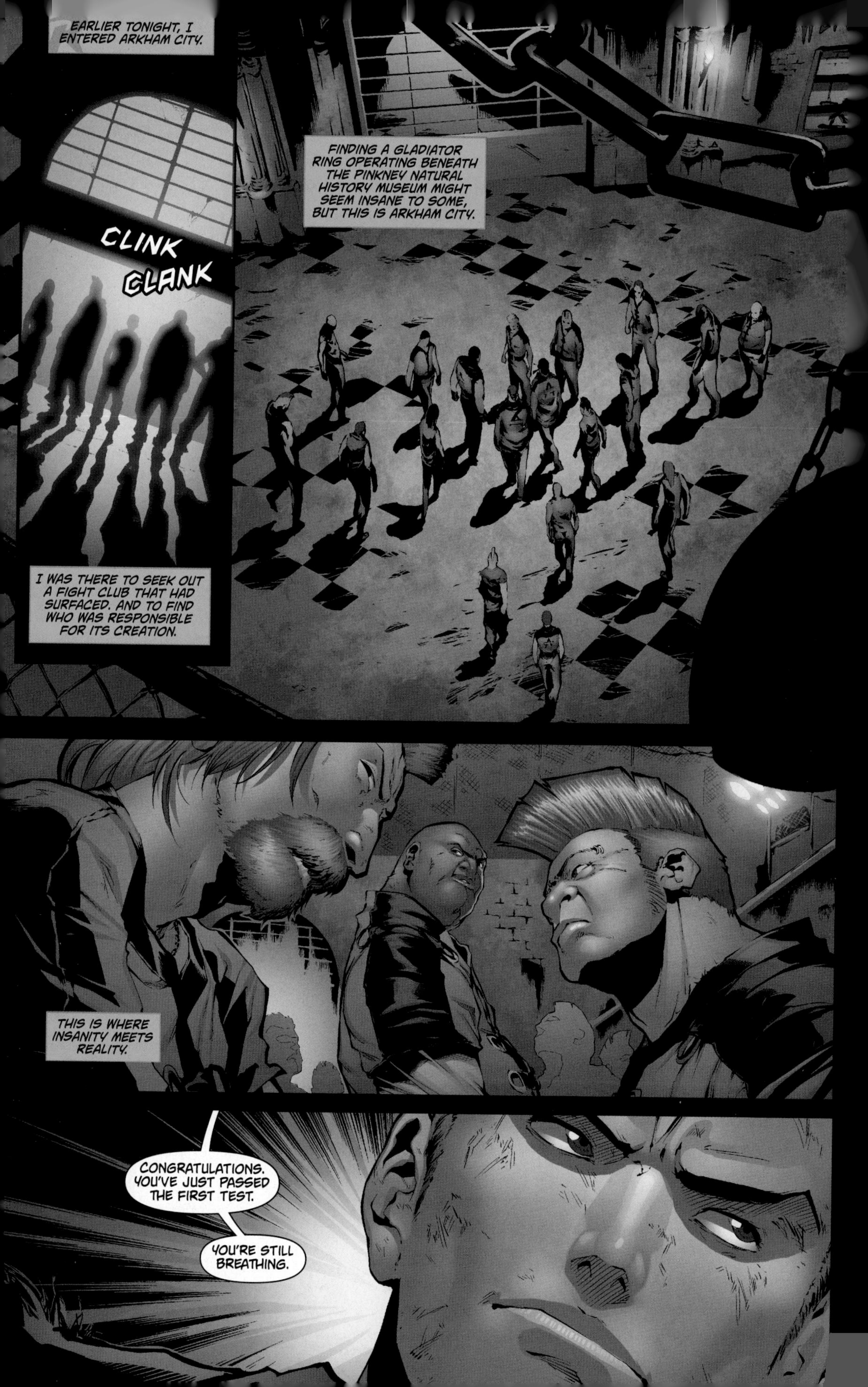
EARLIER TONIGHT, I ENTERED ARKHAM CITY.
CLINK
CLANK
FINDING A GLADIATOR RING OPERATING BENEATH THE PINKNEY NATURAL HISTORY MUSEUM MIGHT SEEM INSANE TO SOME, BUT THIS IS ARKHAM CITY.
I WAS THERE TO SEEK OUT A FIGHT CLUB THAT HAD SURFACED. AND TO FIND WHO WAS RESPONSIBLE FOR ITS CREATION.
THIS IS WHERE INSANITY MEETS REALITY.
CONGRATULATIONS. YOU'VE JUST PASSED THE FIRST TEST.
YOU'RE STILL BREATHING.

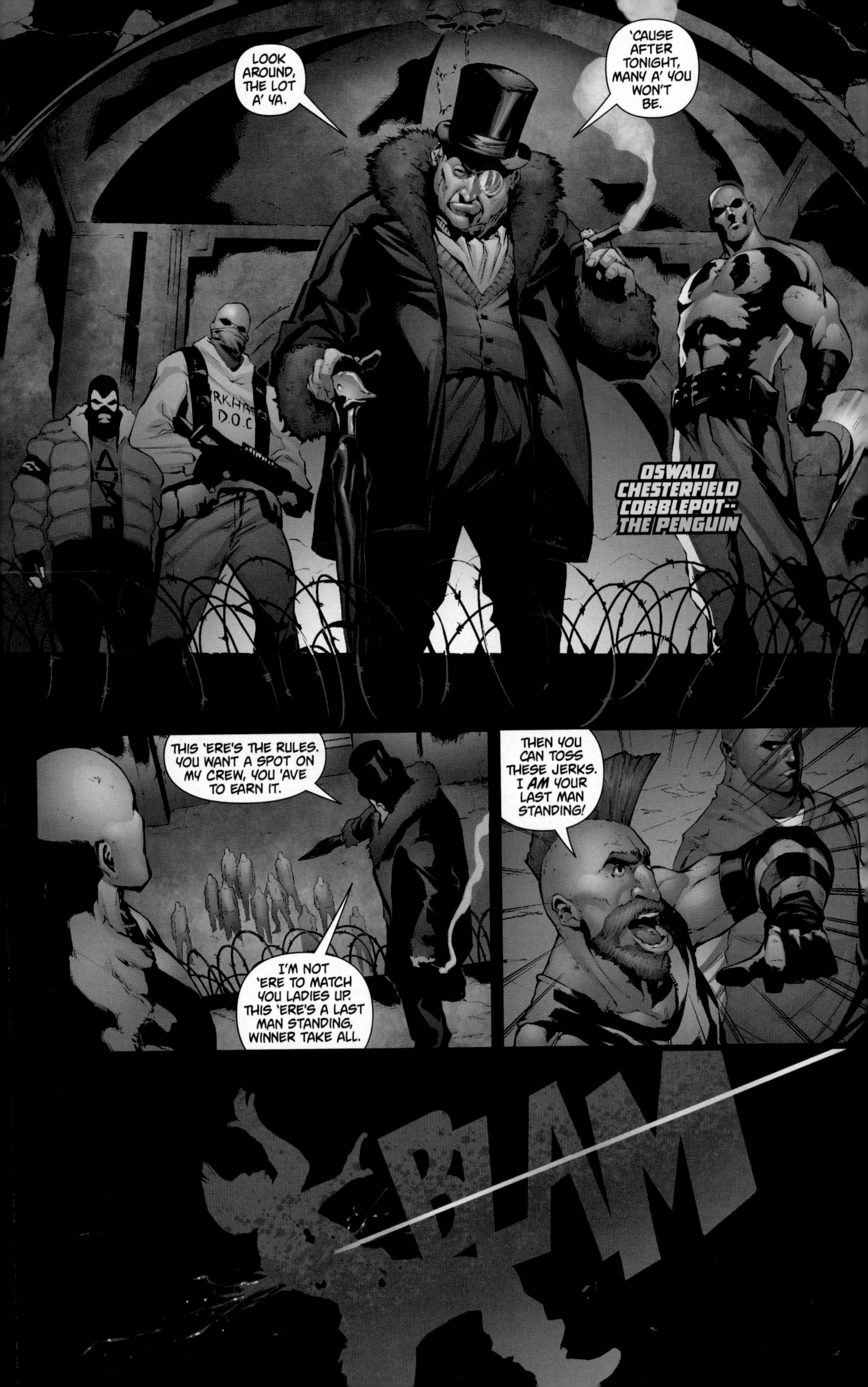
LOOK AROUND, THE LOT A' YA.
'CAUSE AFTER TONIGHT, MANY A' YOU WON'T BE.
OSWALD CHESTERFIELD COBBLEPOT-- THE PENGUIN
THIS 'ERE'S THE RULES. YOU WANT A SPOT ON MY CREW, YOU 'AVE TO EARN IT.
I'M NOT 'ERE TO MATCH YOU LADIES UP. THIS 'ERE'S A LAST MAN STANDING, WINNER TAKE ALL.
THEN YOU CAN TOSS THESE JERKS. I AM YOUR LAST MAN STANDING!
BLAM

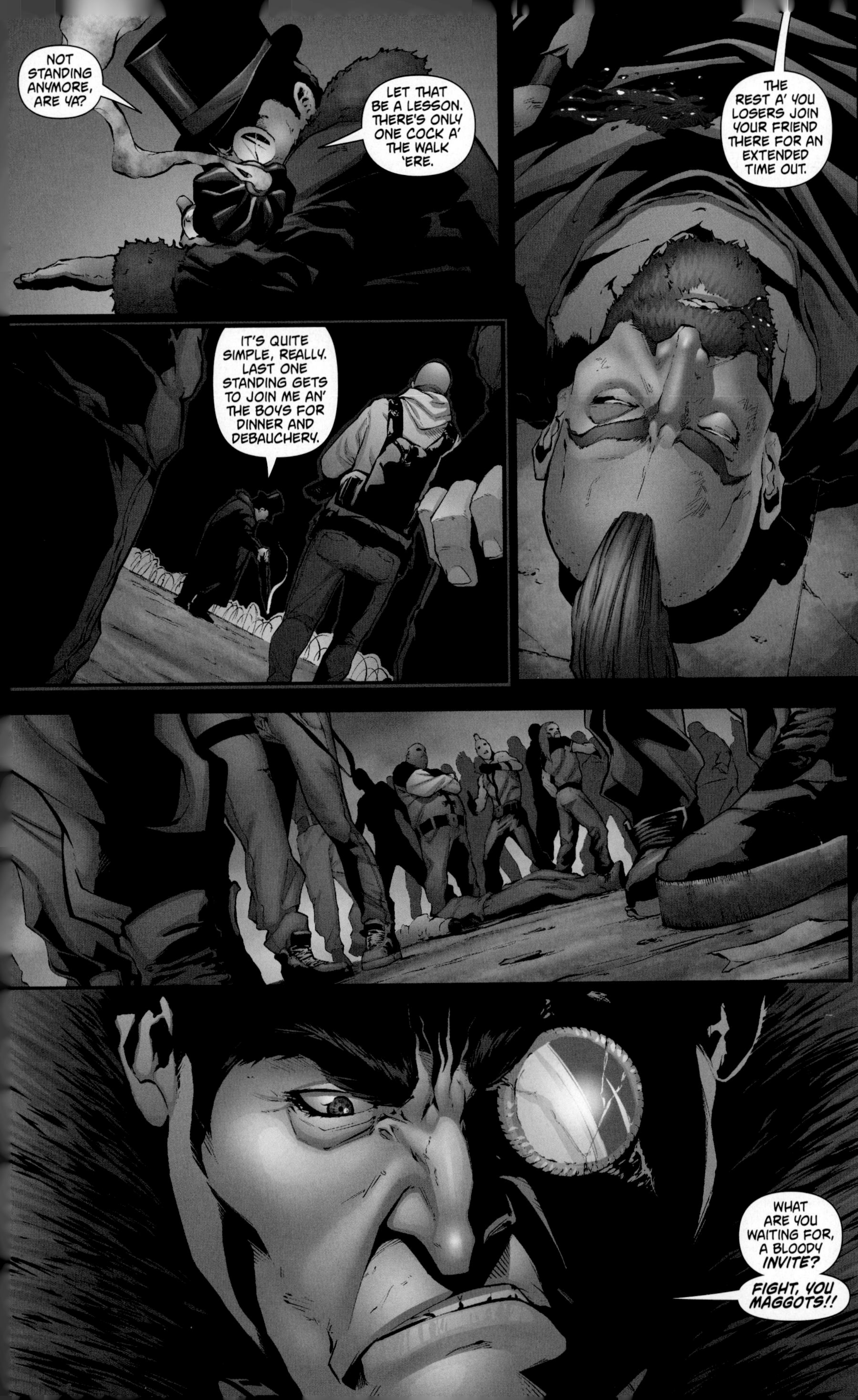
NOT STANDING ANYMORE, ARE YA?
LET THAT BE A LESSON. THERE'S ONLY ONE COCK A' THE WALK 'ERE.
THE REST A' YOU LOSERS JOIN YOUR FRIEND THERE FOR AN EXTENDED TIME OUT.
IT'S QUITE SIMPLE, REALLY. LAST ONE STANDING GETS TO JOIN ME AN' THE BOYS FOR DINNER AND DEBAUCHERY.
WHAT ARE YOU WAITING FOR, A BLOODY INVITE?
FIGHT, YOU MAGGOTS!!

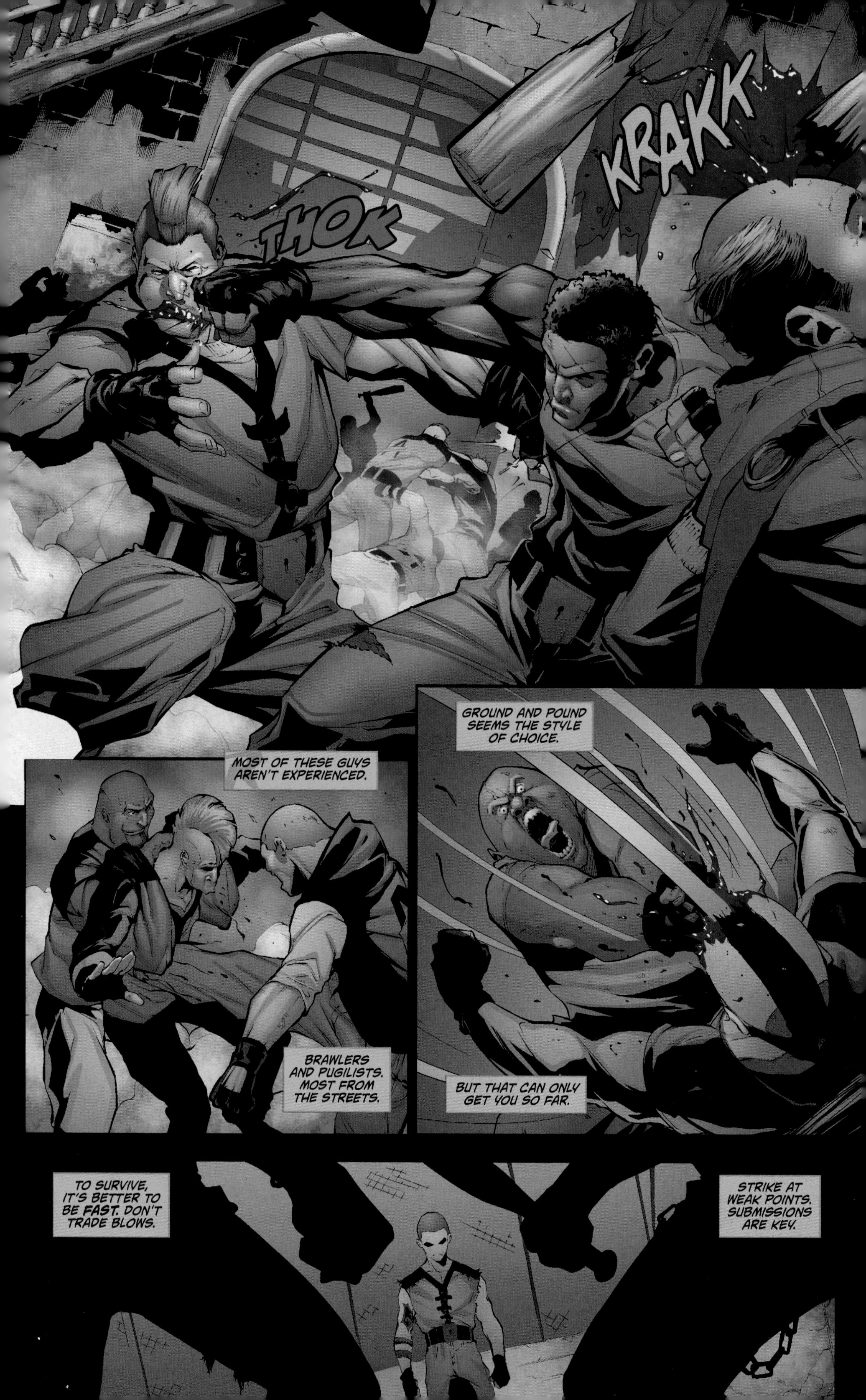
KRAKK
THOK
MOST OF THESE GUYS AREN'T EXPERIENCED.
BRAWLERS AND PUGILISTS. MOST FROM THE STREETS.
GROUND AND POUND SEEMS THE STYLE OF CHOICE.
BUT THAT CAN ONLY GET YOU SO FAR.
TO SURVIVE, IT'S BETTER TO BE FAST. DON'T TRADE BLOWS.
STRIKE AT WEAK POINTS. SUBMISSIONS ARE KEY.

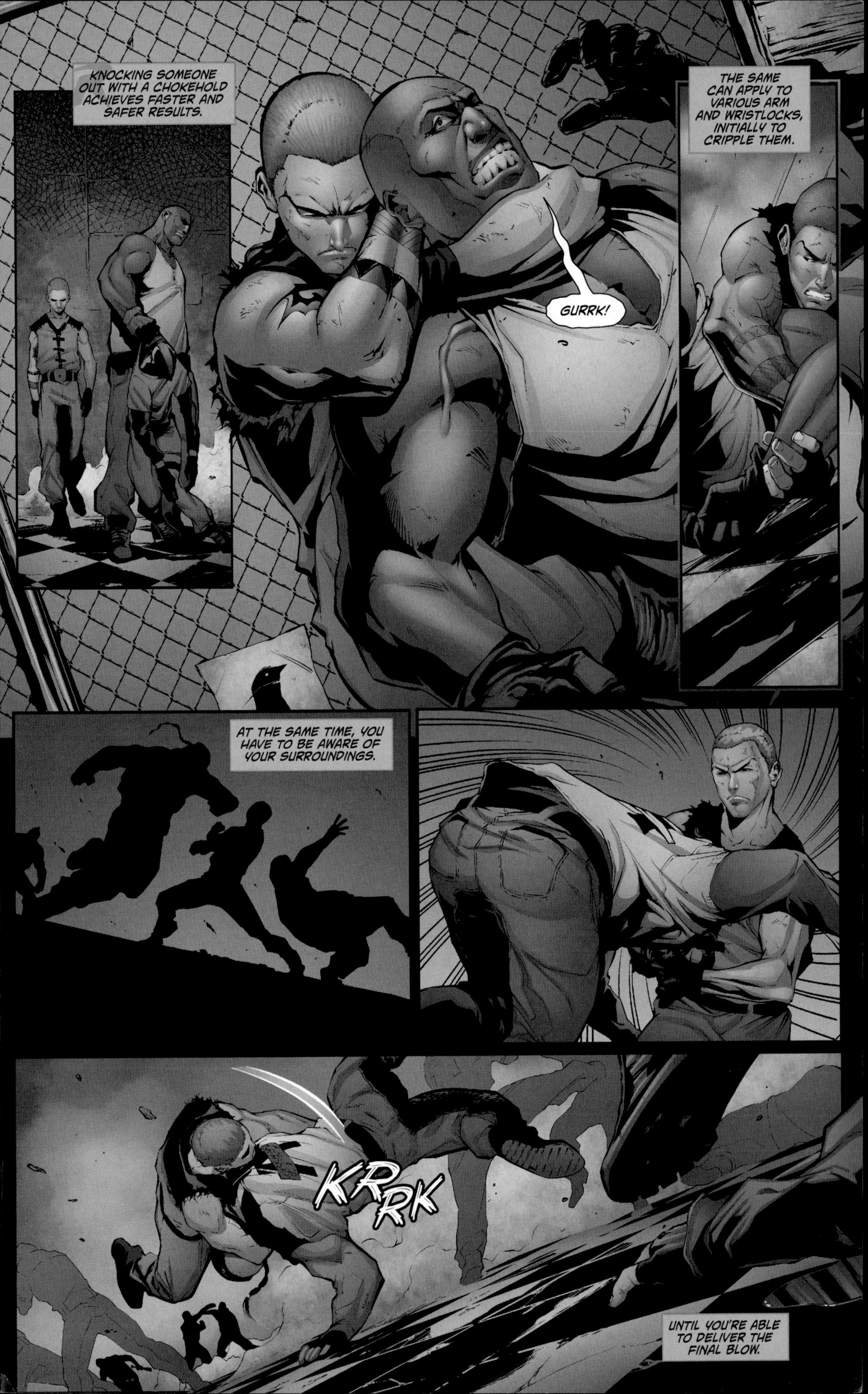
KNOCKING SOMEONE OUT WITH A CHOKEHOLD ACHIEVES FASTER AND SAFER RESULTS.
GURRK!
THE SAME CAN APPLY TO VARIOUS ARM AND WRISTLOCKS, INITIALLY TO CRIPPLE THEM.
AT THE SAME TIME, YOU HAVE TO BE AWARE OF YOUR SURROUNDINGS.
KRRK
UNTIL YOU'RE ABLE TO DELIVER THE FINAL BLOW.

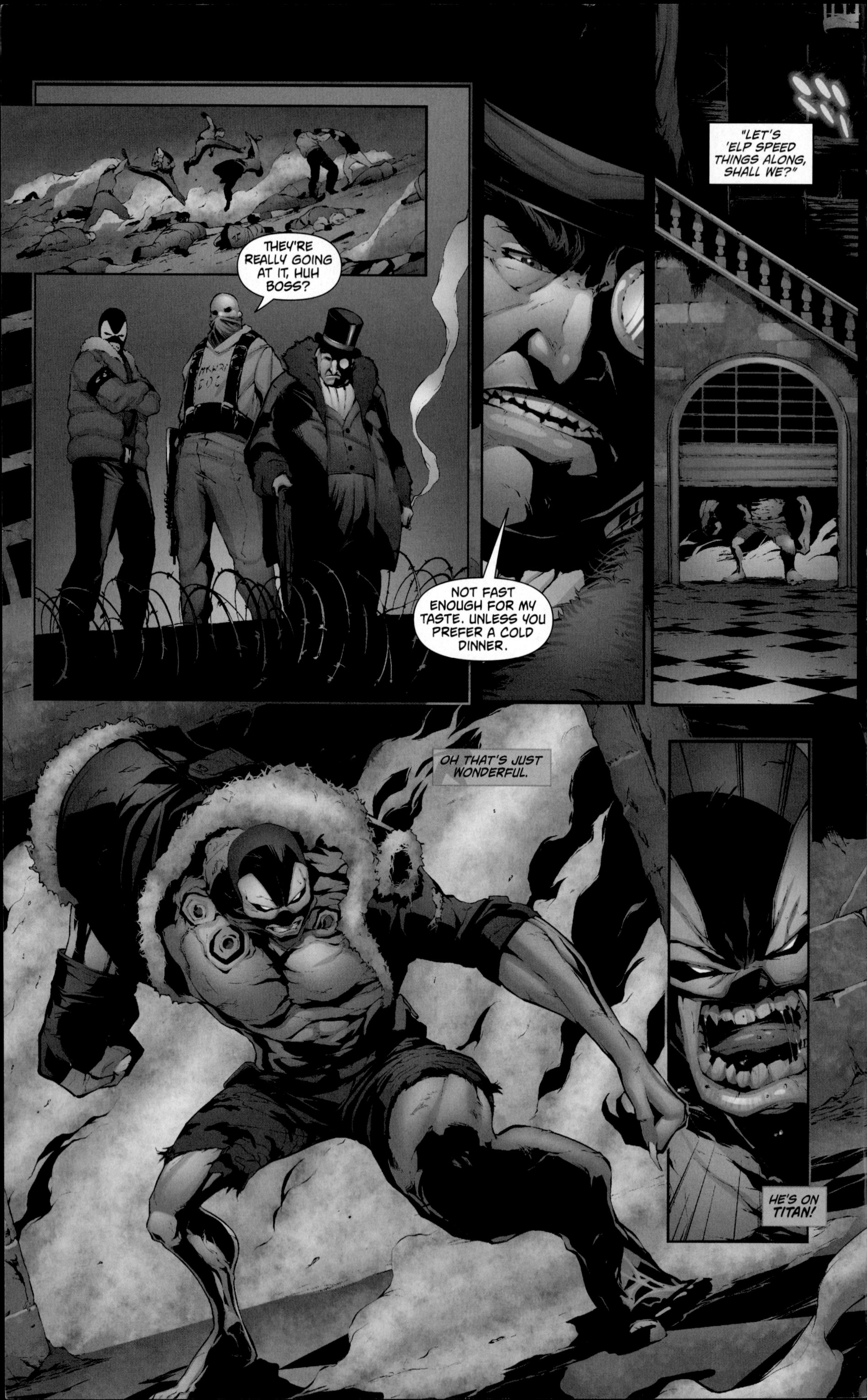
THEY'RE REALLY GOING AT IT, HUH BOSS?
NOT FAST ENOUGH FOR MY TASTE. UNLESS YOU PREFER A COLD DINNER.
"LET'S 'ELP SPEED THINGS ALONG, SHALL WE?"
OH THAT'S JUST WONDERFUL.
HE'S ON TITAN!

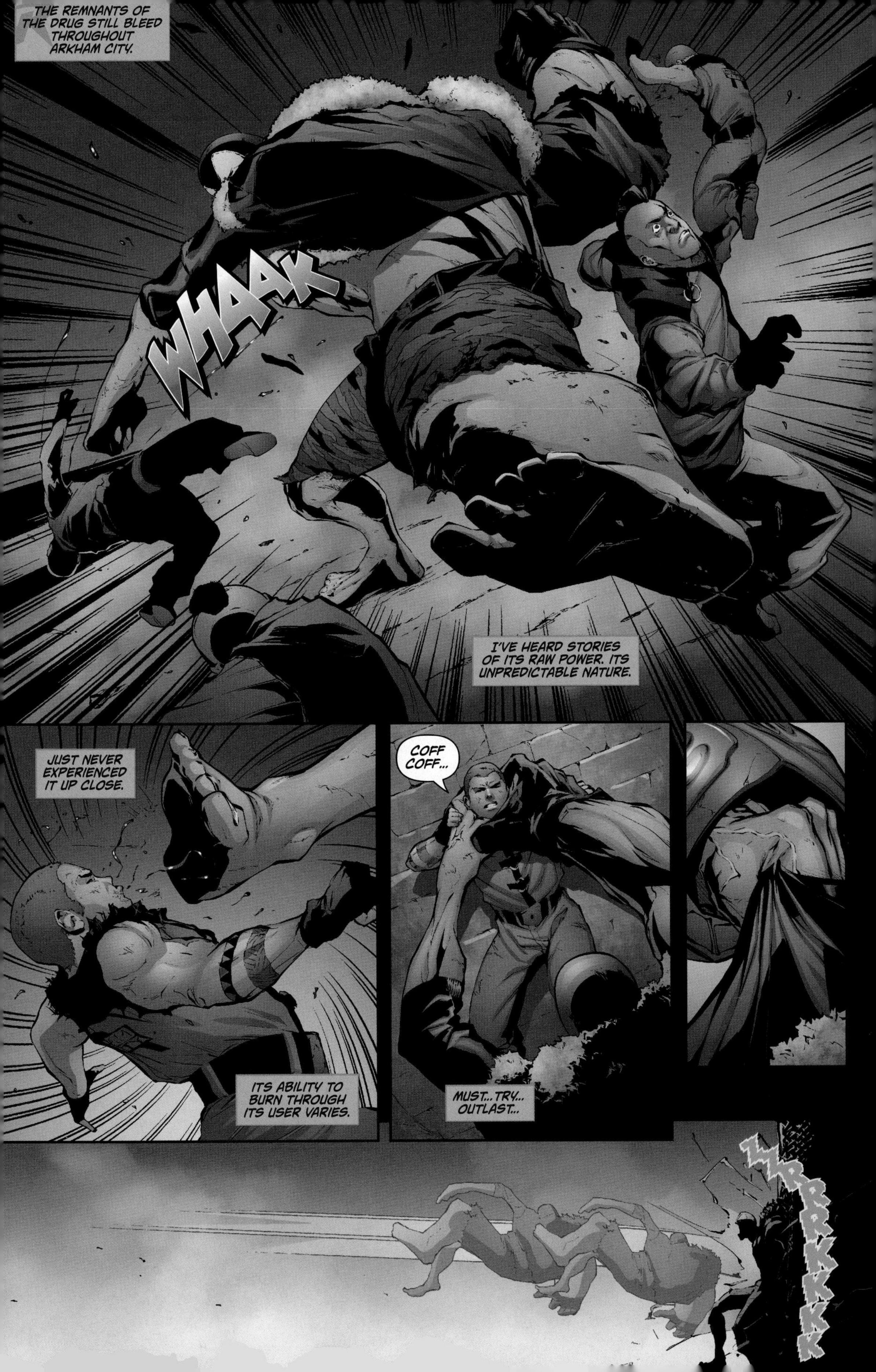
THE REMNANTS OF THE DRUG STILL BLEED THROUGHOUT ARKHAM CITY.
WHAAK
I'VE HEARD STORIES OF ITS RAW POWER. ITS UNPREDICTABLE NATURE.
JUST NEVER EXPERIENCED IT UP CLOSE.
ITS ABILITY TO BURN THROUGH ITS USER VARIES.
COFF COFF...
MUST...TRY... OUTLAST...
ZZRRRKKKK

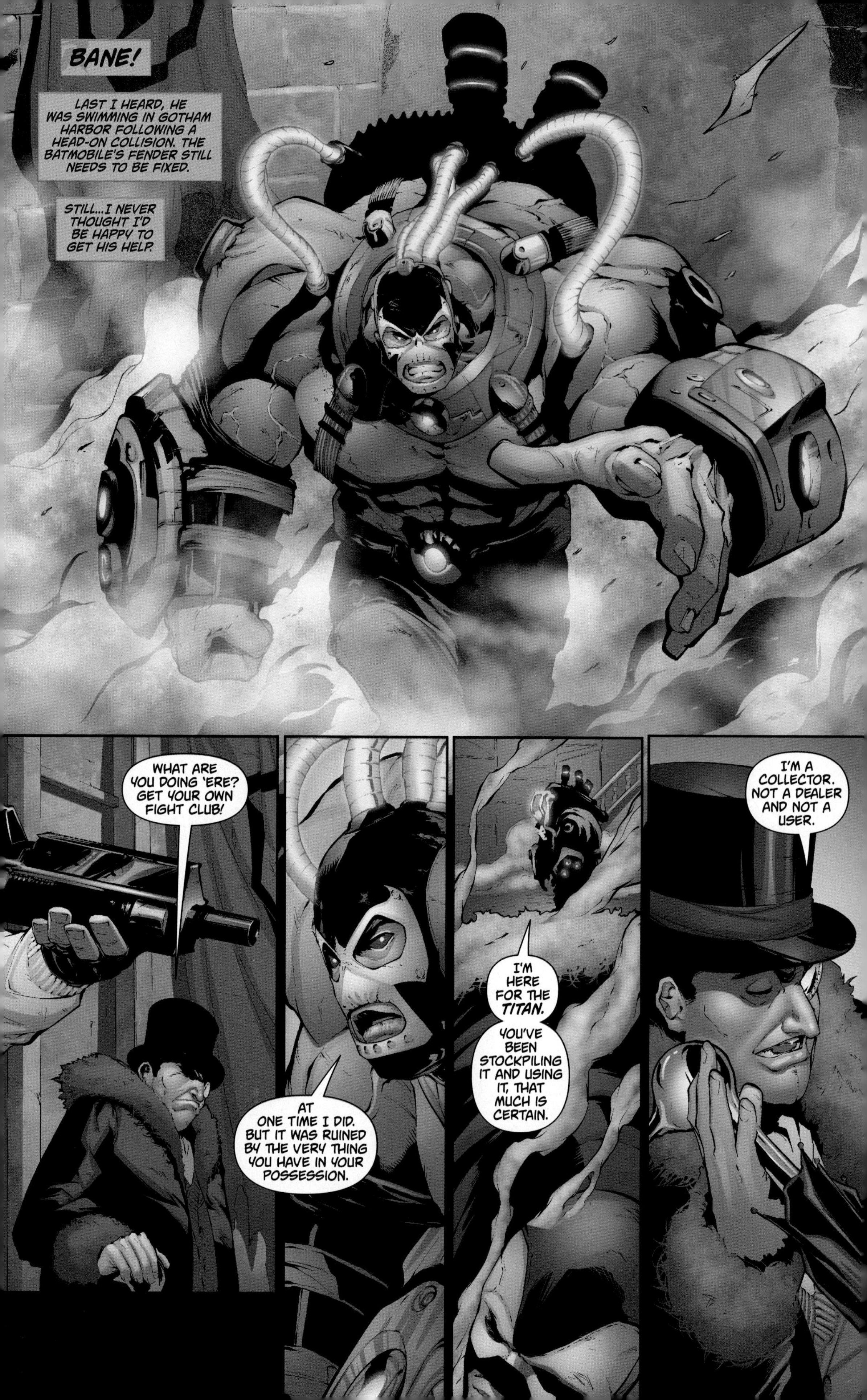
BANE!
LAST I HEARD, HE WAS SWIMMING IN GOTHAM HARBOR FOLLOWING A HEAD-ON COLLISION. THE BATMOBILE'S FENDER STILL NEEDS TO BE FIXED.
STILL...I NEVER THOUGHT I'D BE HAPPY TO GET HIS HELP.
WHAT ARE YOU DOING 'ERE? GET YOUR OWN FIGHT CLUB!
AT ONE TIME I DID. BUT IT WAS RUINED BY THE VERY THING YOU HAVE IN YOUR POSSESSION.
I'M HERE FOR THE *TITAN.*
YOU'VE BEEN STOCKPILING IT AND USING IT, THAT MUCH IS CERTAIN.
I'M A COLLECTOR. NOT A DEALER AND NOT A USER.

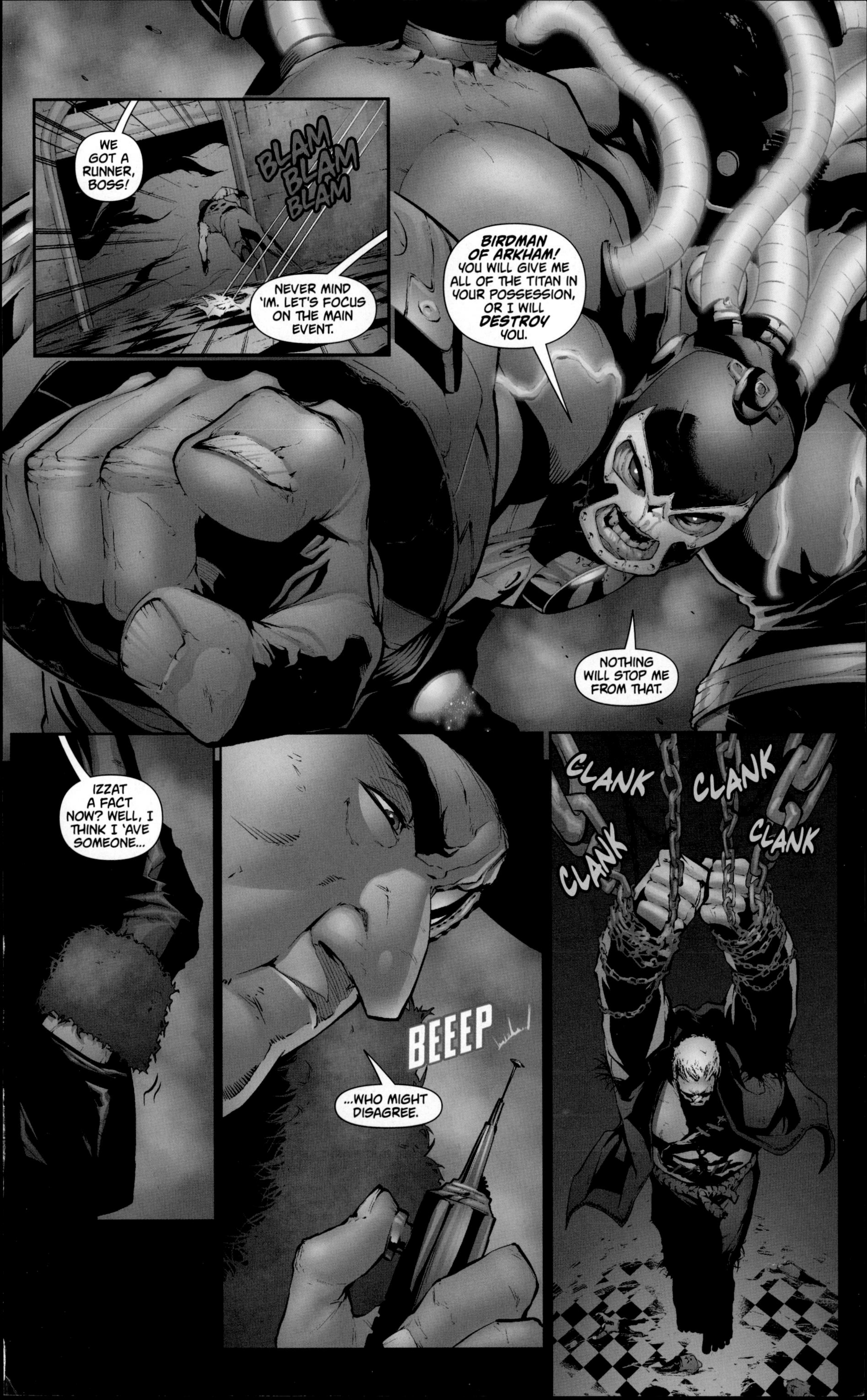
WE GOT A RUNNER, BOSS!
BLAM BLAM BLAM
NEVER MIND 'IM. LET'S FOCUS ON THE MAIN EVENT.
BIRDMAN OF ARKHAM! YOU WILL GIVE ME ALL OF THE TITAN IN YOUR POSSESSION, OR I WILL DESTROY YOU.
NOTHING WILL STOP ME FROM THAT.
IZZAT A FACT NOW? WELL, I THINK I 'AVE SOMEONE...
BEEEP
...WHO MIGHT DISAGREE.
CLANK CLANK CLANK CLANK CLANK

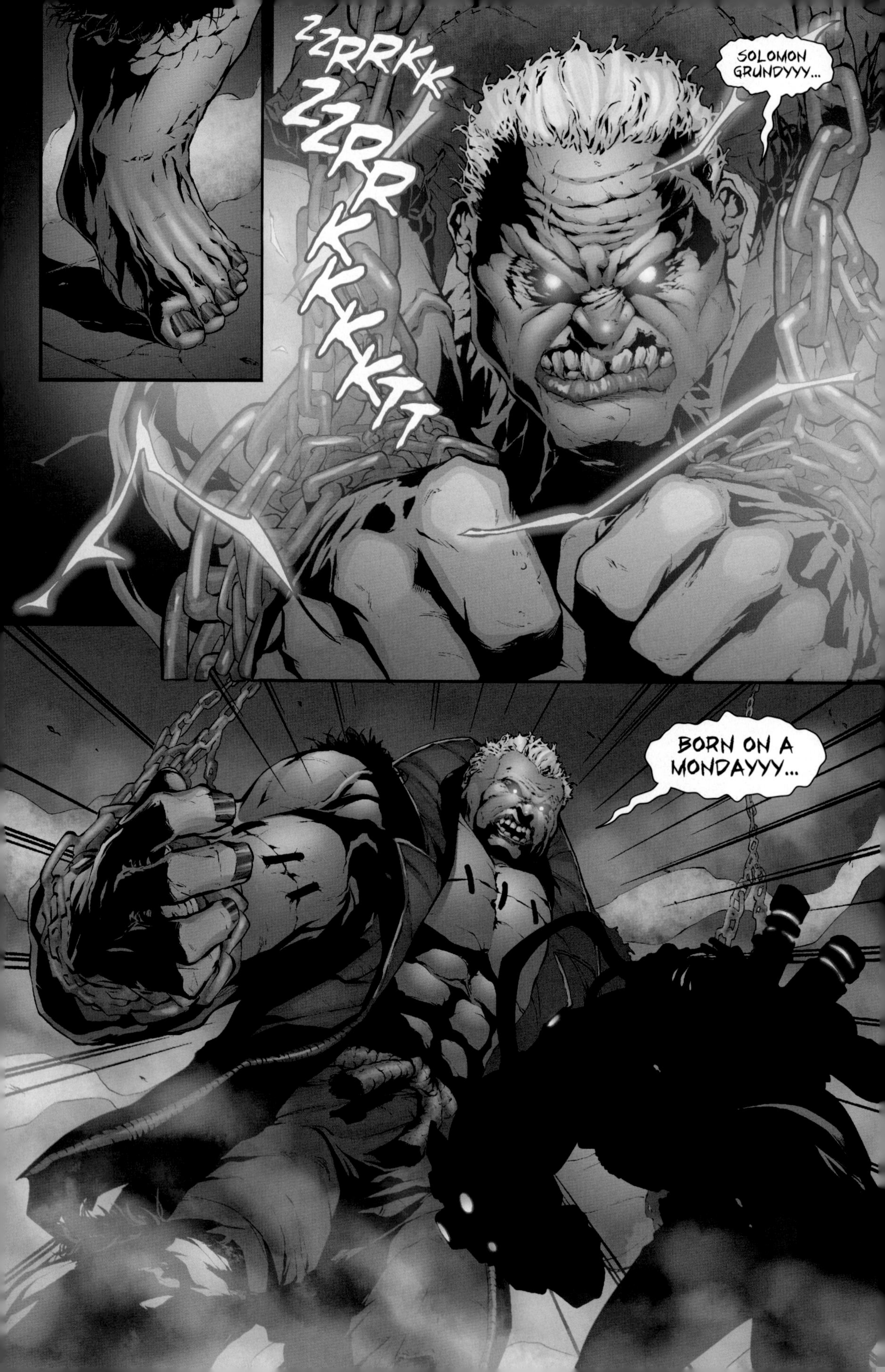
ZZRRKK
ZZRRKKKKTT
SOLOMON GRUNDYYY...
BORN ON A MONDAYYY...

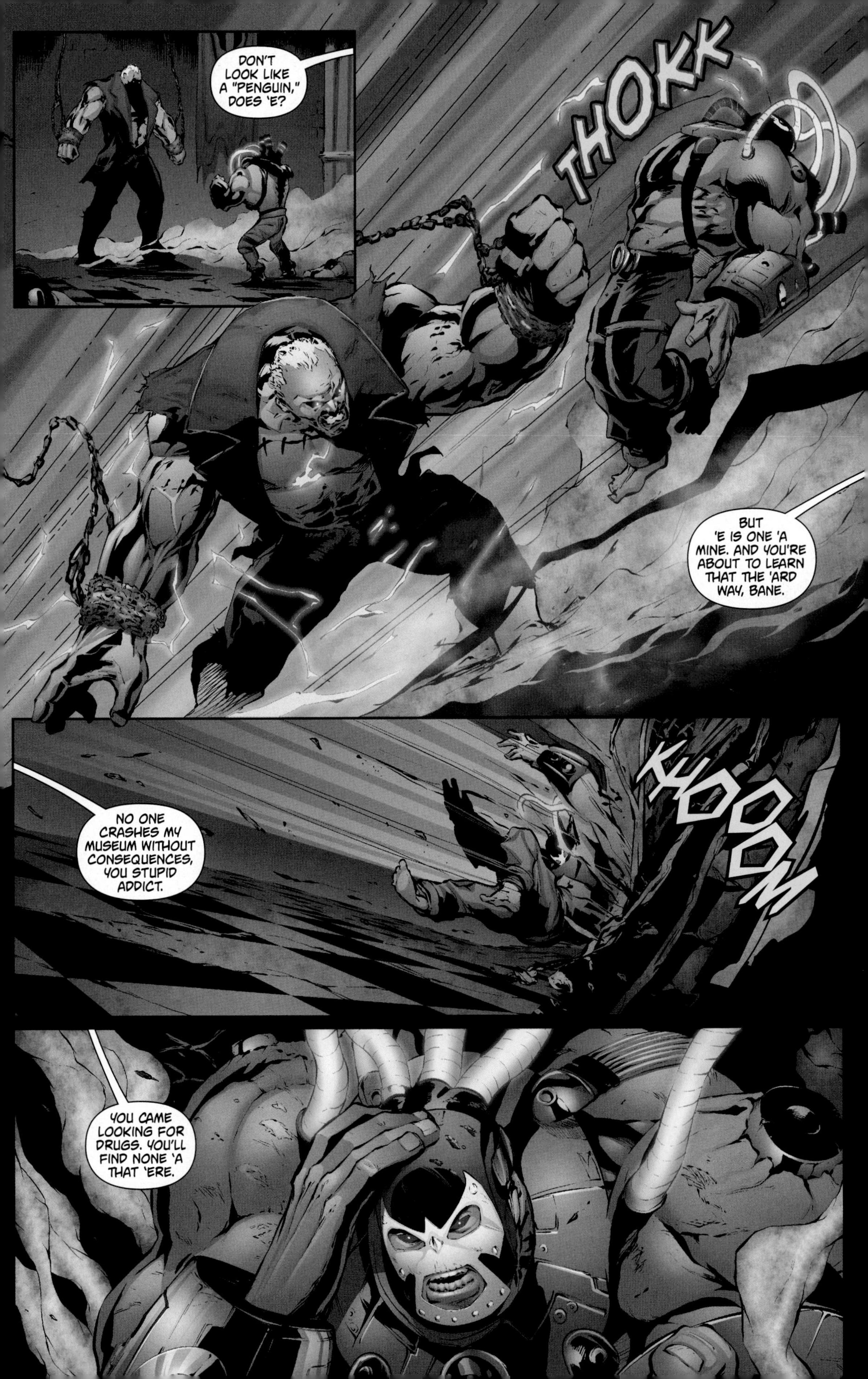
DON'T LOOK LIKE A "PENGUIN," DOES 'E?
THOKK
BUT 'E IS ONE 'A MINE. AND YOU'RE ABOUT TO LEARN THAT THE 'ARD WAY, BANE.
NO ONE CRASHES MY MUSEUM WITHOUT CONSEQUENCES, YOU STUPID ADDICT.
KHOOOM
YOU CAME LOOKING FOR DRUGS. YOU'LL FIND NONE 'A THAT 'ERE.

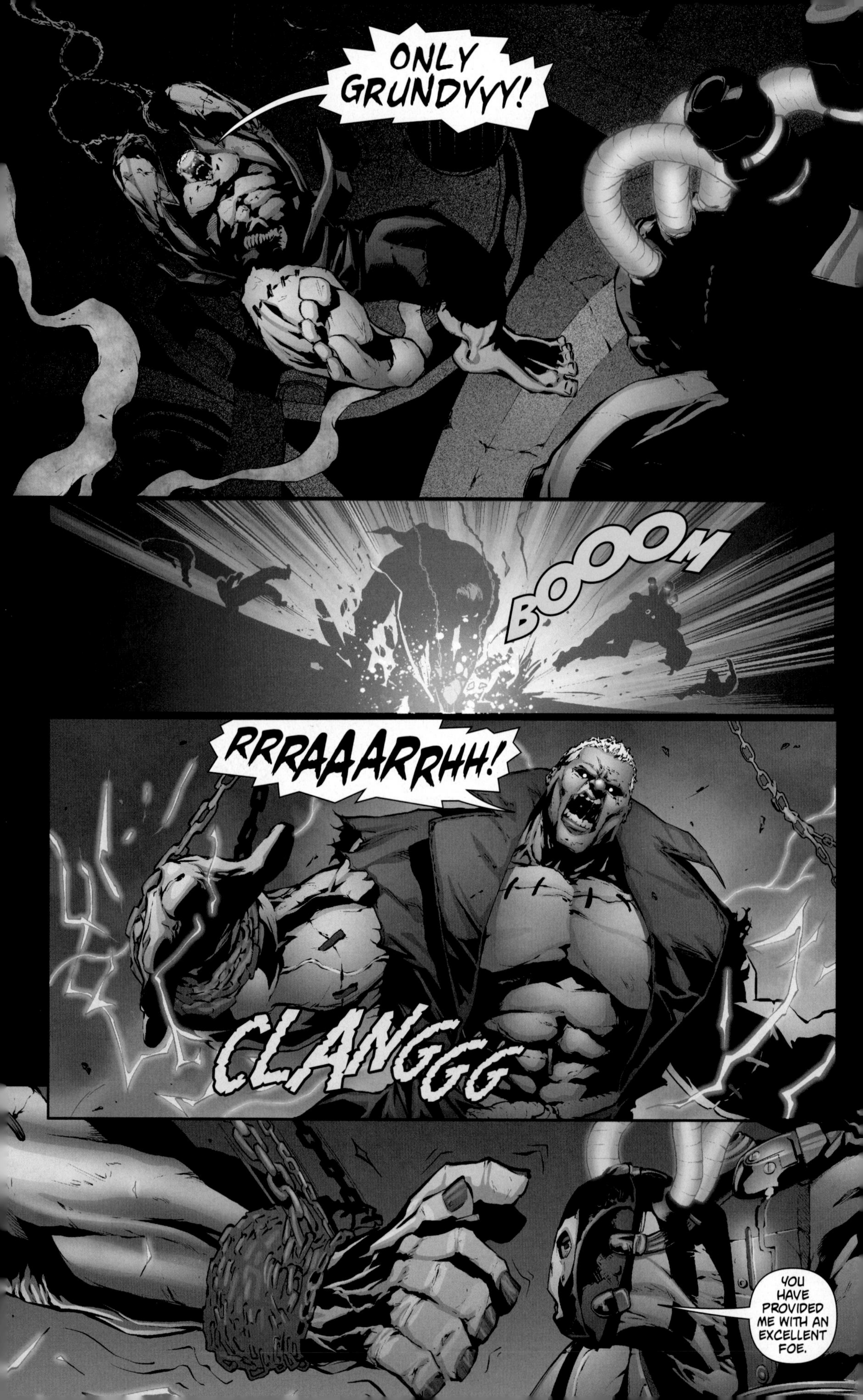
ONLY GRUNDYYY!
BOOOOM
RRRAAARRHH!
CLANGGG
YOU HAVE PROVIDED ME WITH AN EXCELLENT FOE.

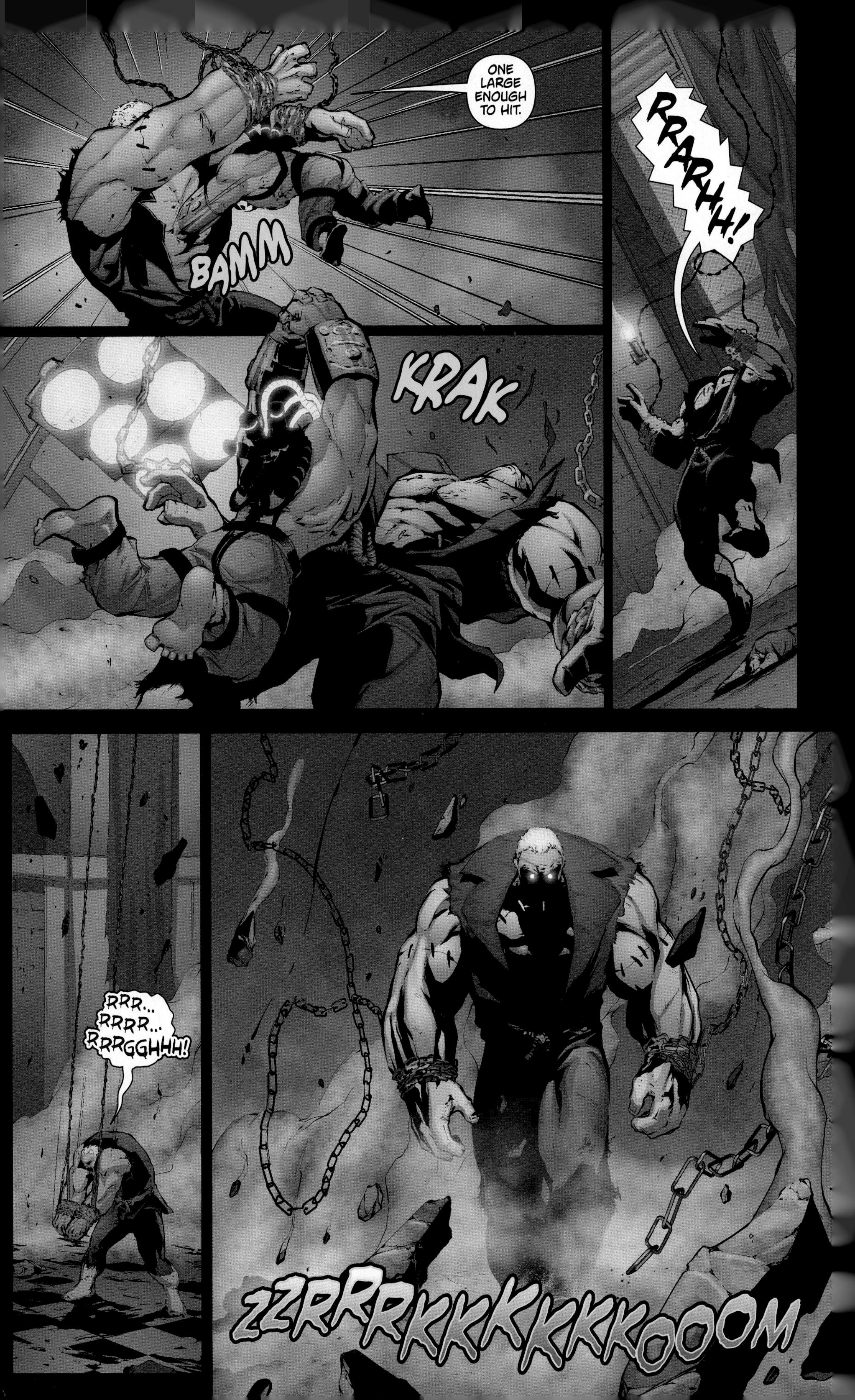
ONE LARGE ENOUGH TO HIT.
BAMM
RRARHH!
KRAK
RRR... RRRR... RRRGGHHH!
ZZRRRRKKKKKKKOOOM

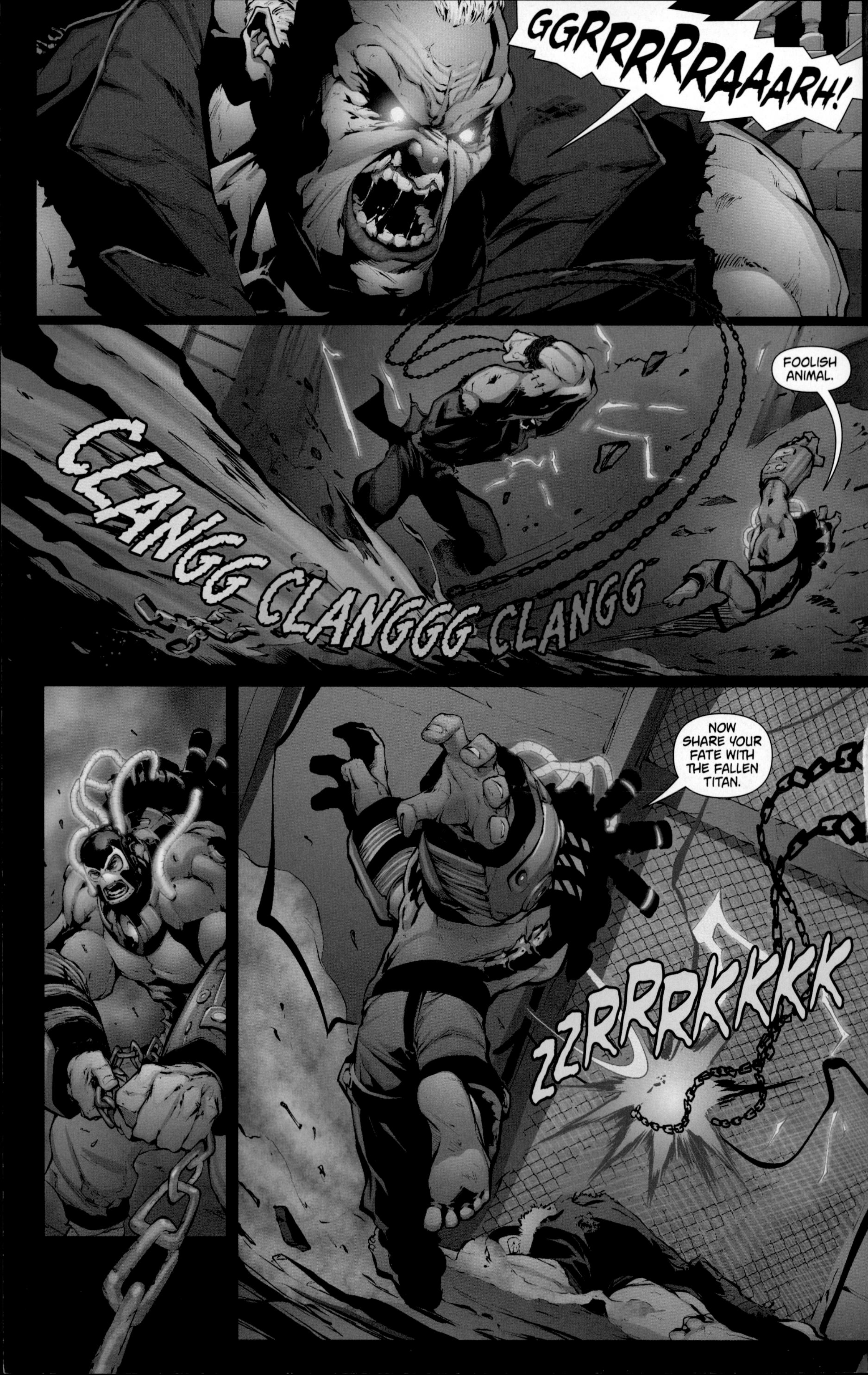
GGRRRRRRAAARH!
FOOLISH ANIMAL.
CLANGG CLANGGG CLANGG
NOW SHARE YOUR FATE WITH THE FALLEN TITAN.
ZZRRRRKKKK

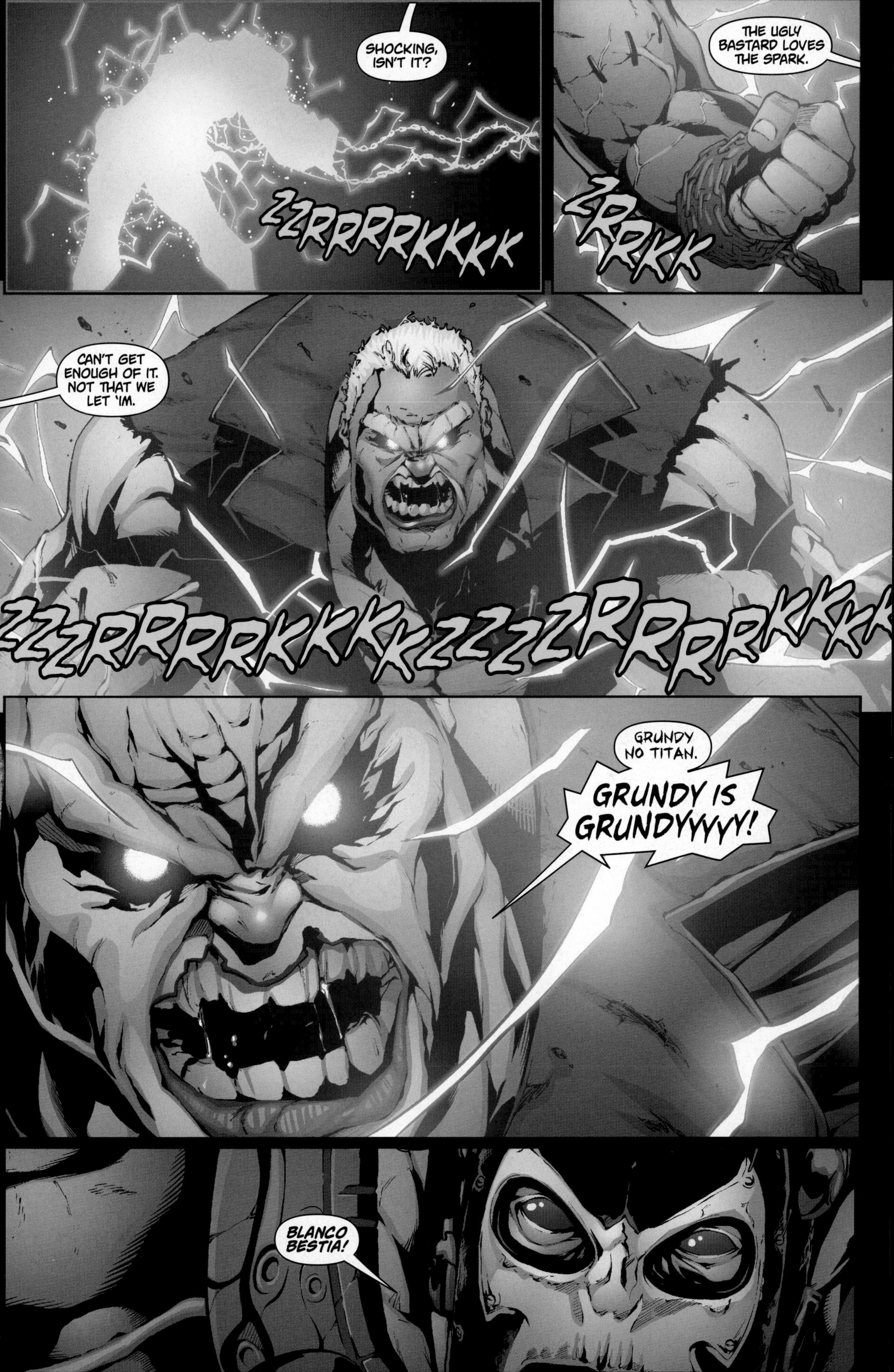
SHOCKING, ISN'T IT?
ZZRRRRRKKKK
THE UGLY BASTARD LOVES THE SPARK.
ZRRKK
CAN'T GET ENOUGH OF IT. NOT THAT WE LET 'IM.
ZZZRRRRKKKKZZZZZRRRRKKKK
GRUNDY NO TITAN.
GRUNDY IS GRUNDYYYYY!
BLANCO BESTIA!

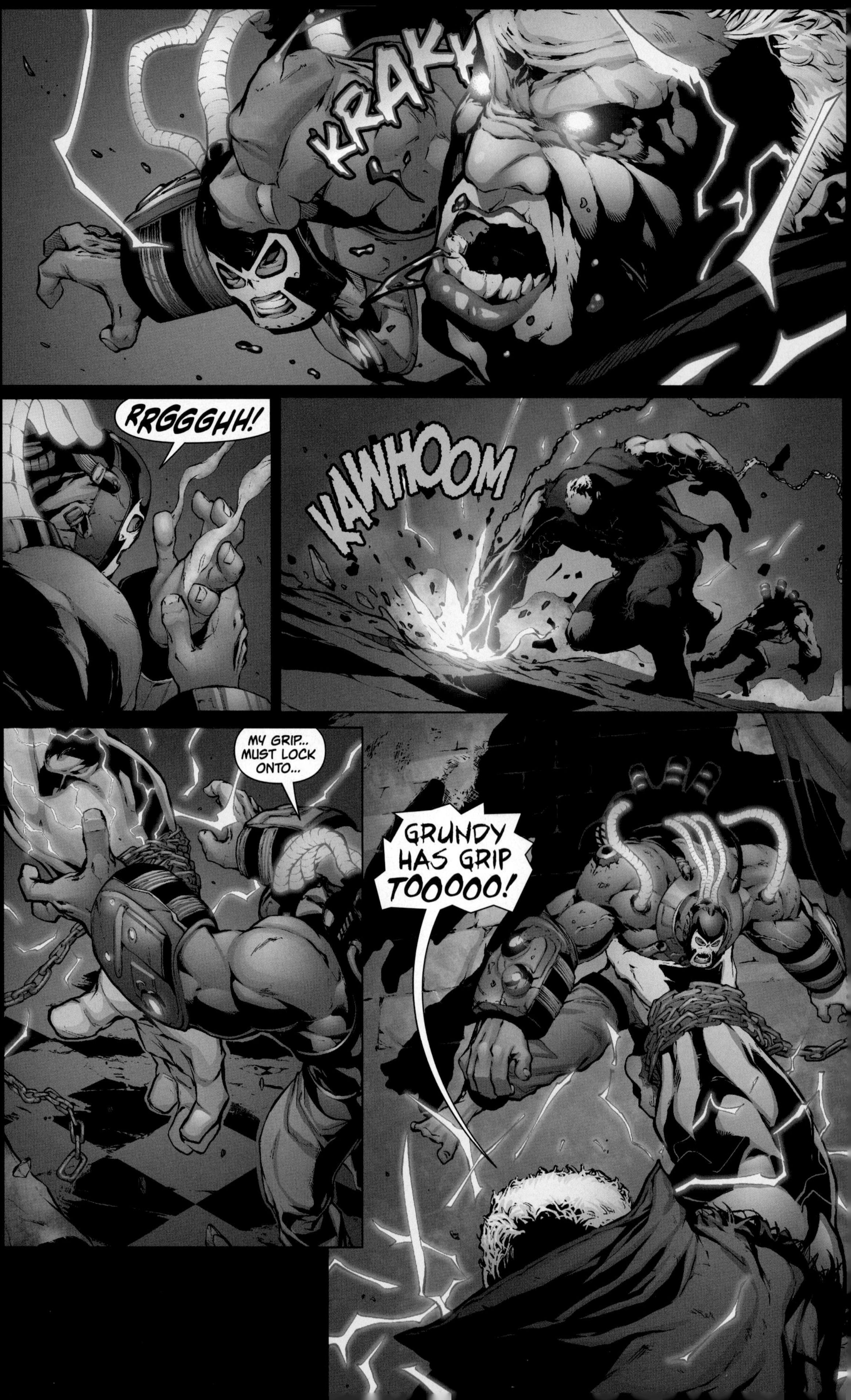
KRAKK
RRGGGHH!
KAWHOOM
MY GRIP... MUST LOCK ONTO...
GRUNDY HAS GRIP TOOOOO!

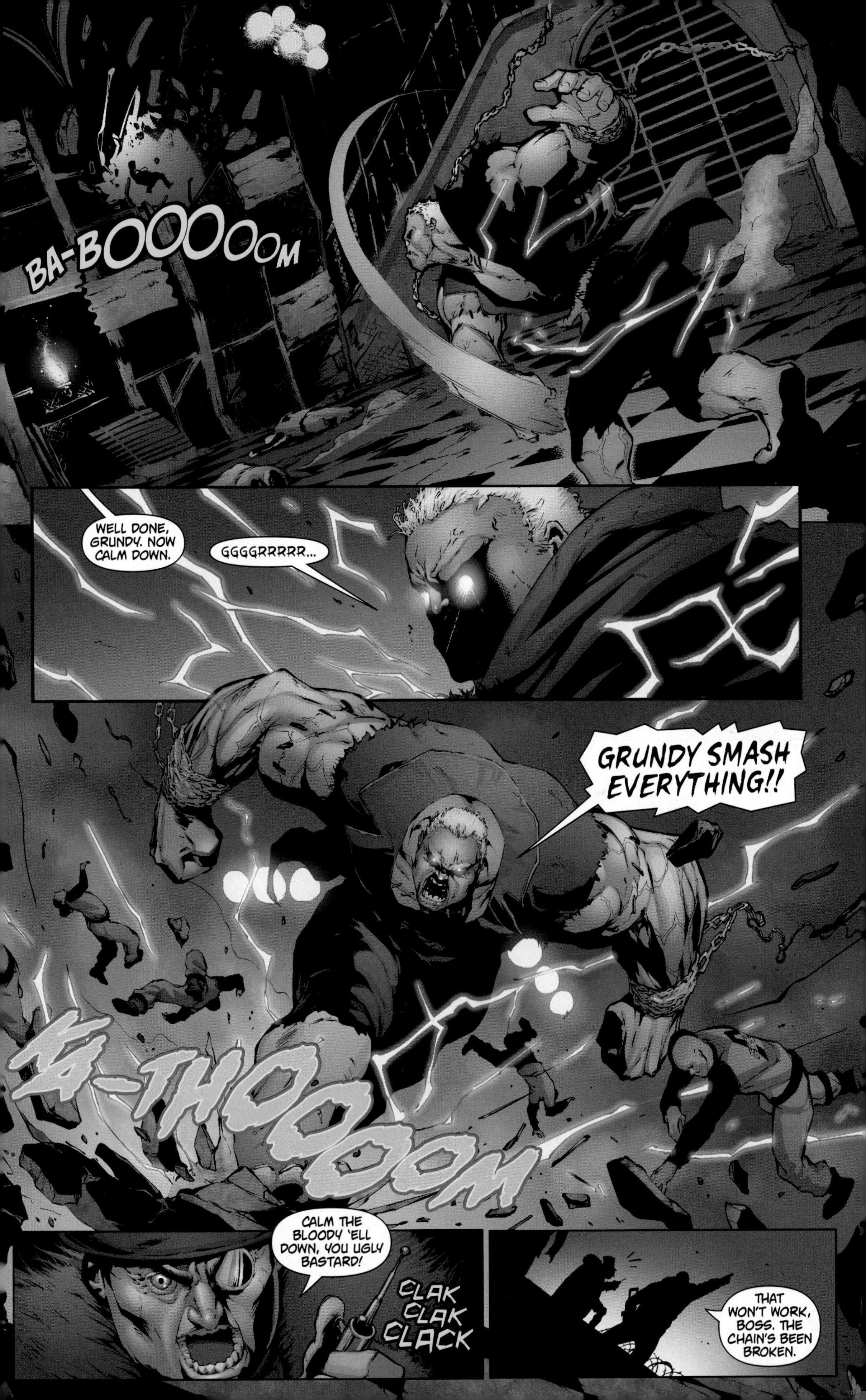
BA-BOOOOoom
WELL DONE, GRUNDY. NOW CALM DOWN.
GGGGRRRRR...
GRUNDY SMASH EVERYTHING!!
KA-THOOOOOM
CALM THE BLOODY 'ELL DOWN, YOU UGLY BASTARD!
CLAK CLAK CLACK
THAT WON'T WORK, BOSS. THE CHAIN'S BEEN BROKEN.

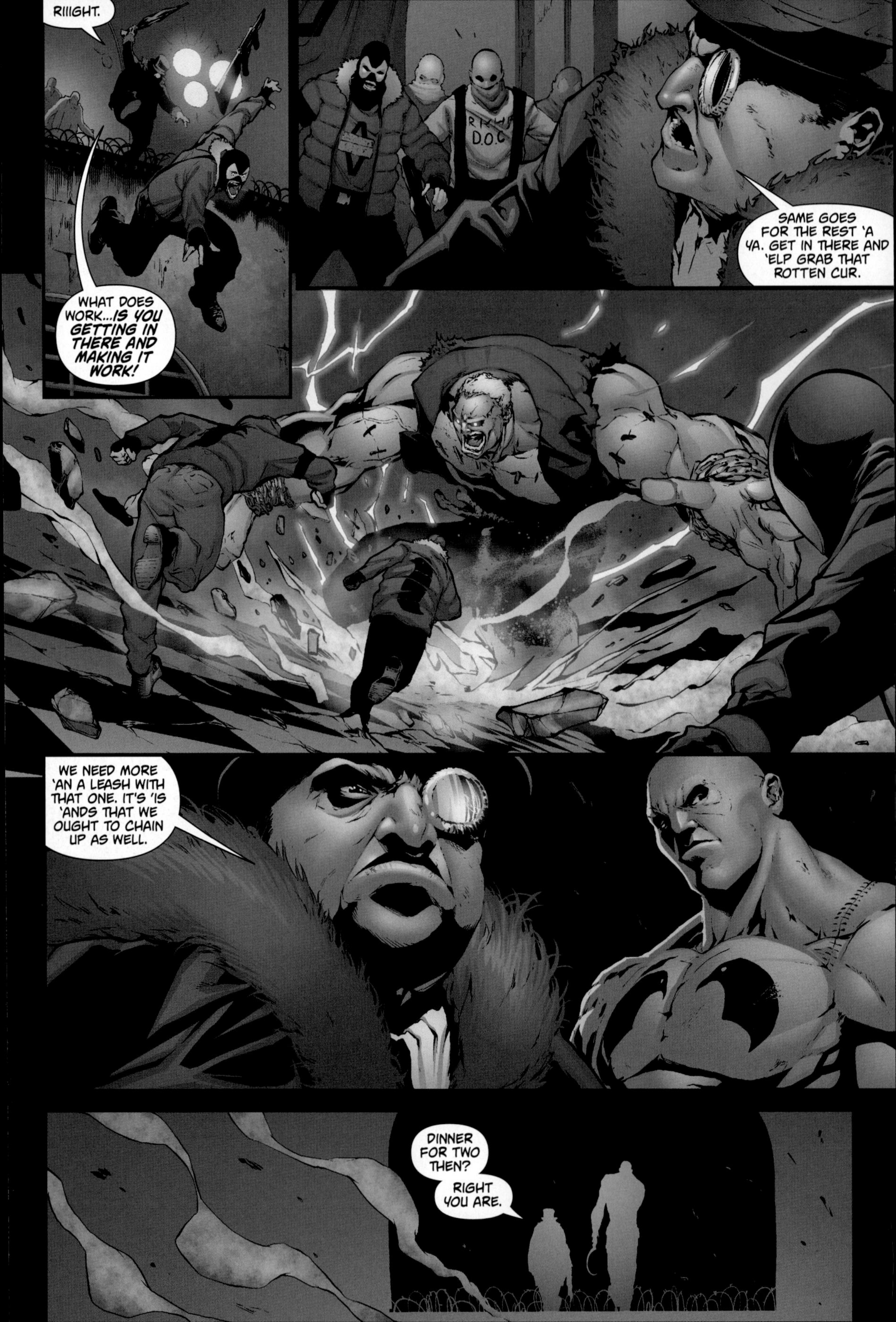

RIIIGHT.
WHAT DOES WORK...IS YOU GETTING IN THERE AND MAKING IT WORK!
SAME GOES FOR THE REST 'A YA. GET IN THERE AND 'ELP GRAB THAT ROTTEN CUR.
WE NEED MORE 'AN A LEASH WITH THAT ONE. IT'S 'IS 'ANDS THAT WE OUGHT TO CHAIN UP AS WELL.
DINNER FOR TWO THEN?
RIGHT YOU ARE.

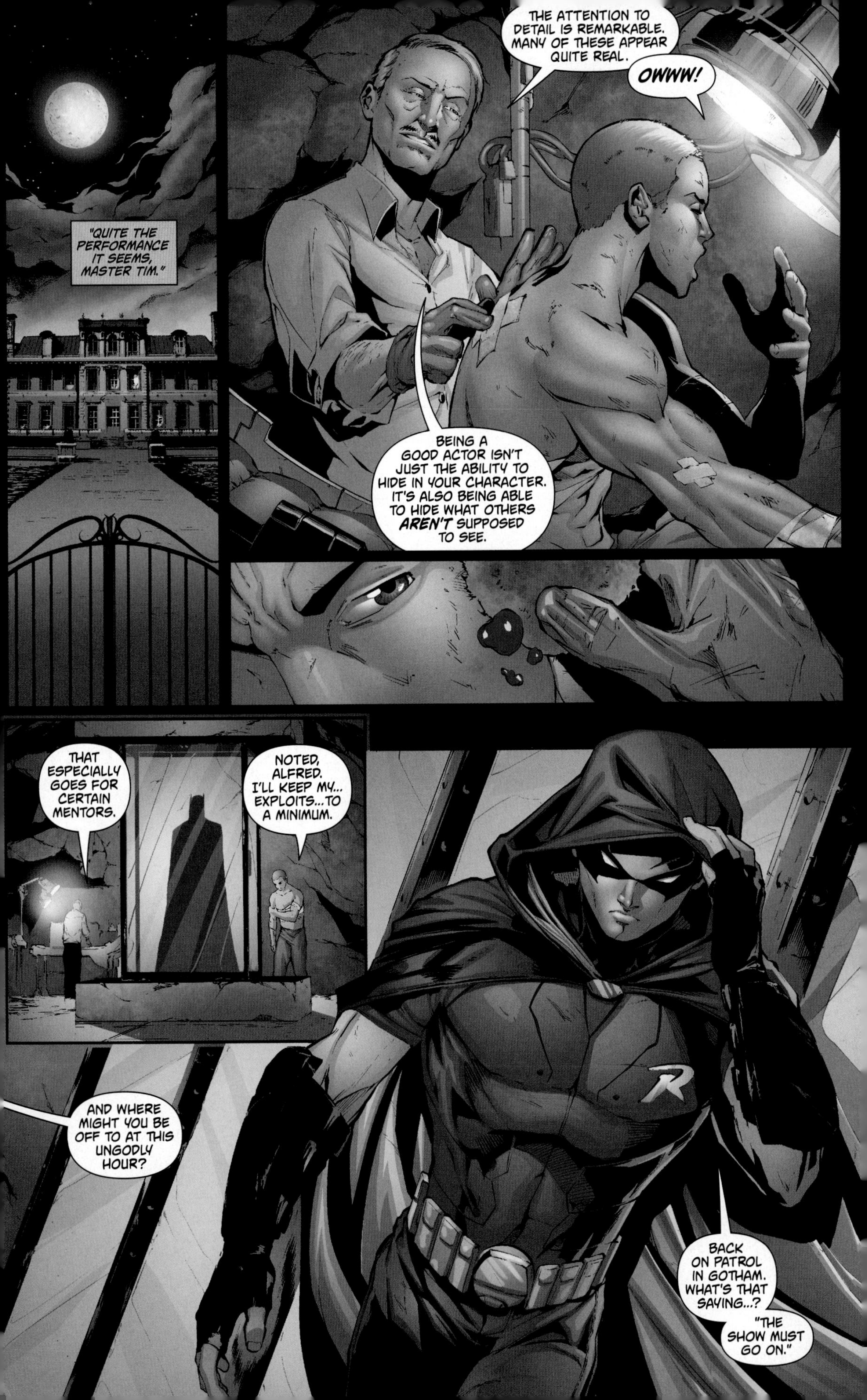
"QUITE THE PERFORMANCE IT SEEMS, MASTER TIM."
THE ATTENTION TO DETAIL IS REMARKABLE. MANY OF THESE APPEAR QUITE REAL.
OWWW!
BEING A GOOD ACTOR ISN'T JUST THE ABILITY TO HIDE IN YOUR CHARACTER. IT'S ALSO BEING ABLE TO HIDE WHAT OTHERS AREN'T SUPPOSED TO SEE.
THAT ESPECIALLY GOES FOR CERTAIN MENTORS.
NOTED, ALFRED. I'LL KEEP MY... EXPLOITS...TO A MINIMUM.
AND WHERE MIGHT YOU BE OFF TO AT THIS UNGODLY HOUR?
BACK ON PATROL IN GOTHAM. WHAT'S THAT SAYING...?
"THE SHOW MUST GO ON."

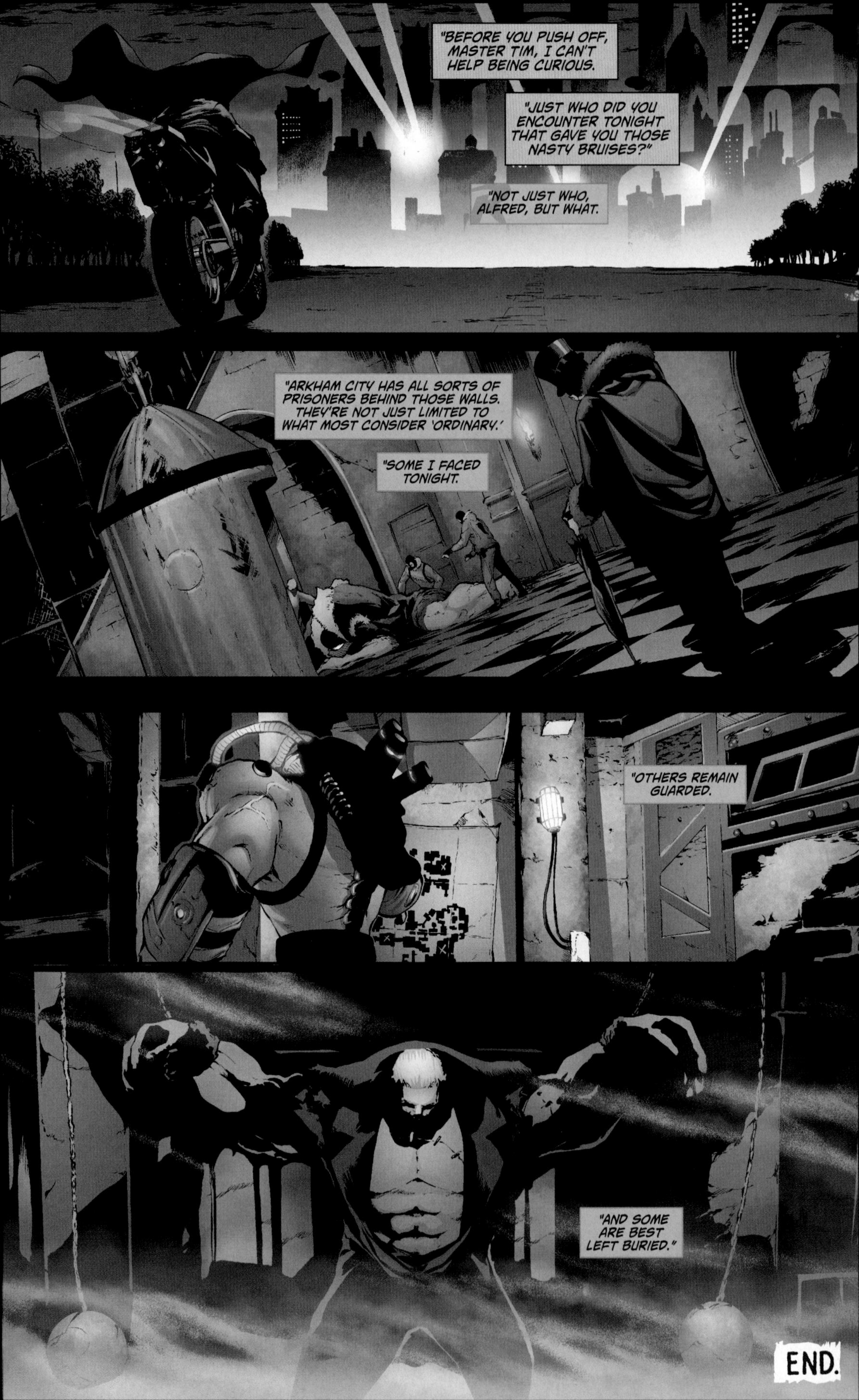
"BEFORE YOU PUSH OFF, MASTER TIM, I CAN'T HELP BEING CURIOUS.
"JUST WHO DID YOU ENCOUNTER TONIGHT THAT GAVE YOU THOSE NASTY BRUISES?"
"NOT JUST WHO, ALFRED, BUT WHAT.
"ARKHAM CITY HAS ALL SORTS OF PRISONERS BEHIND THOSE WALLS. THEY'RE NOT JUST LIMITED TO WHAT MOST CONSIDER 'ORDINARY.'
"SOME I FACED TONIGHT.
"OTHERS REMAIN GUARDED.
"AND SOME ARE BEST LEFT BURIED."
END.

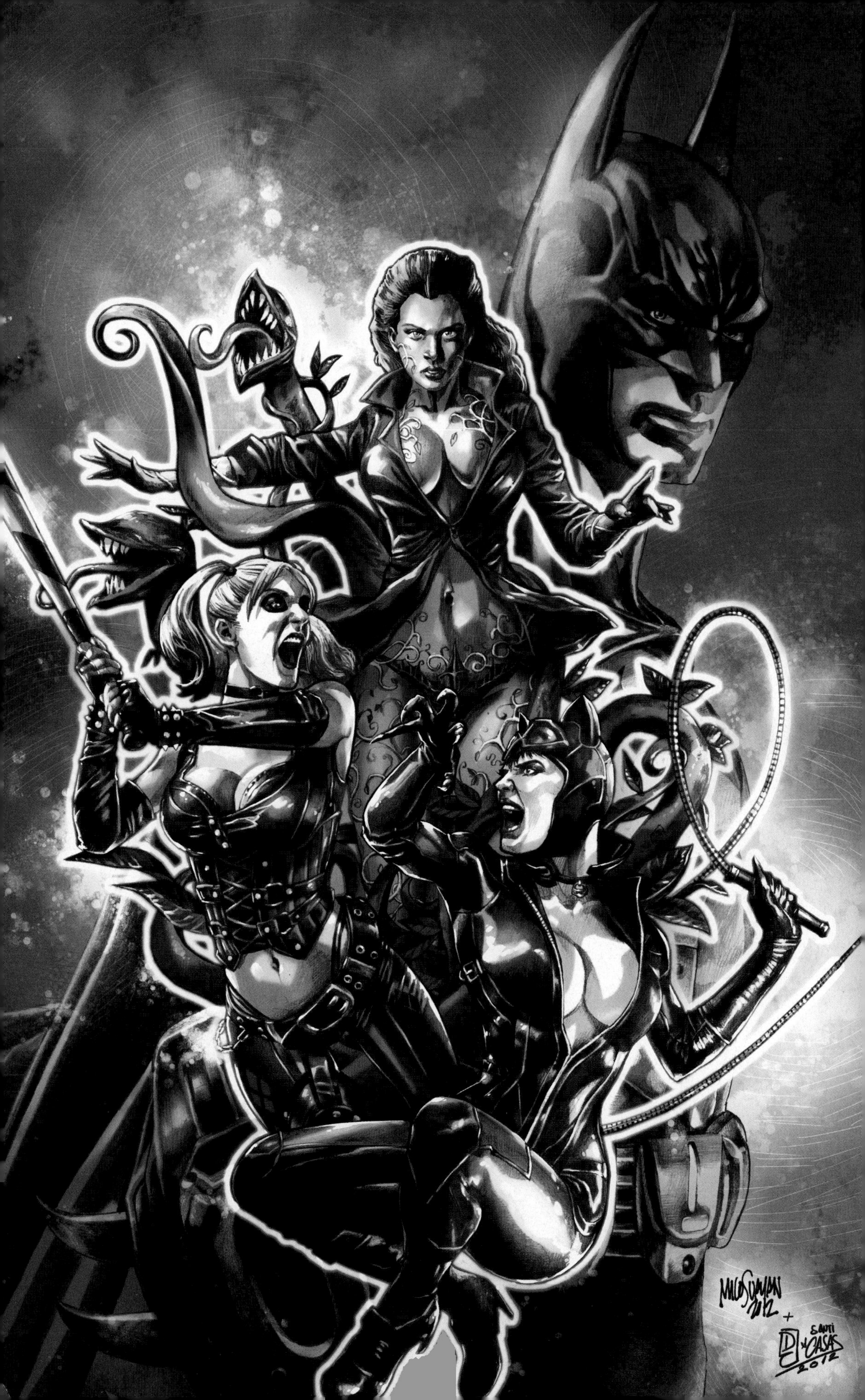

ARKHAM CITY SIRENS

WRITTEN BY: DEREK FRIDOLFS

ART BY: MIKE S. MILLER

COLORS BY: ANDREW ELDER

LETTERS BY: TRAVIS LANHAM

COVER ART BY: MICO SUAYAN

COVER COLORS BY: DAVID LOPEZ

& SANTI CASAS OF IKARI STUDIO

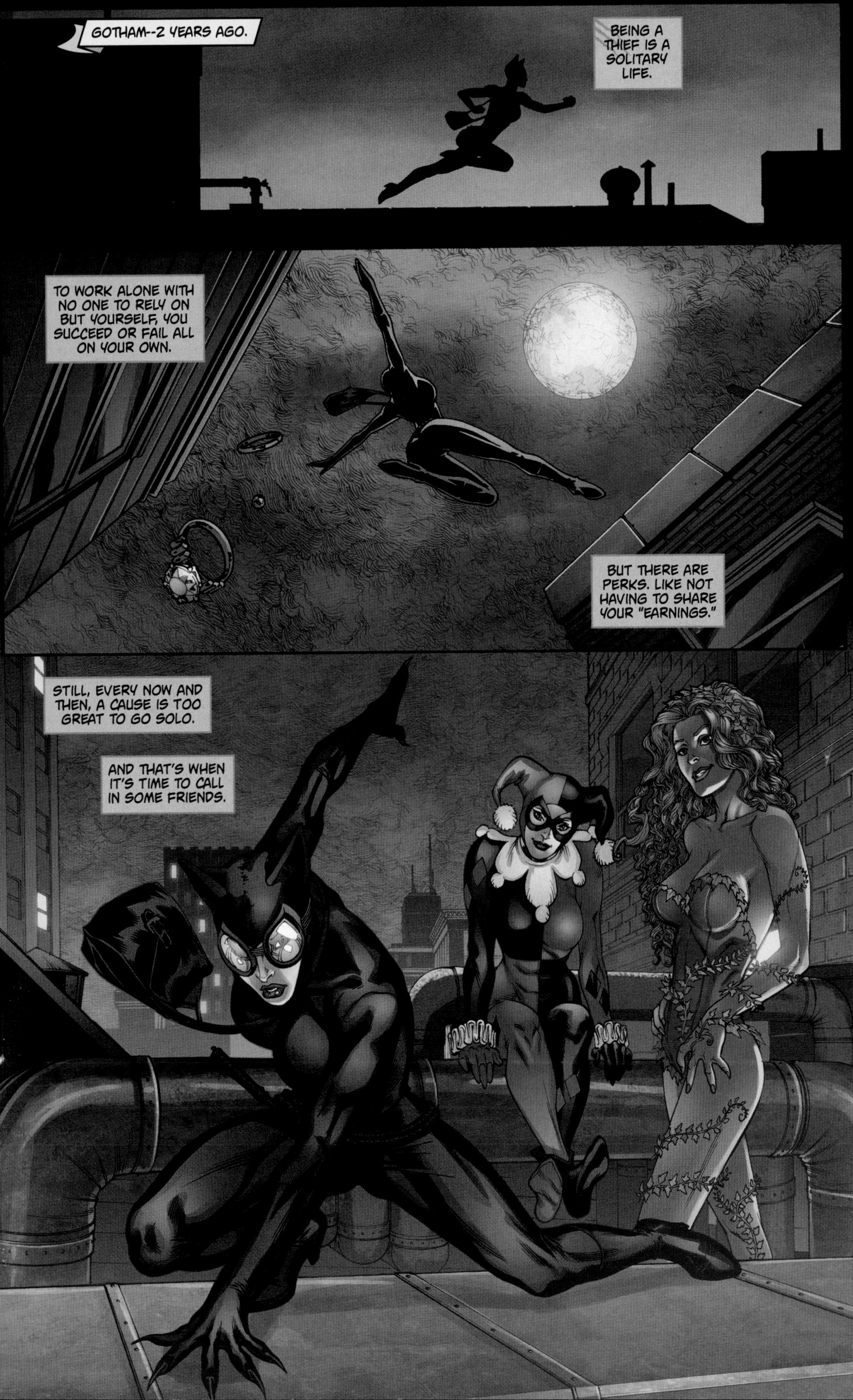
GOTHAM--2 YEARS AGO.
BEING A THIEF IS A SOLITARY LIFE.
TO WORK ALONE WITH NO ONE TO RELY ON BUT YOURSELF, YOU SUCCEED OR FAIL ALL ON YOUR OWN.
BUT THERE ARE PERKS. LIKE NOT HAVING TO SHARE YOUR "EARNINGS."
STILL, EVERY NOW AND THEN, A CAUSE IS TOO GREAT TO GO SOLO.
AND THAT'S WHEN IT'S TIME TO CALL IN SOME FRIENDS.

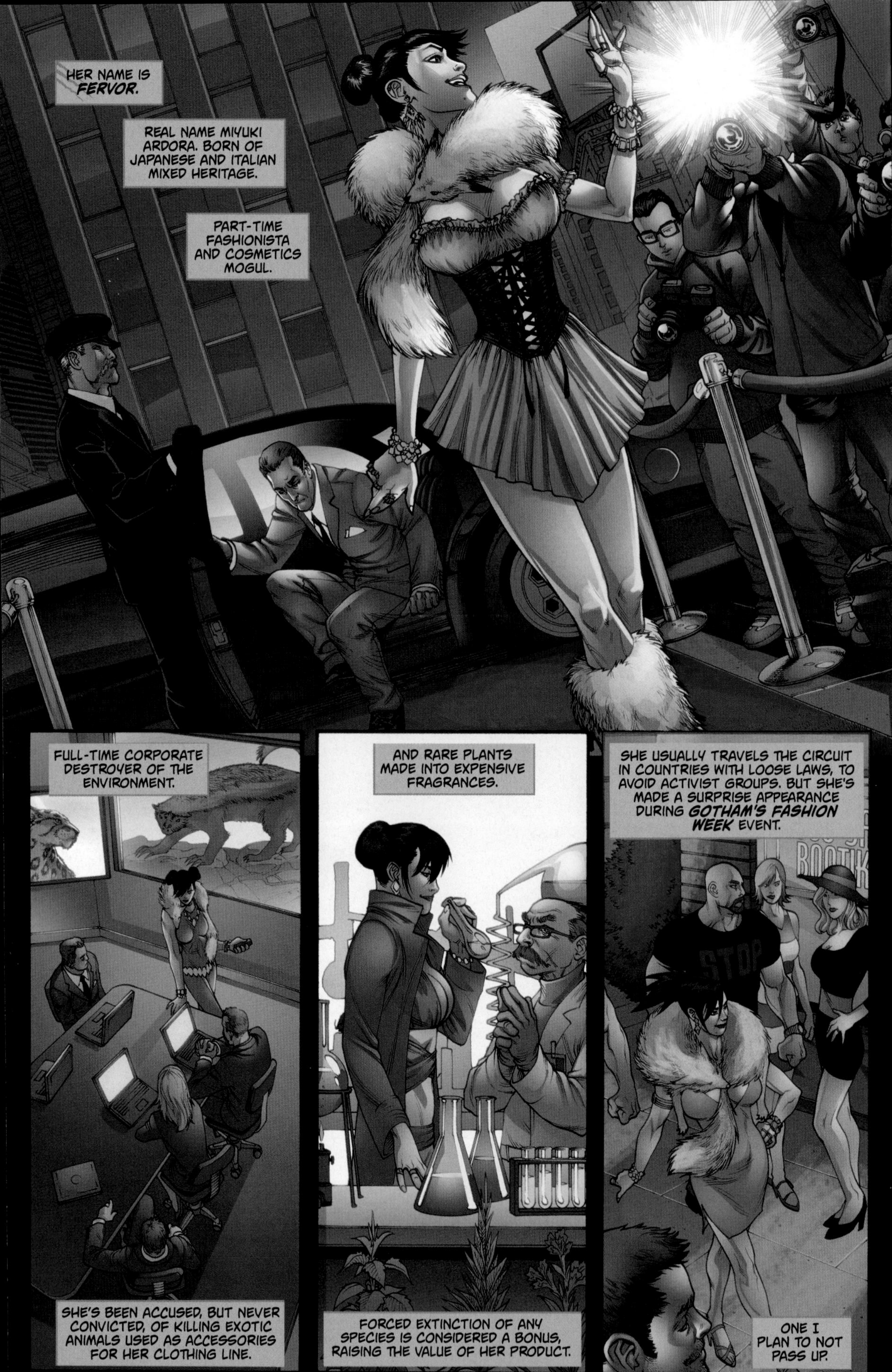
HER NAME IS FERVOR.
REAL NAME MIYUKI ARDORA. BORN OF JAPANESE AND ITALIAN MIXED HERITAGE.
PART-TIME FASHIONISTA AND COSMETICS MOGUL.
FULL-TIME CORPORATE DESTROYER OF THE ENVIRONMENT.
SHE'S BEEN ACCUSED, BUT NEVER CONVICTED, OF KILLING EXOTIC ANIMALS USED AS ACCESSORIES FOR HER CLOTHING LINE.
AND RARE PLANTS MADE INTO EXPENSIVE FRAGRANCES.
FORCED EXTINCTION OF ANY SPECIES IS CONSIDERED A BONUS, RAISING THE VALUE OF HER PRODUCT.
SHE USUALLY TRAVELS THE CIRCUIT IN COUNTRIES WITH LOOSE LAWS, TO AVOID ACTIVIST GROUPS. BUT SHE'S MADE A SURPRISE APPEARANCE DURING GOTHAM'S FASHION WEEK EVENT.
STOP
ONE I PLAN TO NOT PASS UP.

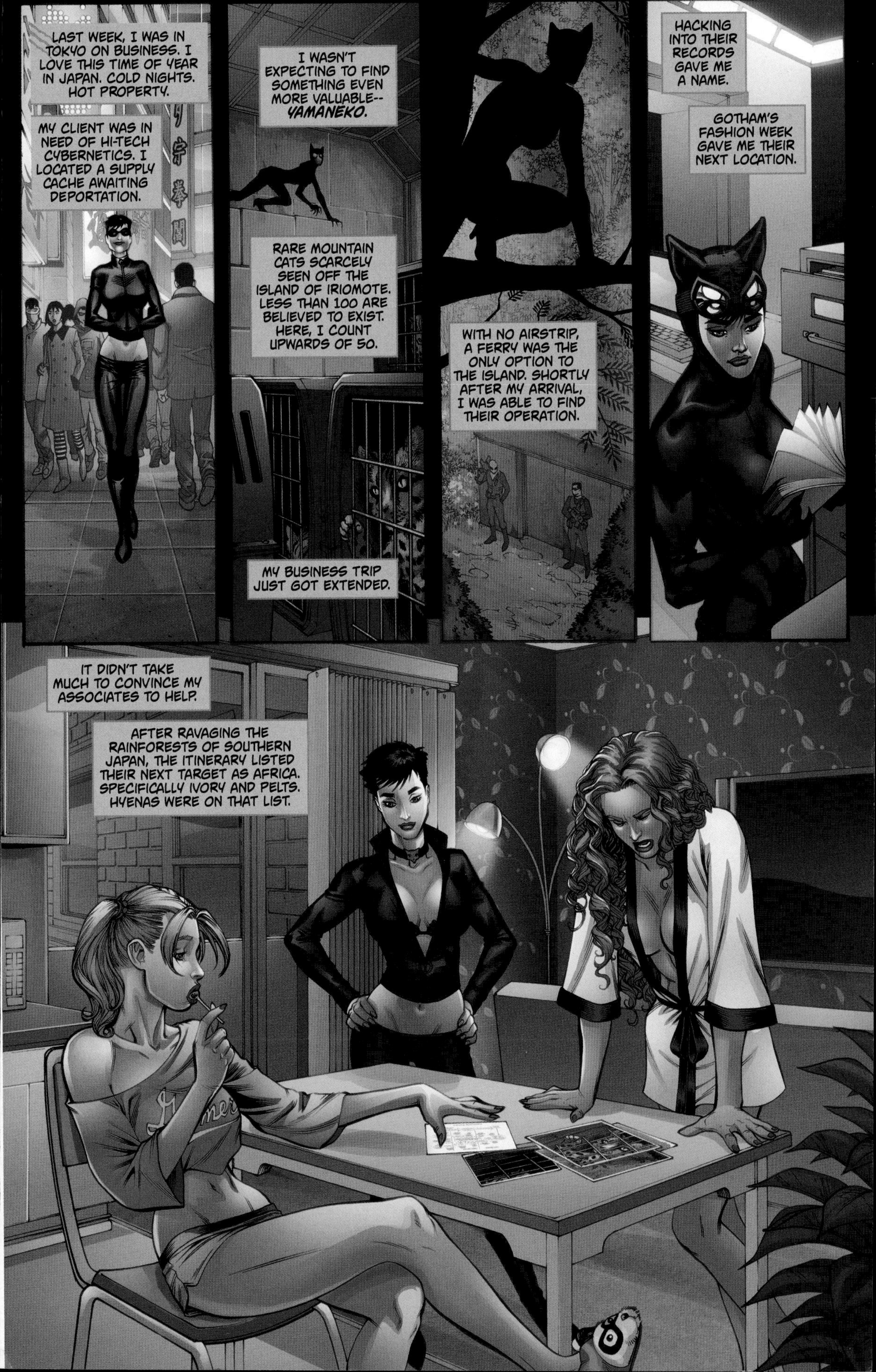

LAST WEEK, I WAS IN TOKYO ON BUSINESS. I LOVE THIS TIME OF YEAR IN JAPAN. COLD NIGHTS. HOT PROPERTY.
MY CLIENT WAS IN NEED OF HI-TECH CYBERNETICS. I LOCATED A SUPPLY CACHE AWAITING DEPORTATION.
I WASN'T EXPECTING TO FIND SOMETHING EVEN MORE VALUABLE-- YAMANEKO.
RARE MOUNTAIN CATS SCARCELY SEEN OFF THE ISLAND OF IRIOMOTE. LESS THAN 100 ARE BELIEVED TO EXIST. HERE, I COUNT UPWARDS OF 50.
MY BUSINESS TRIP JUST GOT EXTENDED.
WITH NO AIRSTRIP, A FERRY WAS THE ONLY OPTION TO THE ISLAND. SHORTLY AFTER MY ARRIVAL, I WAS ABLE TO FIND THEIR OPERATION.
HACKING INTO THEIR RECORDS GAVE ME A NAME.
GOTHAM'S FASHION WEEK GAVE ME THEIR NEXT LOCATION.
IT DIDN'T TAKE MUCH TO CONVINCE MY ASSOCIATES TO HELP.
AFTER RAVAGING THE RAINFORESTS OF SOUTHERN JAPAN, THE ITINERARY LISTED THEIR NEXT TARGET AS AFRICA. SPECIFICALLY IVORY AND PELTS. HYENAS WERE ON THAT LIST.

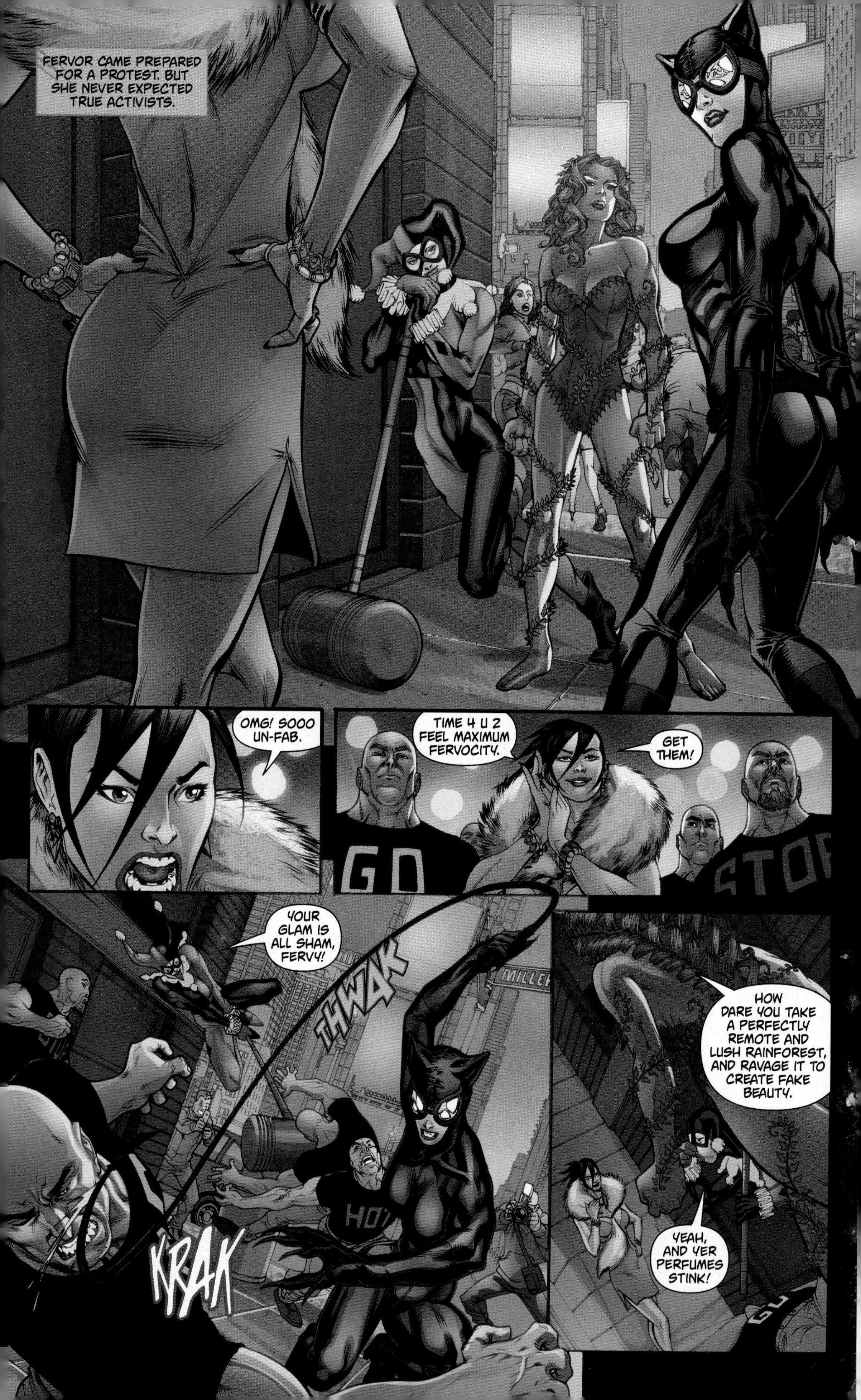
FERVOR CAME PREPARED FOR A PROTEST. BUT SHE NEVER EXPECTED TRUE ACTIVISTS.
OMG! SOOO UN-FAB.
TIME 4 U 2 FEEL MAXIMUM FERVOCITY.
GET THEM!
GO
STOP
YOUR GLAM IS ALL SHAM, FERVY!
THWAK
KRAK
HOW DARE YOU TAKE A PERFECTLY REMOTE AND LUSH RAINFOREST, AND RAVAGE IT TO CREATE FAKE BEAUTY.
YEAH, AND YER PERFUMES STINK!

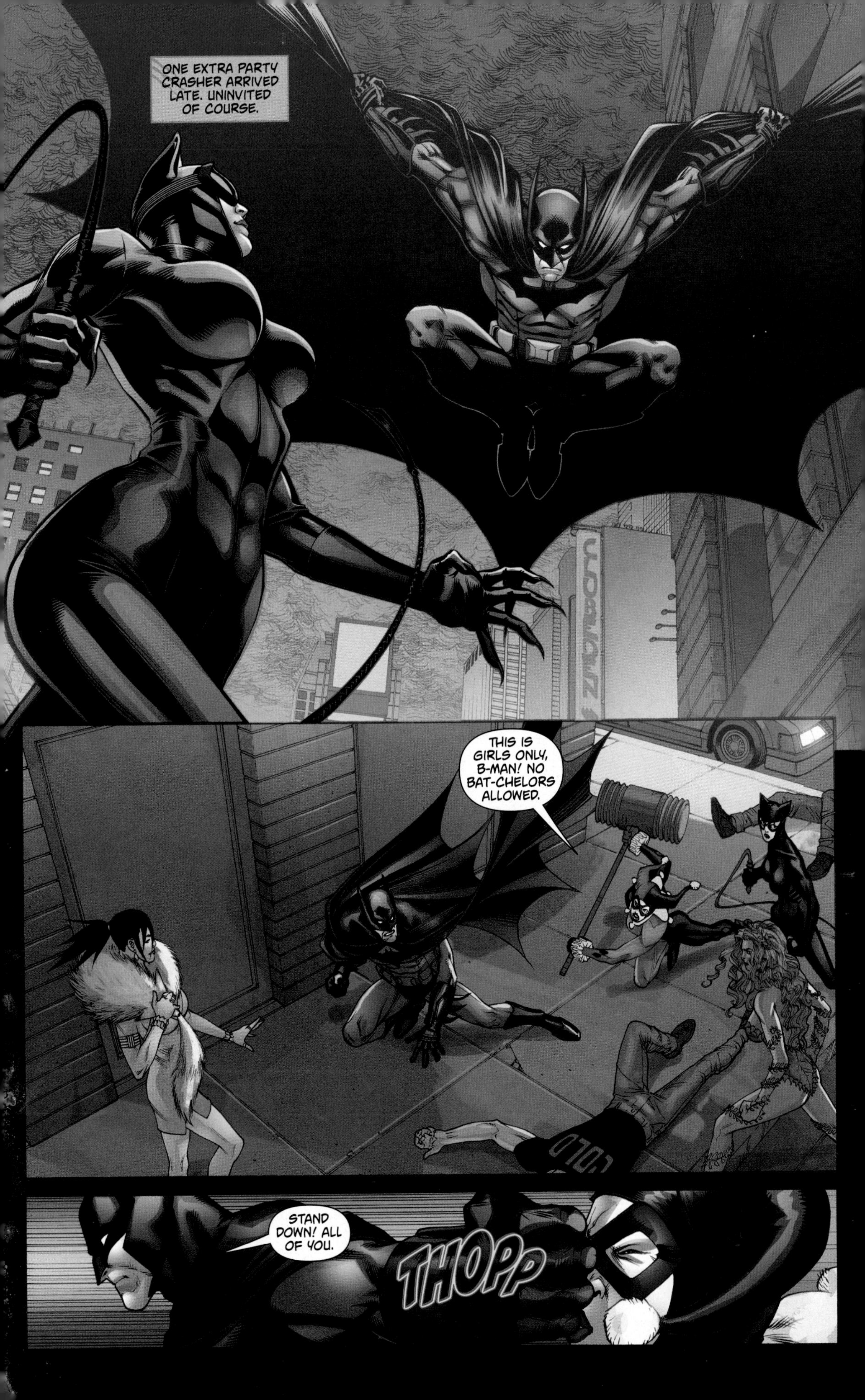
ONE EXTRA PARTY CRASHER ARRIVED LATE. UNINVITED OF COURSE.
THIS IS GIRLS ONLY, B-MAN! NO BAT-CHELORS ALLOWED.
STAND DOWN! ALL OF YOU.
THOPP

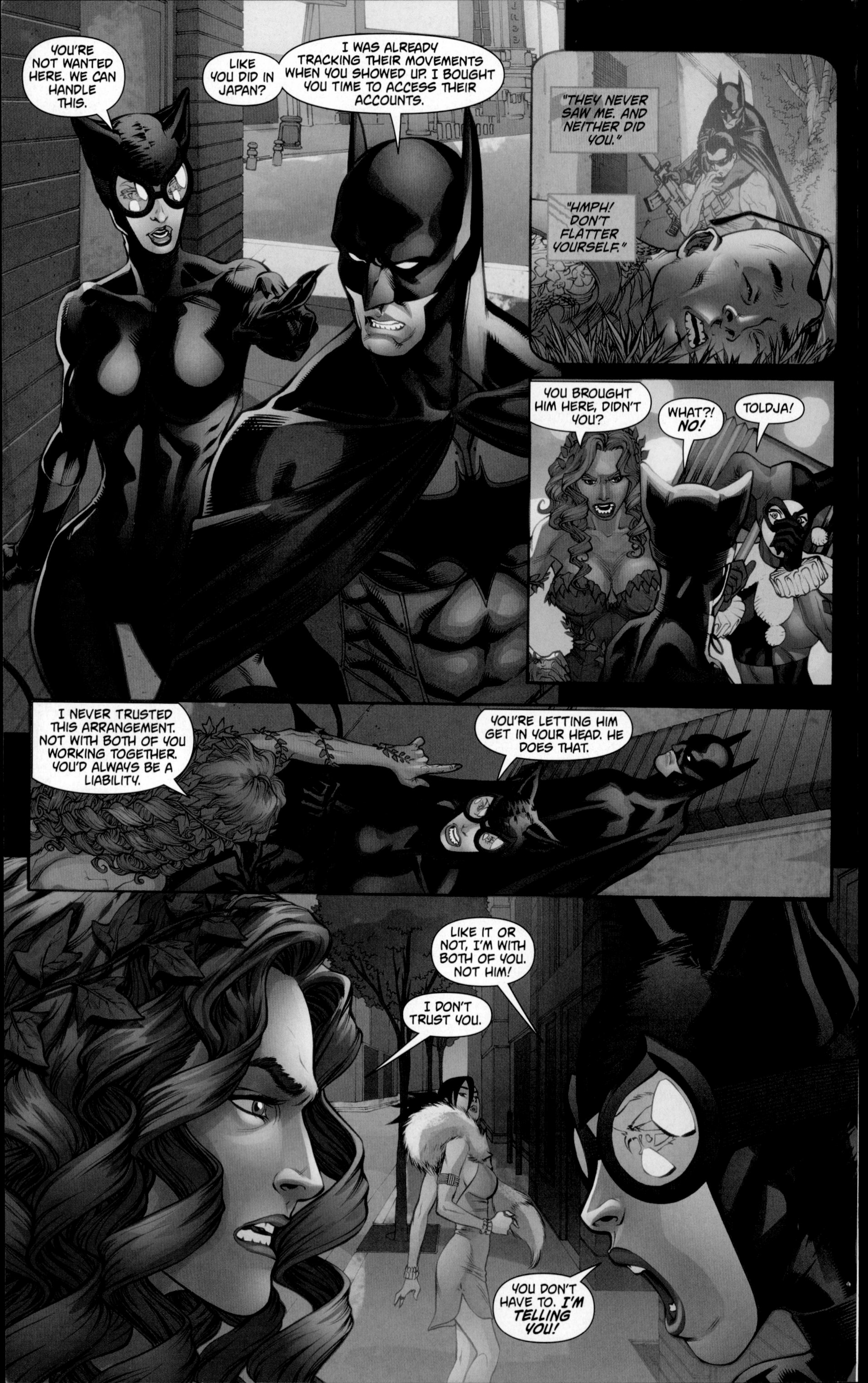
YOU'RE NOT WANTED HERE. WE CAN HANDLE THIS.
LIKE YOU DID IN JAPAN?
I WAS ALREADY TRACKING THEIR MOVEMENTS WHEN YOU SHOWED UP. I BOUGHT YOU TIME TO ACCESS THEIR ACCOUNTS.
"THEY NEVER SAW ME. AND NEITHER DID YOU."
"HMPH! DON'T FLATTER YOURSELF."
YOU BROUGHT HIM HERE, DIDN'T YOU?
WHAT?! NO!
TOLDJA!
I NEVER TRUSTED THIS ARRANGEMENT. NOT WITH BOTH OF YOU WORKING TOGETHER. YOU'D ALWAYS BE A LIABILITY.
YOU'RE LETTING HIM GET IN YOUR HEAD. HE DOES THAT.
LIKE IT OR NOT, I'M WITH BOTH OF YOU. NOT HIM!
I DON'T TRUST YOU.
YOU DON'T HAVE TO. I'M TELLING YOU!

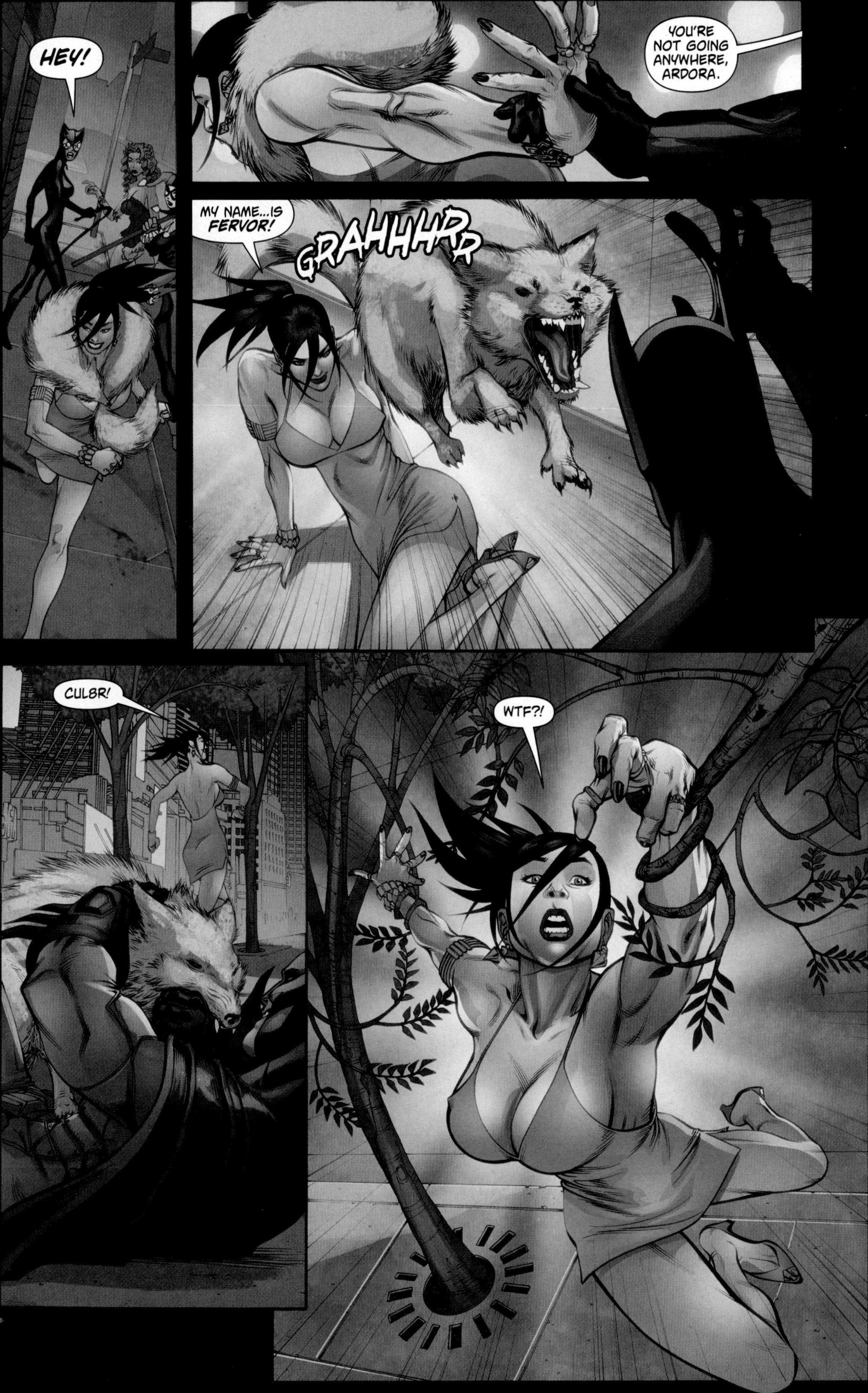
HEY!
YOU'RE NOT GOING ANYWHERE, ARDORA.
MY NAME...IS FERVOR!
GRAHHHRR
CUL8R!
WTF?!

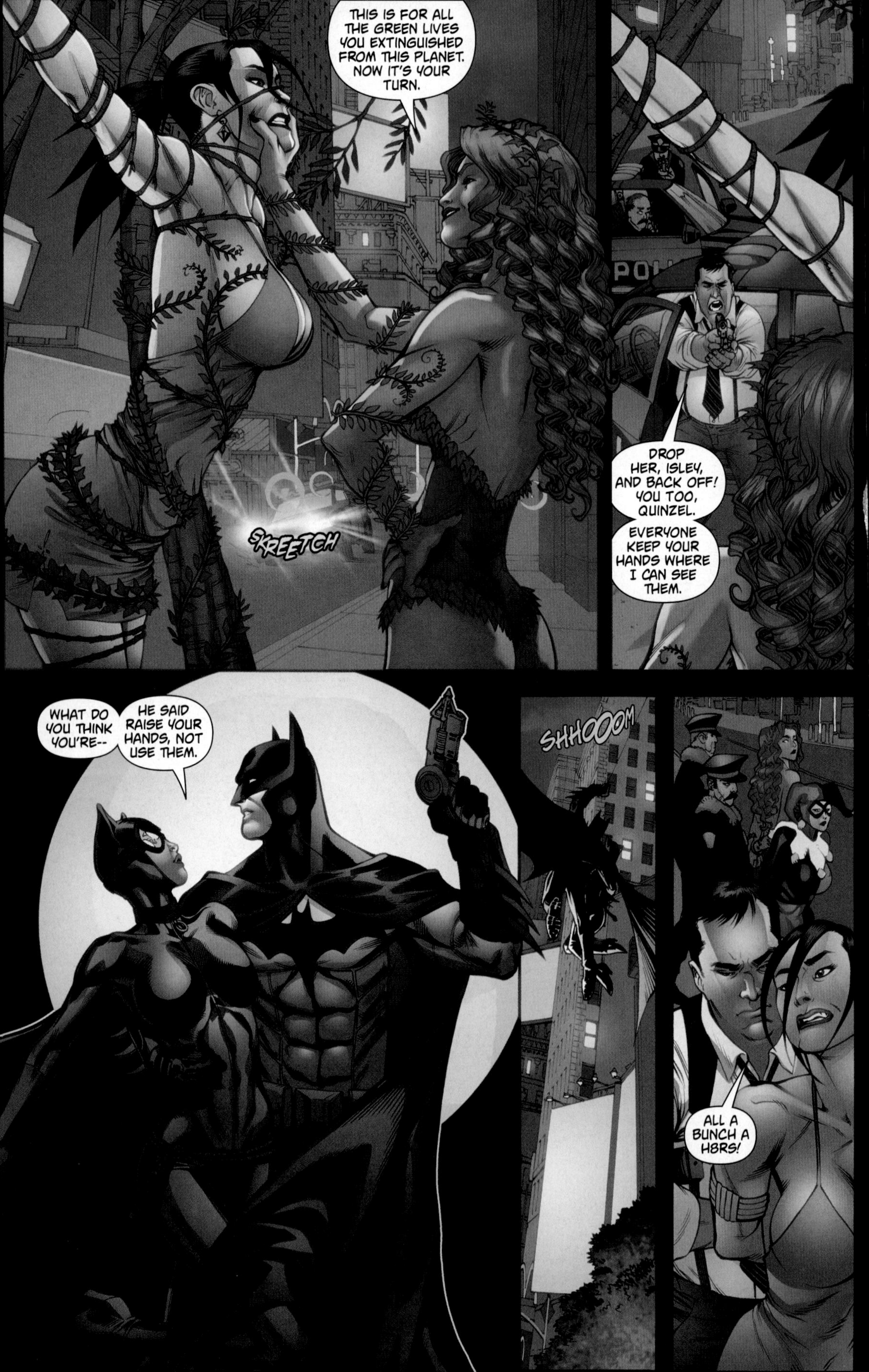
THIS IS FOR ALL THE GREEN LIVES YOU EXTINGUISHED FROM THIS PLANET. NOW IT'S YOUR TURN.
SKREETCH
DROP HER, ISLEY, AND BACK OFF! YOU TOO, QUINZEL.
EVERYONE KEEP YOUR HANDS WHERE I CAN SEE THEM.
WHAT DO YOU THINK YOU'RE--
HE SAID RAISE YOUR HANDS, NOT USE THEM.
SHHOOOM
ALL A BUNCH A H8RS!

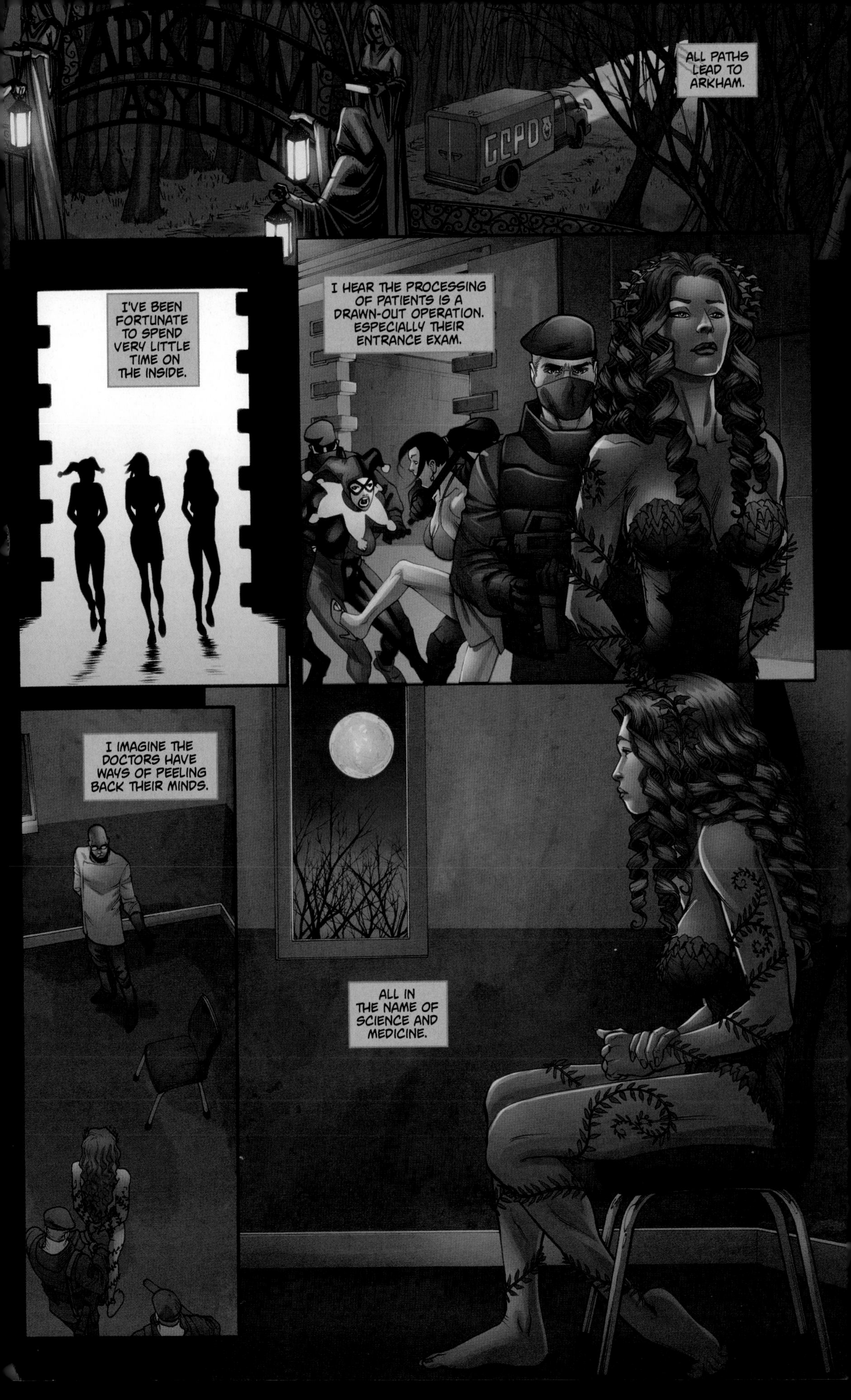
ARKHAM ASYLUM
ALL PATHS LEAD TO ARKHAM.
GCPD
I'VE BEEN FORTUNATE TO SPEND VERY LITTLE TIME ON THE INSIDE.
I HEAR THE PROCESSING OF PATIENTS IS A DRAWN-OUT OPERATION. ESPECIALLY THEIR ENTRANCE EXAM.
I IMAGINE THE DOCTORS HAVE WAYS OF PEELING BACK THEIR MINDS.
ALL IN THE NAME OF SCIENCE AND MEDICINE.

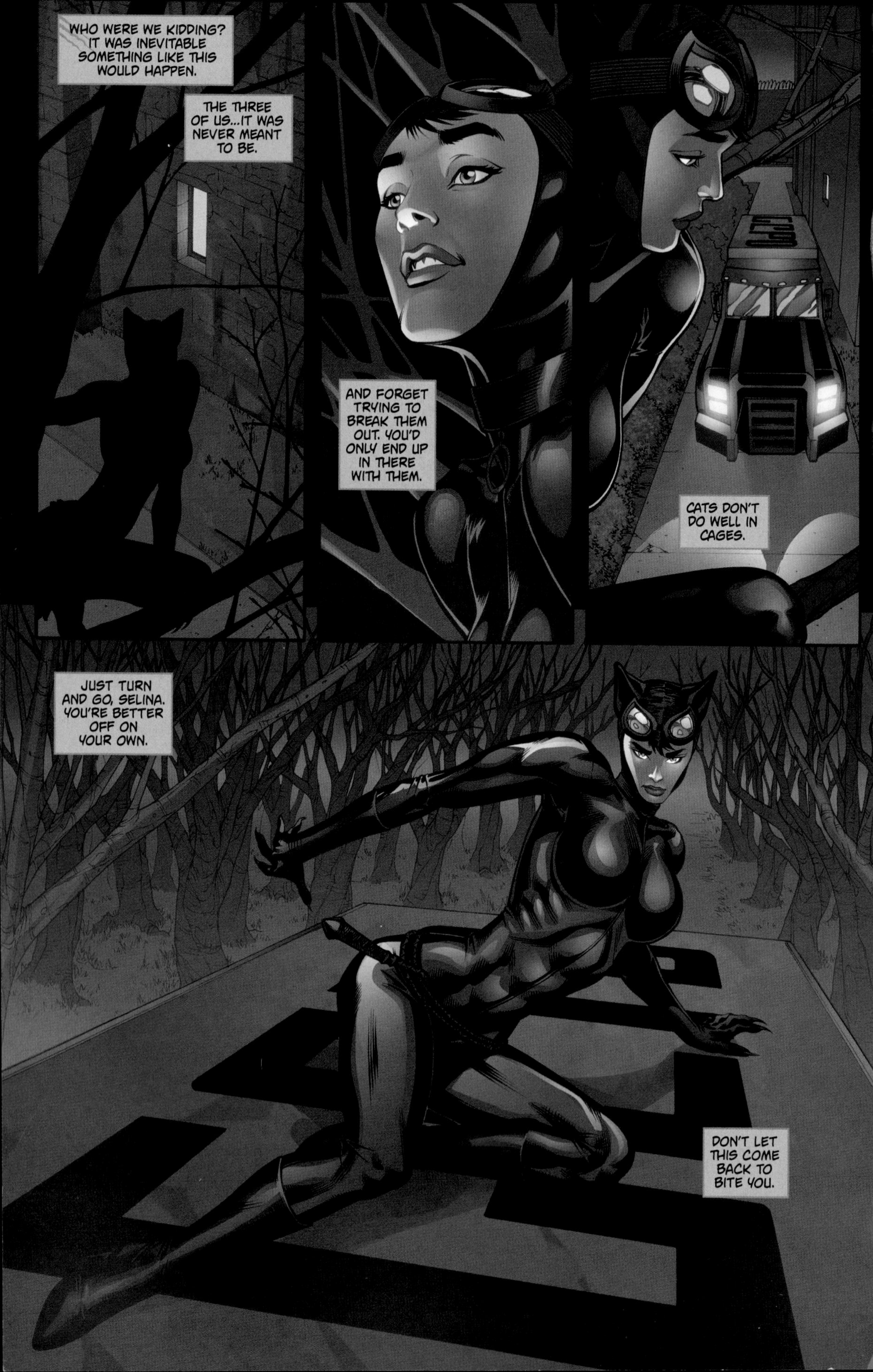
WHO WERE WE KIDDING? IT WAS INEVITABLE SOMETHING LIKE THIS WOULD HAPPEN.
THE THREE OF US...IT WAS NEVER MEANT TO BE.
AND FORGET TRYING TO BREAK THEM OUT. YOU'D ONLY END UP IN THERE WITH THEM.
CATS DON'T DO WELL IN CAGES.
JUST TURN AND GO, SELINA. YOU'RE BETTER OFF ON YOUR OWN.
DON'T LET THIS COME BACK TO BITE YOU.

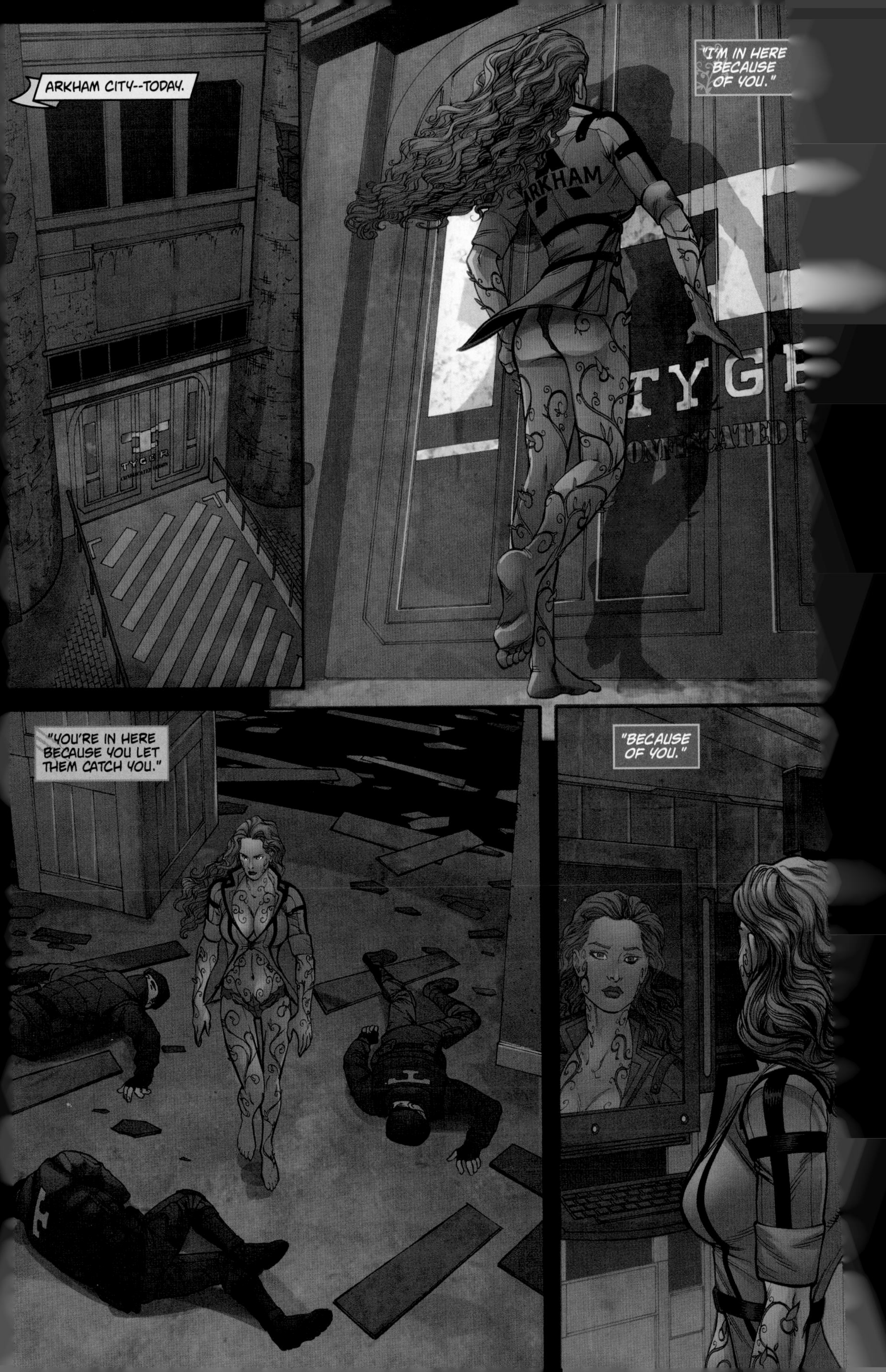

ARKHAM CITY--TODAY.
TYGER
"I'M IN HERE BECAUSE OF YOU."
ARKHAM
TYGE
"YOU'RE IN HERE BECAUSE YOU LET THEM CATCH YOU."
"BECAUSE OF YOU."

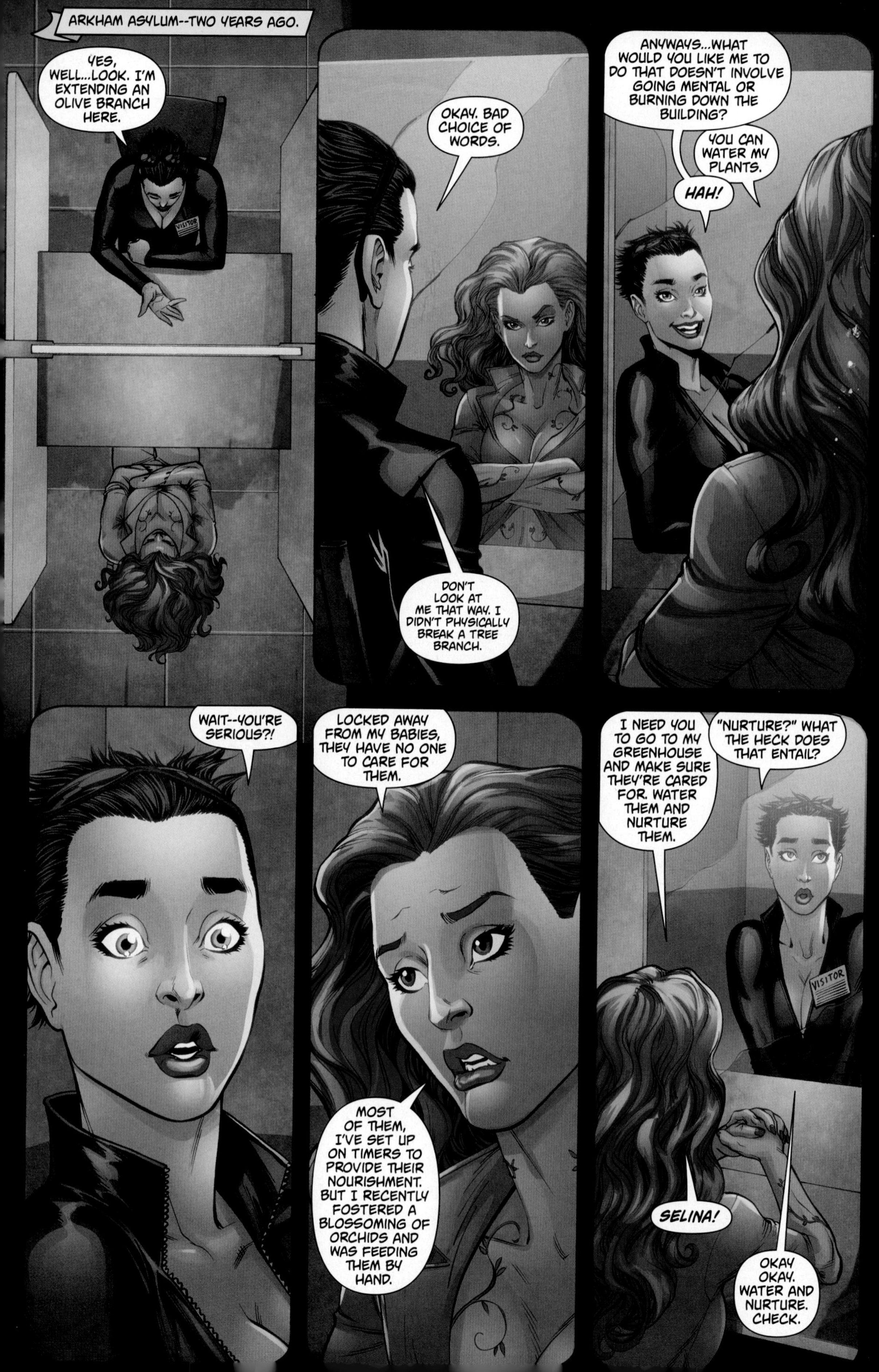
ARKHAM ASYLUM--TWO YEARS AGO.
YES, WELL...LOOK. I'M EXTENDING AN OLIVE BRANCH HERE.
OKAY. BAD CHOICE OF WORDS.
DON'T LOOK AT ME THAT WAY. I DIDN'T PHYSICALLY BREAK A TREE BRANCH.
ANYWAYS...WHAT WOULD YOU LIKE ME TO DO THAT DOESN'T INVOLVE GOING MENTAL OR BURNING DOWN THE BUILDING?
YOU CAN WATER MY PLANTS.
HAH!
WAIT--YOU'RE SERIOUS?!
LOCKED AWAY FROM MY BABIES, THEY HAVE NO ONE TO CARE FOR THEM.
MOST OF THEM, I'VE SET UP ON TIMERS TO PROVIDE THEIR NOURISHMENT. BUT I RECENTLY FOSTERED A BLOSSOMING OF ORCHIDS AND WAS FEEDING THEM BY HAND.
I NEED YOU TO GO TO MY GREENHOUSE AND MAKE SURE THEY'RE CARED FOR. WATER THEM AND NURTURE THEM.
"NURTURE?" WHAT THE HECK DOES THAT ENTAIL?
SELINA!
OKAY OKAY. WATER AND NURTURE. CHECK.
VISITOR

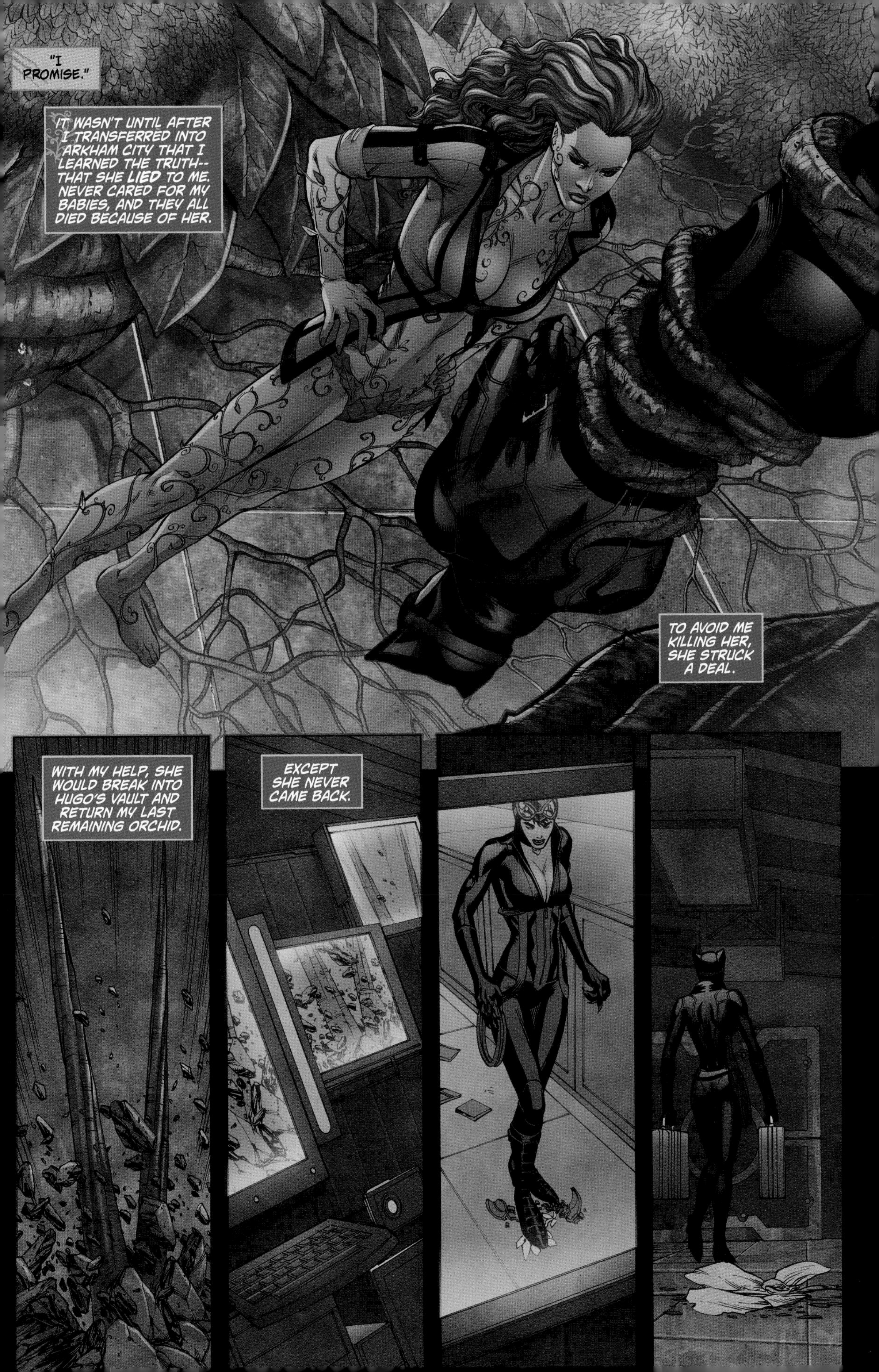
"I PROMISE."
IT WASN'T UNTIL AFTER I TRANSFERRED INTO ARKHAM CITY THAT I LEARNED THE TRUTH-- THAT SHE LIED TO ME. NEVER CARED FOR MY BABIES, AND THEY ALL DIED BECAUSE OF HER.
TO AVOID ME KILLING HER, SHE STRUCK A DEAL.
WITH MY HELP, SHE WOULD BREAK INTO HUGO'S VAULT AND RETURN MY LAST REMAINING ORCHID.
EXCEPT SHE NEVER CAME BACK.

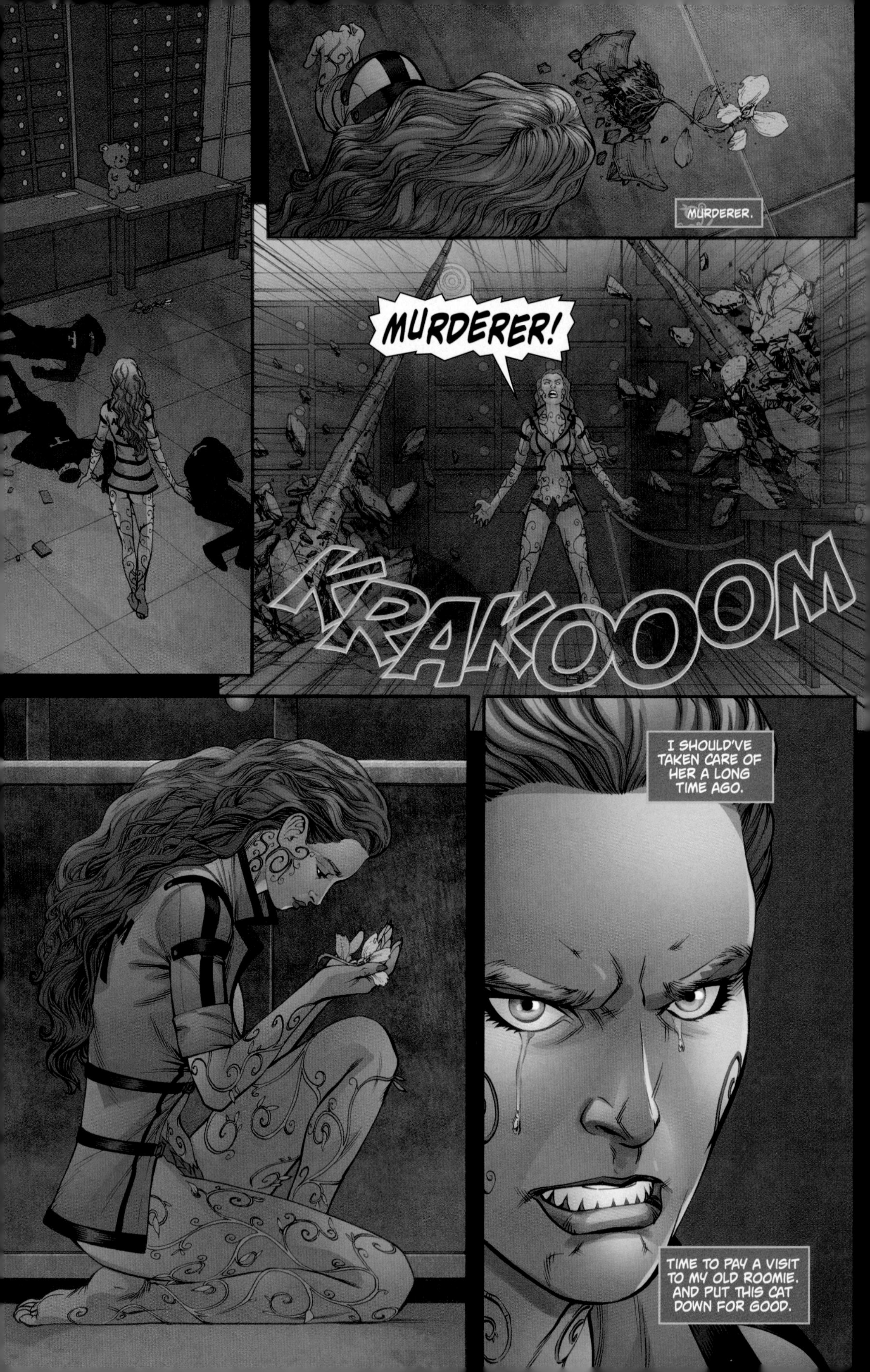
MURDERER.
MURDERER!
KRAKOOOM
I SHOULD'VE TAKEN CARE OF HER A LONG TIME AGO.
TIME TO PAY A VISIT TO MY OLD ROOMIE. AND PUT THIS CAT DOWN FOR GOOD.

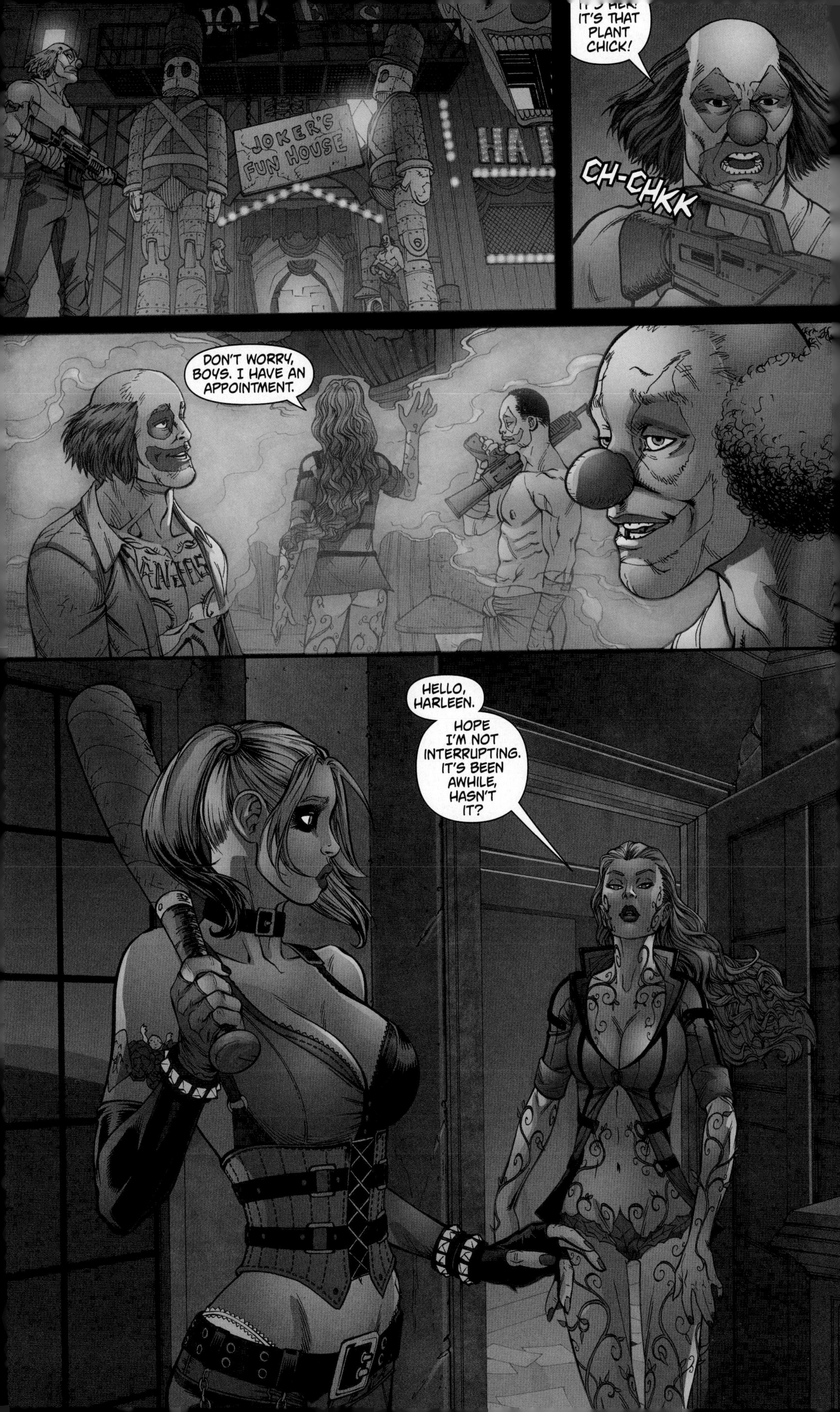
JOKER'S FUN HOUSE
IT'S THAT PLANT CHICK!
CH-CHKK
DON'T WORRY, BOYS. I HAVE AN APPOINTMENT.
HELLO, HARLEEN.
HOPE I'M NOT INTERRUPTING. IT'S BEEN AWHILE, HASN'T IT?

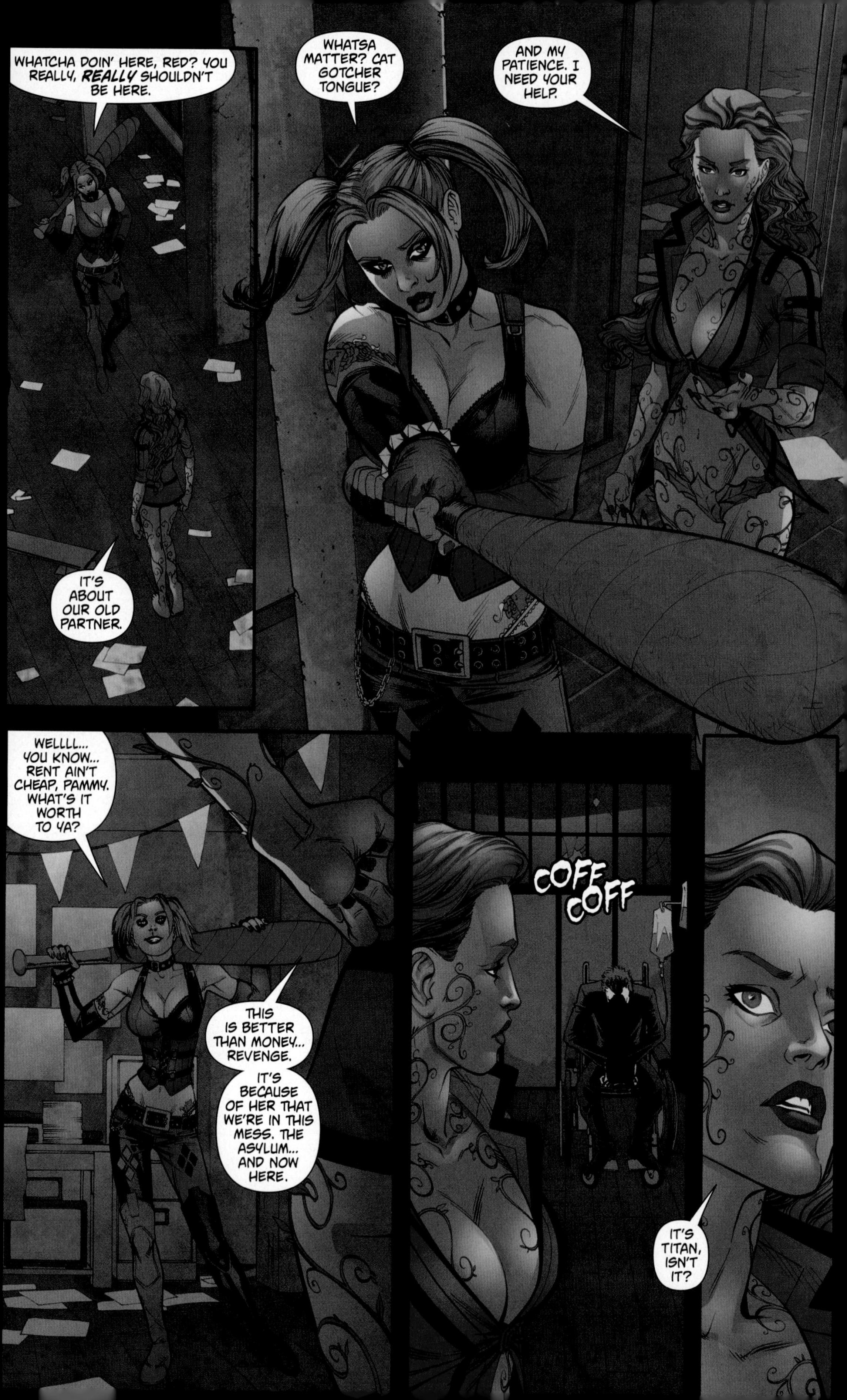
WHATCHA DOIN' HERE, RED? YOU REALLY, *REALLY* SHOULDN'T BE HERE.
IT'S ABOUT OUR OLD PARTNER.
WHATSA MATTER? CAT GOTCHER TONGUE?
AND MY PATIENCE. I NEED YOUR HELP.
WELLLL... YOU KNOW... RENT AIN'T CHEAP, PAMMY. WHAT'S IT WORTH TO YA?
THIS IS BETTER THAN MONEY... REVENGE.
IT'S BECAUSE OF HER THAT WE'RE IN THIS MESS. THE ASYLUM... AND NOW HERE.
COFF COFF
IT'S TITAN, ISN'T IT?

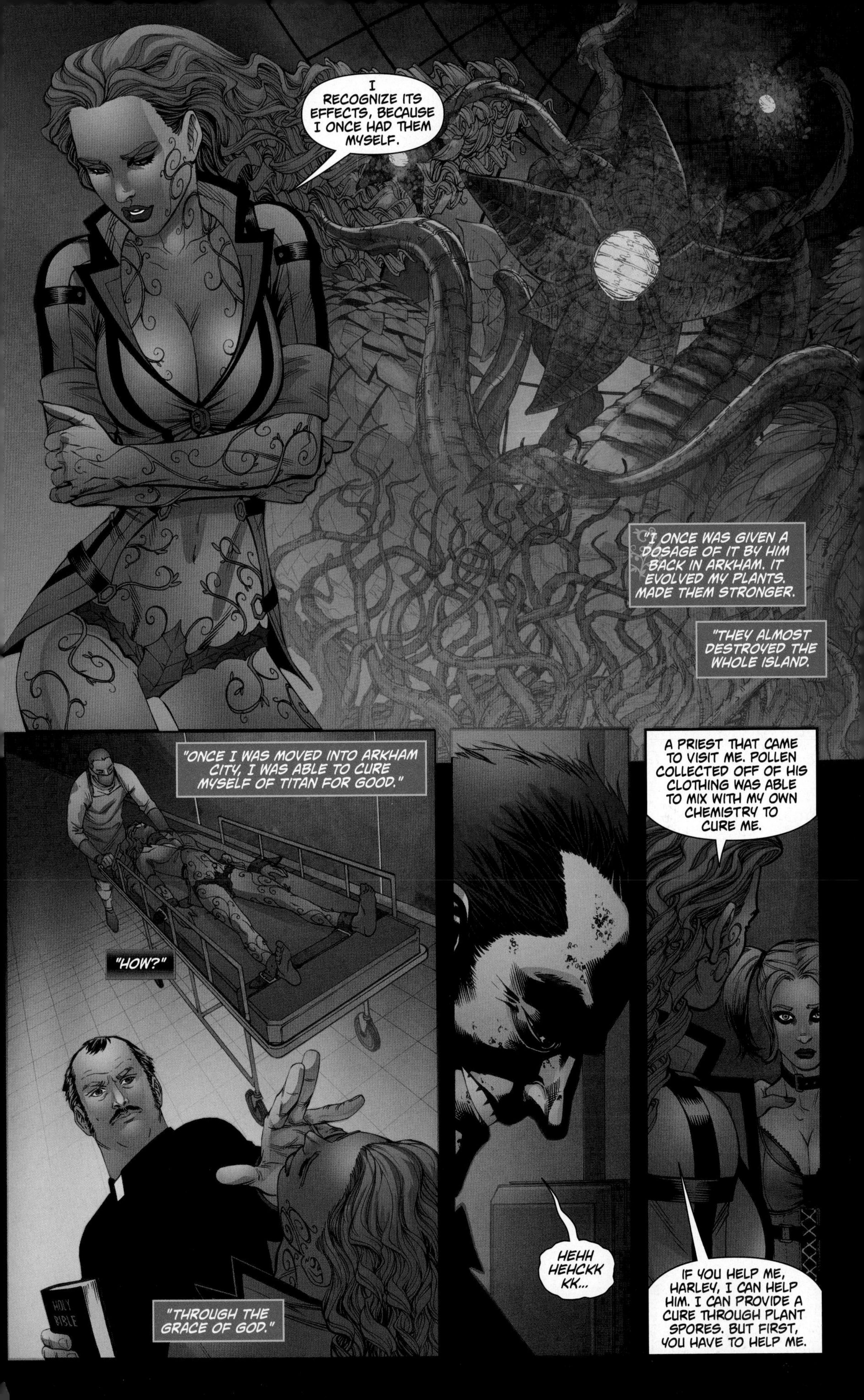
I RECOGNIZE ITS EFFECTS, BECAUSE I ONCE HAD THEM MYSELF.
"I ONCE WAS GIVEN A DOSAGE OF IT BY HIM BACK IN ARKHAM. IT EVOLVED MY PLANTS. MADE THEM STRONGER.
"THEY ALMOST DESTROYED THE WHOLE ISLAND.
"ONCE I WAS MOVED INTO ARKHAM CITY, I WAS ABLE TO CURE MYSELF OF TITAN FOR GOOD."
"HOW?"
"THROUGH THE GRACE OF GOD."
HOLY BIBLE
HEHH HEHCKK KK...
A PRIEST THAT CAME TO VISIT ME. POLLEN COLLECTED OFF OF HIS CLOTHING WAS ABLE TO MIX WITH MY OWN CHEMISTRY TO CURE ME.
IF YOU HELP ME, HARLEY, I CAN HELP HIM. I CAN PROVIDE A CURE THROUGH PLANT SPORES. BUT FIRST, YOU HAVE TO HELP ME.

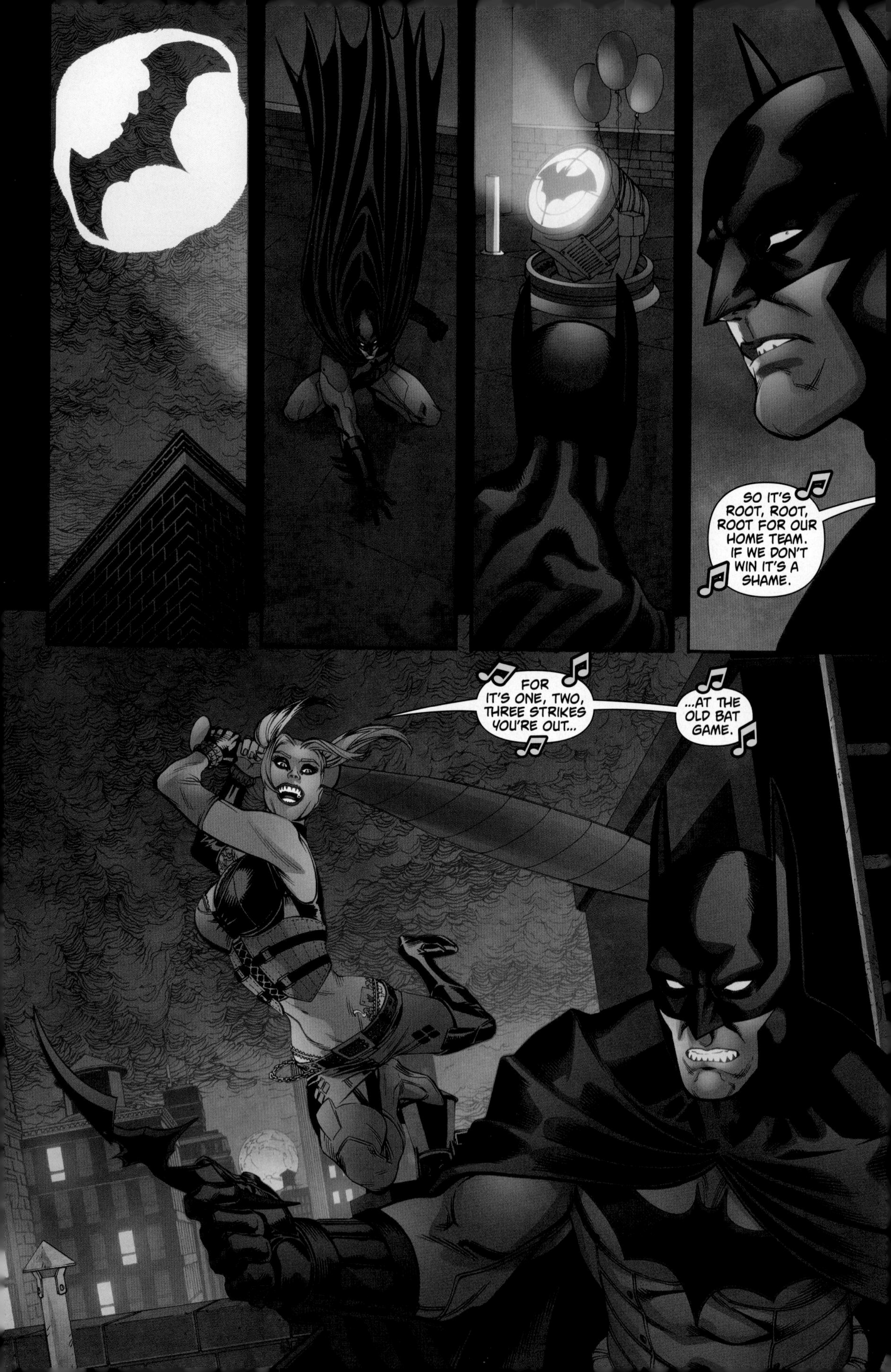
SO IT'S ROOT, ROOT, ROOT FOR OUR HOME TEAM. IF WE DON'T WIN IT'S A SHAME.
FOR IT'S ONE, TWO, THREE STRIKES YOU'RE OUT...
...AT THE OLD BAT GAME.

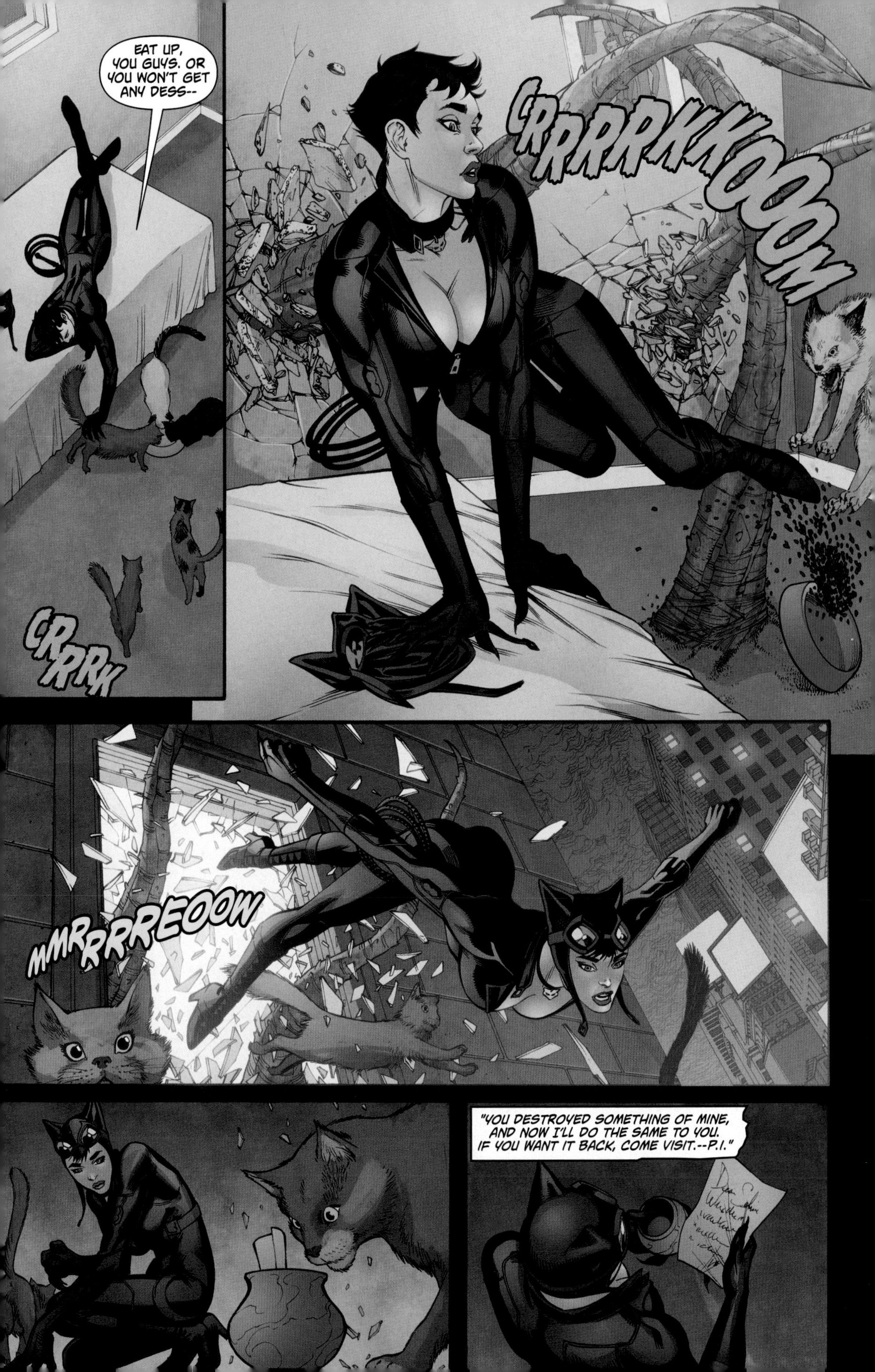
EAT UP, YOU GUYS. OR YOU WON'T GET ANY DESS--
CRRRRKKOOOOM
CRRRK
MMRRRRREOOW
"YOU DESTROYED SOMETHING OF MINE, AND NOW I'LL DO THE SAME TO YOU. IF YOU WANT IT BACK, COME VISIT.--P.I."

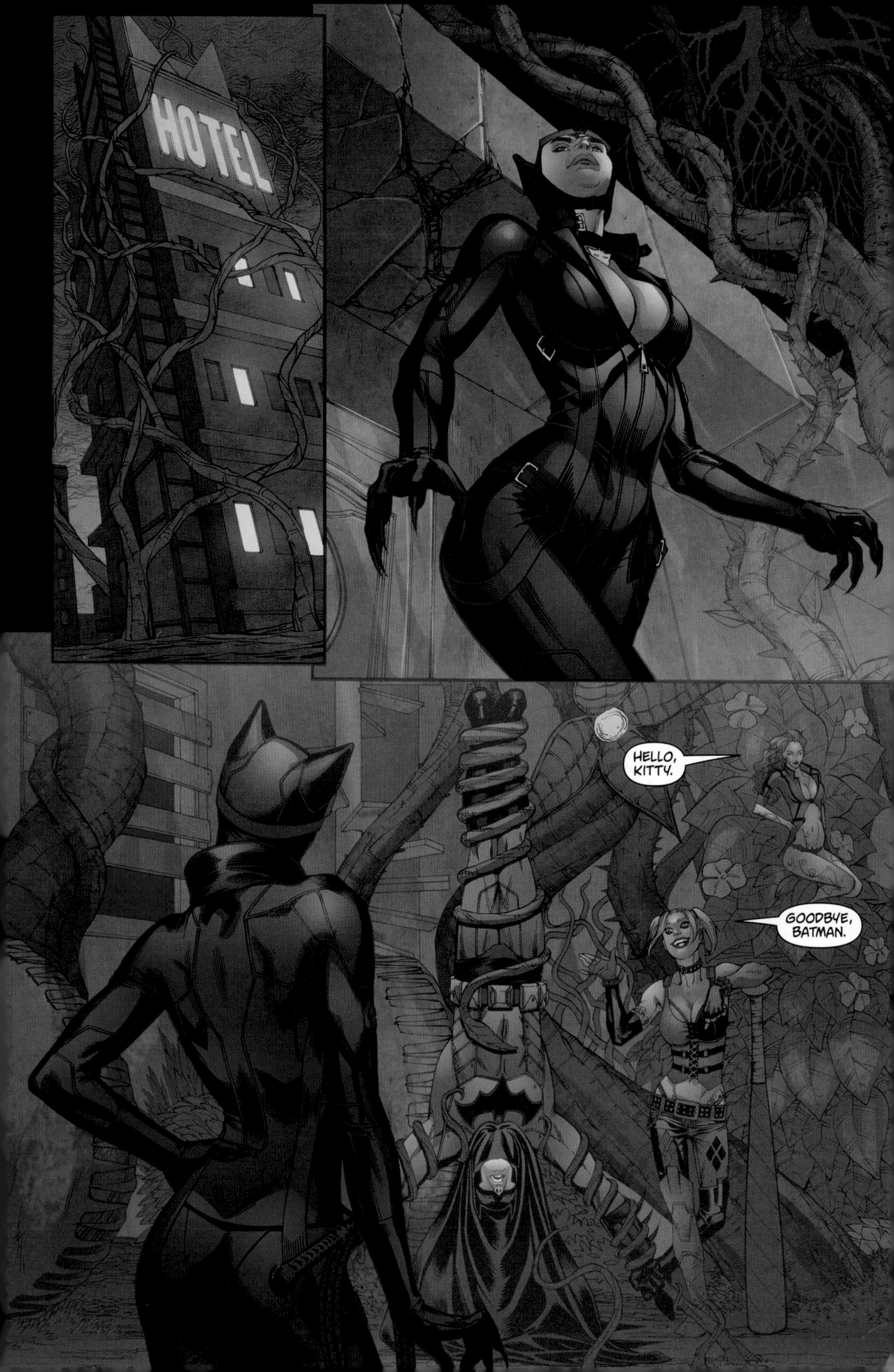
HOTEL
HELLO, KITTY.
GOODBYE, BATMAN.

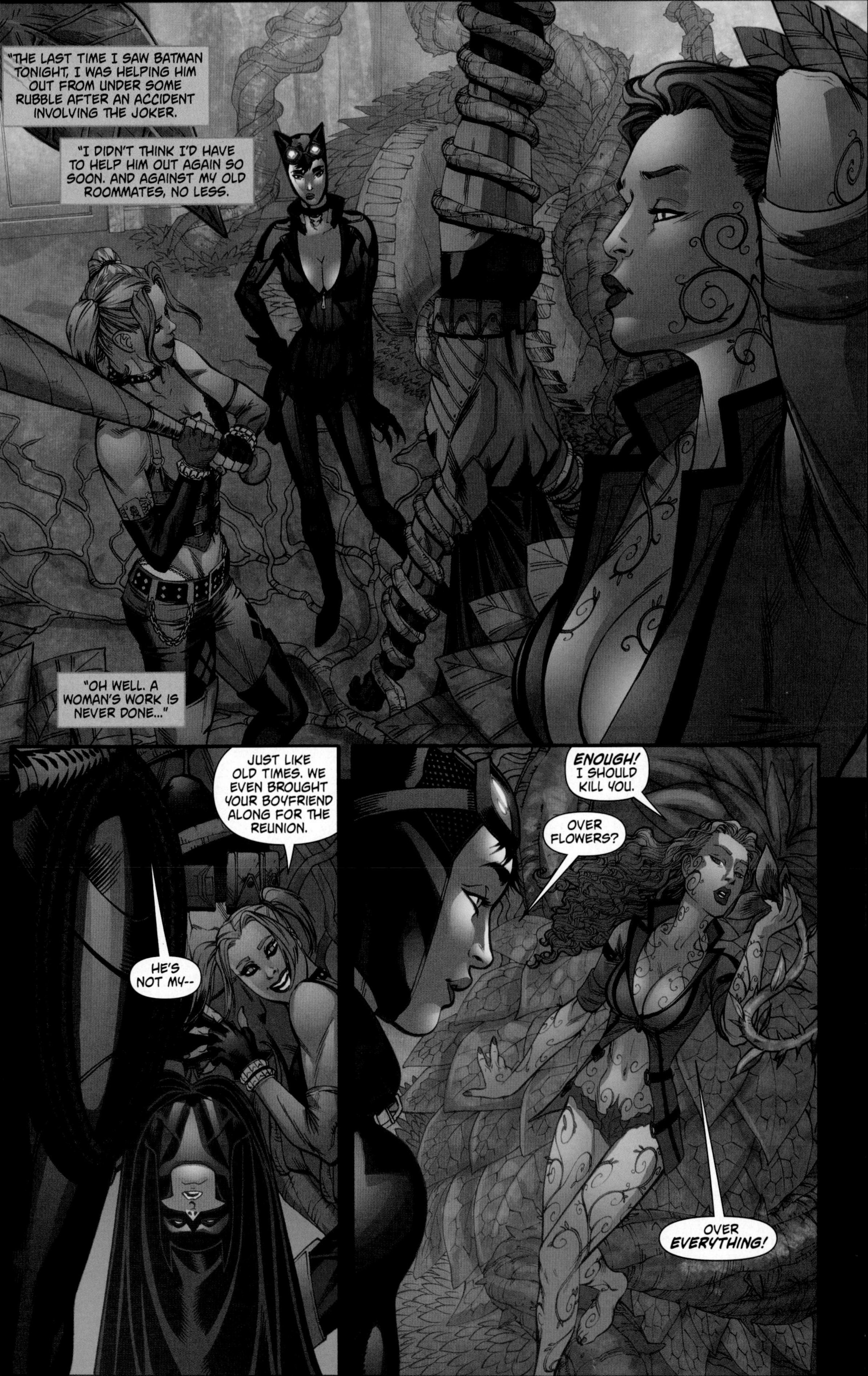
"THE LAST TIME I SAW BATMAN TONIGHT, I WAS HELPING HIM OUT FROM UNDER SOME RUBBLE AFTER AN ACCIDENT INVOLVING THE JOKER.
"I DIDN'T THINK I'D HAVE TO HELP HIM OUT AGAIN SO SOON. AND AGAINST MY OLD ROOMMATES, NO LESS.
"OH WELL. A WOMAN'S WORK IS NEVER DONE..."
JUST LIKE OLD TIMES. WE EVEN BROUGHT YOUR BOYFRIEND ALONG FOR THE REUNION.
HE'S NOT MY--
ENOUGH! I SHOULD KILL YOU.
OVER FLOWERS?
OVER EVERYTHING!

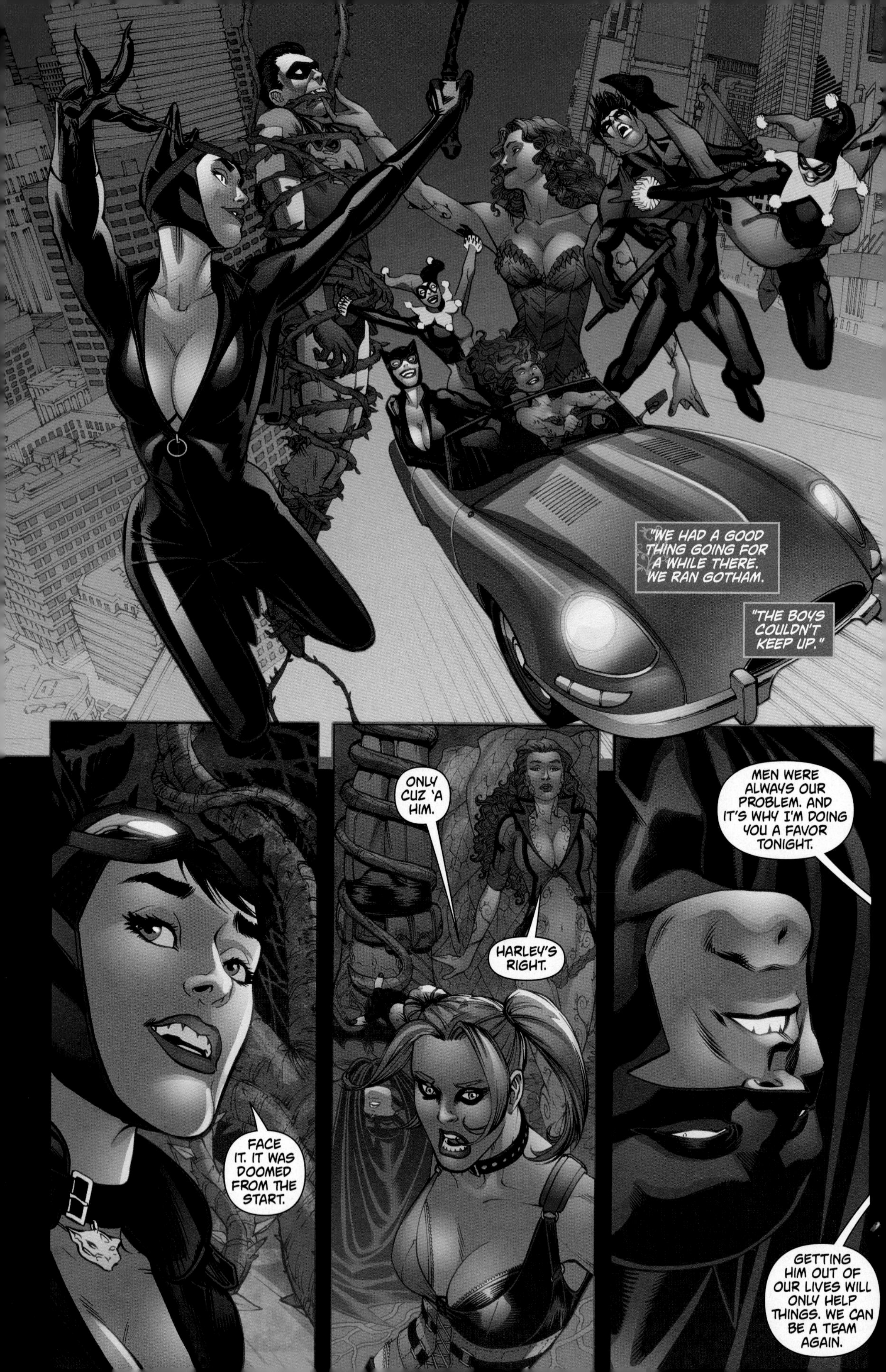
"WE HAD A GOOD THING GOING FOR A WHILE THERE. WE RAN GOTHAM.
"THE BOYS COULDN'T KEEP UP."
FACE IT. IT WAS DOOMED FROM THE START.
ONLY CUZ 'A HIM.
HARLEY'S RIGHT.
MEN WERE ALWAYS OUR PROBLEM. AND IT'S WHY I'M DOING YOU A FAVOR TONIGHT.
GETTING HIM OUT OF OUR LIVES WILL ONLY HELP THINGS. WE CAN BE A TEAM AGAIN.

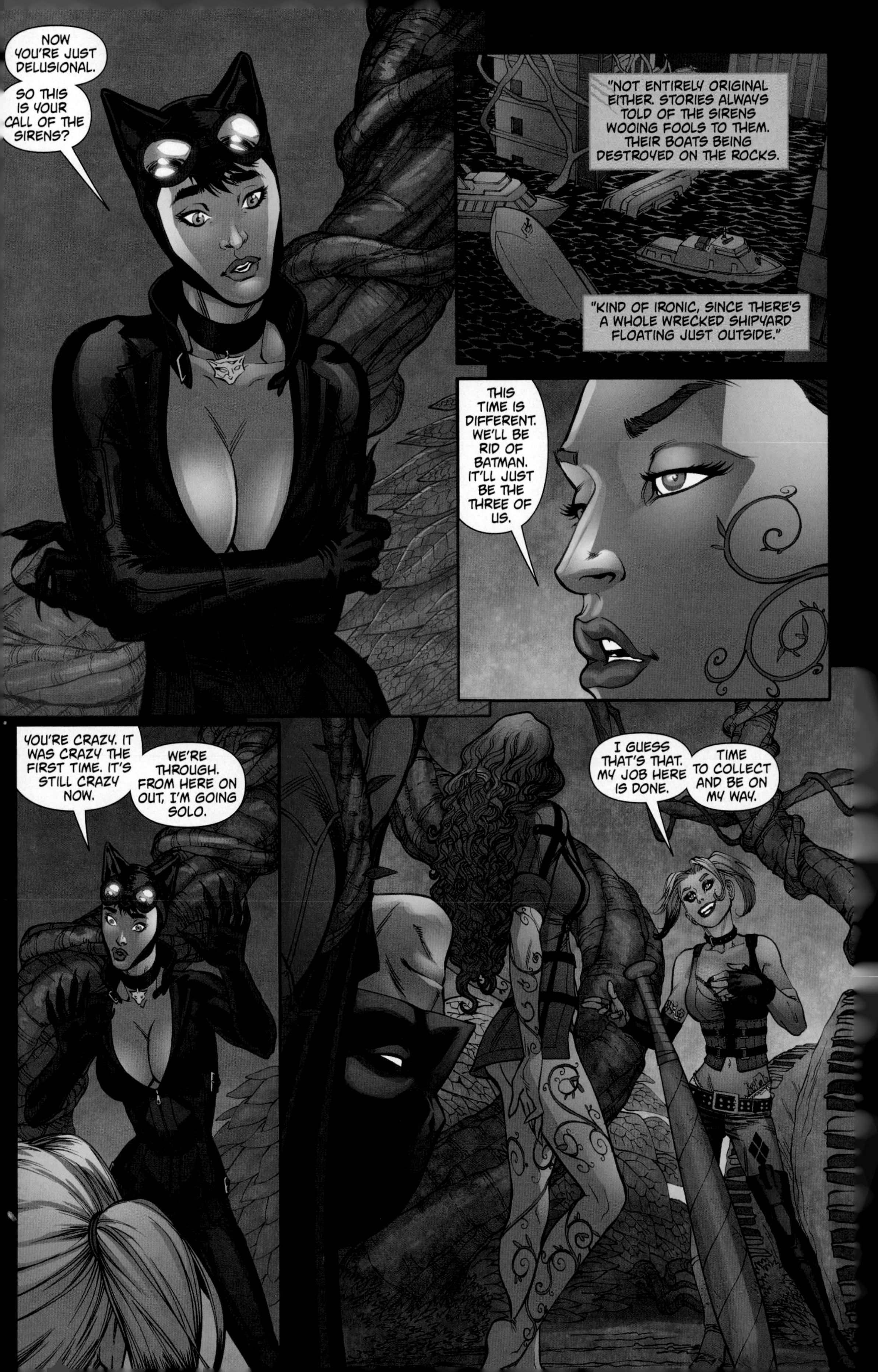
NOW YOU'RE JUST DELUSIONAL.
SO THIS IS YOUR CALL OF THE SIRENS?
"NOT ENTIRELY ORIGINAL EITHER. STORIES ALWAYS TOLD OF THE SIRENS WOOING FOOLS TO THEM. THEIR BOATS BEING DESTROYED ON THE ROCKS.
"KIND OF IRONIC, SINCE THERE'S A WHOLE WRECKED SHIPYARD FLOATING JUST OUTSIDE."
THIS TIME IS DIFFERENT. WE'LL BE RID OF BATMAN. IT'LL JUST BE THE THREE OF US.
YOU'RE CRAZY. IT WAS CRAZY THE FIRST TIME. IT'S STILL CRAZY NOW.
WE'RE THROUGH. FROM HERE ON OUT, I'M GOING SOLO.
I GUESS THAT'S THAT. MY JOB HERE IS DONE.
TIME TO COLLECT AND BE ON MY WAY.

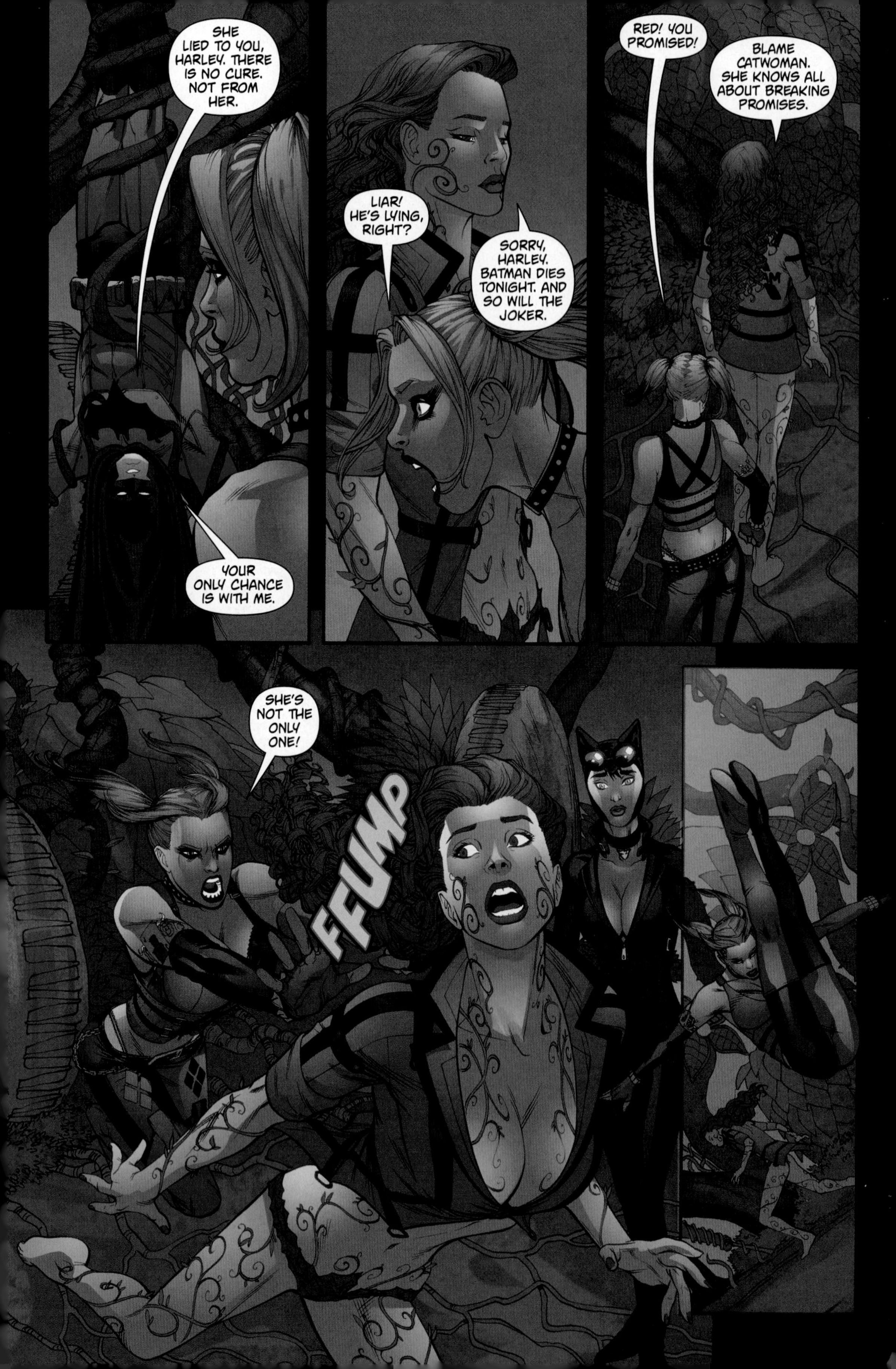
SHE LIED TO YOU, HARLEY. THERE IS NO CURE. NOT FROM HER.
YOUR ONLY CHANCE IS WITH ME.
LIAR! HE'S LYING, RIGHT?
SORRY, HARLEY. BATMAN DIES TONIGHT. AND SO WILL THE JOKER.
RED! YOU PROMISED!
BLAME CATWOMAN. SHE KNOWS ALL ABOUT BREAKING PROMISES.
SHE'S NOT THE ONLY ONE!
FFUMP

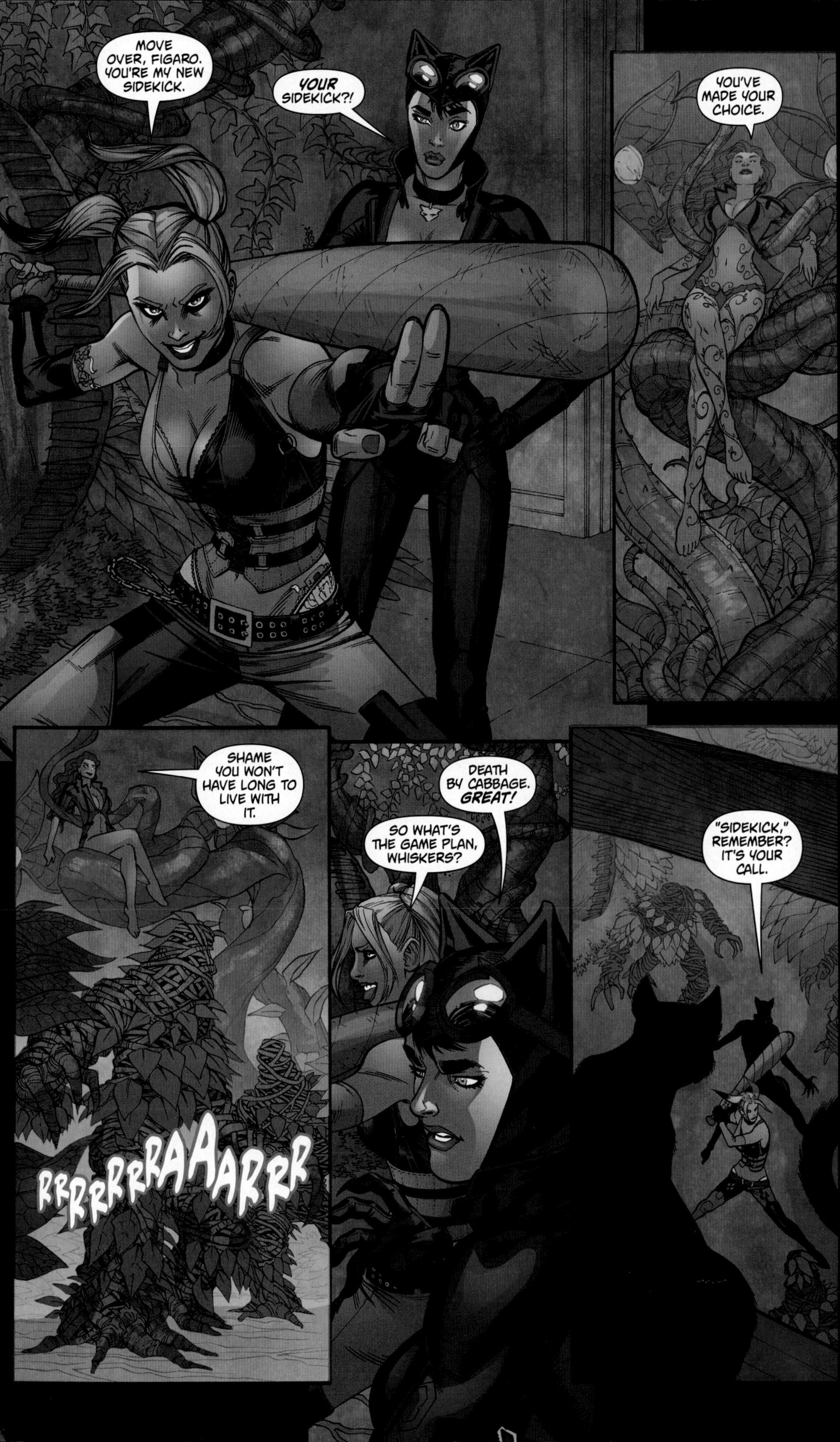
MOVE OVER, FIGARO. YOU'RE MY NEW SIDEKICK.
YOUR SIDEKICK?!
YOU'VE MADE YOUR CHOICE.
SHAME YOU WON'T HAVE LONG TO LIVE WITH IT.
RRRRRRRAAAARRR
DEATH BY CABBAGE. GREAT!
SO WHAT'S THE GAME PLAN, WHISKERS?
"SIDEKICK," REMEMBER? IT'S YOUR CALL.

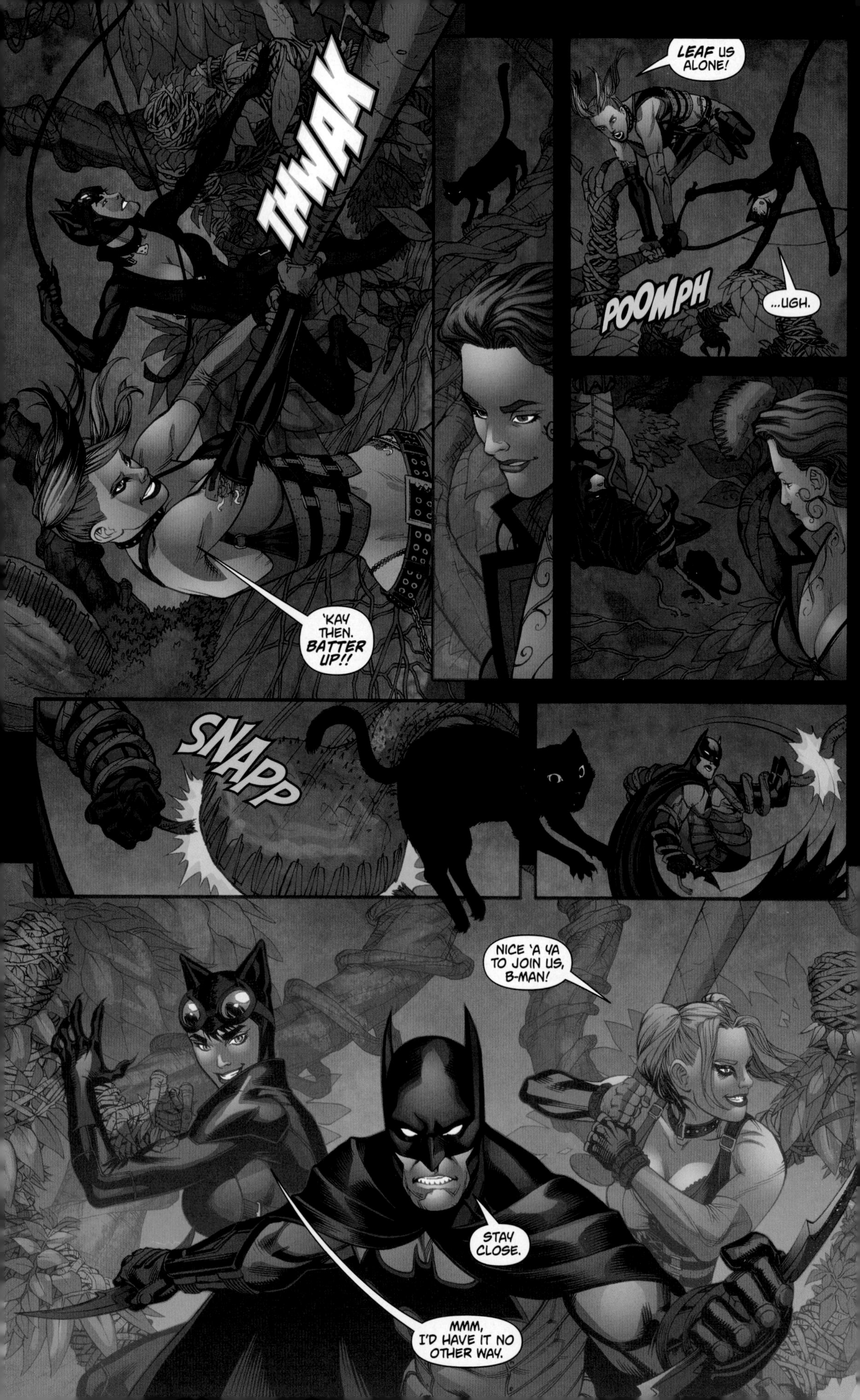
THWAK
'KAY THEN. BATTER UP!!
LEAF US ALONE!
POOMPH
...UGH.
SNAPP
NICE 'A YA TO JOIN US, B-MAN!
STAY CLOSE.
MMM, I'D HAVE IT NO OTHER WAY.

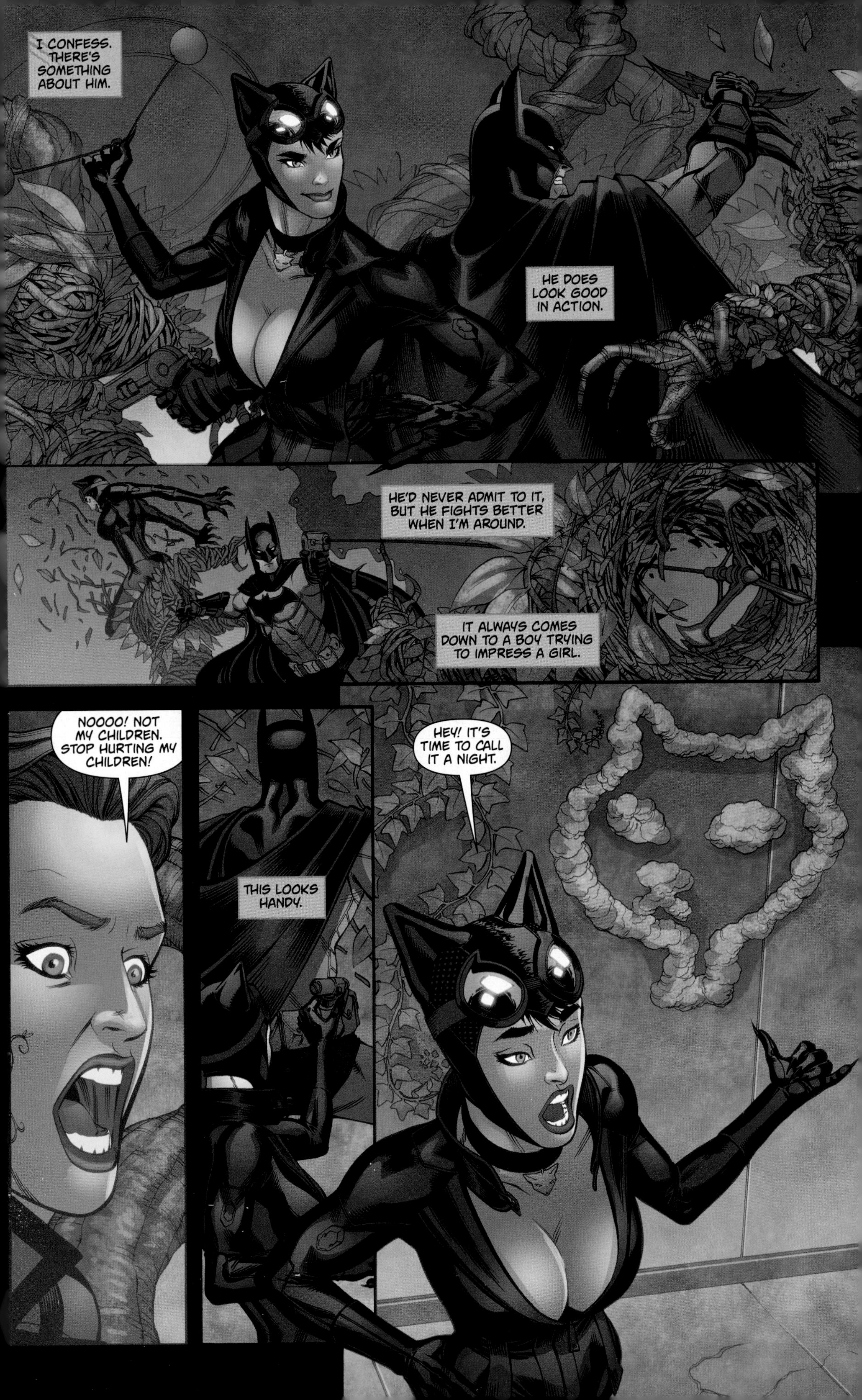
I CONFESS. THERE'S SOMETHING ABOUT HIM.
HE DOES LOOK GOOD IN ACTION.
HE'D NEVER ADMIT TO IT, BUT HE FIGHTS BETTER WHEN I'M AROUND.
IT ALWAYS COMES DOWN TO A BOY TRYING TO IMPRESS A GIRL.
NOOOO! NOT MY CHILDREN. STOP HURTING MY CHILDREN!
THIS LOOKS HANDY.
HEY! IT'S TIME TO CALL IT A NIGHT.

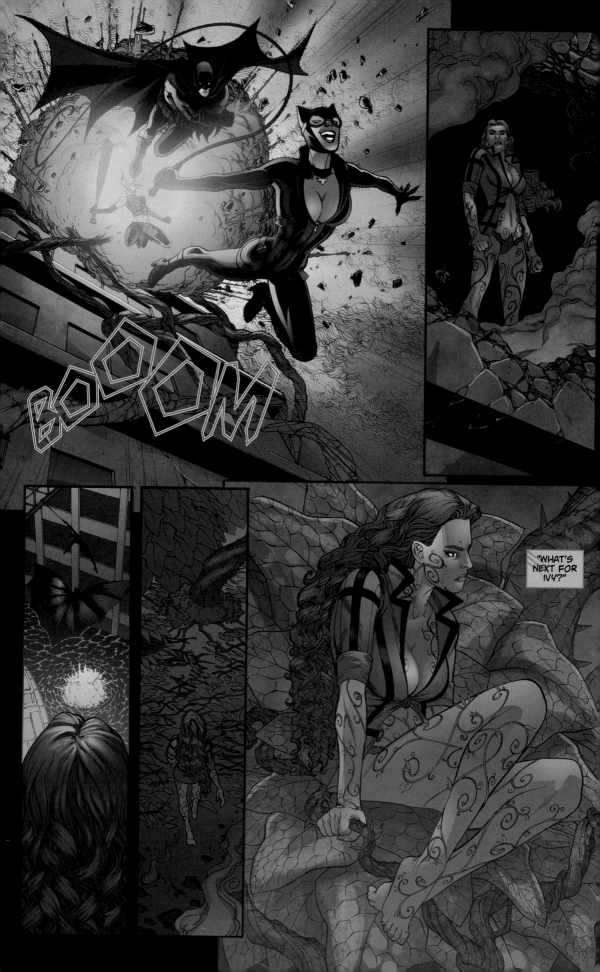

BOOOOM

"WHAT'S NEXT FOR IVY?"

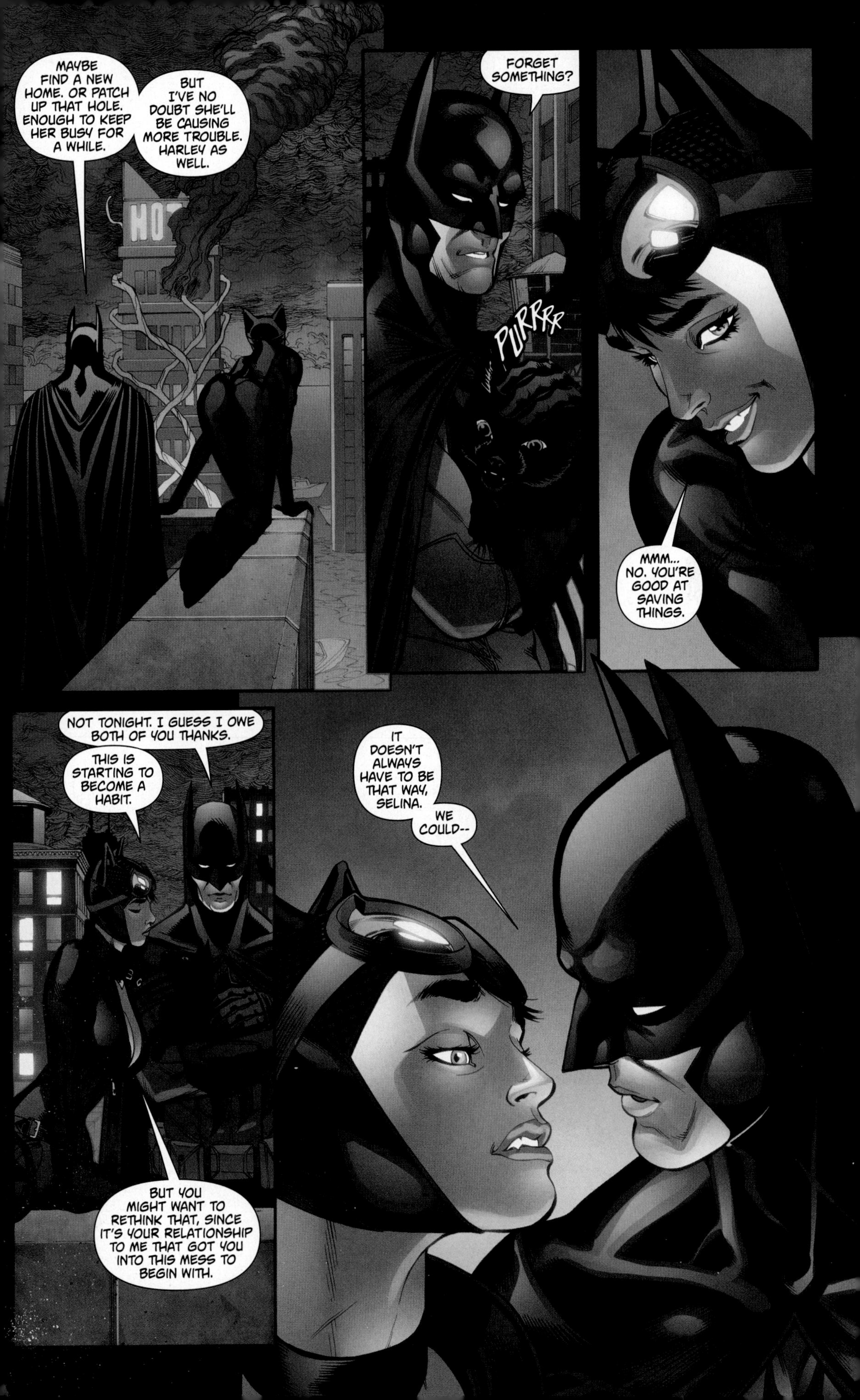
MAYBE FIND A NEW HOME. OR PATCH UP THAT HOLE. ENOUGH TO KEEP HER BUSY FOR A WHILE.
BUT I'VE NO DOUBT SHE'LL BE CAUSING MORE TROUBLE. HARLEY AS WELL.
FORGET SOMETHING?
PURRRR
MMM... NO. YOU'RE GOOD AT SAVING THINGS.
NOT TONIGHT. I GUESS I OWE BOTH OF YOU THANKS.
THIS IS STARTING TO BECOME A HABIT.
BUT YOU MIGHT WANT TO RETHINK THAT, SINCE IT'S YOUR RELATIONSHIP TO ME THAT GOT YOU INTO THIS MESS TO BEGIN WITH.
IT DOESN'T ALWAYS HAVE TO BE THAT WAY, SELINA.
WE COULD--

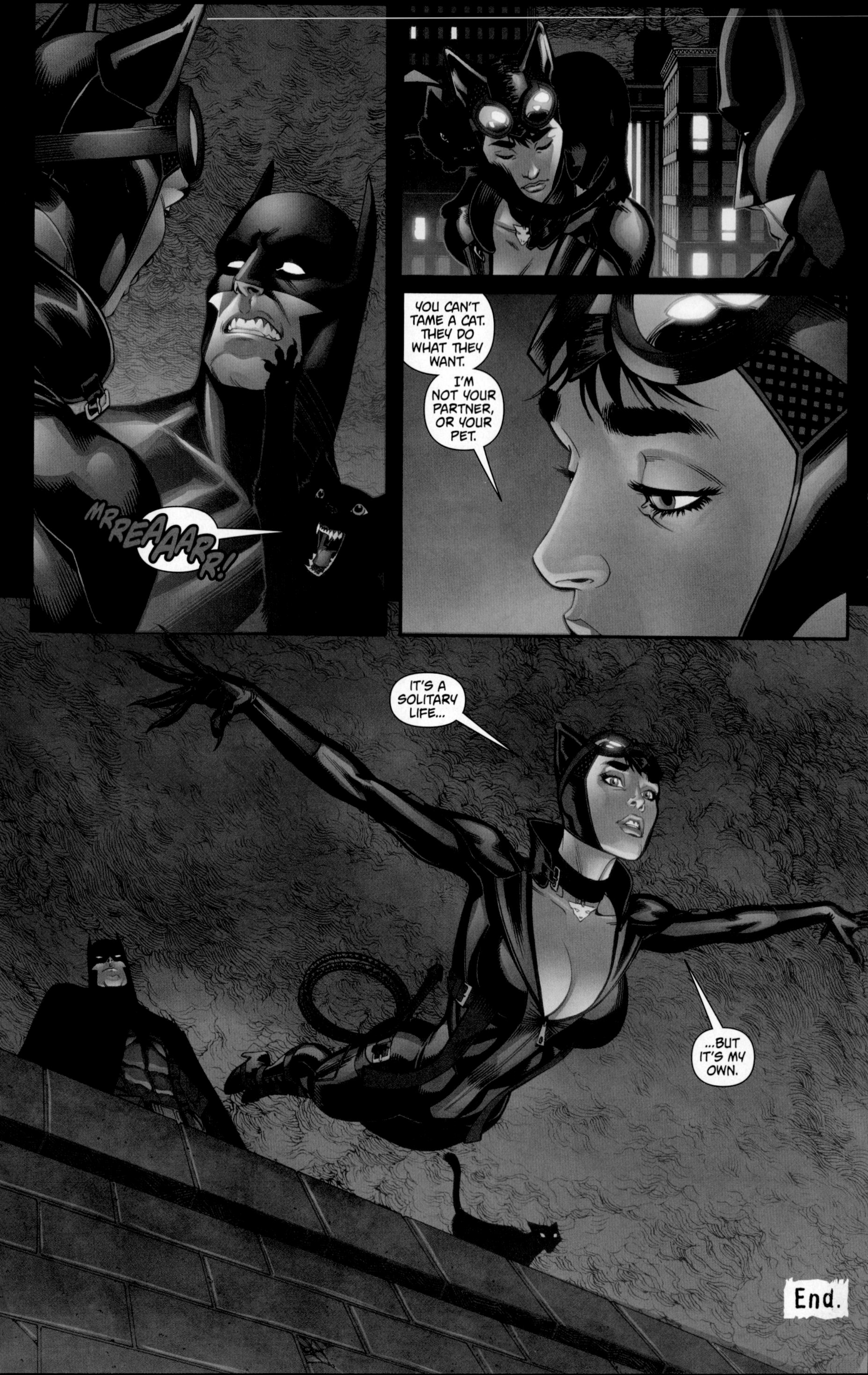
MRREAAAARR!
YOU CAN'T TAME A CAT. THEY DO WHAT THEY WANT.
I'M NOT YOUR PARTNER, OR YOUR PET.
IT'S A SOLITARY LIFE...
...BUT IT'S MY OWN.
End.

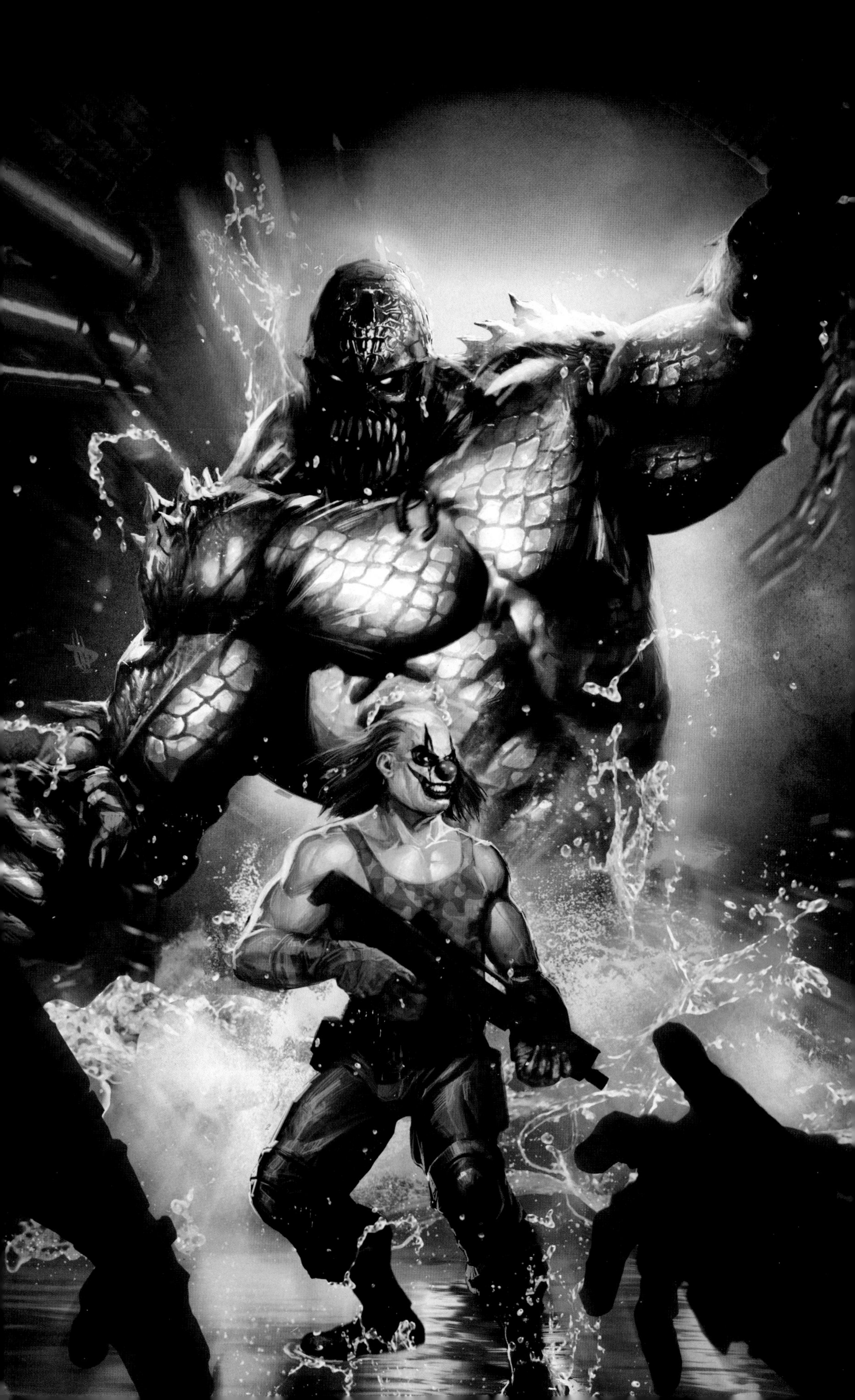

CROCODILE TEARS

WRITTEN BY: DEREK FRIDOLFS
PENCILS BY: DARICK ROBERTSON
INKS BY: RICHARD P. CLARK
COLORS BY: GABE ELTAEB
LETTERS BY: TRAVIS LANHAM
COVER ART BY: DAVE WILKINS

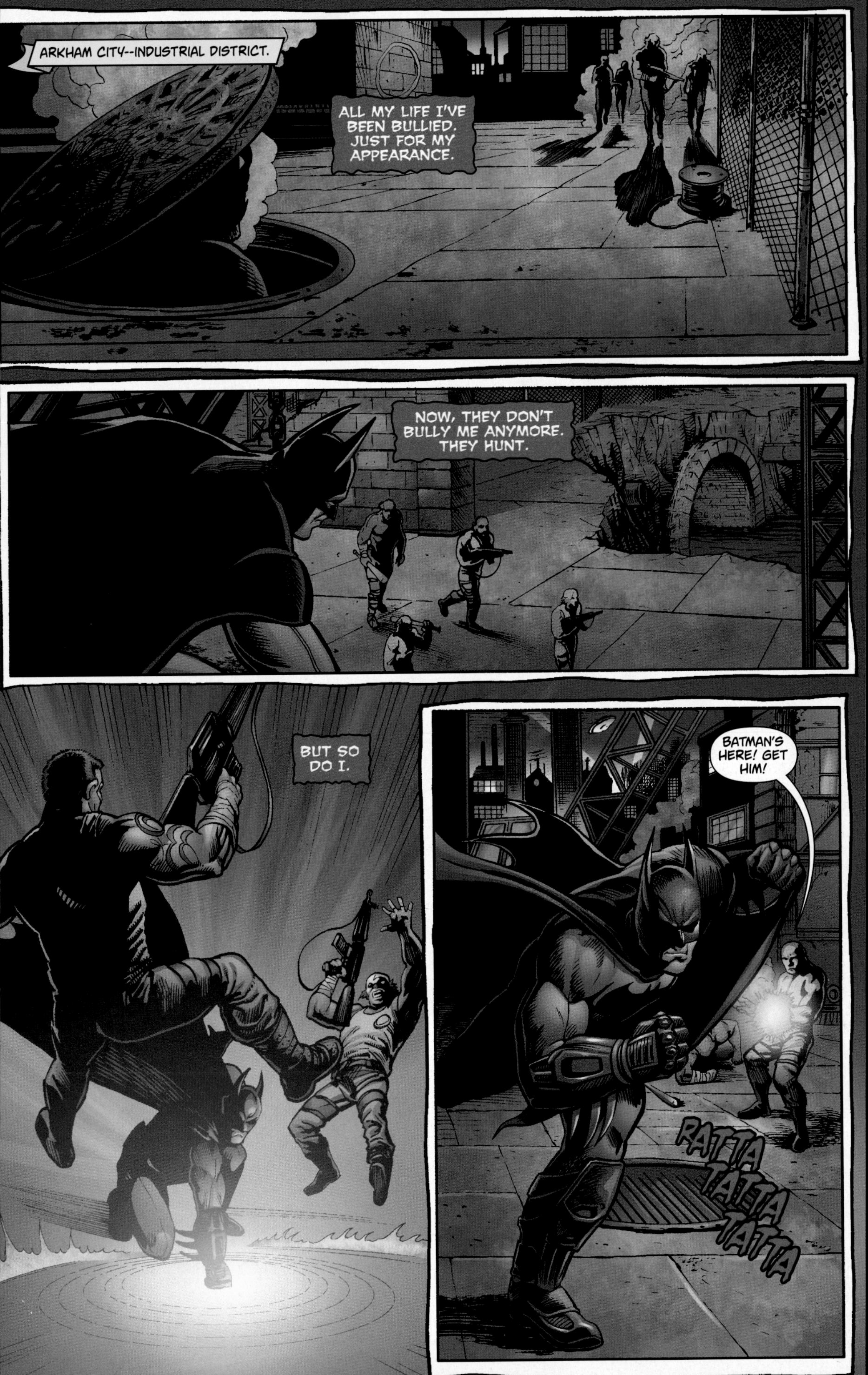
ARKHAM CITY--INDUSTRIAL DISTRICT.
ALL MY LIFE I'VE BEEN BULLIED. JUST FOR MY APPEARANCE.
NOW, THEY DON'T BULLY ME ANYMORE. THEY HUNT.
BUT SO DO I.
BATMAN'S HERE! GET HIM!
RATTA TATTA TATTA

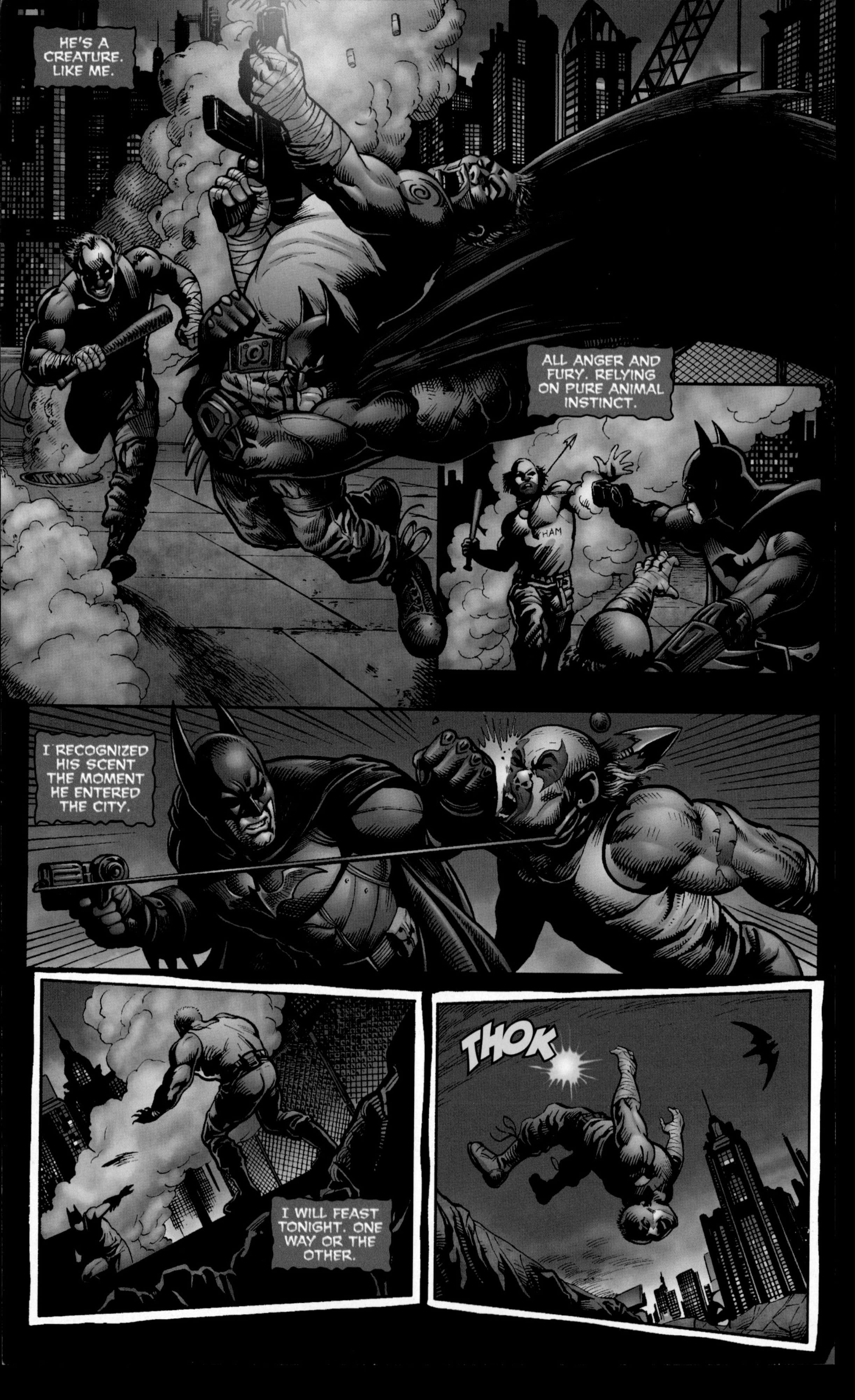
HE'S A CREATURE. LIKE ME.
ALL ANGER AND FURY. RELYING ON PURE ANIMAL INSTINCT.
HAM
I RECOGNIZED HIS SCENT THE MOMENT HE ENTERED THE CITY.
I WILL FEAST TONIGHT. ONE WAY OR THE OTHER.
THOK

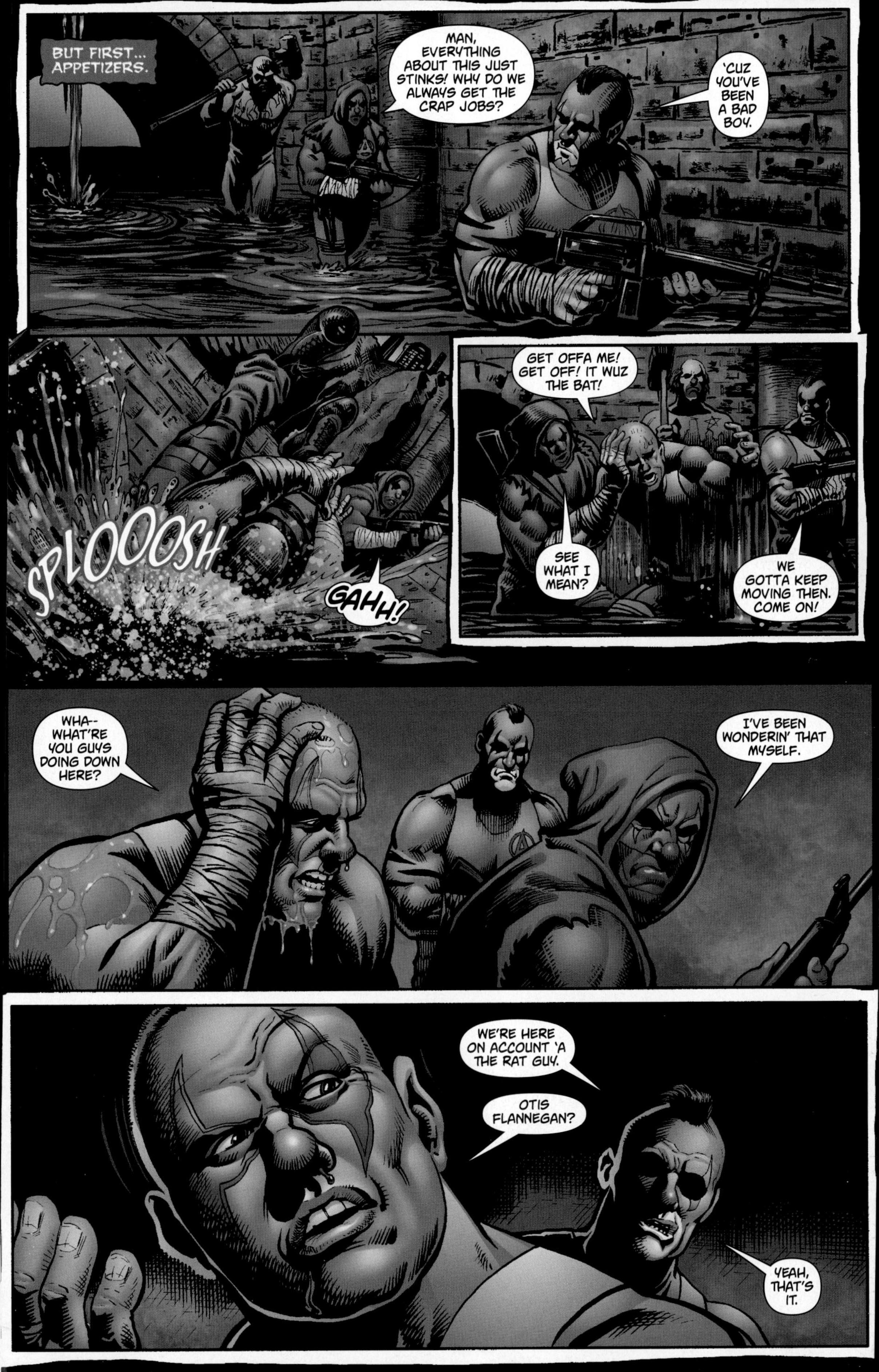
BUT FIRST... APPETIZERS.
MAN, EVERYTHING ABOUT THIS JUST STINKS! WHY DO WE ALWAYS GET THE CRAP JOBS?
'CUZ YOU'VE BEEN A BAD BOY.
SPLOOOSH
GAHH!
GET OFFA ME! GET OFF! IT WUZ THE BAT!
SEE WHAT I MEAN?
WE GOTTA KEEP MOVING THEN. COME ON!
WHA-- WHAT'RE YOU GUYS DOING DOWN HERE?
I'VE BEEN WONDERIN' THAT MYSELF.
WE'RE HERE ON ACCOUNT 'A THE RAT GUY.
OTIS FLANNEGAN?
YEAH, THAT'S IT.

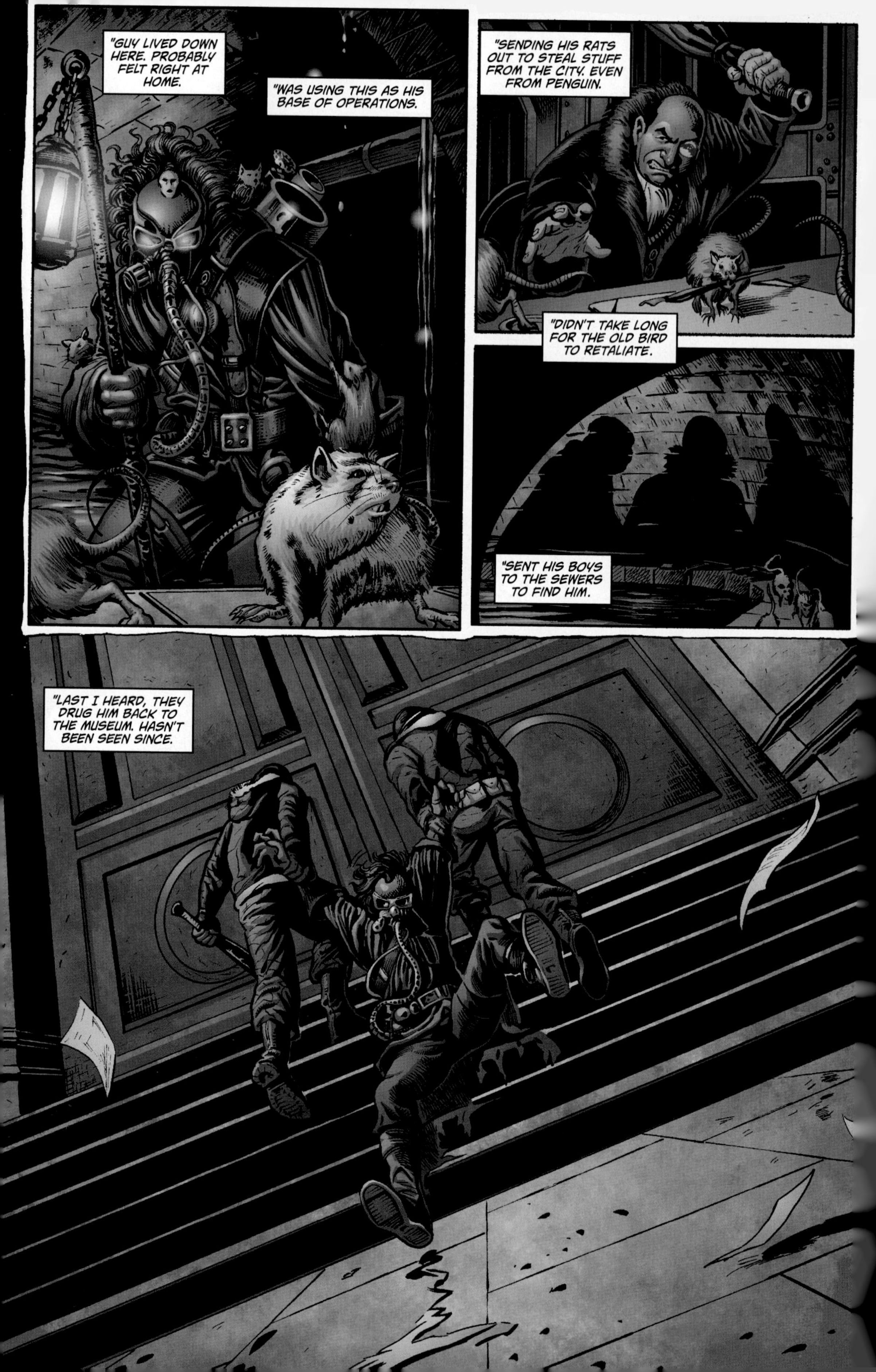
"GUY LIVED DOWN HERE. PROBABLY FELT RIGHT AT HOME.
"WAS USING THIS AS HIS BASE OF OPERATIONS.
"SENDING HIS RATS OUT TO STEAL STUFF FROM THE CITY. EVEN FROM PENGUIN.
"DIDN'T TAKE LONG FOR THE OLD BIRD TO RETALIATE.
"SENT HIS BOYS TO THE SEWERS TO FIND HIM.
"LAST I HEARD, THEY DRUG HIM BACK TO THE MUSEUM. HASN'T BEEN SEEN SINCE.

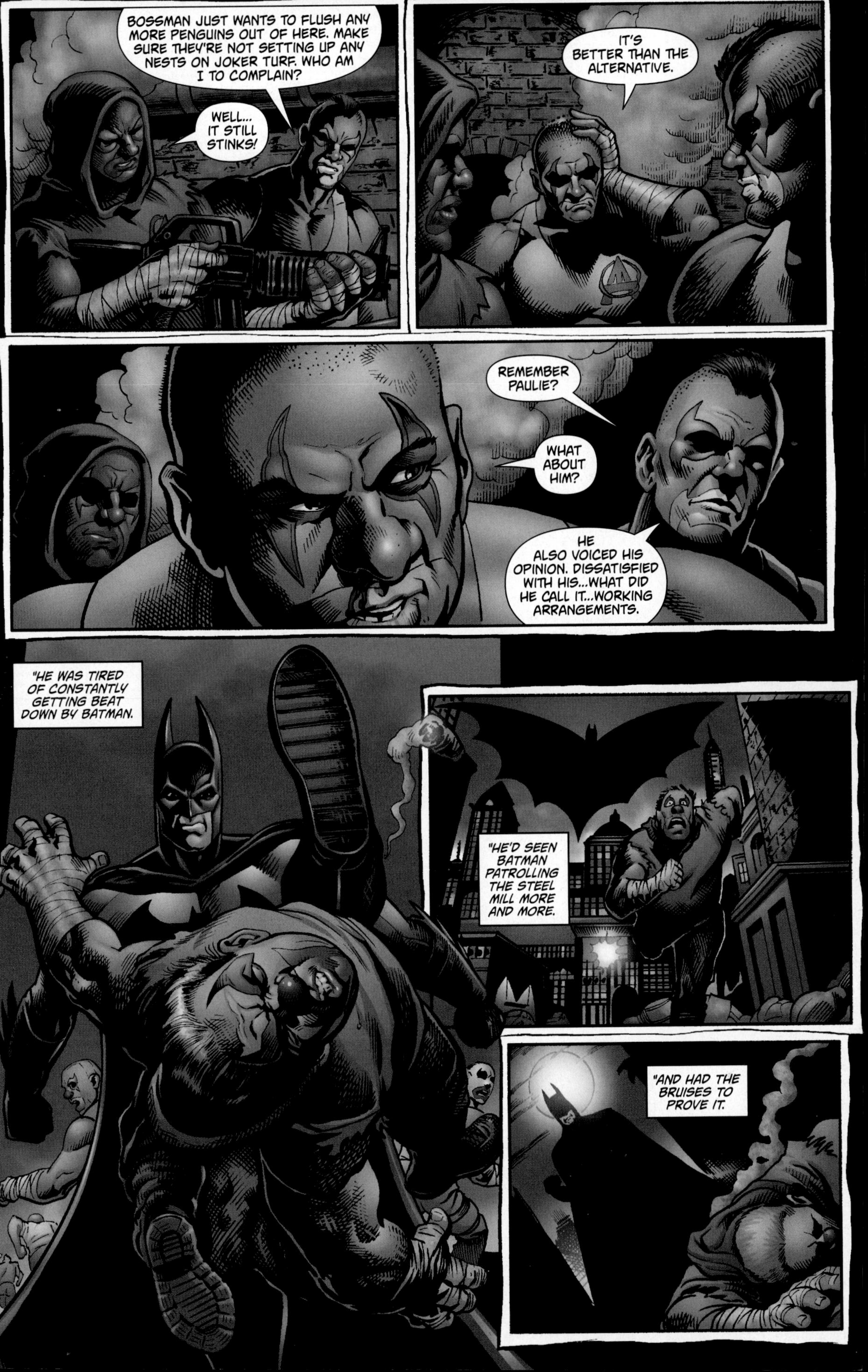
BOSSMAN JUST WANTS TO FLUSH ANY MORE PENGUINS OUT OF HERE. MAKE SURE THEY'RE NOT SETTING UP ANY NESTS ON JOKER TURF. WHO AM I TO COMPLAIN?
WELL... IT STILL STINKS!
IT'S BETTER THAN THE ALTERNATIVE.
REMEMBER PAULIE?
WHAT ABOUT HIM?
HE ALSO VOICED HIS OPINION. DISSATISFIED WITH HIS...WHAT DID HE CALL IT...WORKING ARRANGEMENTS.
"HE WAS TIRED OF CONSTANTLY GETTING BEAT DOWN BY BATMAN.
"HE'D SEEN BATMAN PATROLLING THE STEEL MILL MORE AND MORE.
"AND HAD THE BRUISES TO PROVE IT.

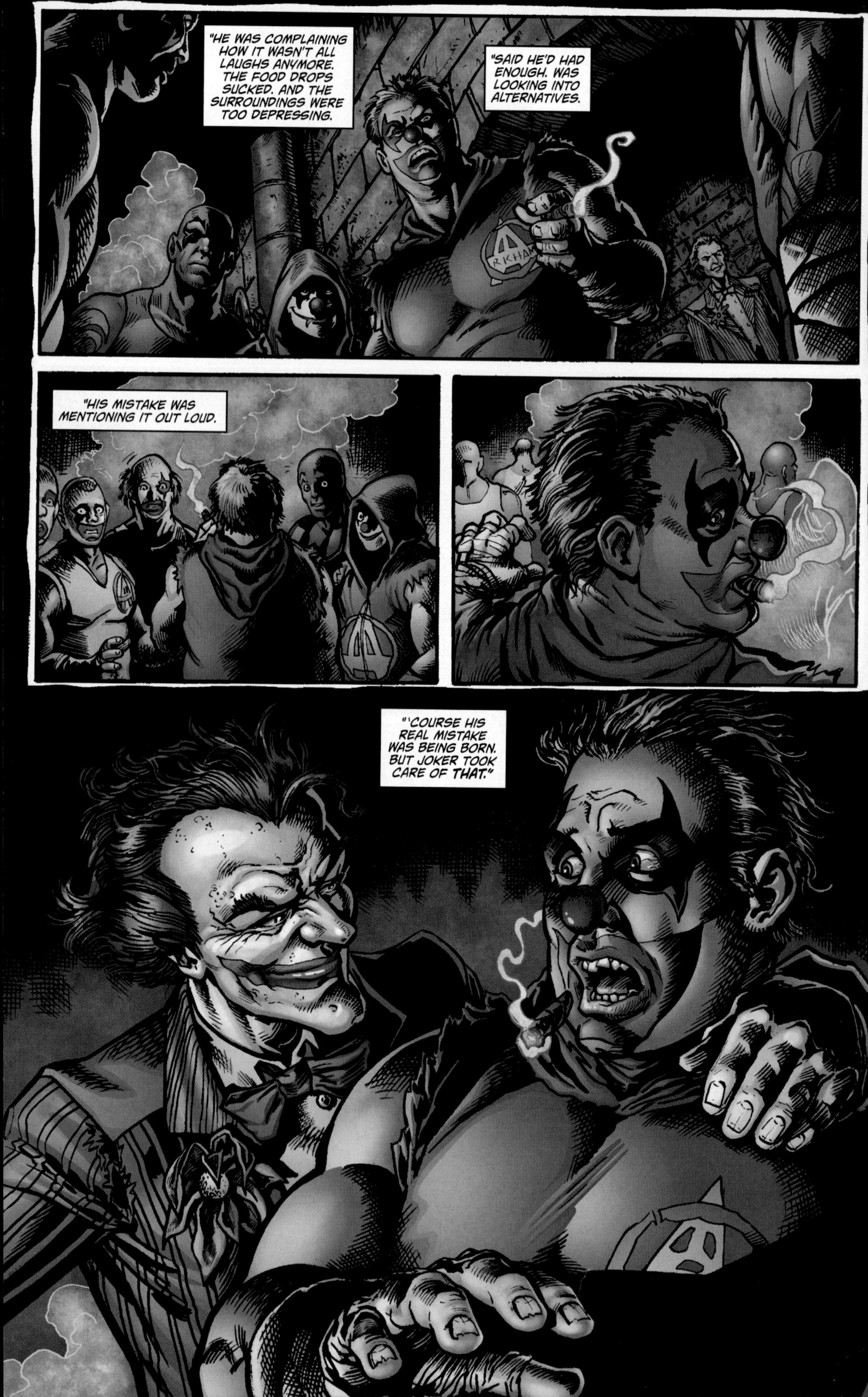
"HE WAS COMPLAINING HOW IT WASN'T ALL LAUGHS ANYMORE. THE FOOD DROPS SUCKED. AND THE SURROUNDINGS WERE TOO DEPRESSING.
"SAID HE'D HAD ENOUGH. WAS LOOKING INTO ALTERNATIVES.
"HIS MISTAKE WAS MENTIONING IT OUT LOUD.
"'COURSE HIS REAL MISTAKE WAS BEING BORN. BUT JOKER TOOK CARE OF THAT."

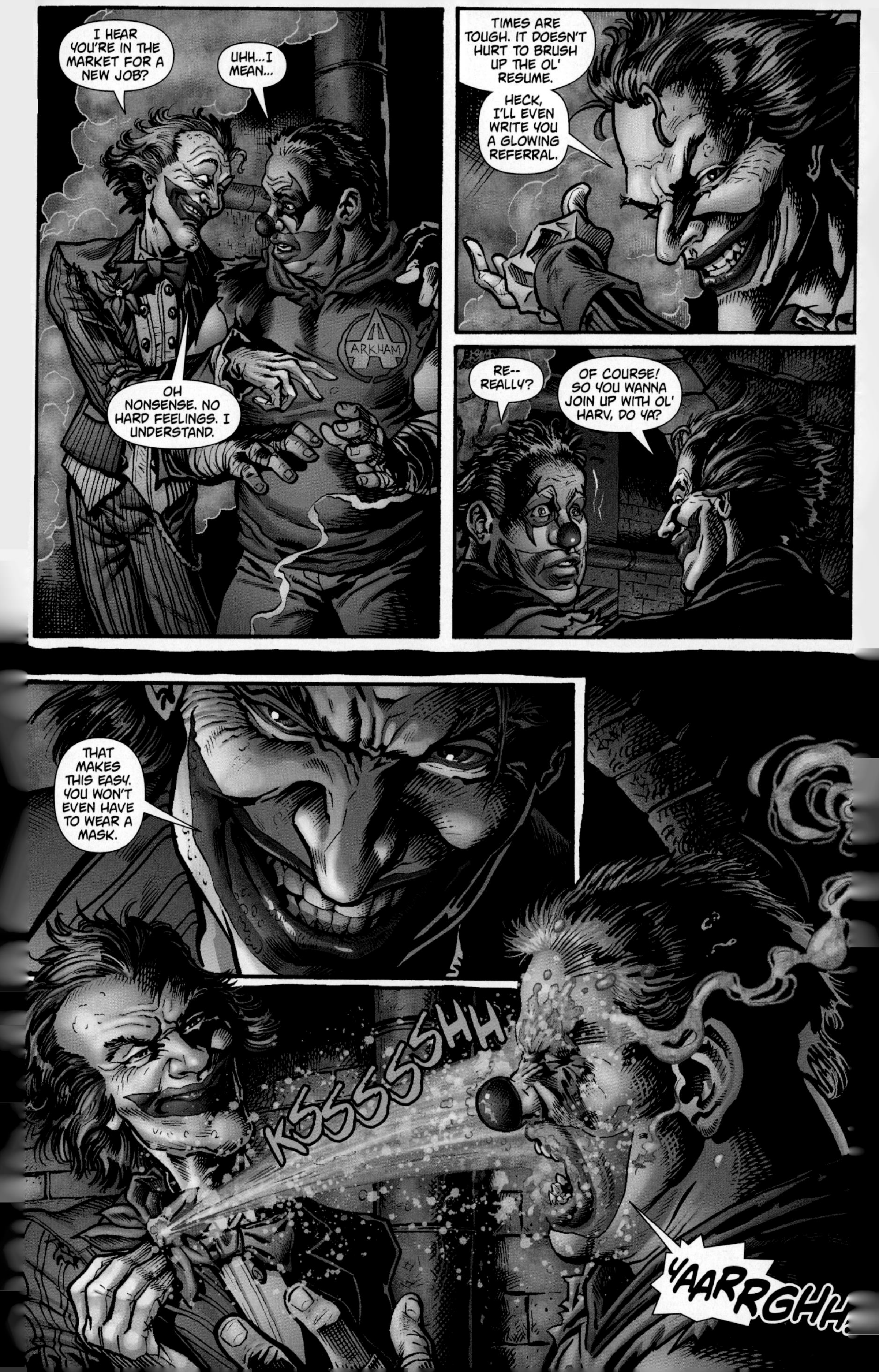
I HEAR YOU'RE IN THE MARKET FOR A NEW JOB?
UHH...I MEAN...
OH NONSENSE. NO HARD FEELINGS. I UNDERSTAND.
TIMES ARE TOUGH. IT DOESN'T HURT TO BRUSH UP THE OL' RESUME.
HECK, I'LL EVEN WRITE YOU A GLOWING REFERRAL.
RE--REALLY?
OF COURSE! SO YOU WANNA JOIN UP WITH OL' HARV, DO YA?
THAT MAKES THIS EASY. YOU WON'T EVEN HAVE TO WEAR A MASK.
KSSSSSSHH
YAARRGHH

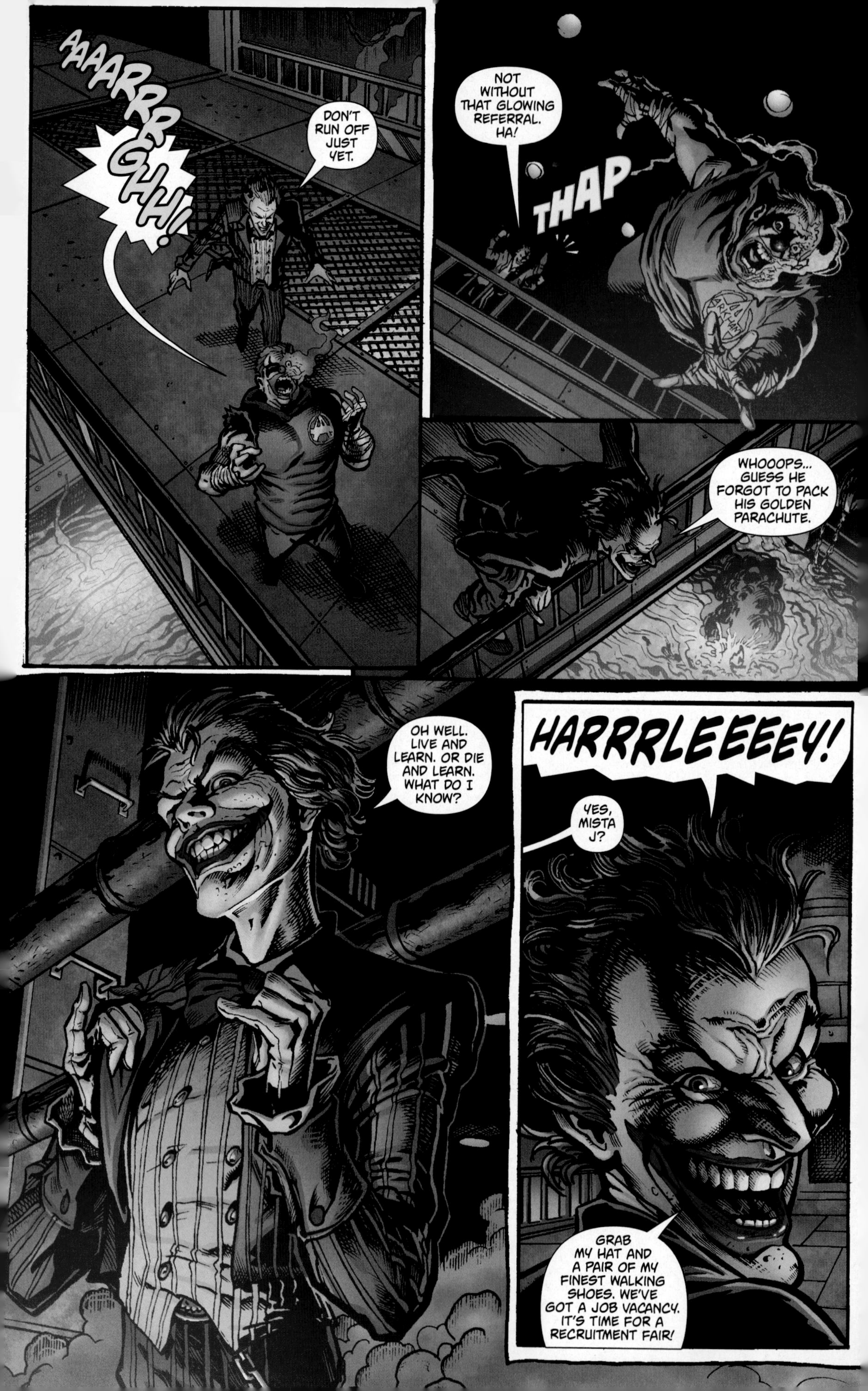
AAAARRRGHH!
DON'T RUN OFF JUST YET.
NOT WITHOUT THAT GLOWING REFERRAL. HA!
THAP
WHOOOPS... GUESS HE FORGOT TO PACK HIS GOLDEN PARACHUTE.
OH WELL. LIVE AND LEARN. OR DIE AND LEARN. WHAT DO I KNOW?
HARRRLEEEEY!
YES, MISTA J?
GRAB MY HAT AND A PAIR OF MY FINEST WALKING SHOES. WE'VE GOT A JOB VACANCY. IT'S TIME FOR A RECRUITMENT FAIR!

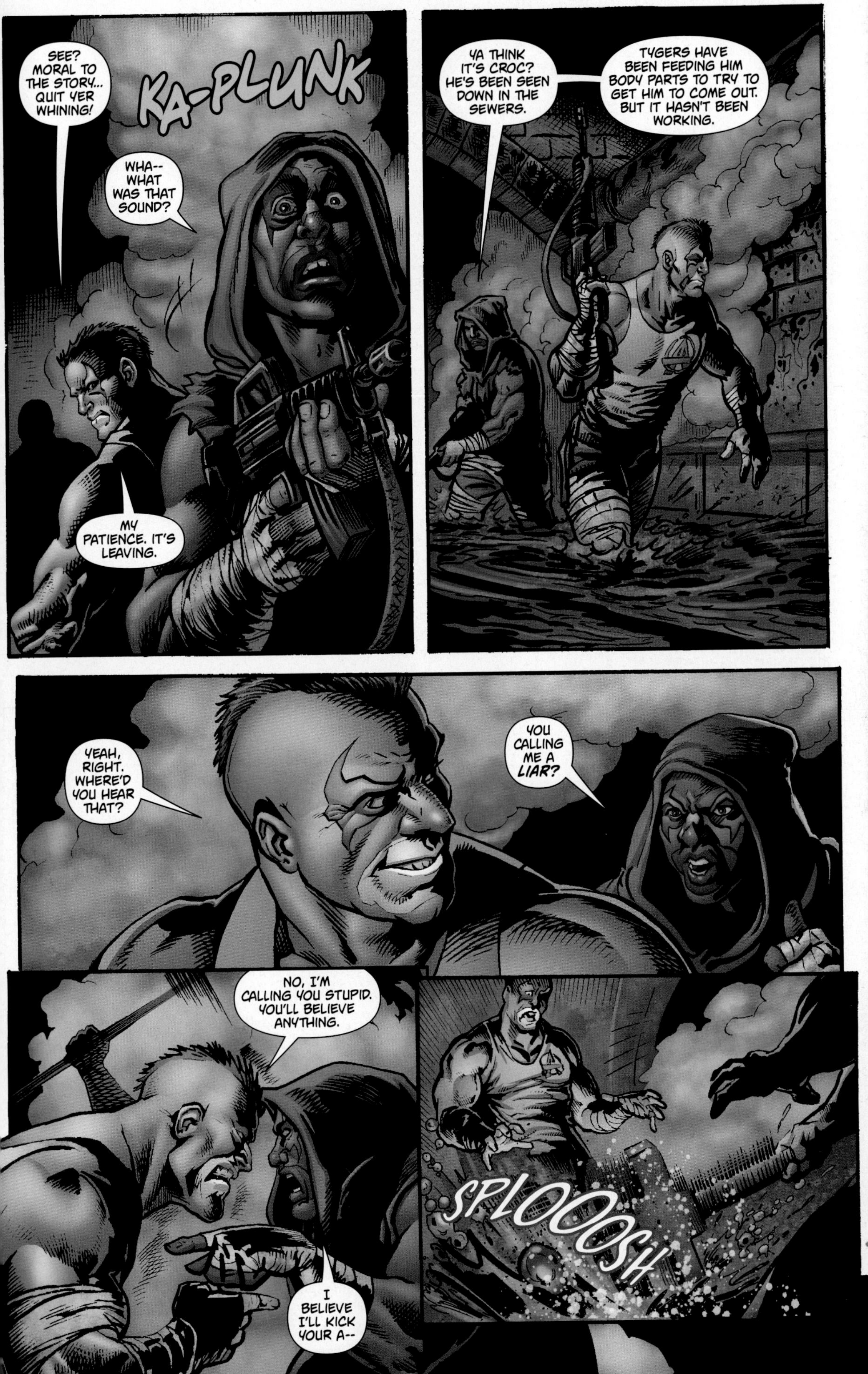
SEE? MORAL TO THE STORY... QUIT YER WHINING!
KA-PLUNK
WHA-- WHAT WAS THAT SOUND?
MY PATIENCE. IT'S LEAVING.
YA THINK IT'S CROC? HE'S BEEN SEEN DOWN IN THE SEWERS.
TYGERS HAVE BEEN FEEDING HIM BODY PARTS TO TRY TO GET HIM TO COME OUT. BUT IT HASN'T BEEN WORKING.
YEAH, RIGHT. WHERE'D YOU HEAR THAT?
YOU CALLING ME A *LIAR?*
NO, I'M CALLING YOU STUPID. YOU'LL BELIEVE ANYTHING.
I BELIEVE I'LL KICK YOUR A--
SPLOOOSH

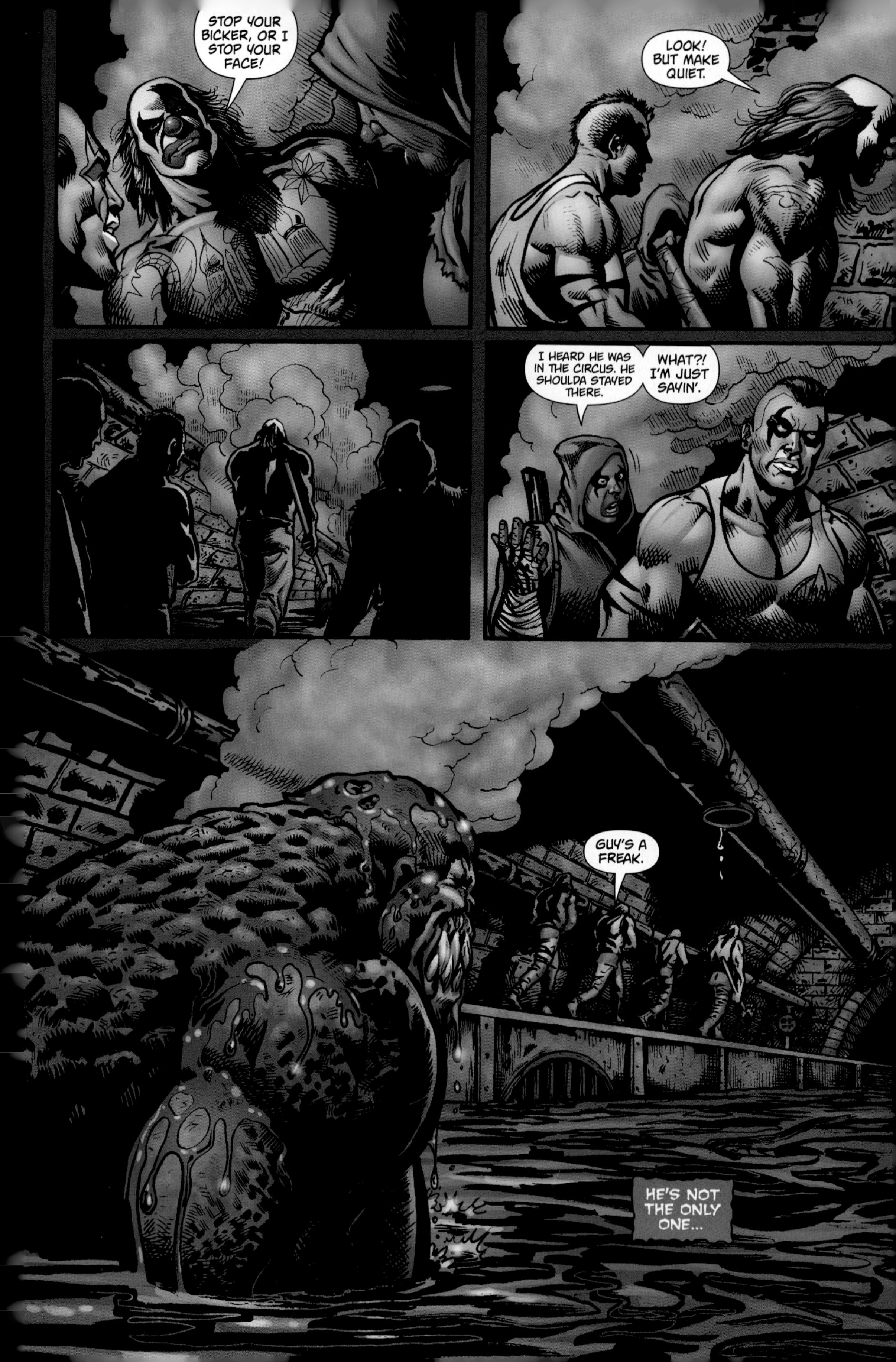
STOP YOUR BICKER, OR I STOP YOUR FACE!
LOOK! BUT MAKE QUIET.
I HEARD HE WAS IN THE CIRCUS. HE SHOULDA STAYED THERE.
WHAT?! I'M JUST SAYIN'.
GUY'S A FREAK.
HE'S NOT THE ONLY ONE...

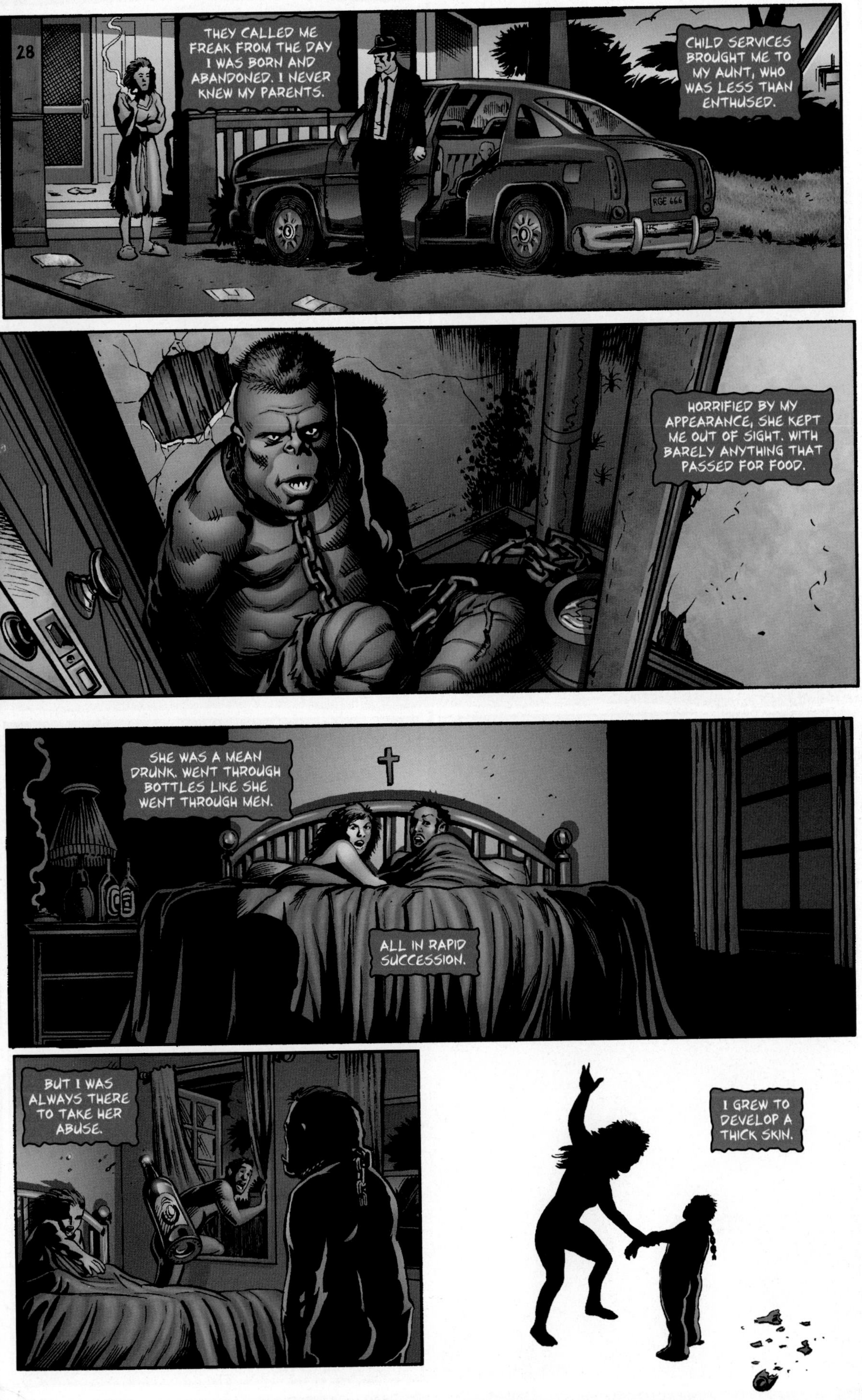
28
THEY CALLED ME FREAK FROM THE DAY I WAS BORN AND ABANDONED. I NEVER KNEW MY PARENTS.
CHILD SERVICES BROUGHT ME TO MY AUNT, WHO WAS LESS THAN ENTHUSED.
RGE 666
HORRIFIED BY MY APPEARANCE, SHE KEPT ME OUT OF SIGHT. WITH BARELY ANYTHING THAT PASSED FOR FOOD.
SHE WAS A MEAN DRUNK. WENT THROUGH BOTTLES LIKE SHE WENT THROUGH MEN.
ALL IN RAPID SUCCESSION.
BUT I WAS ALWAYS THERE TO TAKE HER ABUSE.
I GREW TO DEVELOP A THICK SKIN.

EVERY DAY I WAS THE SUBJECT OF THEIR HATRED. RELENTLESSLY BULLIED AT SCHOOL...

...AS WELL AS AT HOME.

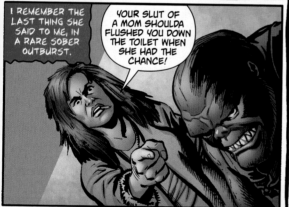

I REMEMBER THE LAST THING SHE SAID TO ME, IN A RARE SOBER OUTBURST.

YOUR SLUT OF A MOM SHOULDA FLUSHED YOU DOWN THE TOILET WHEN SHE HAD THE CHANCE!

FINALLY I SNAPPED.

AND I DIDN'T STOP SNAPPING, UNTIL SHE WAS ALL GONE.

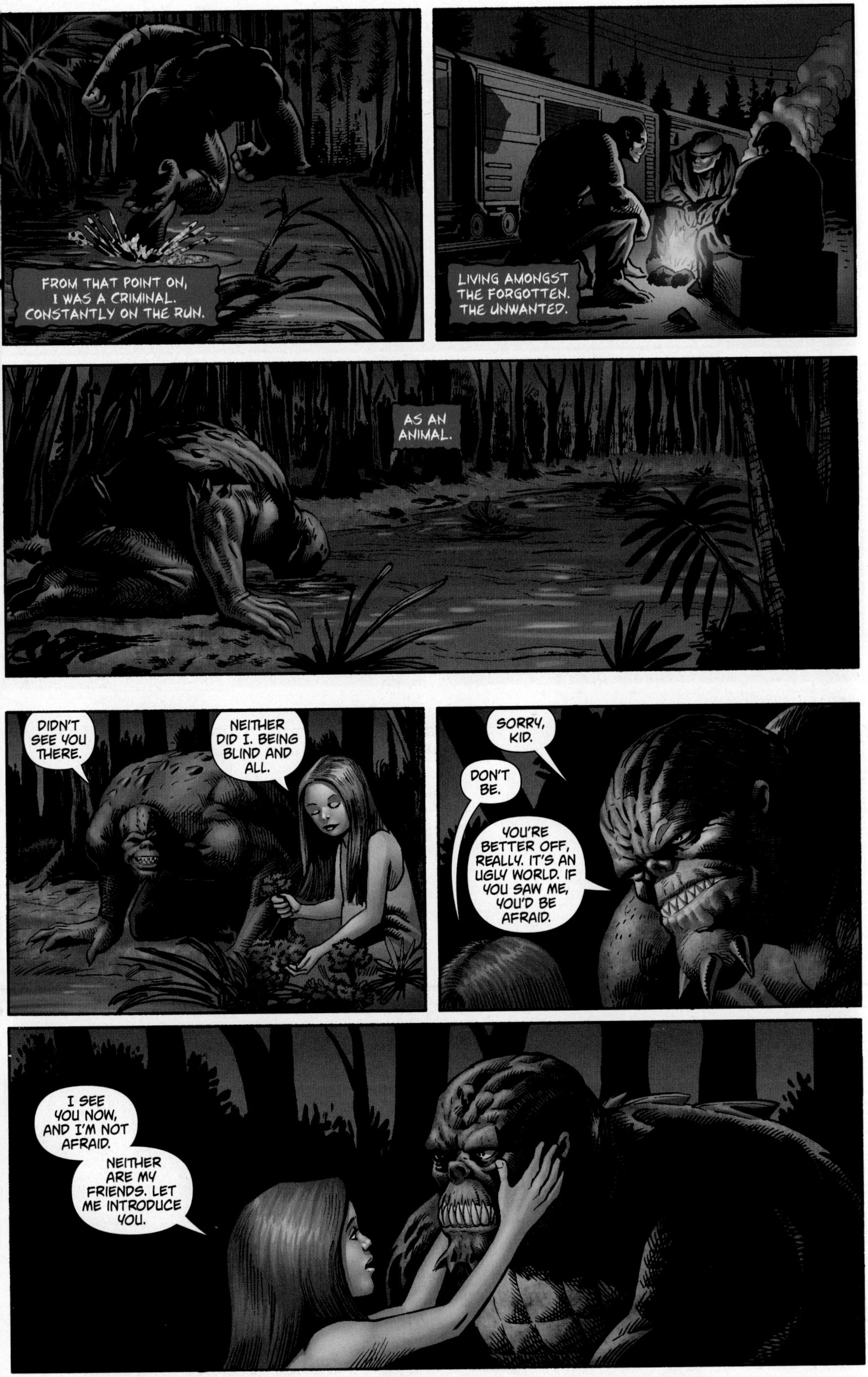
FROM THAT POINT ON, I WAS A CRIMINAL. CONSTANTLY ON THE RUN.
LIVING AMONGST THE FORGOTTEN. THE UNWANTED.
AS AN ANIMAL.
DIDN'T SEE YOU THERE.
NEITHER DID I. BEING BLIND AND ALL.
SORRY, KID.
DON'T BE.
YOU'RE BETTER OFF, REALLY. IT'S AN UGLY WORLD. IF YOU SAW ME, YOU'D BE AFRAID.
I SEE YOU NOW, AND I'M NOT AFRAID.
NEITHER ARE MY FRIENDS. LET ME INTRODUCE YOU.

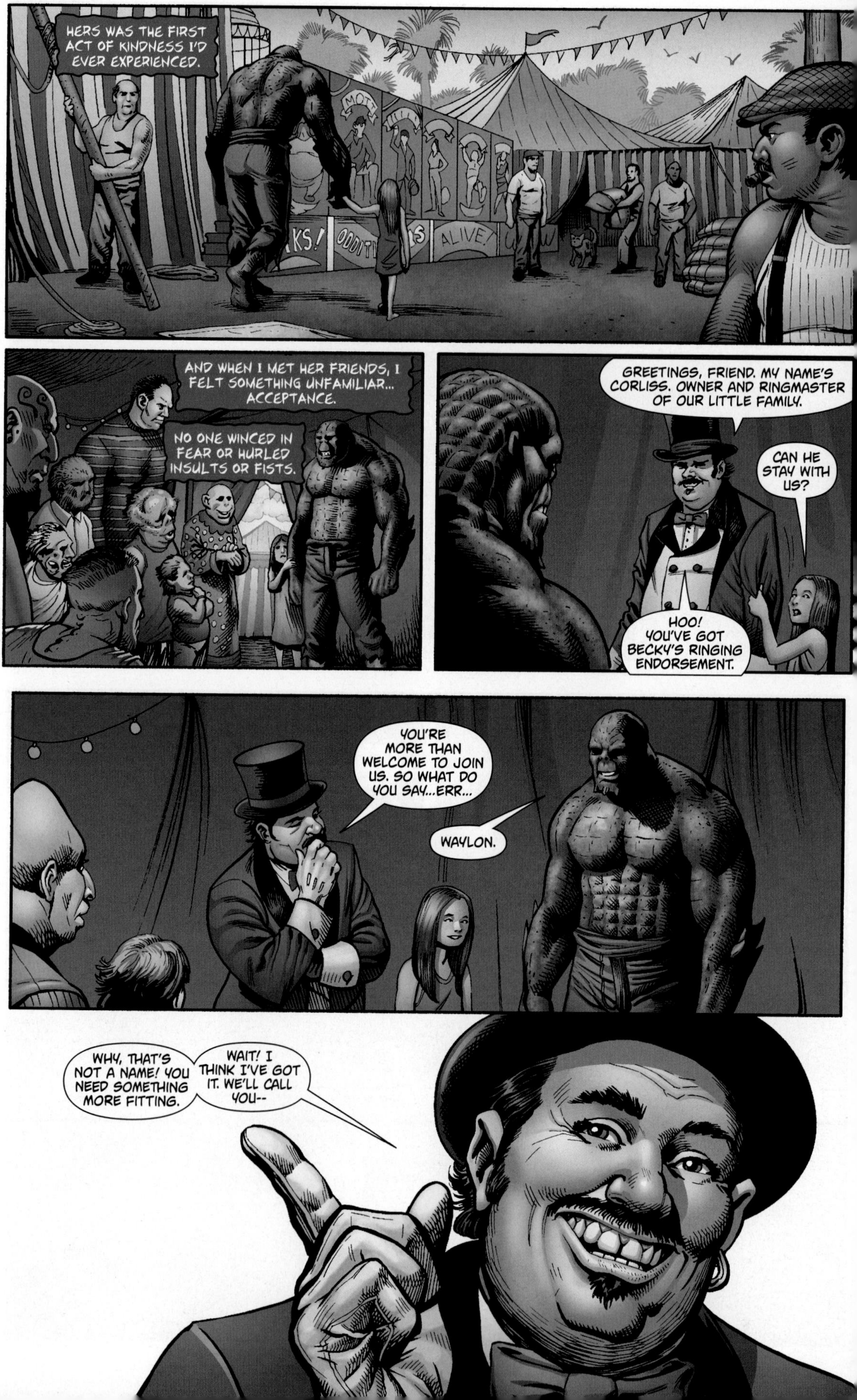
HERS WAS THE FIRST ACT OF KINDNESS I'D EVER EXPERIENCED.
ALIVE!
AND WHEN I MET HER FRIENDS, I FELT SOMETHING UNFAMILIAR... ACCEPTANCE.
NO ONE WINCED IN FEAR OR HURLED INSULTS OR FISTS.
GREETINGS, FRIEND. MY NAME'S CORLISS. OWNER AND RINGMASTER OF OUR LITTLE FAMILY.
CAN HE STAY WITH US?
HOO! YOU'VE GOT BECKY'S RINGING ENDORSEMENT.
YOU'RE MORE THAN WELCOME TO JOIN US. SO WHAT DO YOU SAY...ERR...
WAYLON.
WHY, THAT'S NOT A NAME! YOU NEED SOMETHING MORE FITTING.
WAIT! I THINK I'VE GOT IT. WE'LL CALL YOU--

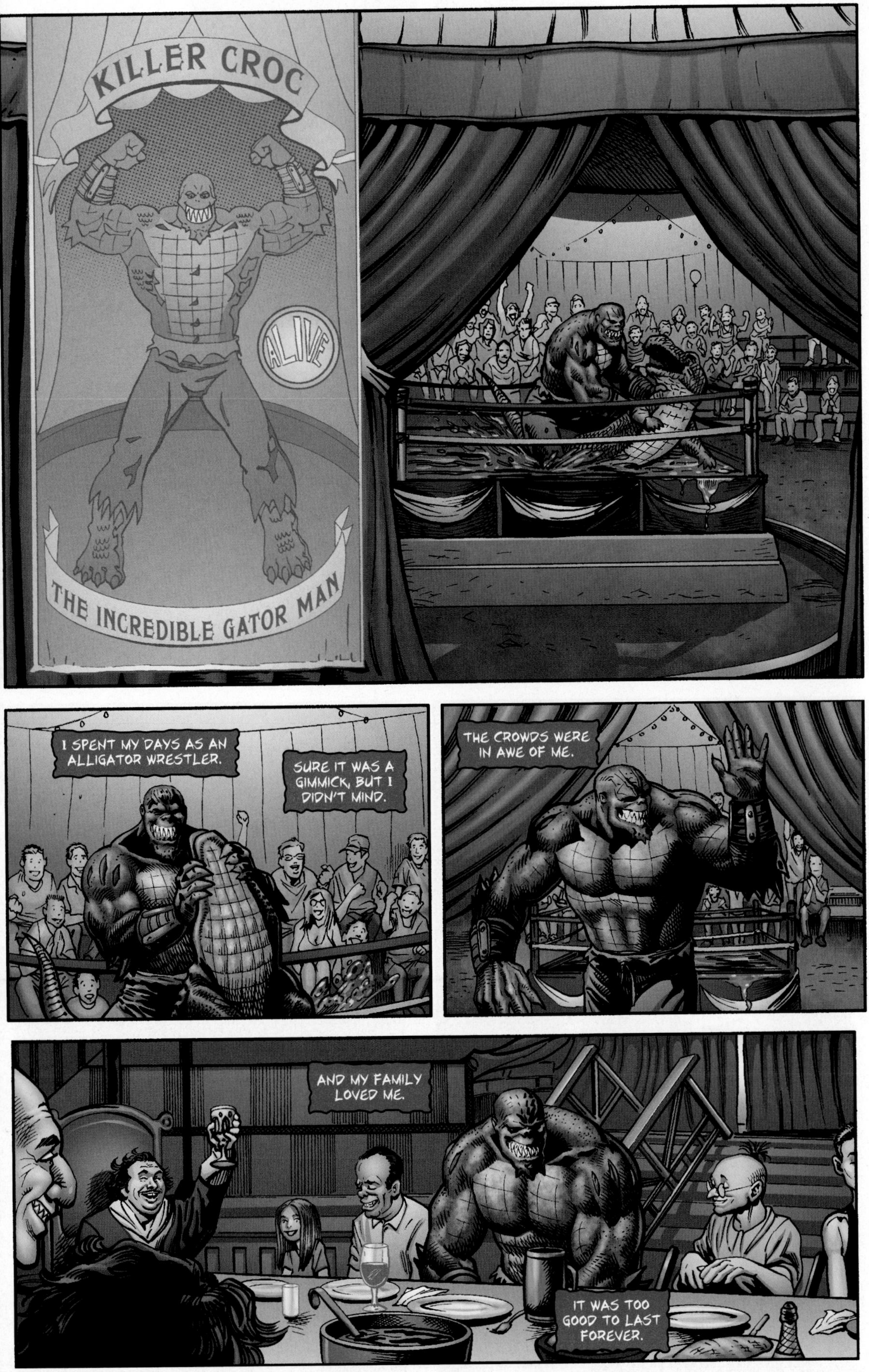
KILLER CROC
ALIVE
THE INCREDIBLE GATOR MAN
I SPENT MY DAYS AS AN ALLIGATOR WRESTLER.
SURE IT WAS A GIMMICK, BUT I DIDN'T MIND.
THE CROWDS WERE IN AWE OF ME.
AND MY FAMILY LOVED ME.
IT WAS TOO GOOD TO LAST FOREVER.

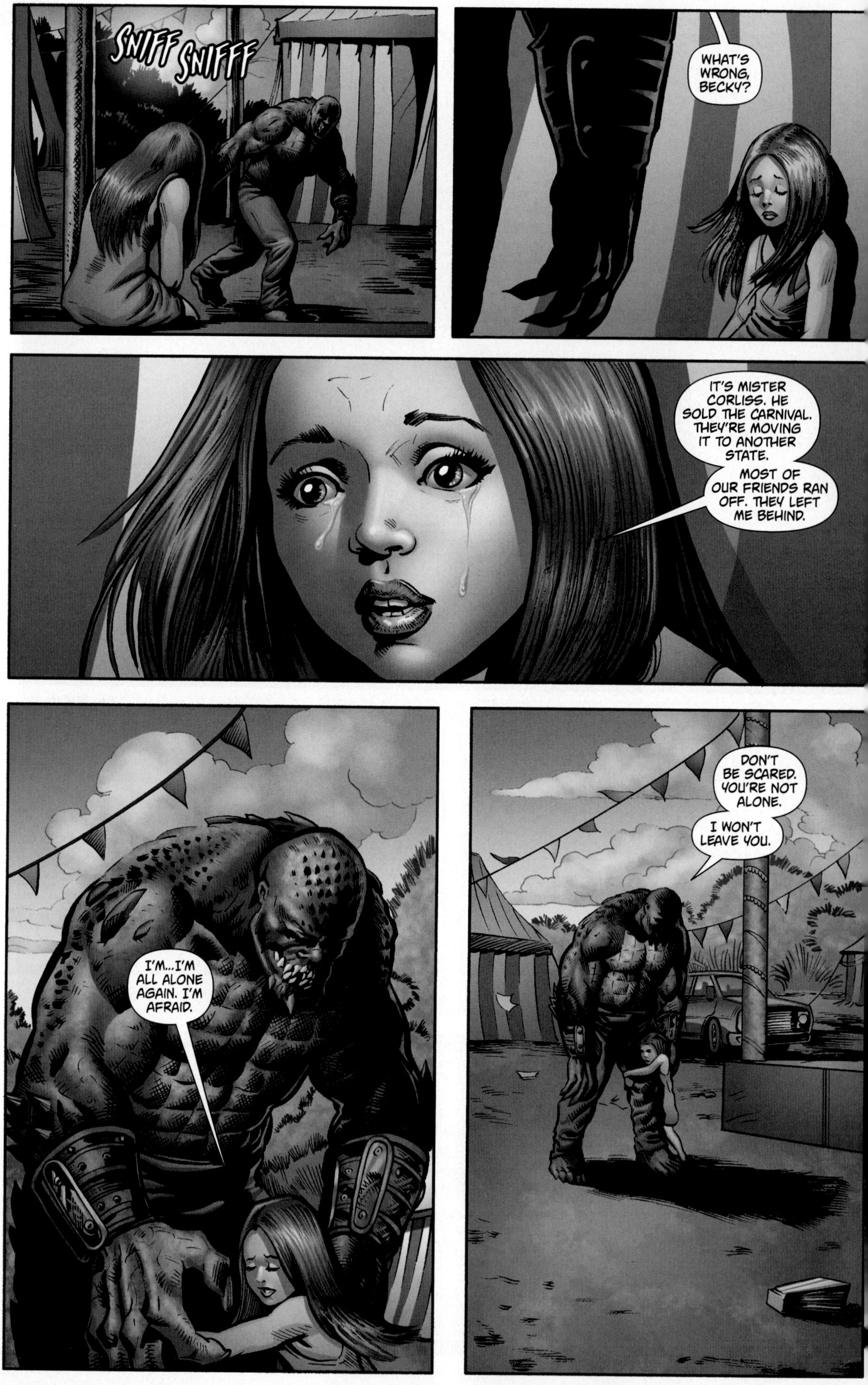
SNIFF SNIFFF
WHAT'S WRONG, BECKY?
IT'S MISTER CORLISS. HE SOLD THE CARNIVAL. THEY'RE MOVING IT TO ANOTHER STATE.
MOST OF OUR FRIENDS RAN OFF. THEY LEFT ME BEHIND.
I'M...I'M ALL ALONE AGAIN. I'M AFRAID.
DON'T BE SCARED. YOU'RE NOT ALONE.
I WON'T LEAVE YOU.

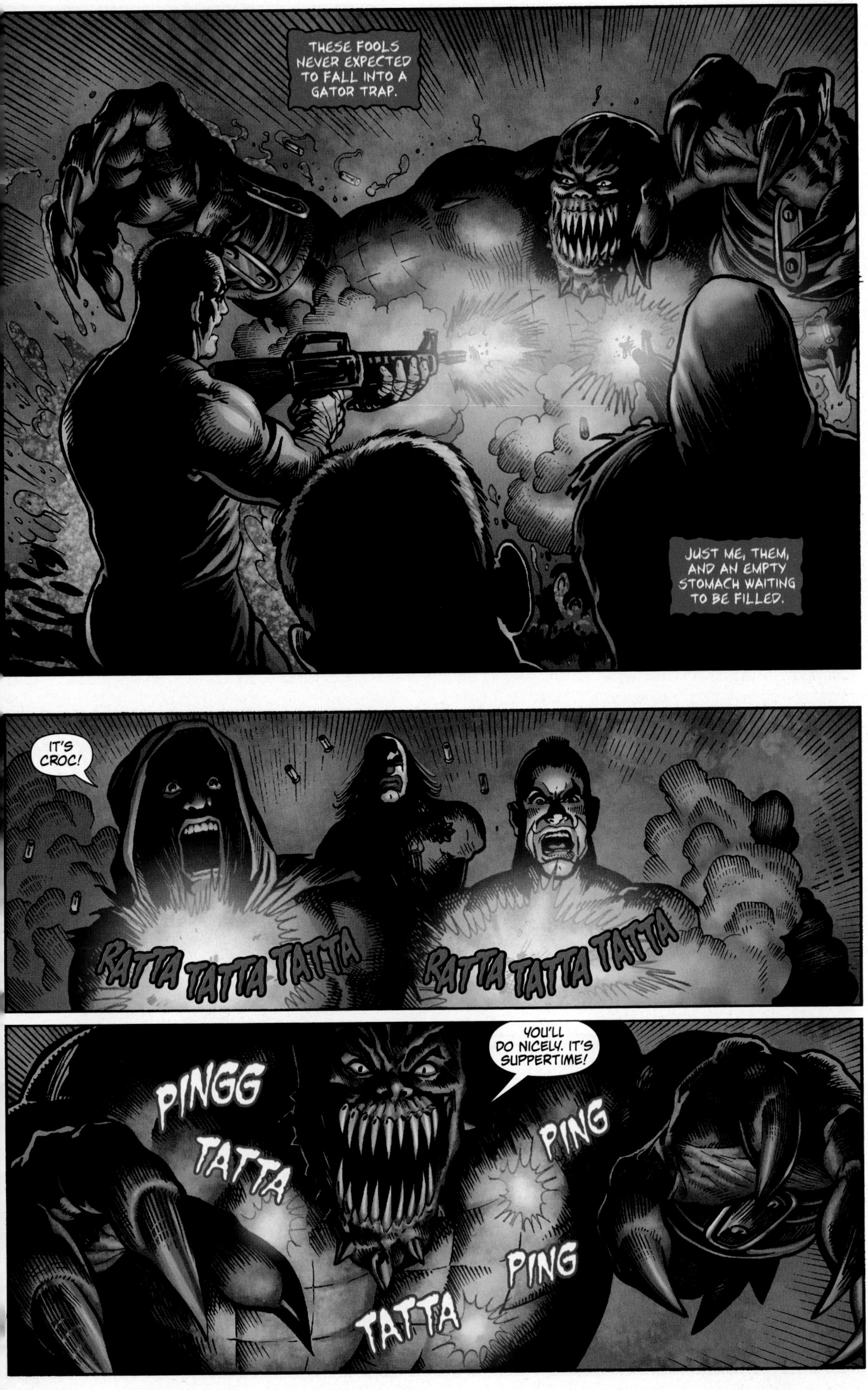
THESE FOOLS NEVER EXPECTED TO FALL INTO A GATOR TRAP.
JUST ME, THEM, AND AN EMPTY STOMACH WAITING TO BE FILLED.
IT'S CROC!
RATTA TATTA TATTA
RATTA TATTA TATTA
YOU'LL DO NICELY. IT'S SUPPERTIME!
PINGG
TATTA
PING
PING
TATTA

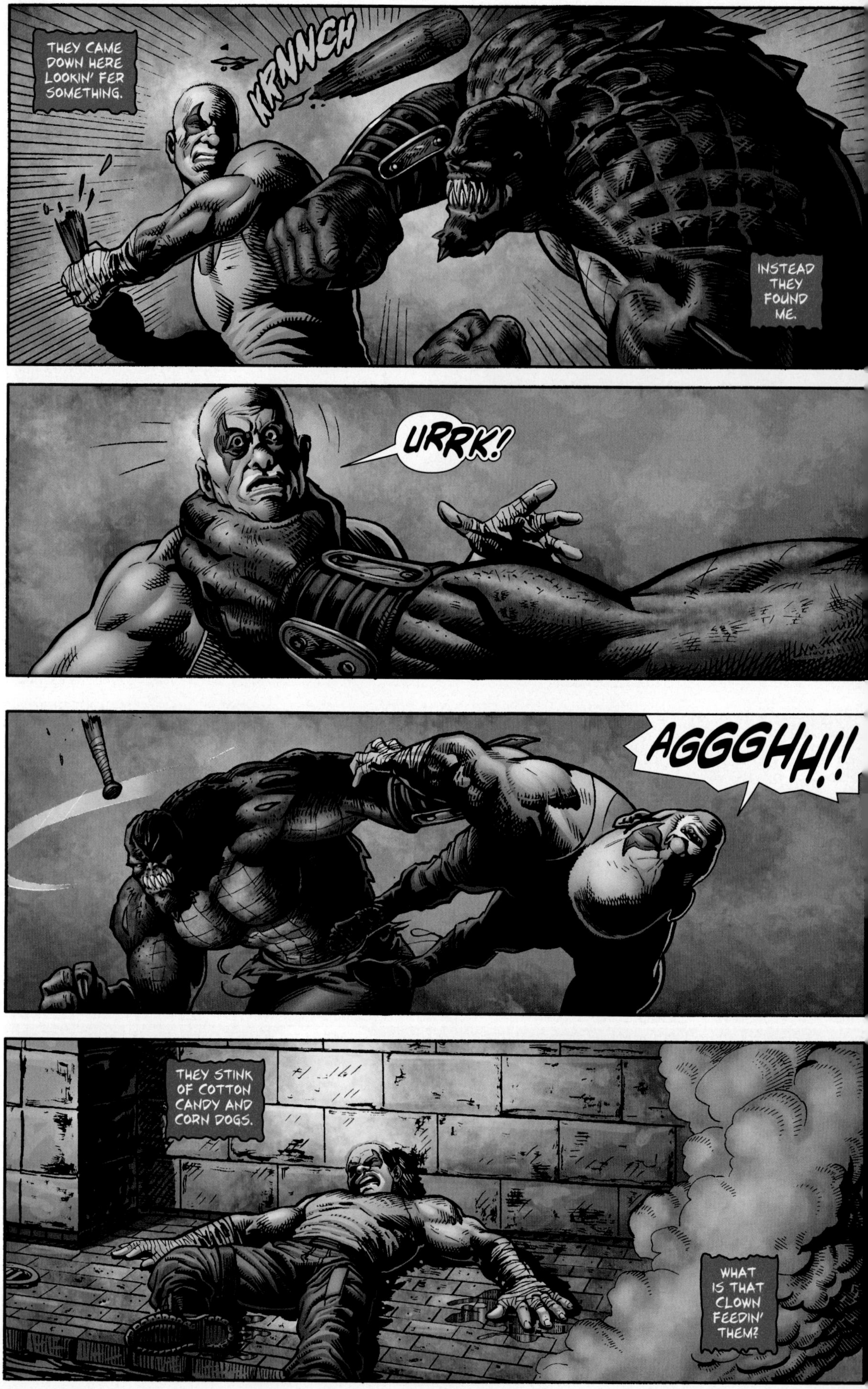
THEY CAME DOWN HERE LOOKIN' FER SOMETHING.
KRNNCH
INSTEAD THEY FOUND ME.
URRK!
AGGGHH!!
THEY STINK OF COTTON CANDY AND CORN DOGS.
WHAT IS THAT CLOWN FEEDIN' THEM?

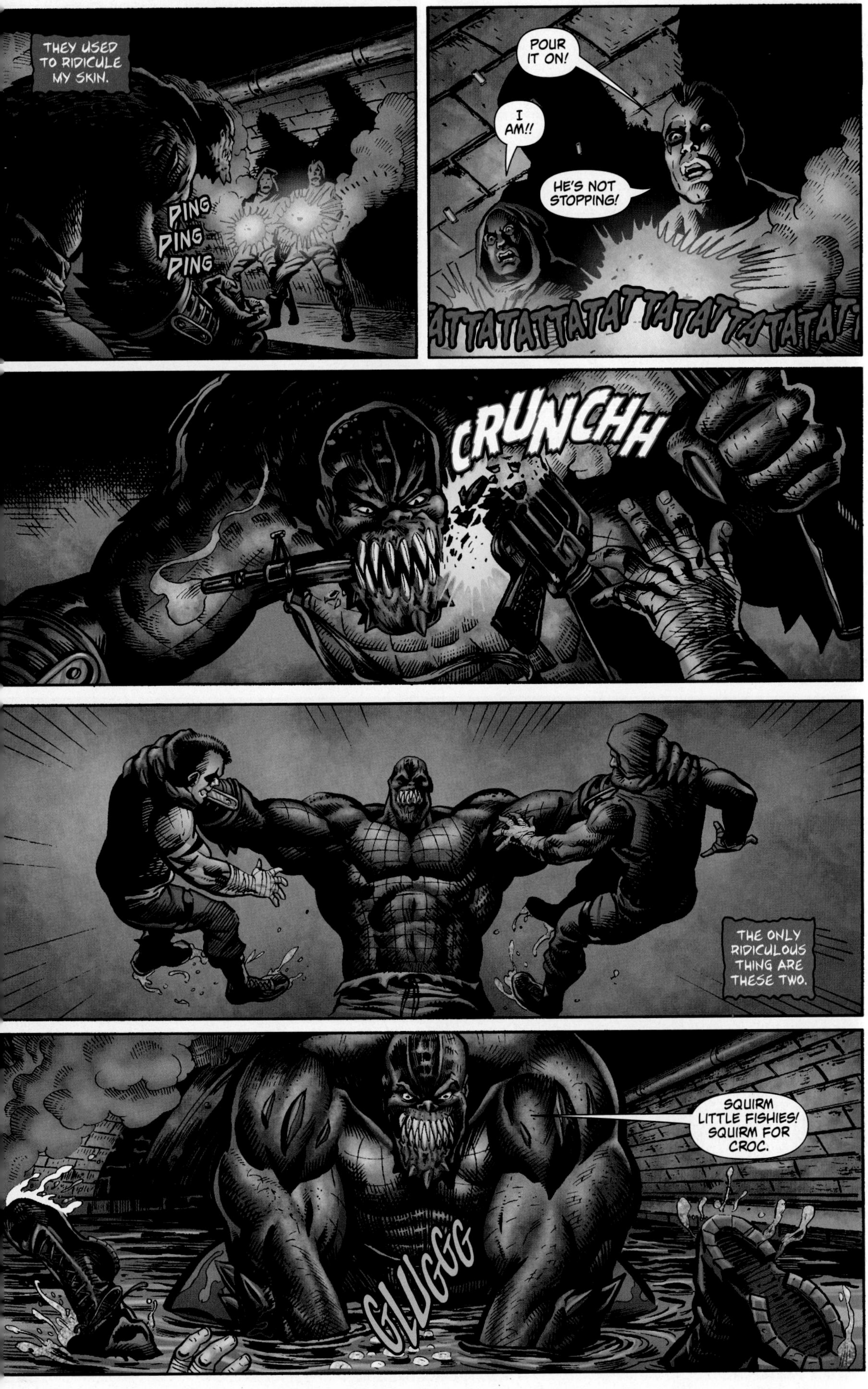
THEY USED TO RIDICULE MY SKIN.
PING
PING
PING
POUR IT ON!
I AM!!
HE'S NOT STOPPING!
TATATATTATATTATATTATATATTATATAT
CRUNCHH
THE ONLY RIDICULOUS THING ARE THESE TWO.
SQUIRM LITTLE FISHIES! SQUIRM FOR CROC.
GLUGGG

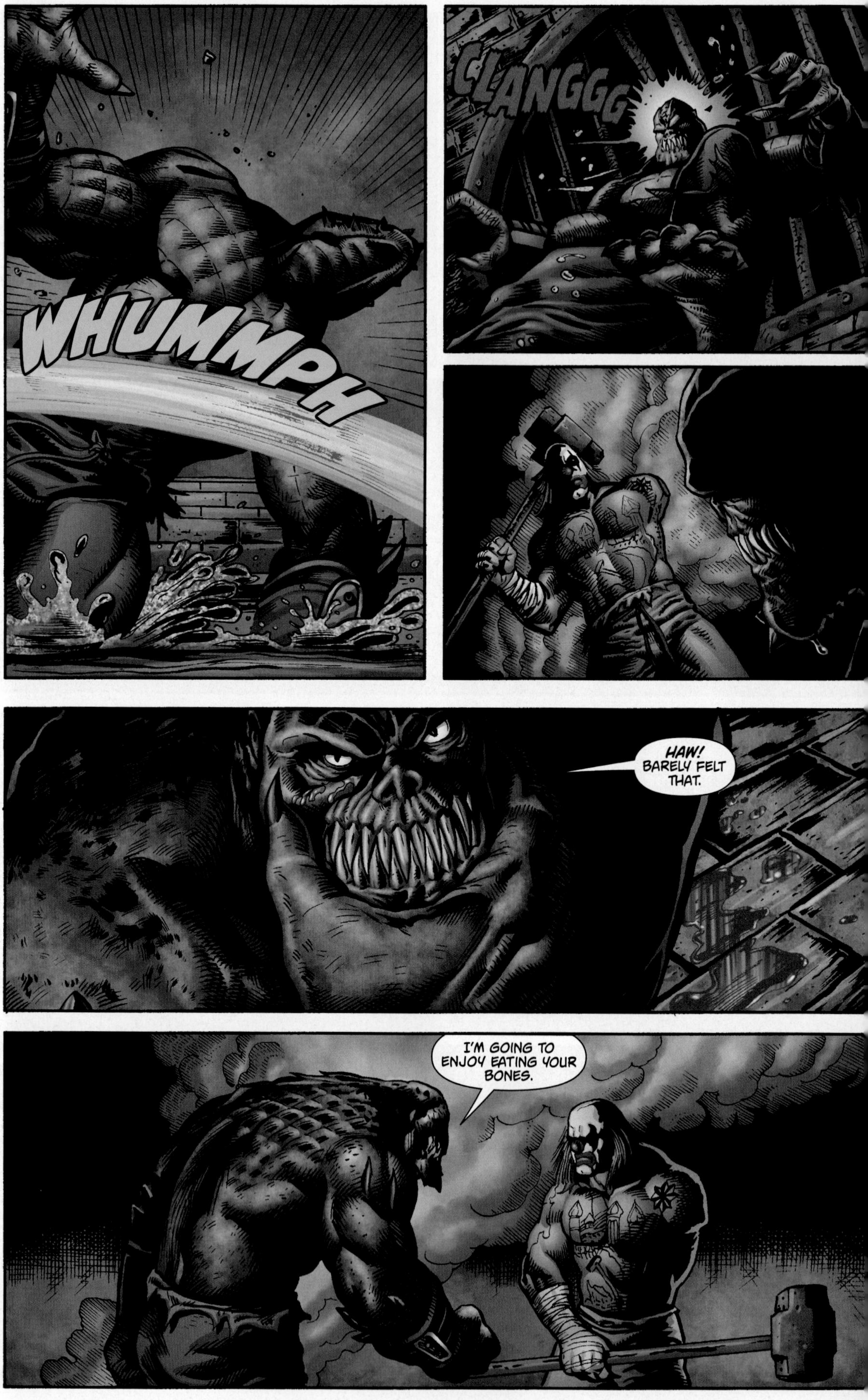
WHUMMPH
CLANGGG
HAW! BARELY FELT THAT.
I'M GOING TO ENJOY EATING YOUR BONES.

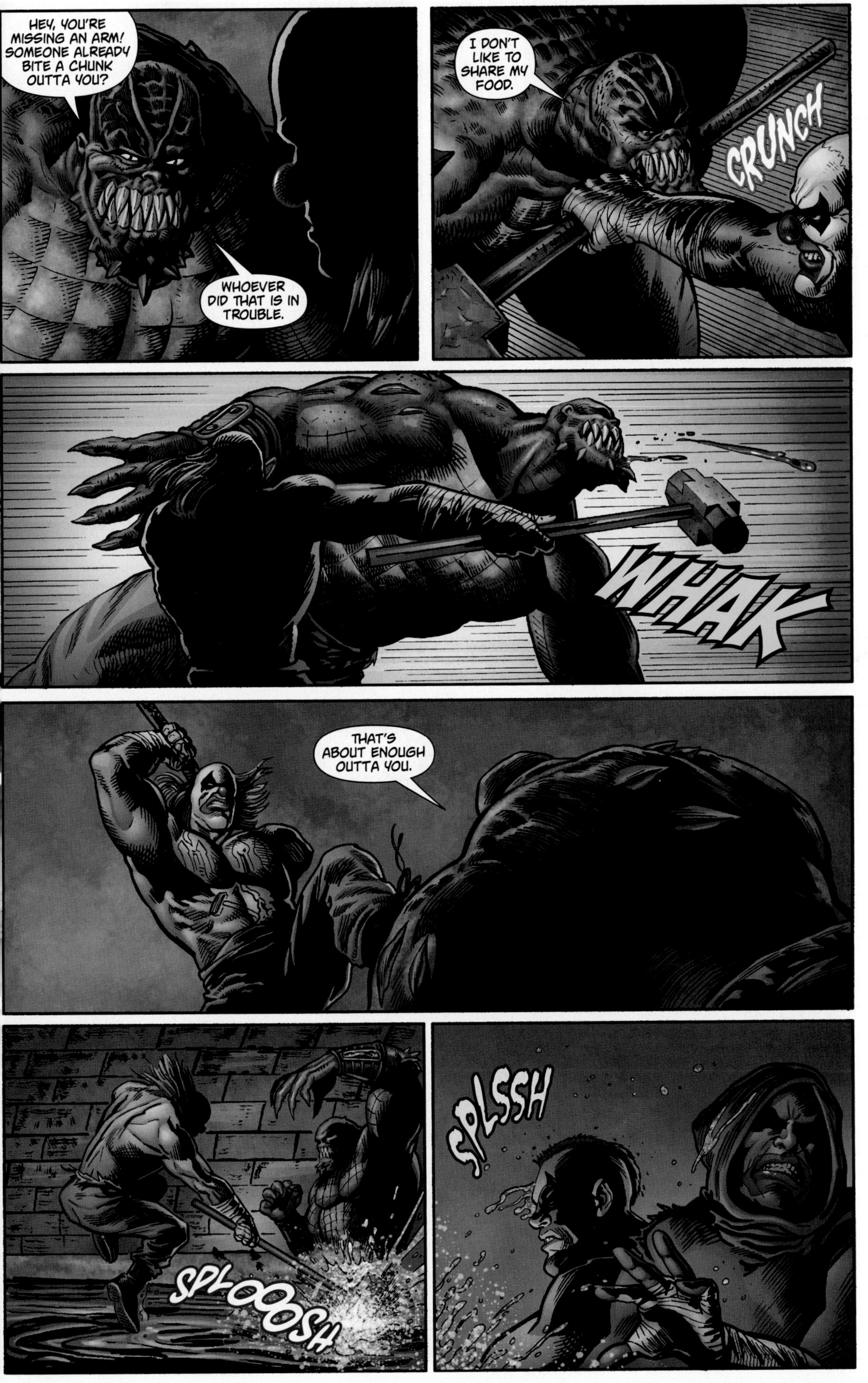
HEY, YOU'RE MISSING AN ARM! SOMEONE ALREADY BITE A CHUNK OUTTA YOU?
WHOEVER DID THAT IS IN TROUBLE.
I DON'T LIKE TO SHARE MY FOOD.
CRUNCH
WHAK
THAT'S ABOUT ENOUGH OUTTA YOU.
SPLOOOSH
SPLSSH

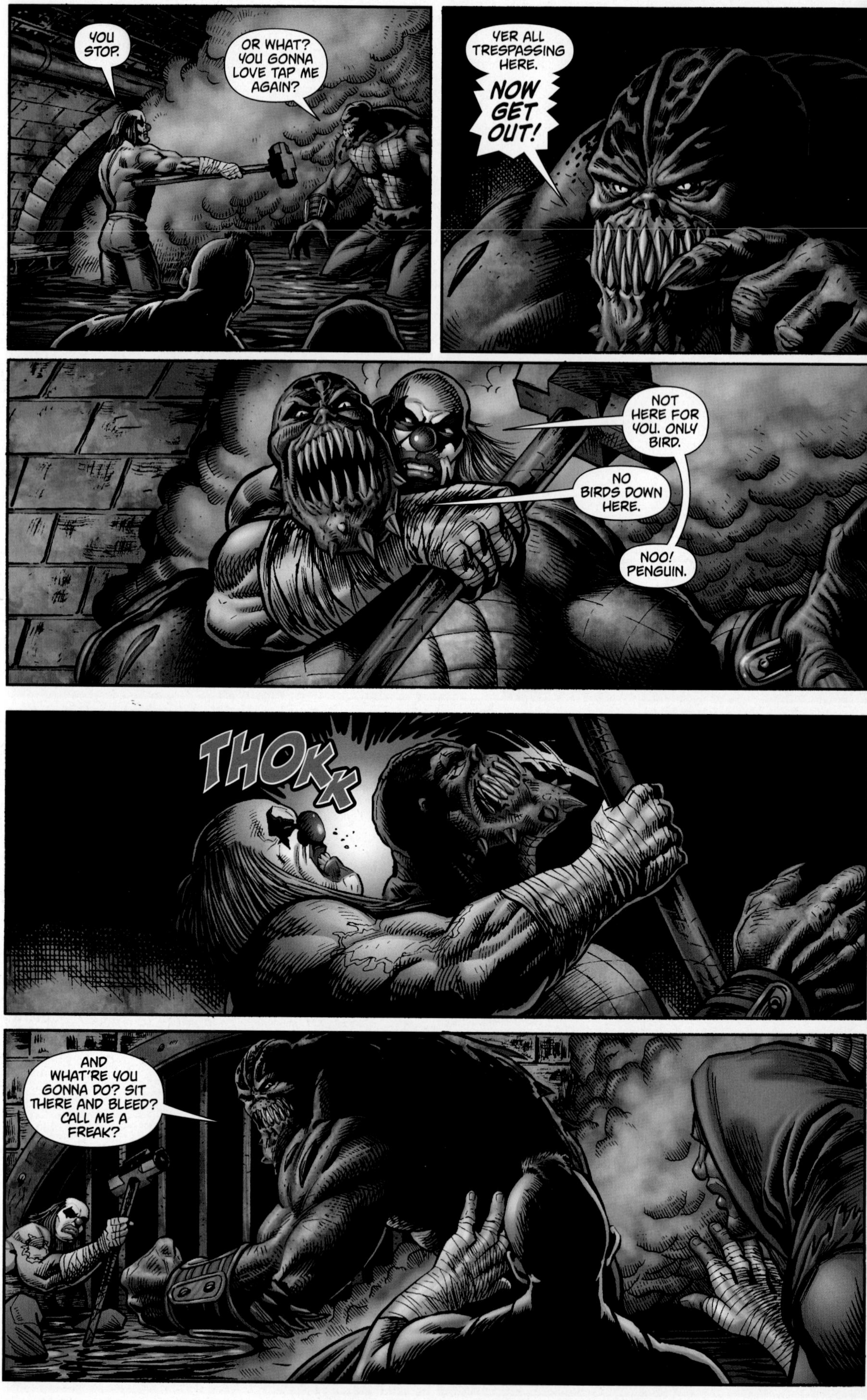
YOU STOP.
OR WHAT? YOU GONNA LOVE TAP ME AGAIN?
YER ALL TRESPASSING HERE.
NOW GET OUT!
NOT HERE FOR YOU. ONLY BIRD.
NO BIRDS DOWN HERE.
NOO! PENGUIN.
THOKK
AND WHAT'RE YOU GONNA DO? SIT THERE AND BLEED? CALL ME A FREAK?

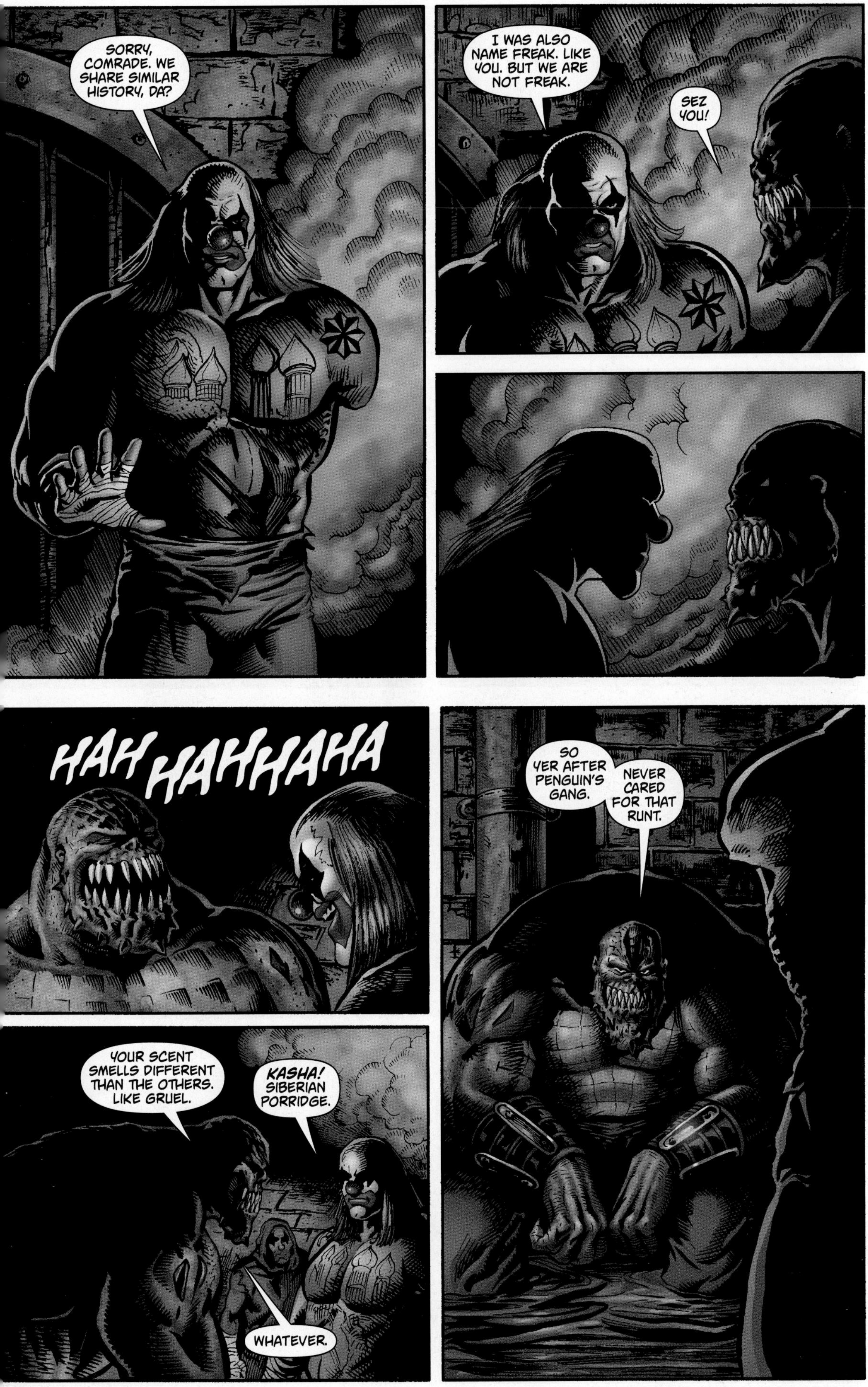
SORRY, COMRADE. WE SHARE SIMILAR HISTORY, DA?
I WAS ALSO NAME FREAK. LIKE YOU. BUT WE ARE NOT FREAK.
SEZ YOU!
HAH HAHHAHA
YOUR SCENT SMELLS DIFFERENT THAN THE OTHERS. LIKE GRUEL.
KASHA! SIBERIAN PORRIDGE.
WHATEVER.
SO YER AFTER PENGUIN'S GANG.
NEVER CARED FOR THAT RUNT.

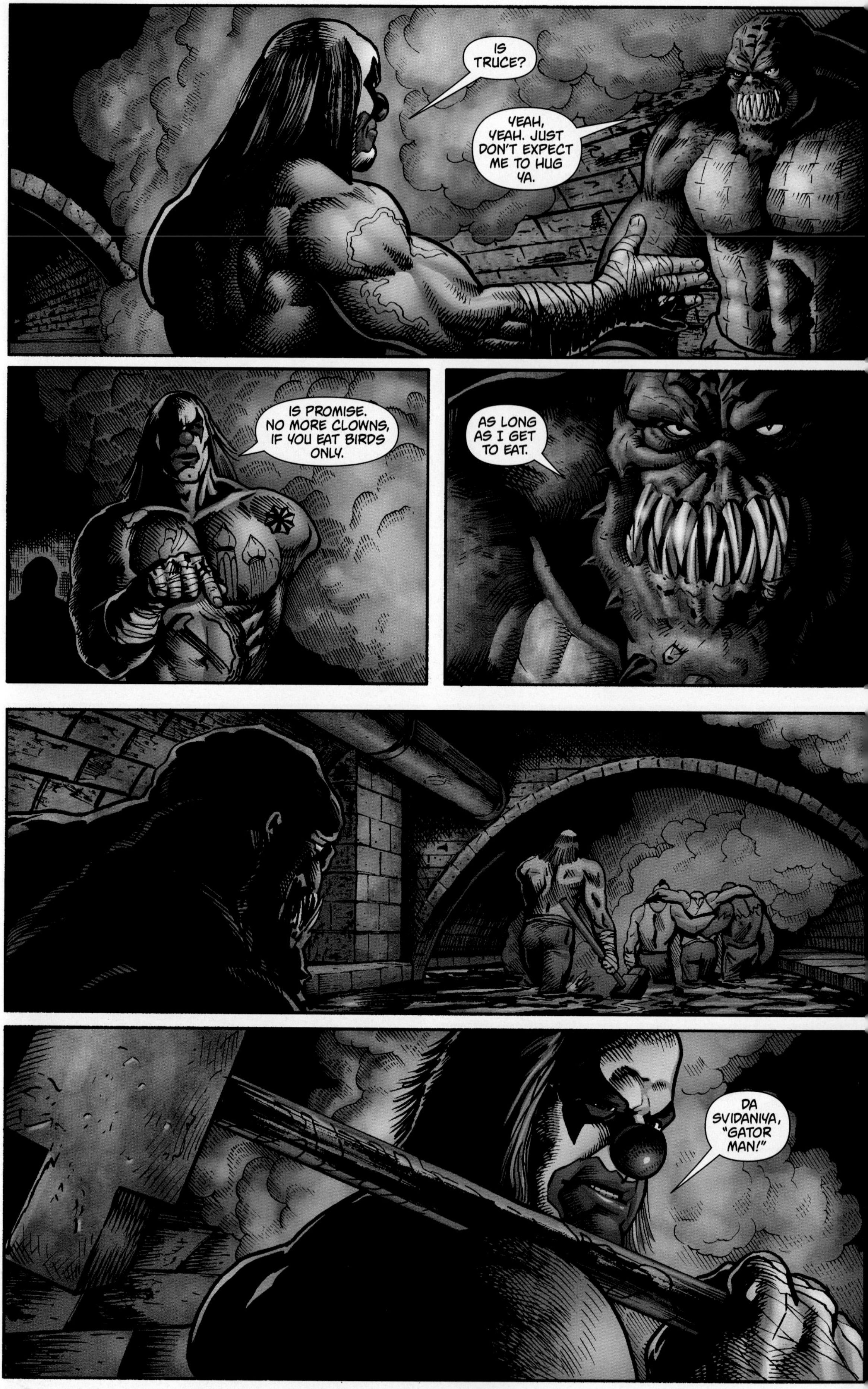
IS TRUCE?
YEAH, YEAH. JUST DON'T EXPECT ME TO HUG YA.
IS PROMISE. NO MORE CLOWNS, IF YOU EAT BIRDS ONLY.
AS LONG AS I GET TO EAT.
DA SVIDANIYA, "GATOR MAN!"

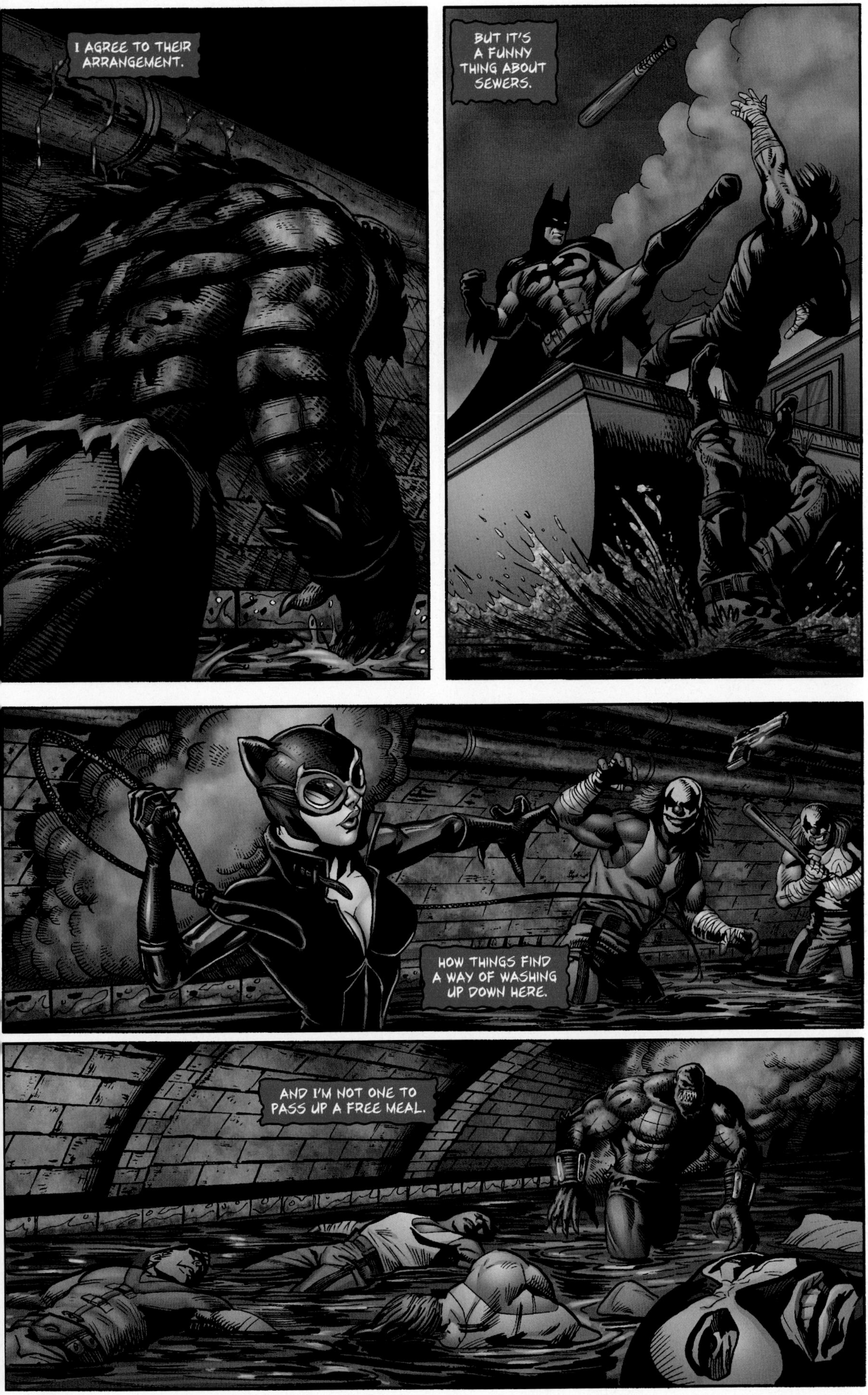
I AGREE TO THEIR ARRANGEMENT.
BUT IT'S A FUNNY THING ABOUT SEWERS.
HOW THINGS FIND A WAY OF WASHING UP DOWN HERE.
AND I'M NOT ONE TO PASS UP A FREE MEAL.

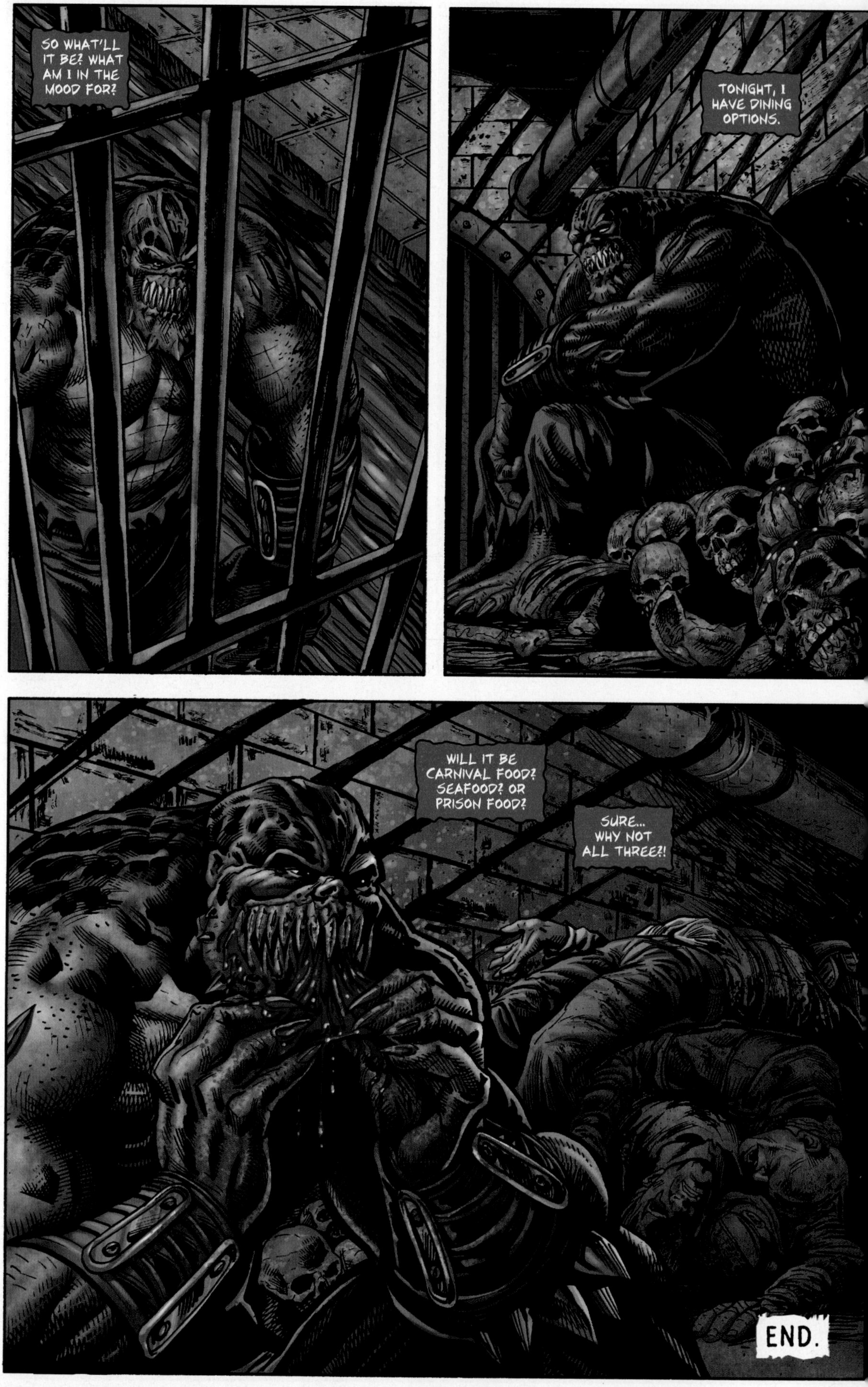
SO WHAT'LL IT BE? WHAT AM I IN THE MOOD FOR?
TONIGHT, I HAVE DINING OPTIONS.
WILL IT BE CARNIVAL FOOD? SEAFOOD? OR PRISON FOOD?
SURE... WHY NOT ALL THREE?!
END.

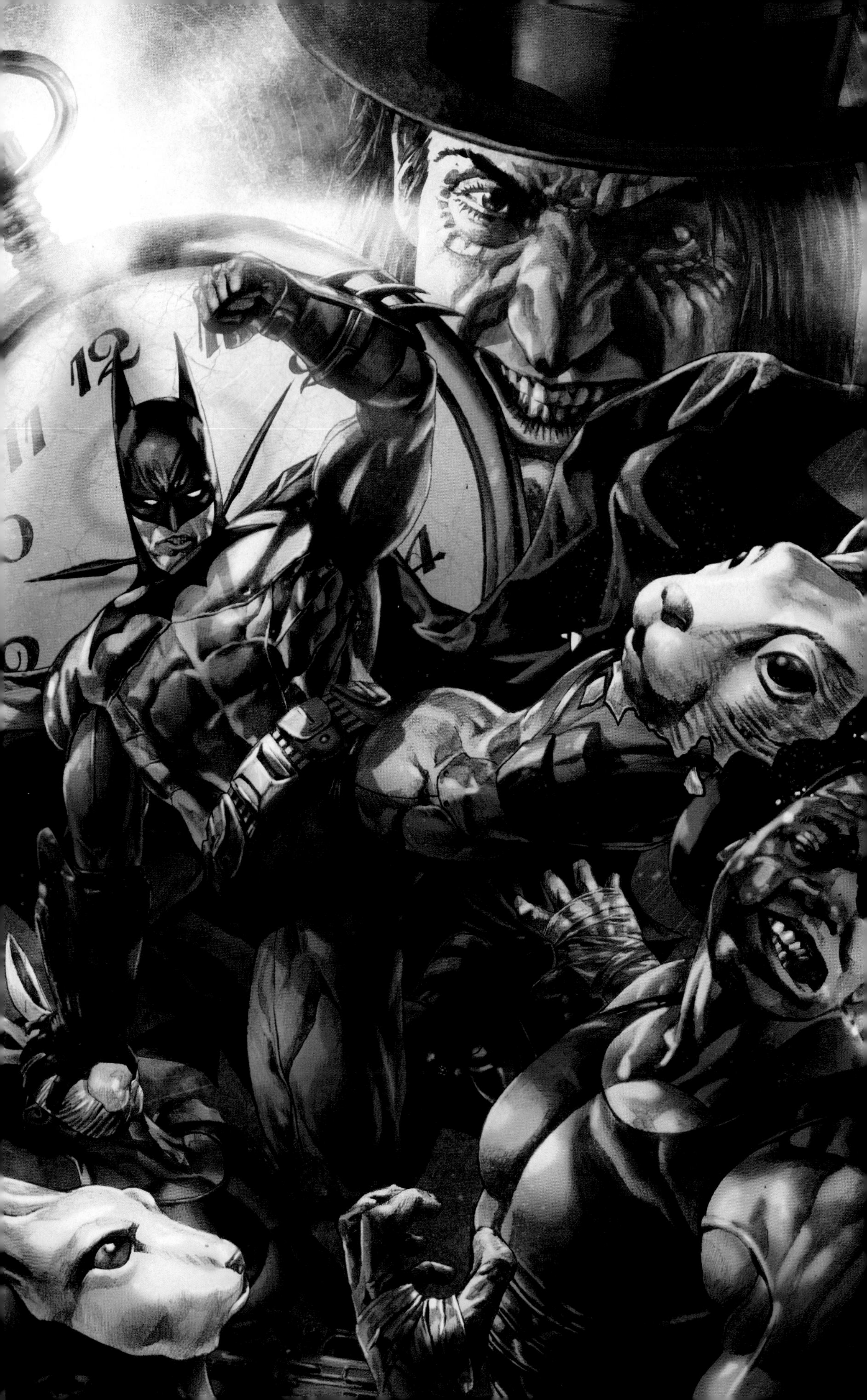

VICKI IN WONDERLAND

WRITTEN BY: DEREK FRIDOLFS

PENCILS BY: PETER NGUYEN

INKS BY: CRAIG YEUNG

COLORS BY: ANDREW ELDER

LETTERS BY: TRAVIS LANHAM

COVER ART BY: MICO SUAYAN

COVER COLORS BY: DAVID LOPEZ

& SANTI CASAS OF IKARI STUDIO

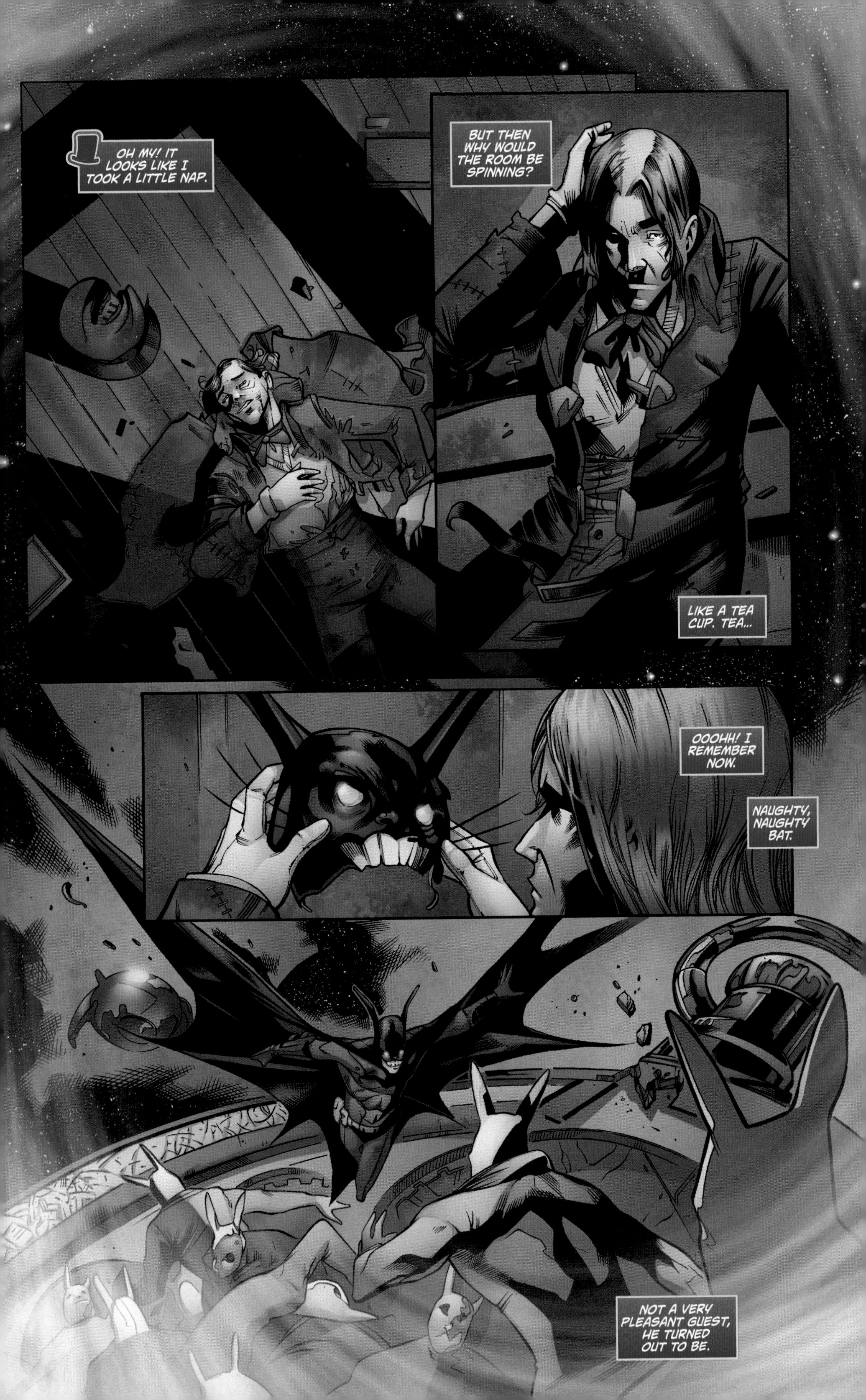
OH MY! IT LOOKS LIKE I TOOK A LITTLE NAP.
BUT THEN WHY WOULD THE ROOM BE SPINNING?
LIKE A TEA CUP. TEA...
OOOHH! I REMEMBER NOW.
NAUGHTY, NAUGHTY BAT.
NOT A VERY PLEASANT GUEST, HE TURNED OUT TO BE.

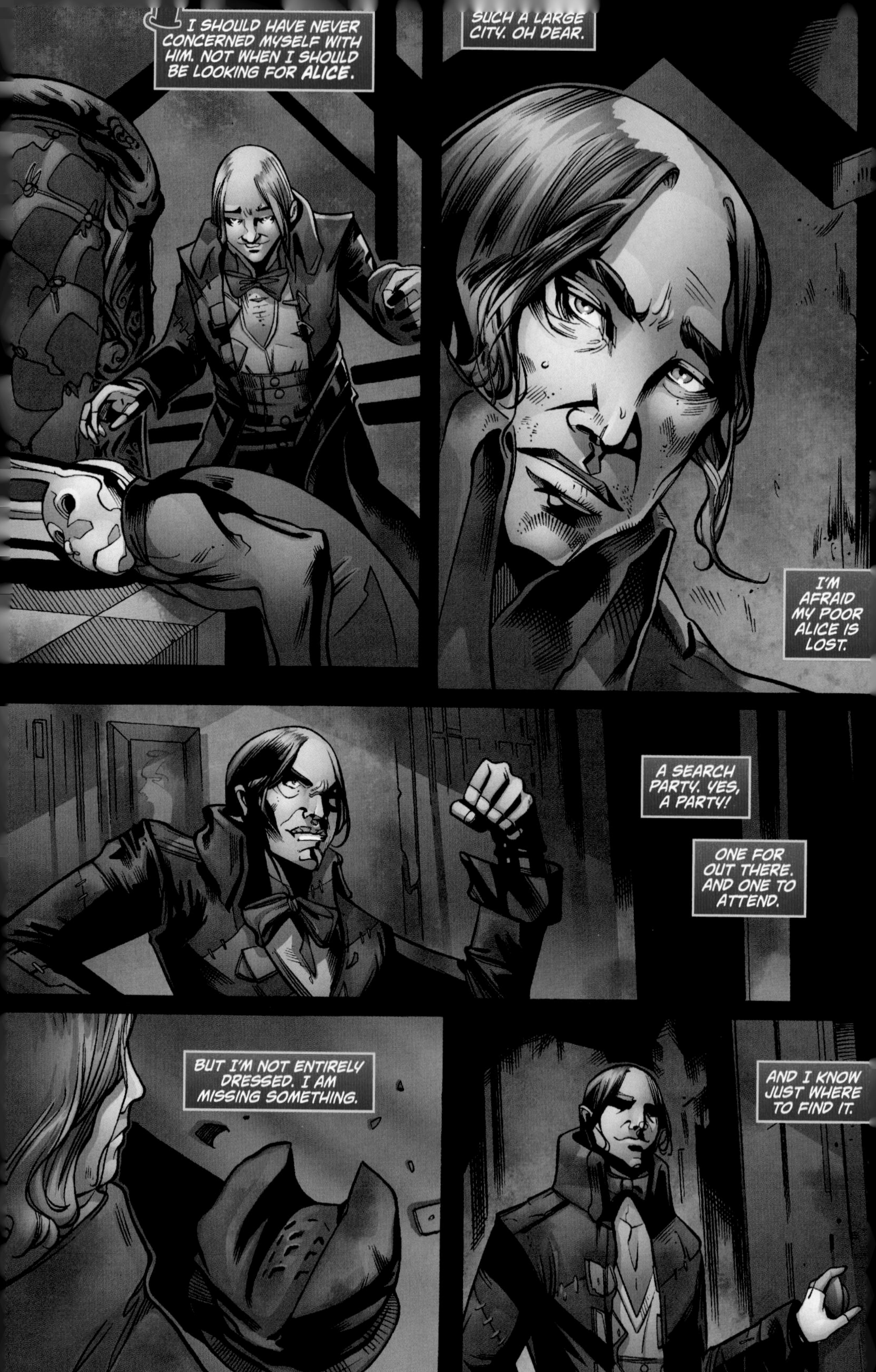
I SHOULD HAVE NEVER CONCERNED MYSELF WITH HIM. NOT WHEN I SHOULD BE LOOKING FOR ALICE.
SUCH A LARGE CITY. OH DEAR.
I'M AFRAID MY POOR ALICE IS LOST.
A SEARCH PARTY. YES, A PARTY!
ONE FOR OUT THERE. AND ONE TO ATTEND.
BUT I'M NOT ENTIRELY DRESSED. I AM MISSING SOMETHING.
AND I KNOW JUST WHERE TO FIND IT.

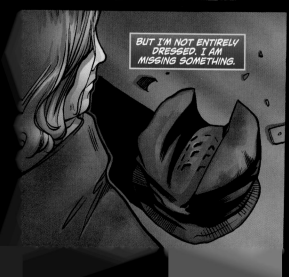

ARKHAM CITY IS A DANGEROUS PLACE. I FOUND THAT OUT WHEN OUR CHANNEL 3 NEWS HELICOPTER WAS SHOT DOWN.

SINCE THEN, THIS CITY HAS ERUPTED IN GUNFIRE. YOU CAN HEAR IT EVERYWHERE.

STILL...THERE'S A STORY OUT THERE, WAITING TO BE TOLD.

AND THE ONLY WAY TO DO THAT IS TO GO OUT THERE AND FIND IT.

FLAP FLAP FLAP

RAT-A-TAT-ATATTATA

KEEP IT TOGETHER, VICKI.

YOU DON'T HAVE TO JUMP AT EVERY LITTLE--

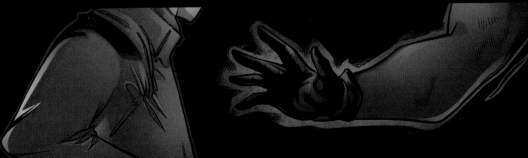

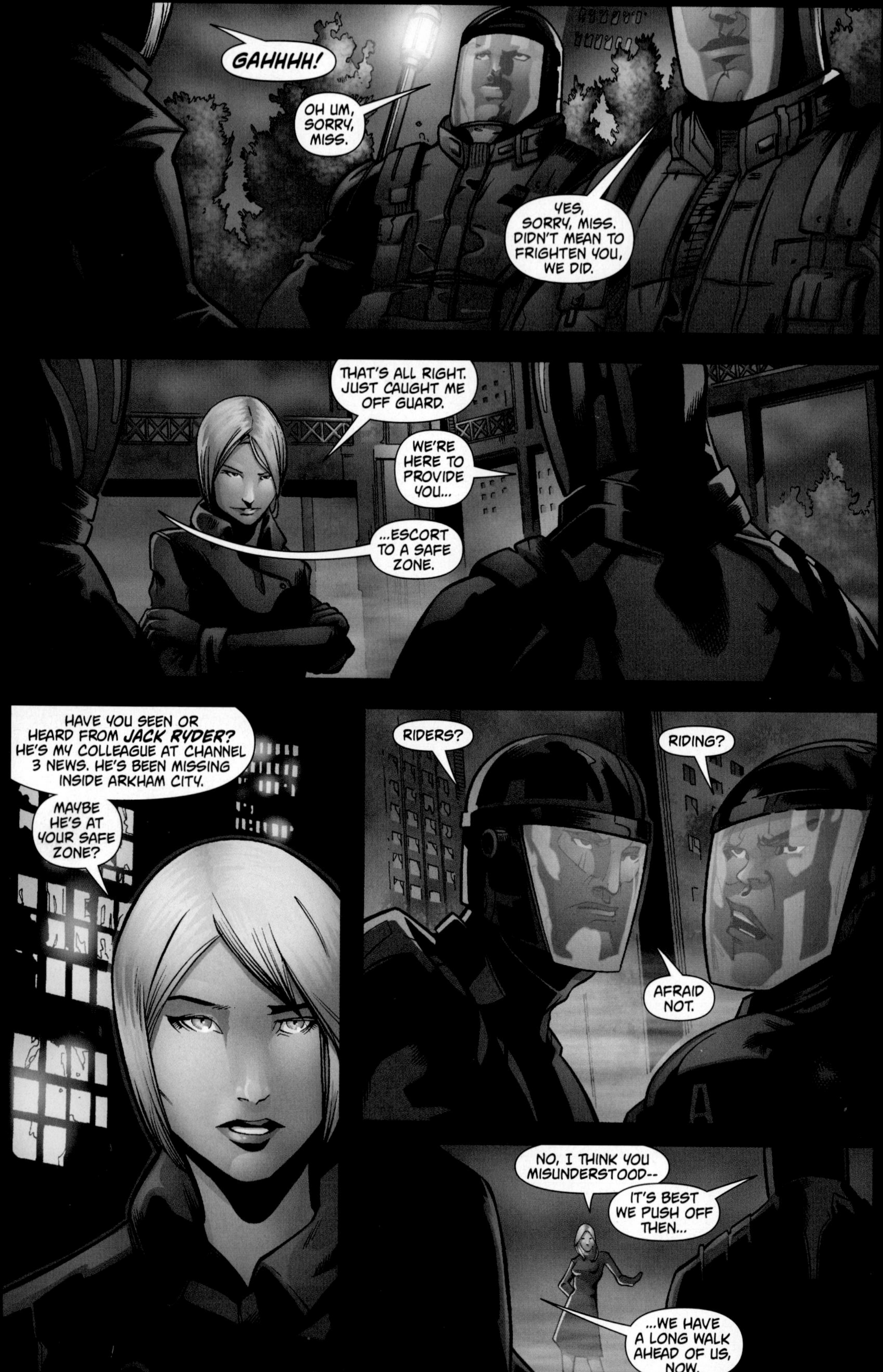
GAHHHH!
OH UM, SORRY, MISS.
YES, SORRY, MISS. DIDN'T MEAN TO FRIGHTEN YOU, WE DID.
THAT'S ALL RIGHT. JUST CAUGHT ME OFF GUARD.
WE'RE HERE TO PROVIDE YOU...
...ESCORT TO A SAFE ZONE.
HAVE YOU SEEN OR HEARD FROM JACK RYDER? HE'S MY COLLEAGUE AT CHANNEL 3 NEWS. HE'S BEEN MISSING INSIDE ARKHAM CITY.
MAYBE HE'S AT YOUR SAFE ZONE?
RIDERS?
RIDING?
AFRAID NOT.
NO, I THINK YOU MISUNDERSTOOD--
IT'S BEST WE PUSH OFF THEN...
...WE HAVE A LONG WALK AHEAD OF US, NOW.

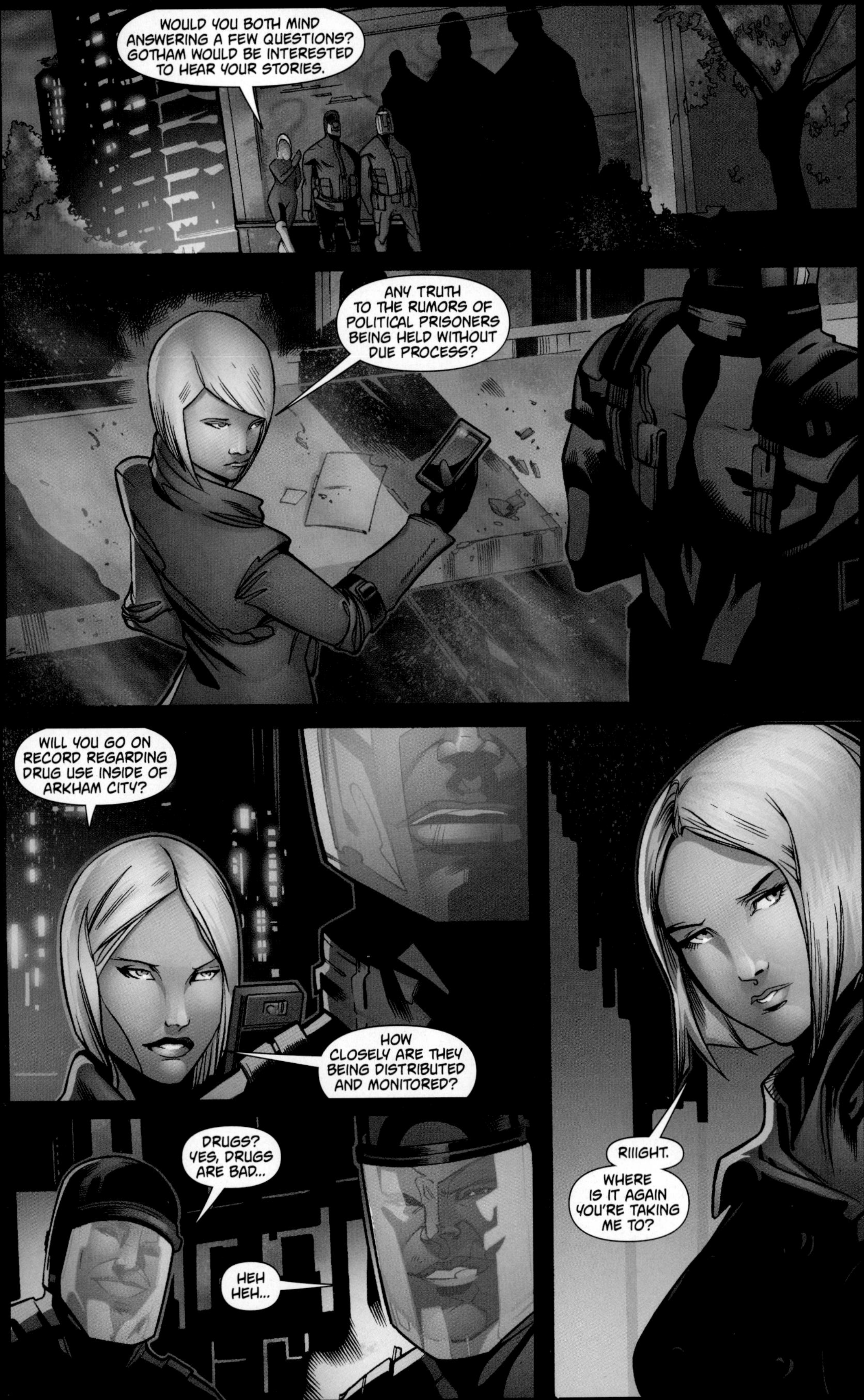
WOULD YOU BOTH MIND ANSWERING A FEW QUESTIONS? GOTHAM WOULD BE INTERESTED TO HEAR YOUR STORIES.
ANY TRUTH TO THE RUMORS OF POLITICAL PRISONERS BEING HELD WITHOUT DUE PROCESS?
WILL YOU GO ON RECORD REGARDING DRUG USE INSIDE OF ARKHAM CITY?
HOW CLOSELY ARE THEY BEING DISTRIBUTED AND MONITORED?
DRUGS? YES, DRUGS ARE BAD...
HEH HEH...
RIIIGHT.
WHERE IS IT AGAIN YOU'RE TAKING ME TO?

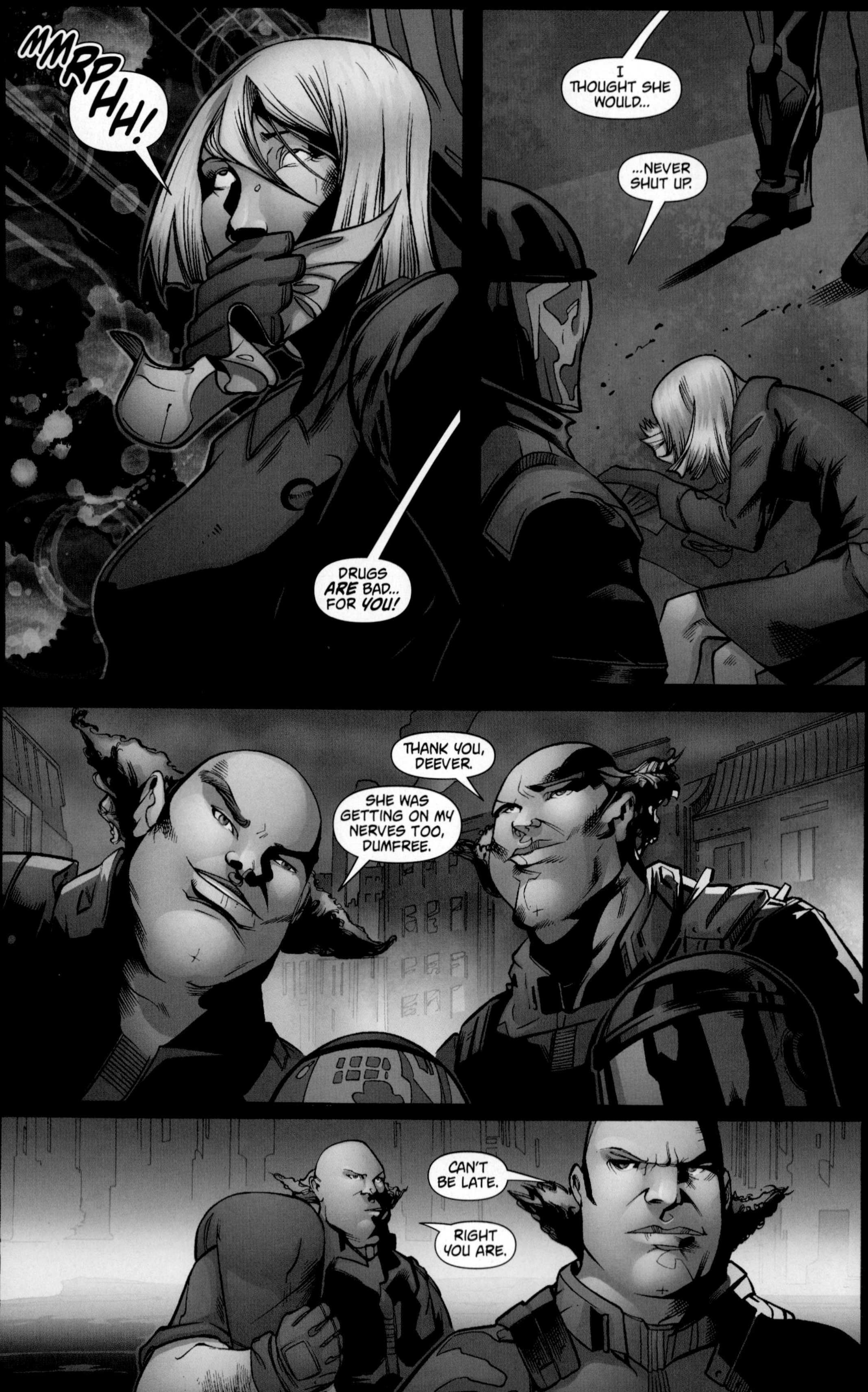
MMRPHH!
DRUGS ARE BAD... FOR YOU!
I THOUGHT SHE WOULD...
...NEVER SHUT UP.
THANK YOU, DEEVER.
SHE WAS GETTING ON MY NERVES TOO, DUMFREE.
CAN'T BE LATE.
RIGHT YOU ARE.

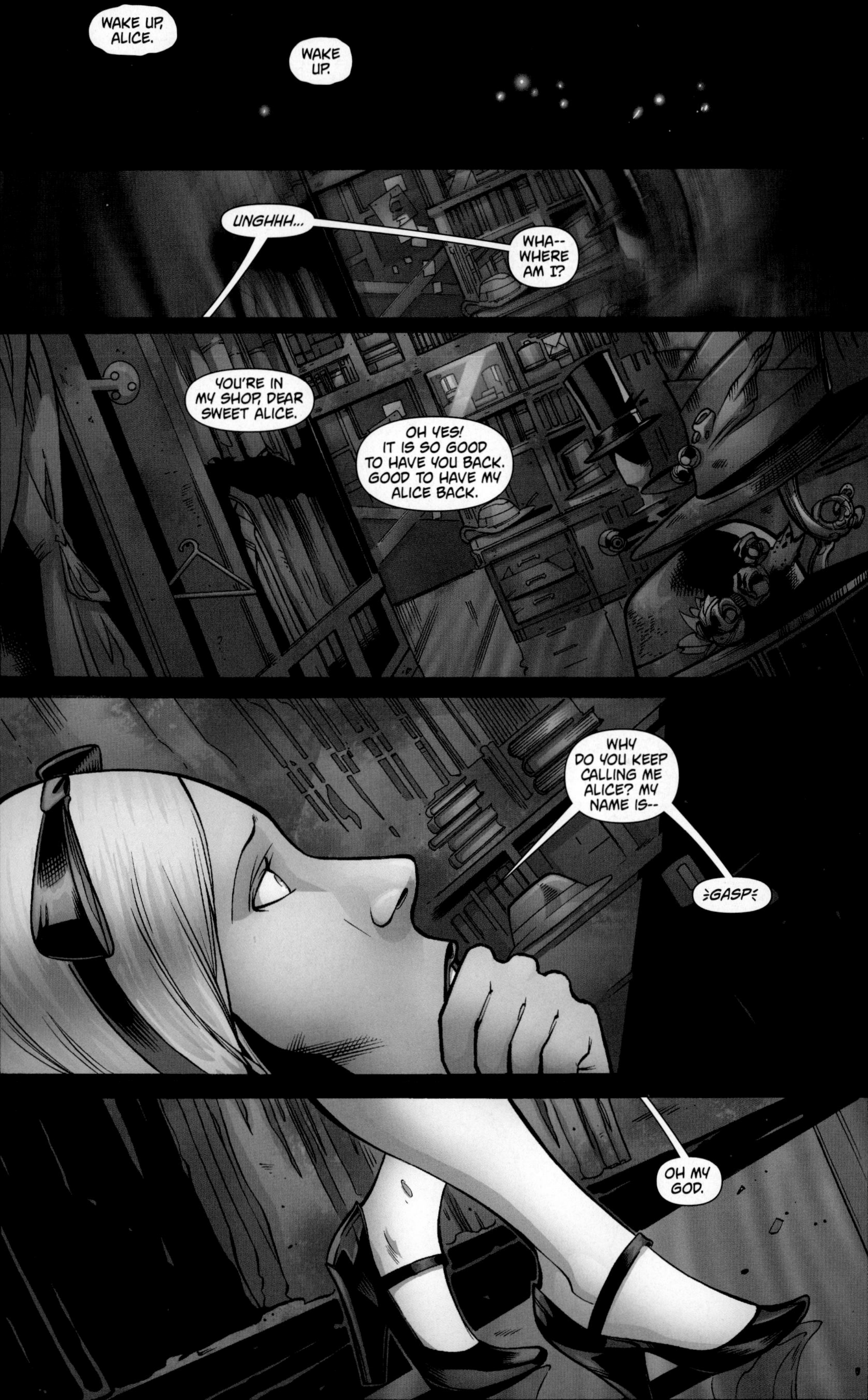
WAKE UP, ALICE.
WAKE UP.
UNGHHH...
WHA-- WHERE AM I?
YOU'RE IN MY SHOP, DEAR SWEET ALICE.
OH YES! IT IS SO GOOD TO HAVE YOU BACK. GOOD TO HAVE MY ALICE BACK.
WHY DO YOU KEEP CALLING ME ALICE? MY NAME IS--
GASP
OH MY GOD.

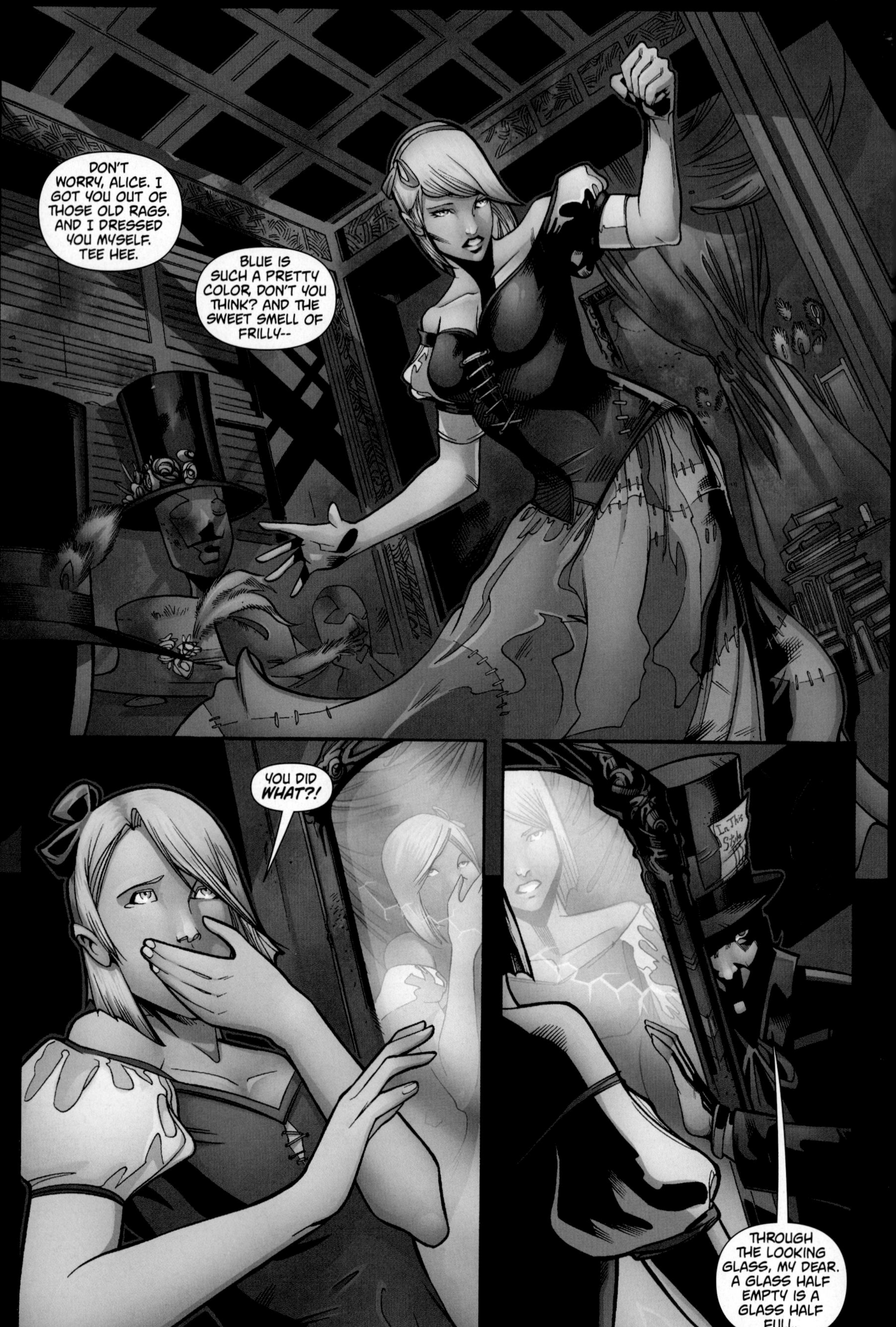
DON'T WORRY, ALICE. I GOT YOU OUT OF THOSE OLD RAGS. AND I DRESSED YOU MYSELF. TEE HEE.
BLUE IS SUCH A PRETTY COLOR, DON'T YOU THINK? AND THE SWEET SMELL OF FRILLY--
YOU DID WHAT?!
THROUGH THE LOOKING GLASS, MY DEAR. A GLASS HALF EMPTY IS A GLASS HALF FULL.

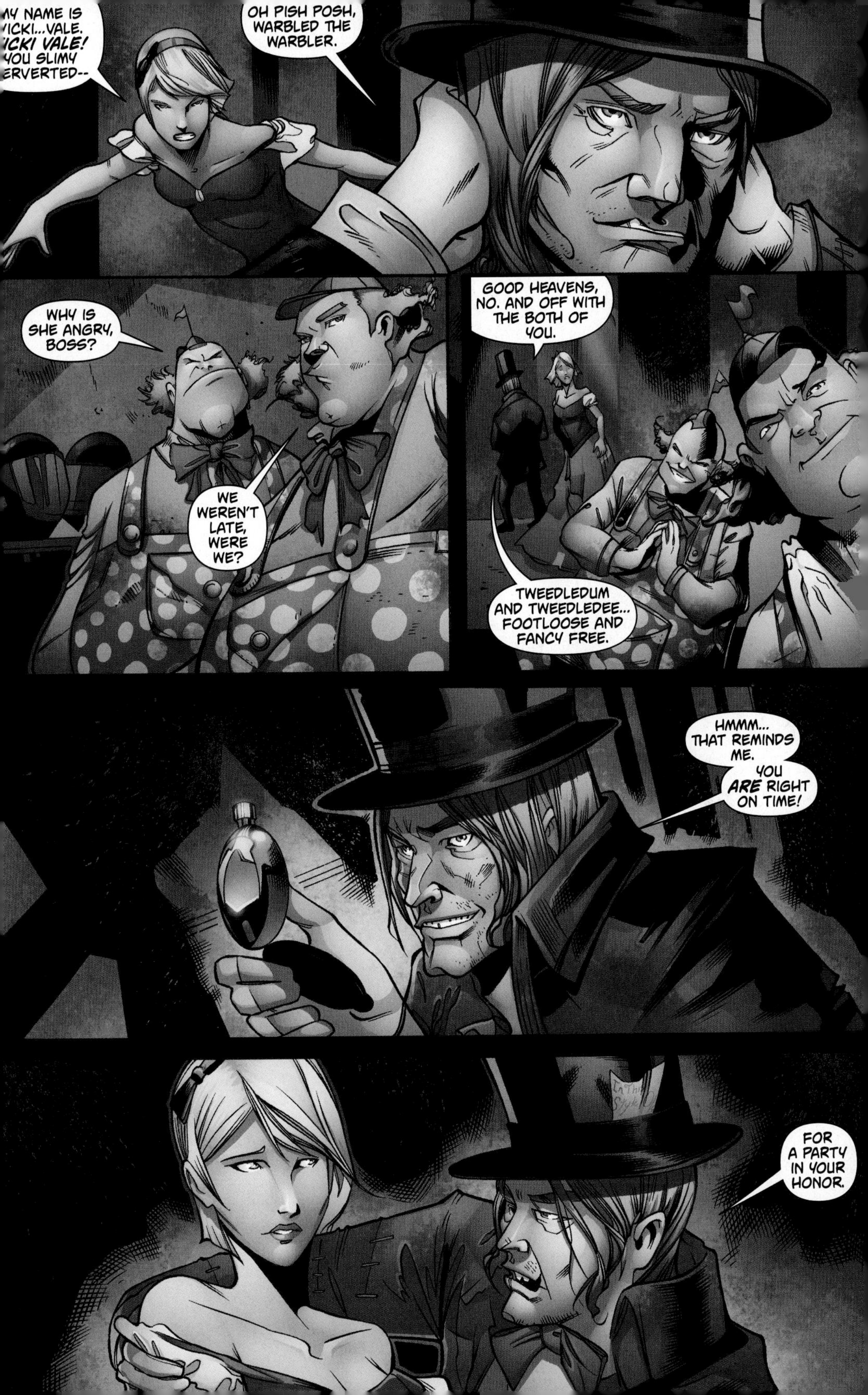
MY NAME IS VICKI...VALE. VICKI VALE! YOU SLIMY PERVERTED--
OH PISH POSH, WARBLED THE WARBLER.
WHY IS SHE ANGRY, BOSS?
WE WEREN'T LATE, WERE WE?
GOOD HEAVENS, NO. AND OFF WITH THE BOTH OF YOU.
TWEEDLEDUM AND TWEEDLEDEE... FOOTLOOSE AND FANCY FREE.
HMMM... THAT REMINDS ME.
YOU ARE RIGHT ON TIME!
FOR A PARTY IN YOUR HONOR.

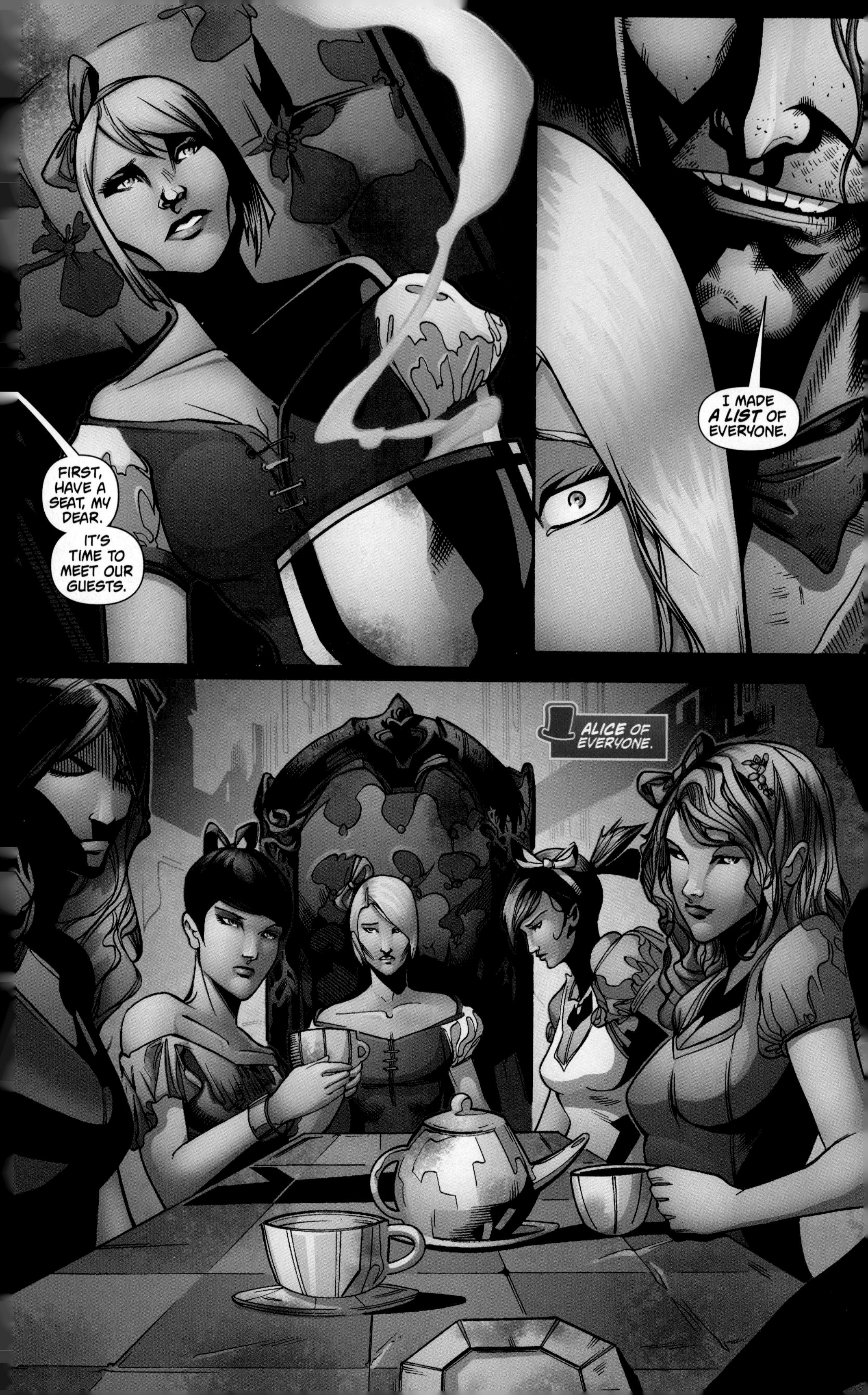
FIRST, HAVE A SEAT, MY DEAR.
IT'S TIME TO MEET OUR GUESTS.
I MADE A LIST OF EVERYONE.
ALICE OF EVERYONE.

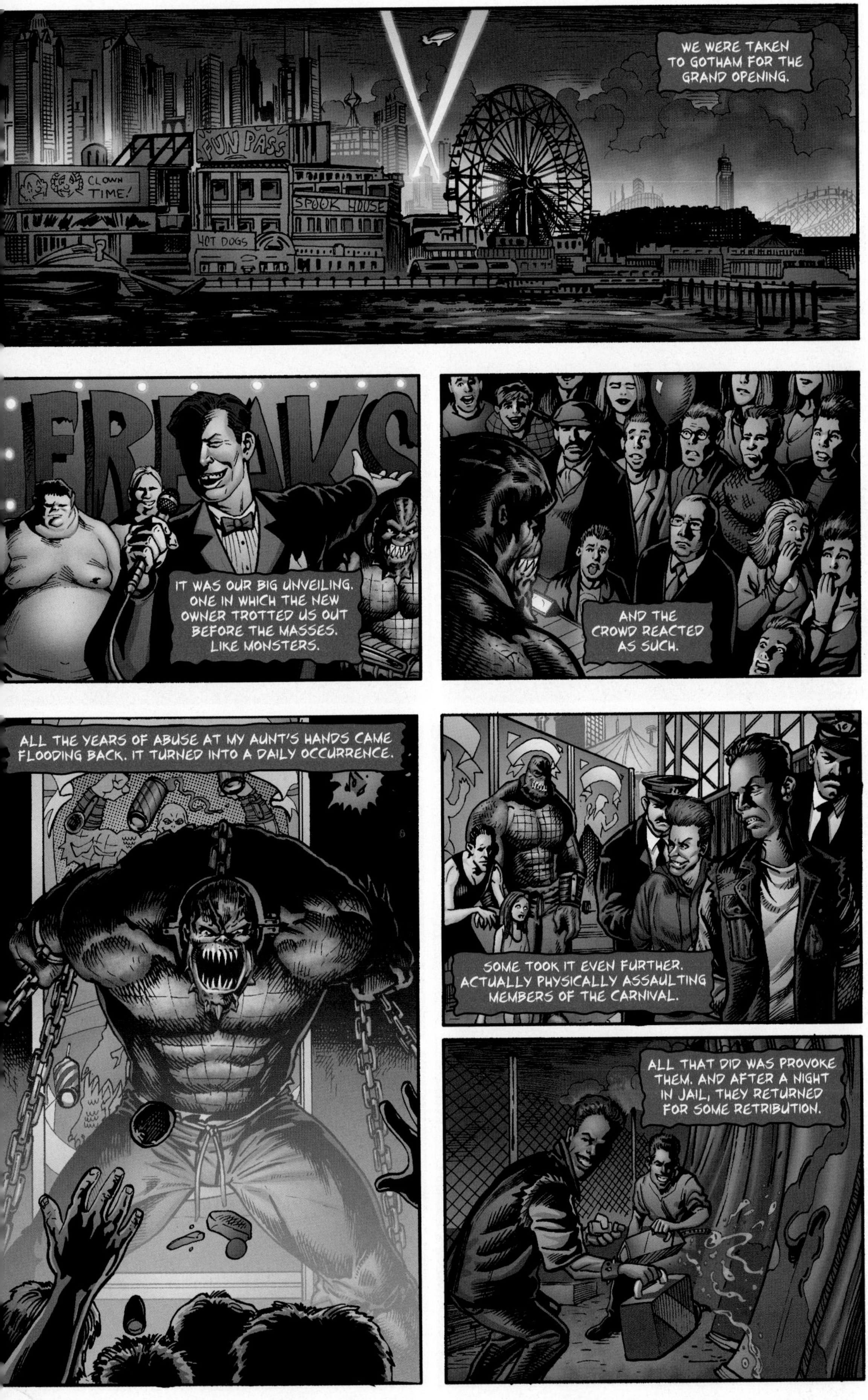
WE WERE TAKEN TO GOTHAM FOR THE GRAND OPENING.
CLOWN TIME!
FUN PASS
SPOOK HOUSE
HOT DOGS
FREAKS
IT WAS OUR BIG UNVEILING. ONE IN WHICH THE NEW OWNER TROTTED US OUT BEFORE THE MASSES. LIKE MONSTERS.
AND THE CROWD REACTED AS SUCH.
ALL THE YEARS OF ABUSE AT MY AUNT'S HANDS CAME FLOODING BACK. IT TURNED INTO A DAILY OCCURRENCE.
SOME TOOK IT EVEN FURTHER. ACTUALLY PHYSICALLY ASSAULTING MEMBERS OF THE CARNIVAL.
ALL THAT DID WAS PROVOKE THEM. AND AFTER A NIGHT IN JAIL, THEY RETURNED FOR SOME RETRIBUTION.

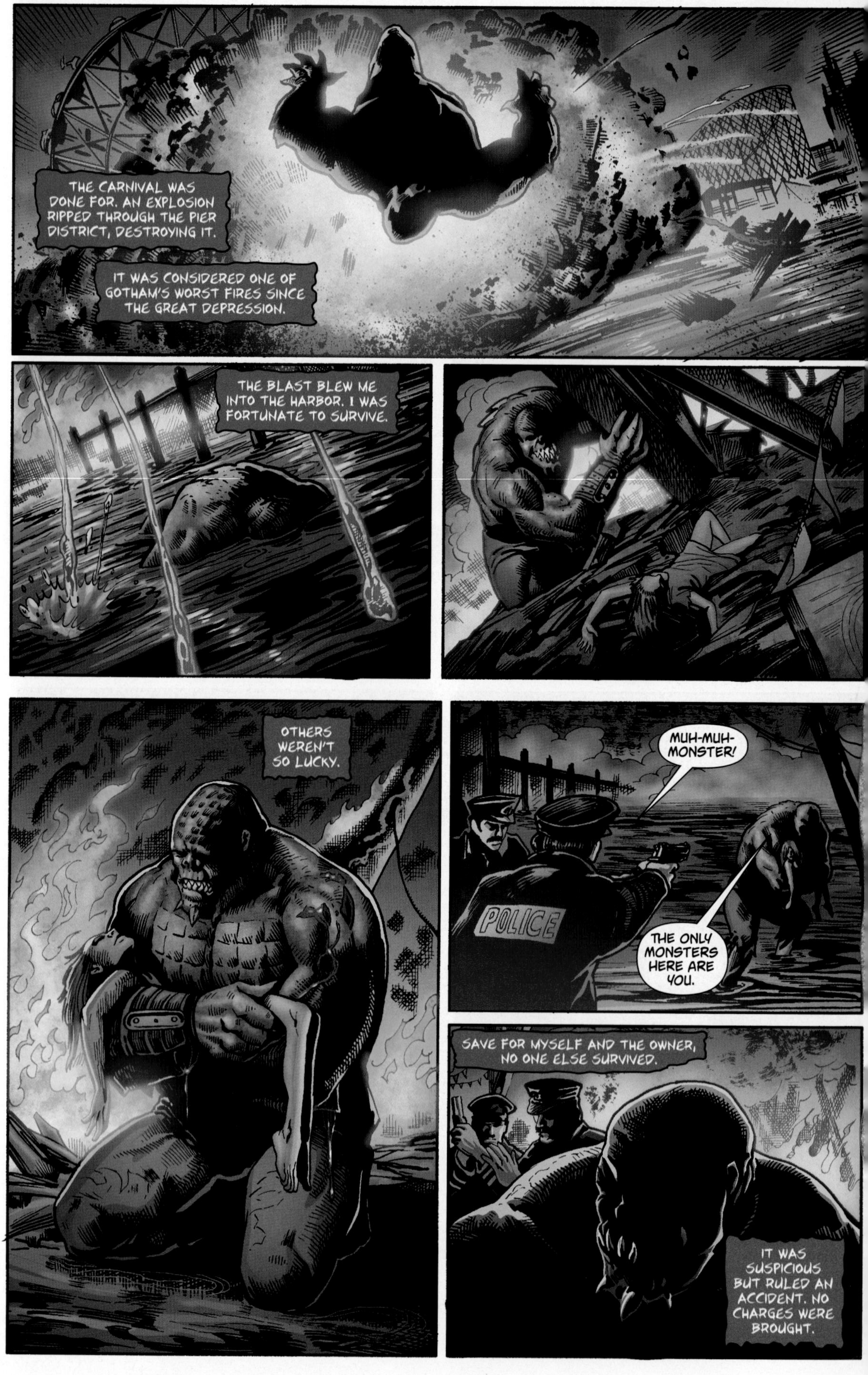
THE CARNIVAL WAS DONE FOR. AN EXPLOSION RIPPED THROUGH THE PIER DISTRICT, DESTROYING IT.
IT WAS CONSIDERED ONE OF GOTHAM'S WORST FIRES SINCE THE GREAT DEPRESSION.
THE BLAST BLEW ME INTO THE HARBOR. I WAS FORTUNATE TO SURVIVE.
OTHERS WEREN'T SO LUCKY.
MUH-MUH-MONSTER!
THE ONLY MONSTERS HERE ARE YOU.
POLICE
SAVE FOR MYSELF AND THE OWNER, NO ONE ELSE SURVIVED.
IT WAS SUSPICIOUS BUT RULED AN ACCIDENT. NO CHARGES WERE BROUGHT.

I WAS NOW STUCK IN GOTHAM, WITHOUT A HOME, FAMILY, OR A JOB.

WITH NOTHING LEFT TO LOSE, I FELL BACK INTO OLD HABITS.

AND I NEVER FORGET A SCENT.

I FOUND A NEW JOB. I BECAME A HEAVY IN THE MOB. AN ENFORCER FOR HIRE.

BUT USUALLY I WORKED ALONE AND DREW A LOT OF ATTENTION IN BOTH GOTHAM AND BLUDHAVEN.

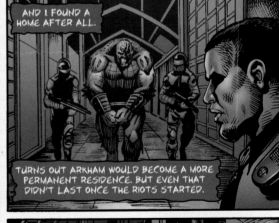

AND I FOUND A HOME AFTER ALL.

TURNS OUT ARKHAM WOULD BECOME A MORE PERMANENT RESIDENCE. BUT EVEN THAT DIDN'T LAST ONCE THE RIOTS STARTED.

DURING ALL THE CONFUSION, I WAS ABLE TO ESCAPE BACK TO THE CITY. ONLY TO FIND AN ALL-NEW CAGE BUILT AROUND ME.

ARKHAM CITY
REHABILITATION FACILITY

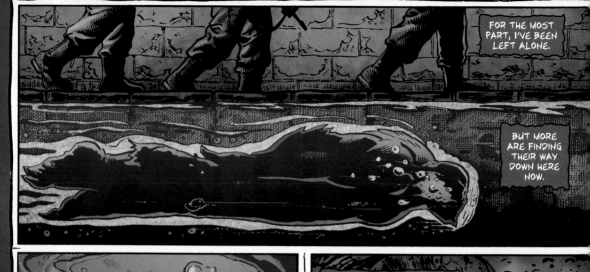

FOR THE MOST PART, I'VE BEEN LEFT ALONE.

BUT MORE ARE FINDING THEIR WAY DOWN HERE NOW.

FOOD HAS ALWAYS BEEN A CONCERN. I'VE SURVIVED OFF THE RATS AND RUMMAGING THROUGH TRASH.

BUT IT'S EVEN BETTER WHEN IT'S DELIVERED RIGHT TO YOUR DOORSTEP.

AND I'VE BUILT UP A MONSTER APPETITE!

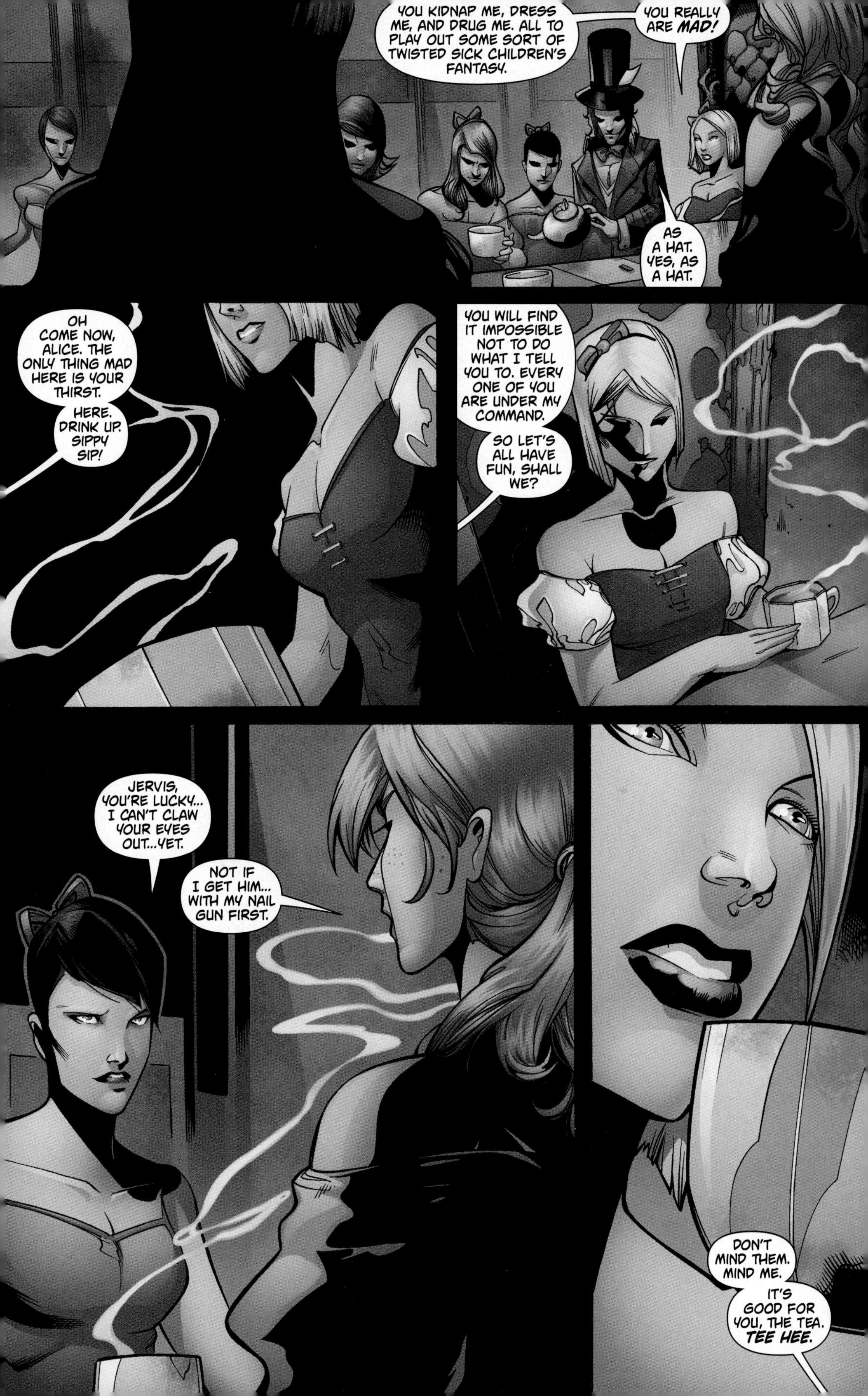
YOU KIDNAP ME, DRESS ME, AND DRUG ME. ALL TO PLAY OUT SOME SORT OF TWISTED SICK CHILDREN'S FANTASY.
YOU REALLY ARE MAD!
AS A HAT. YES, AS A HAT.
OH COME NOW, ALICE. THE ONLY THING MAD HERE IS YOUR THIRST.
HERE. DRINK UP. SIPPY SIP!
YOU WILL FIND IT IMPOSSIBLE NOT TO DO WHAT I TELL YOU TO. EVERY ONE OF YOU ARE UNDER MY COMMAND.
SO LET'S ALL HAVE FUN, SHALL WE?
JERVIS, YOU'RE LUCKY... I CAN'T CLAW YOUR EYES OUT...YET.
NOT IF I GET HIM... WITH MY NAIL GUN FIRST.
DON'T MIND THEM. MIND ME.
IT'S GOOD FOR YOU, THE TEA. TEE HEE.

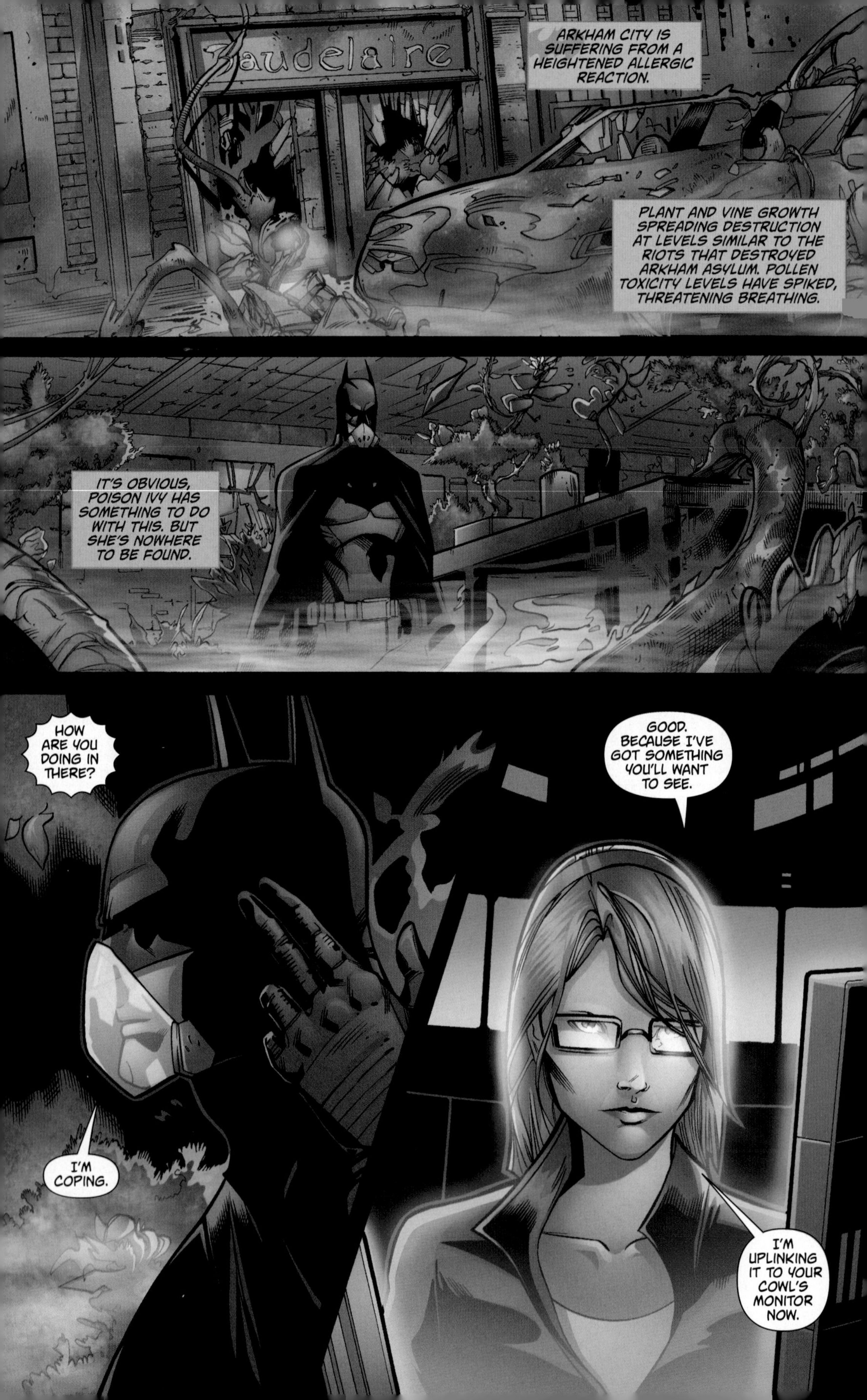
Baudelaire
ARKHAM CITY IS SUFFERING FROM A HEIGHTENED ALLERGIC REACTION.
PLANT AND VINE GROWTH SPREADING DESTRUCTION AT LEVELS SIMILAR TO THE RIOTS THAT DESTROYED ARKHAM ASYLUM. POLLEN TOXICITY LEVELS HAVE SPIKED, THREATENING BREATHING.
IT'S OBVIOUS, POISON IVY HAS SOMETHING TO DO WITH THIS. BUT SHE'S NOWHERE TO BE FOUND.
HOW ARE YOU DOING IN THERE?
I'M COPING.
GOOD. BECAUSE I'VE GOT SOMETHING YOU'LL WANT TO SEE.
I'M UPLINKING IT TO YOUR COWL'S MONITOR NOW.

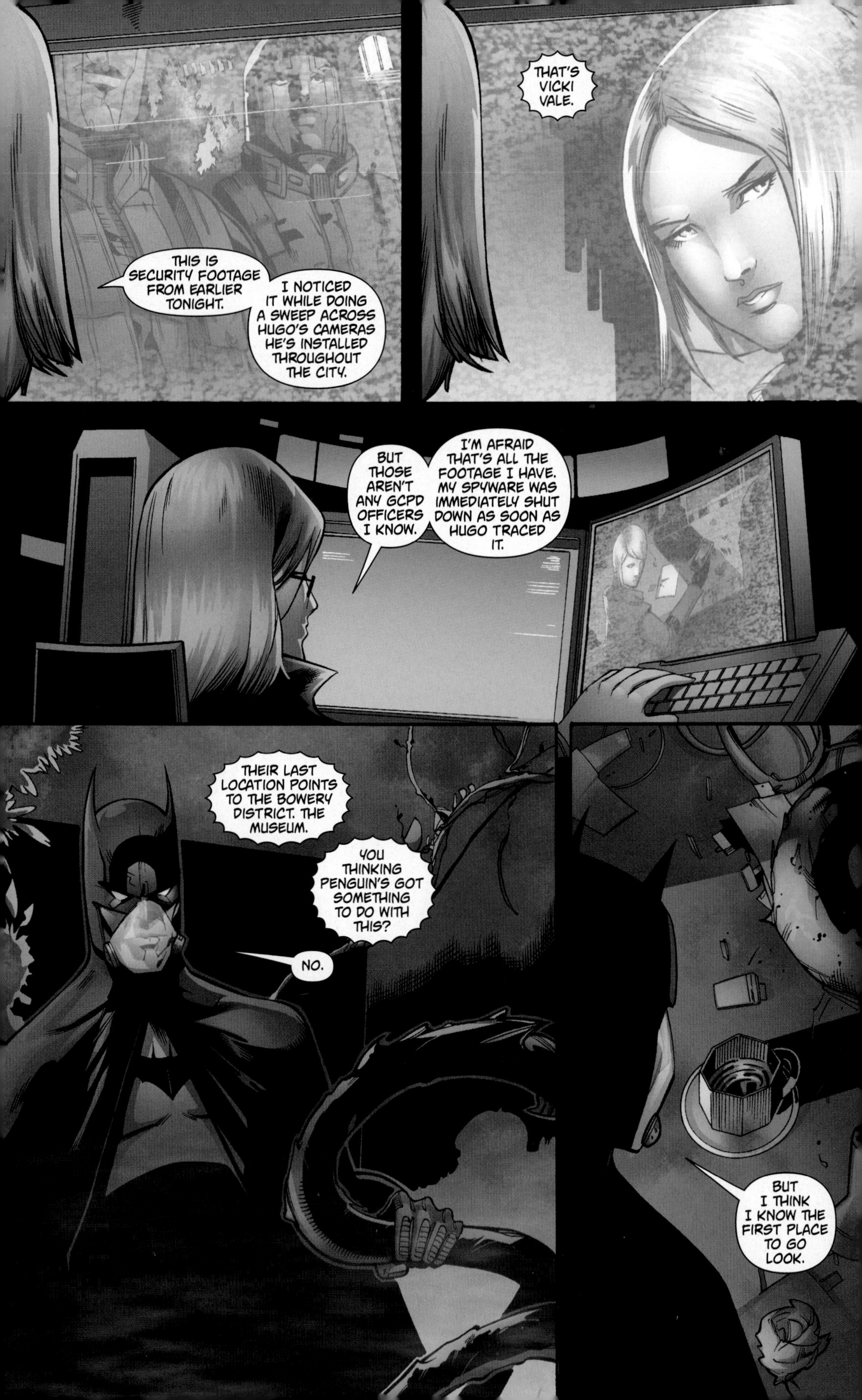
THIS IS SECURITY FOOTAGE FROM EARLIER TONIGHT.
I NOTICED IT WHILE DOING A SWEEP ACROSS HUGO'S CAMERAS HE'S INSTALLED THROUGHOUT THE CITY.
THAT'S VICKI VALE.
BUT THOSE AREN'T ANY GCPD OFFICERS I KNOW.
I'M AFRAID THAT'S ALL THE FOOTAGE I HAVE. MY SPYWARE WAS IMMEDIATELY SHUT DOWN AS SOON AS HUGO TRACED IT.
THEIR LAST LOCATION POINTS TO THE BOWERY DISTRICT. THE MUSEUM.
YOU THINKING PENGUIN'S GOT SOMETHING TO DO WITH THIS?
NO.
BUT I THINK I KNOW THE FIRST PLACE TO GO LOOK.

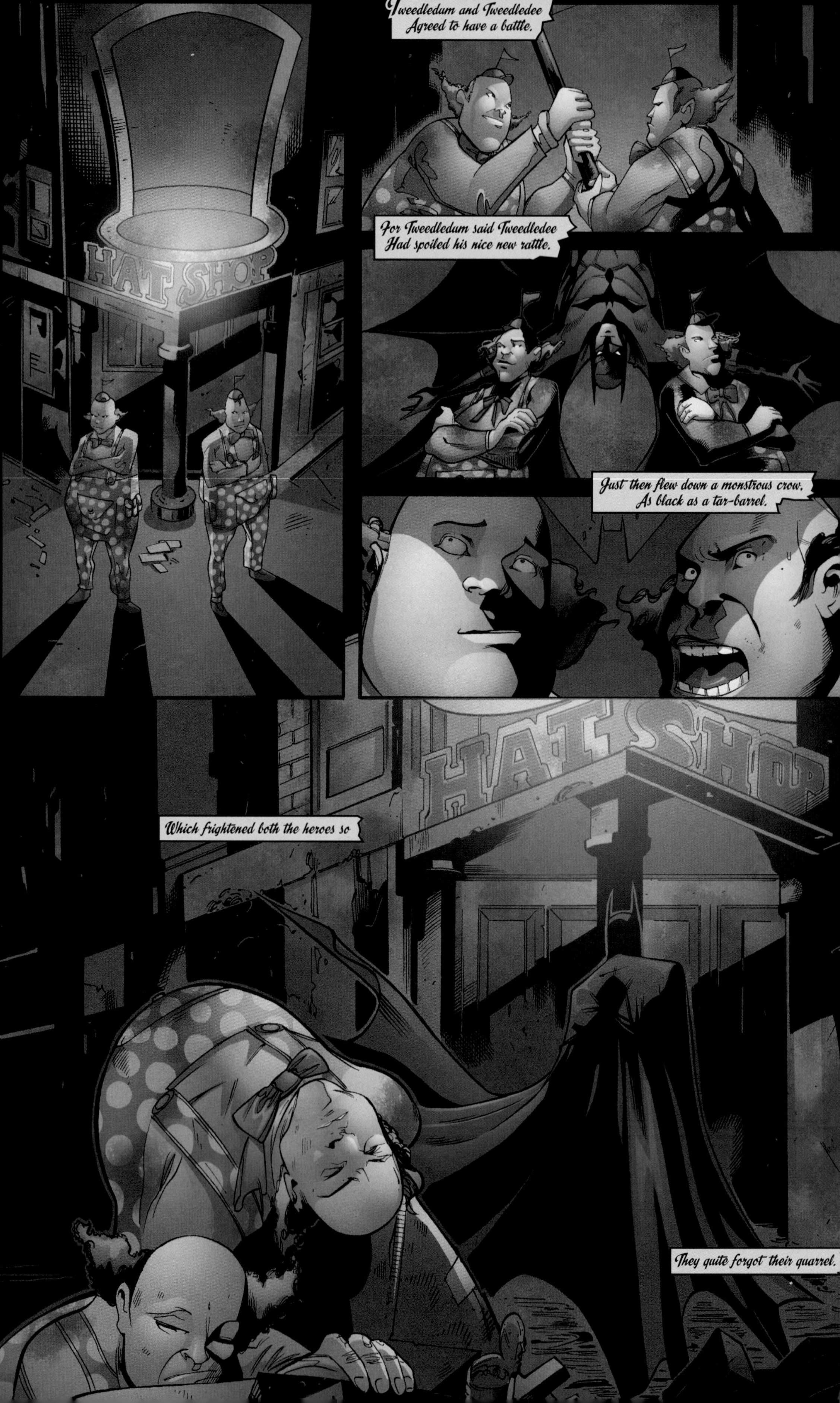
HAT SHOP
Tweedledum and Tweedledee
Agreed to have a battle.
For Tweedledum said Tweedledee
Had spoiled his nice new rattle.
Just then flew down a monstrous crow,
As black as a tar-barrel.
HAT SHOP
Which frightened both the heroes so
They quite forgot their quarrel.

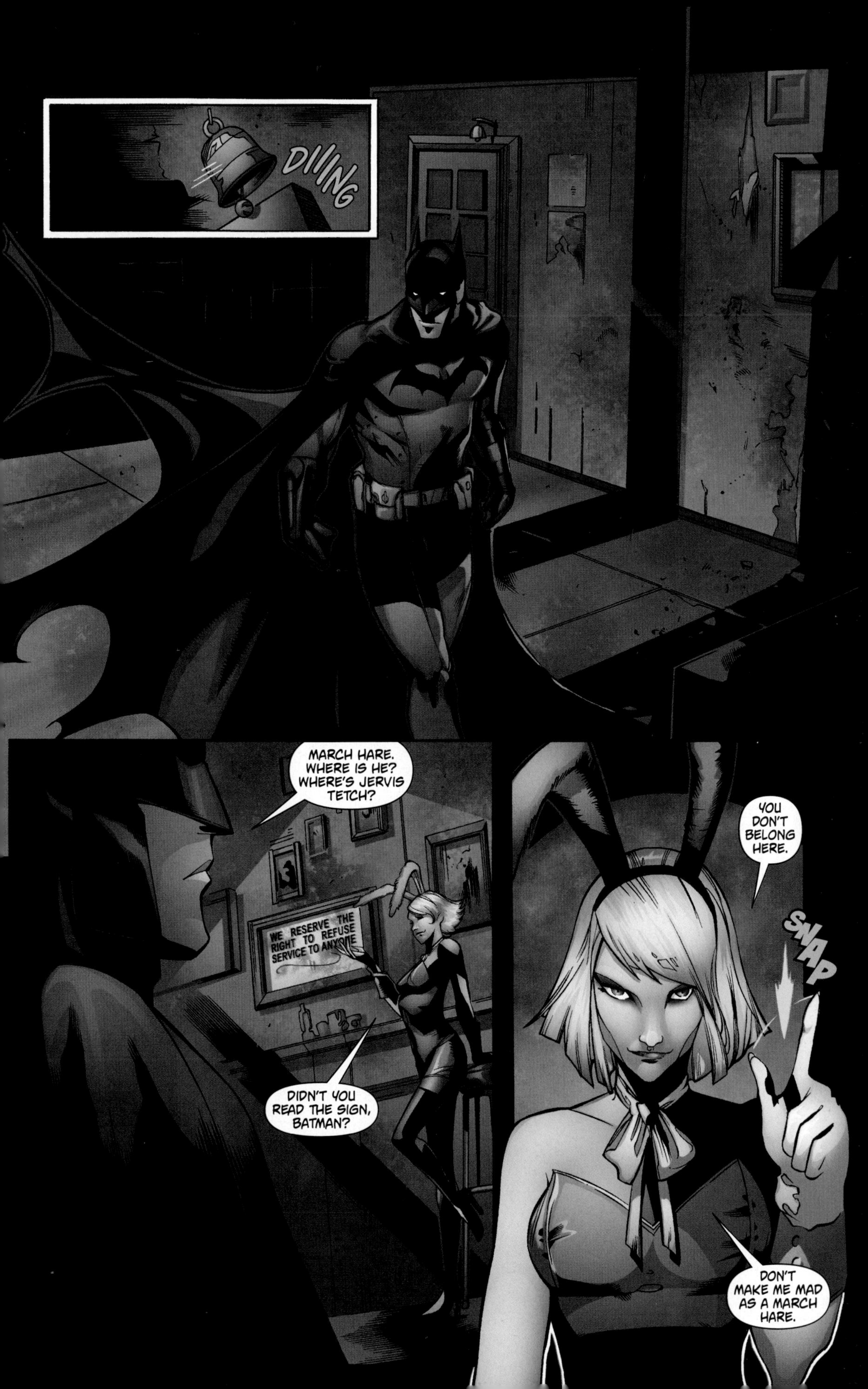
DIIING
MARCH HARE. WHERE IS HE? WHERE'S JERVIS TETCH?
WE RESERVE THE RIGHT TO REFUSE SERVICE TO ANYONE
DIDN'T YOU READ THE SIGN, BATMAN?
YOU DON'T BELONG HERE.
SNAP
DON'T MAKE ME MAD AS A MARCH HARE.

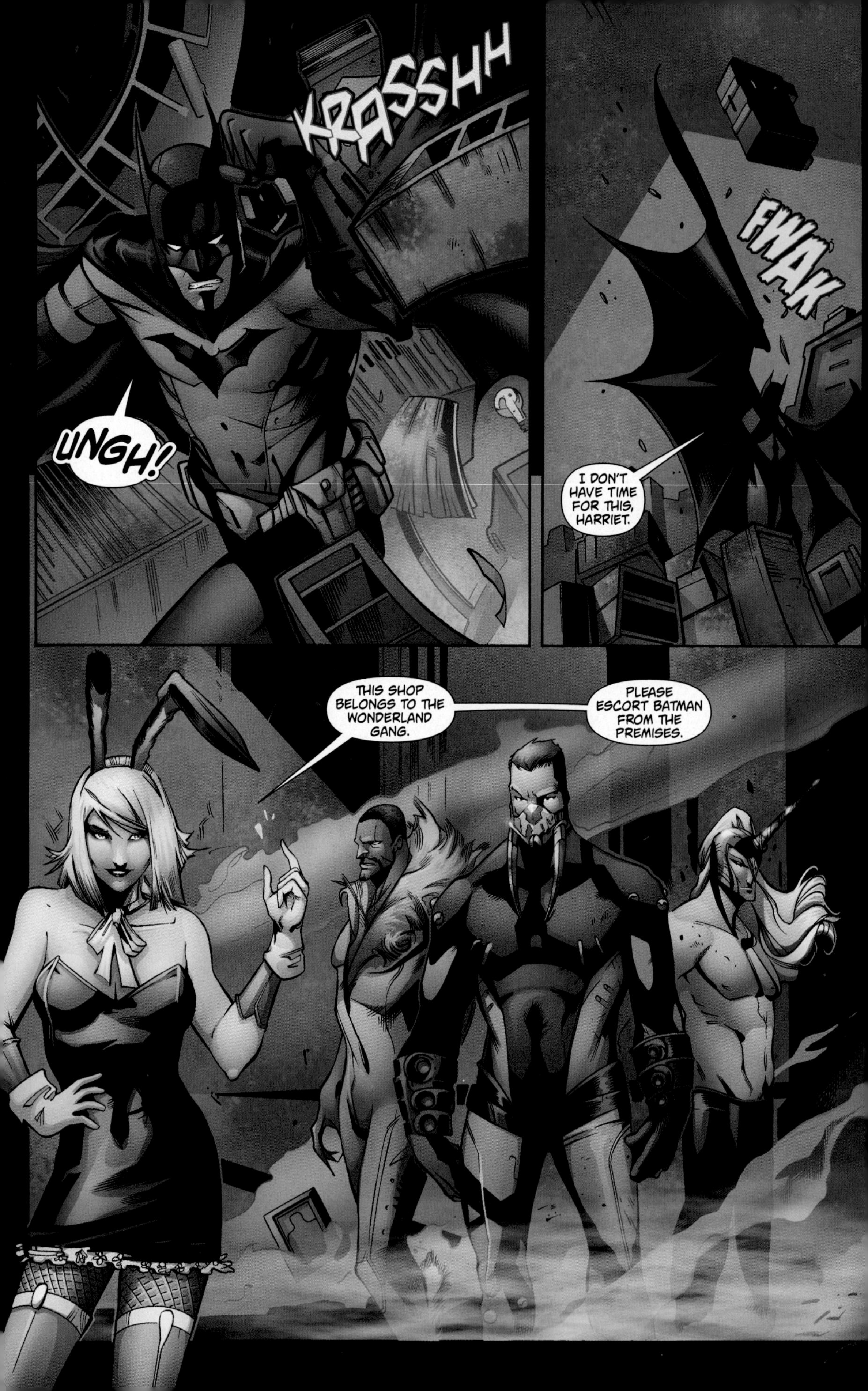
KRASSHH
UNGH!
FWAK
I DON'T HAVE TIME FOR THIS, HARRIET.
THIS SHOP BELONGS TO THE WONDERLAND GANG.
PLEASE ESCORT BATMAN FROM THE PREMISES.

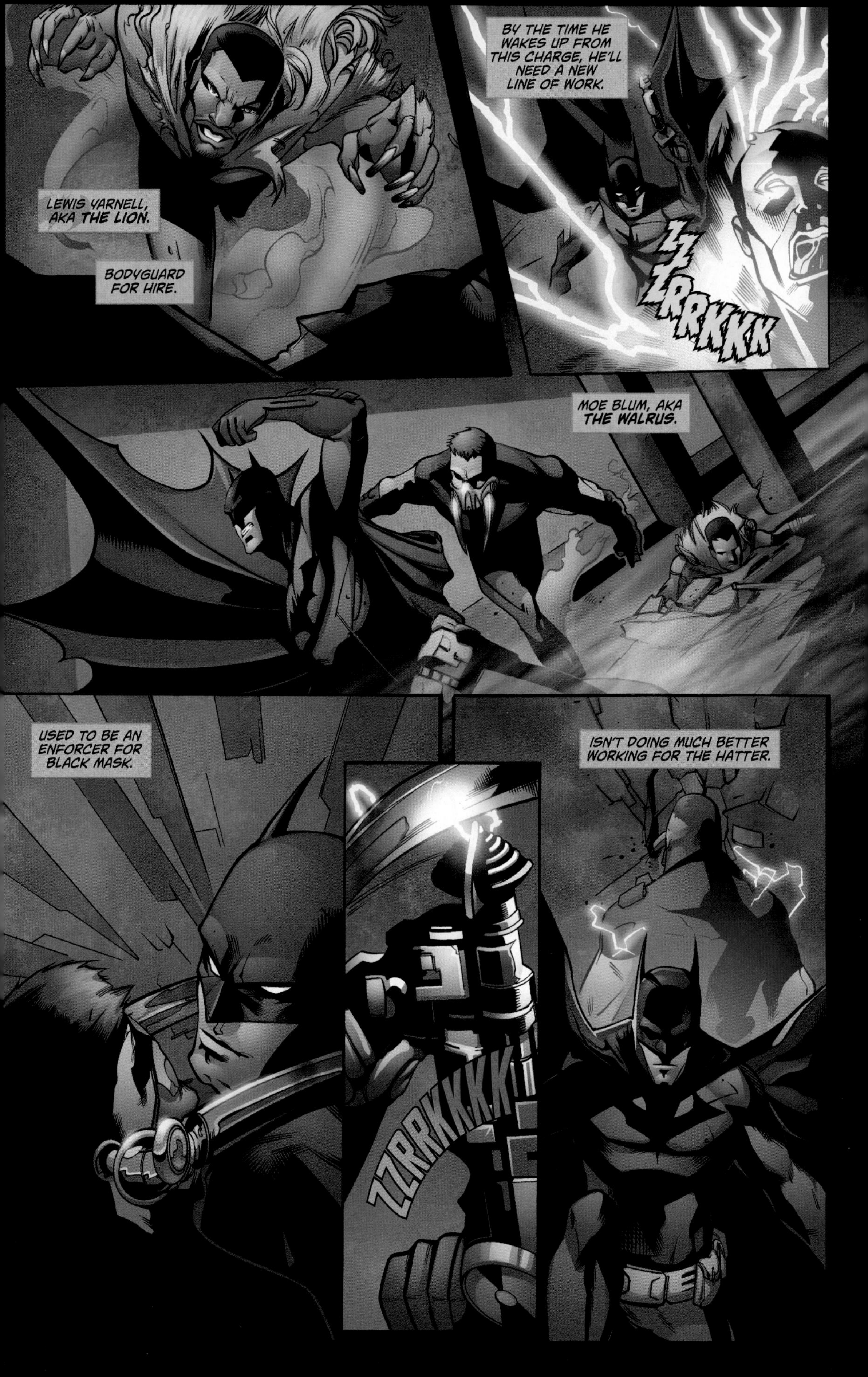
LEWIS YARNELL, AKA THE LION.
BODYGUARD FOR HIRE.
BY THE TIME HE WAKES UP FROM THIS CHARGE, HE'LL NEED A NEW LINE OF WORK.
ZZZRRKKKK
MOE BLUM, AKA THE WALRUS.
USED TO BE AN ENFORCER FOR BLACK MASK.
ZZRRKKKKK
ISN'T DOING MUCH BETTER WORKING FOR THE HATTER.

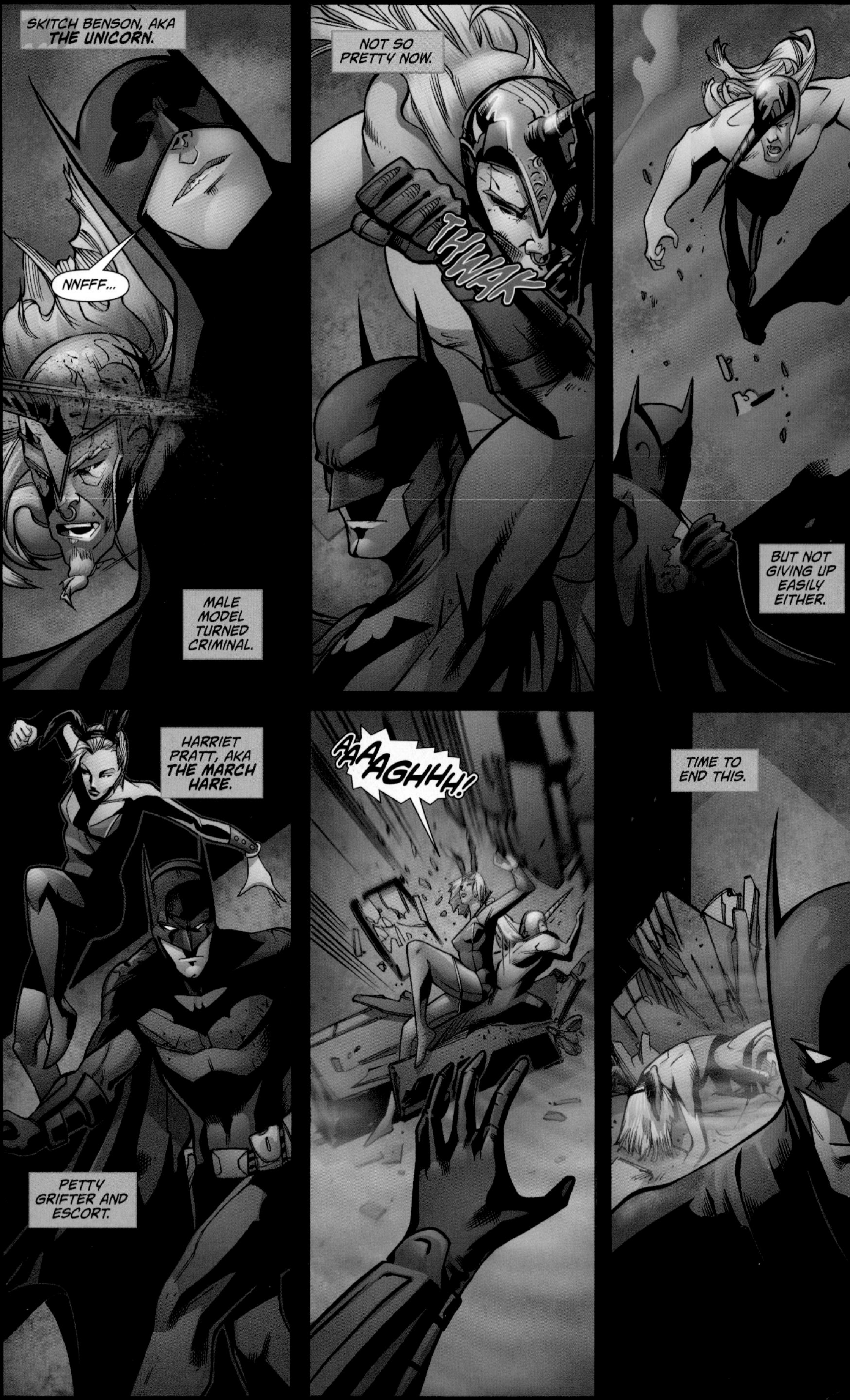
SKITCH BENSON, AKA THE UNICORN.
NNFFF...
MALE MODEL TURNED CRIMINAL.
NOT SO PRETTY NOW.
THWAK
BUT NOT GIVING UP EASILY EITHER.
HARRIET PRATT, AKA THE MARCH HARE.
PETTY GRIFTER AND ESCORT.
AAAAGHHH!
TIME TO END THIS.

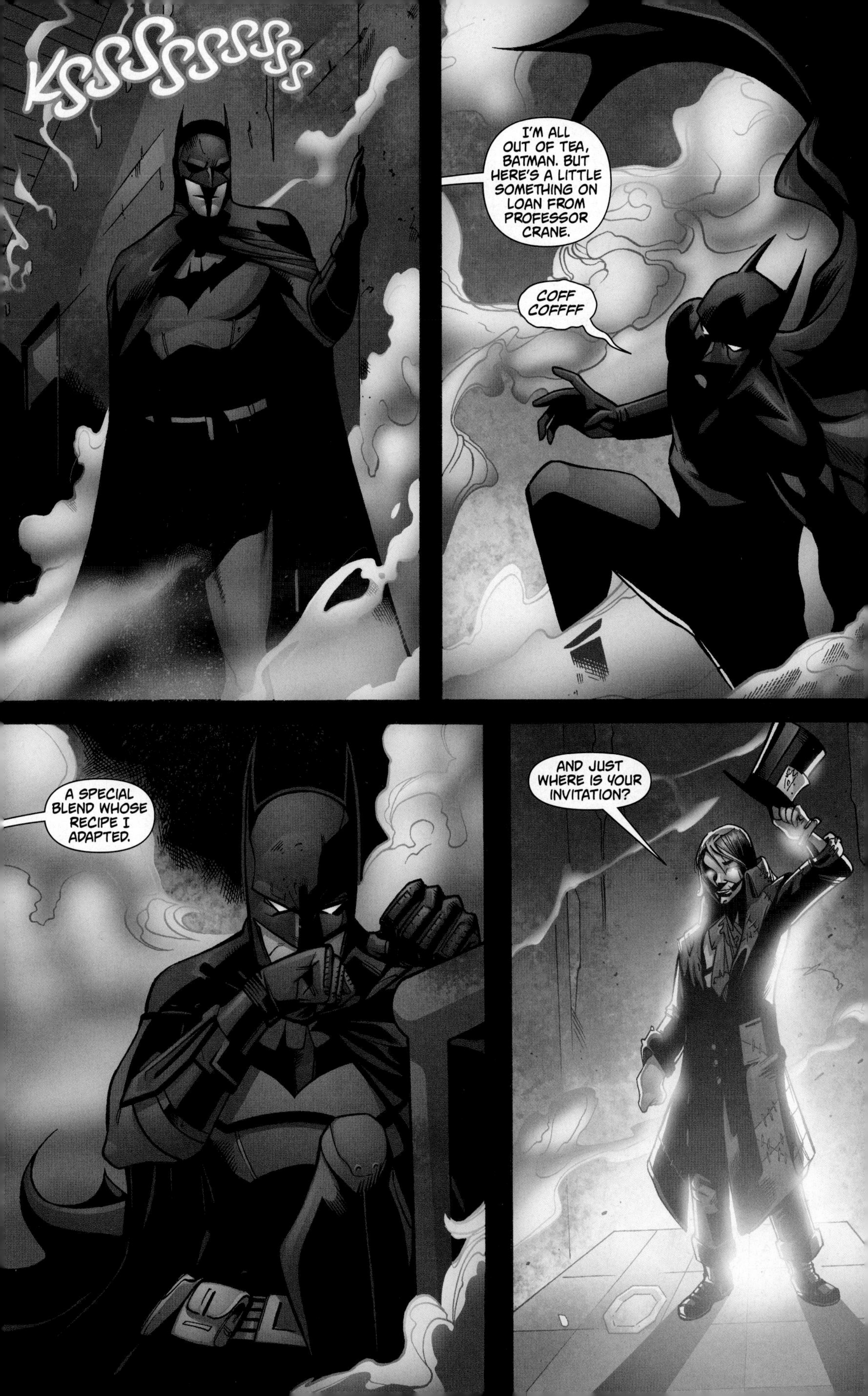
KSSSSSSSSS
I'M ALL OUT OF TEA, BATMAN. BUT HERE'S A LITTLE SOMETHING ON LOAN FROM PROFESSOR CRANE.
COFF COFFFF
A SPECIAL BLEND WHOSE RECIPE I ADAPTED.
AND JUST WHERE IS YOUR INVITATION?

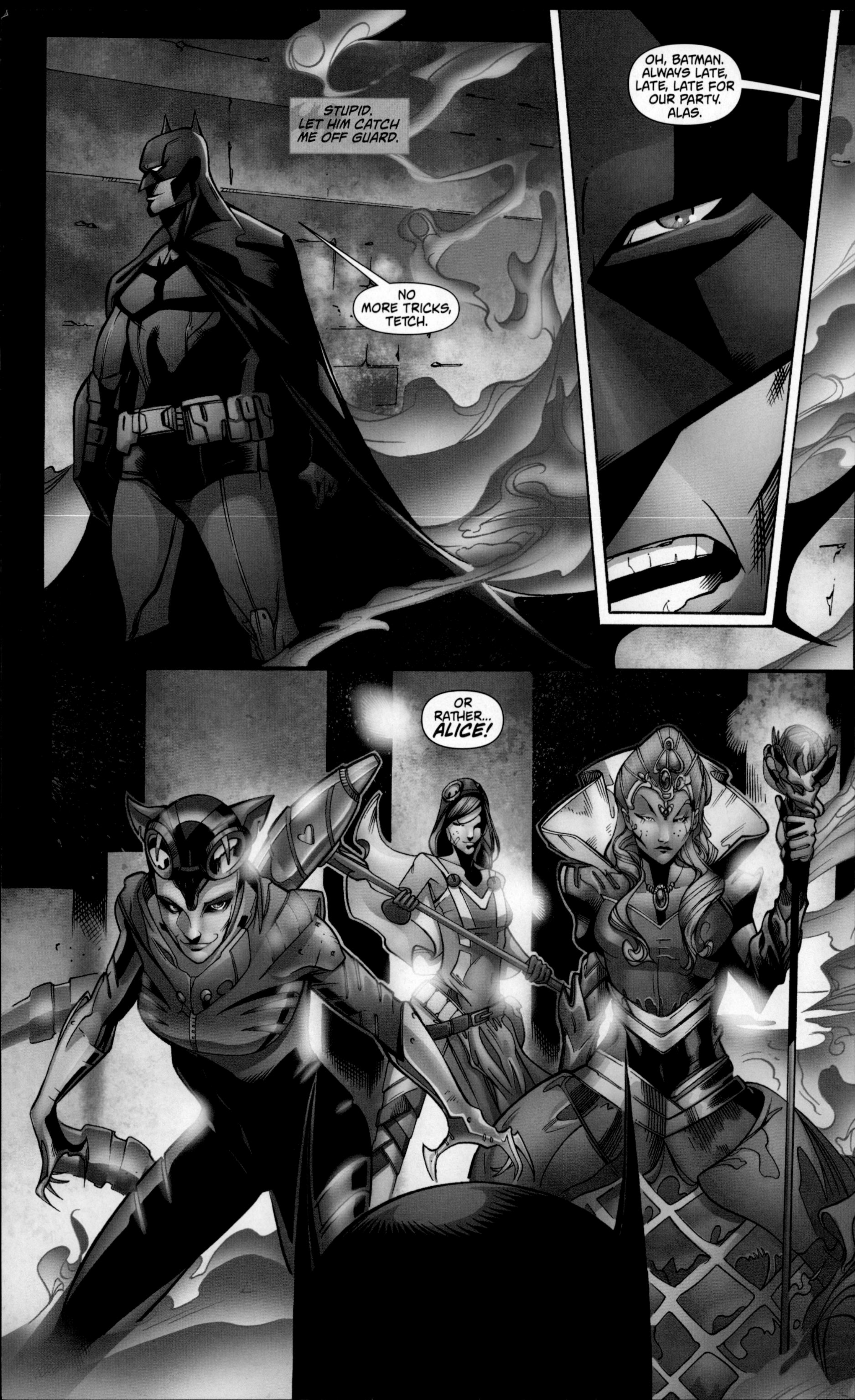
STUPID. LET HIM CATCH ME OFF GUARD.
NO MORE TRICKS, TETCH.
OH, BATMAN. ALWAYS LATE, LATE, LATE FOR OUR PARTY. ALAS.
OR RATHER... ALICE!

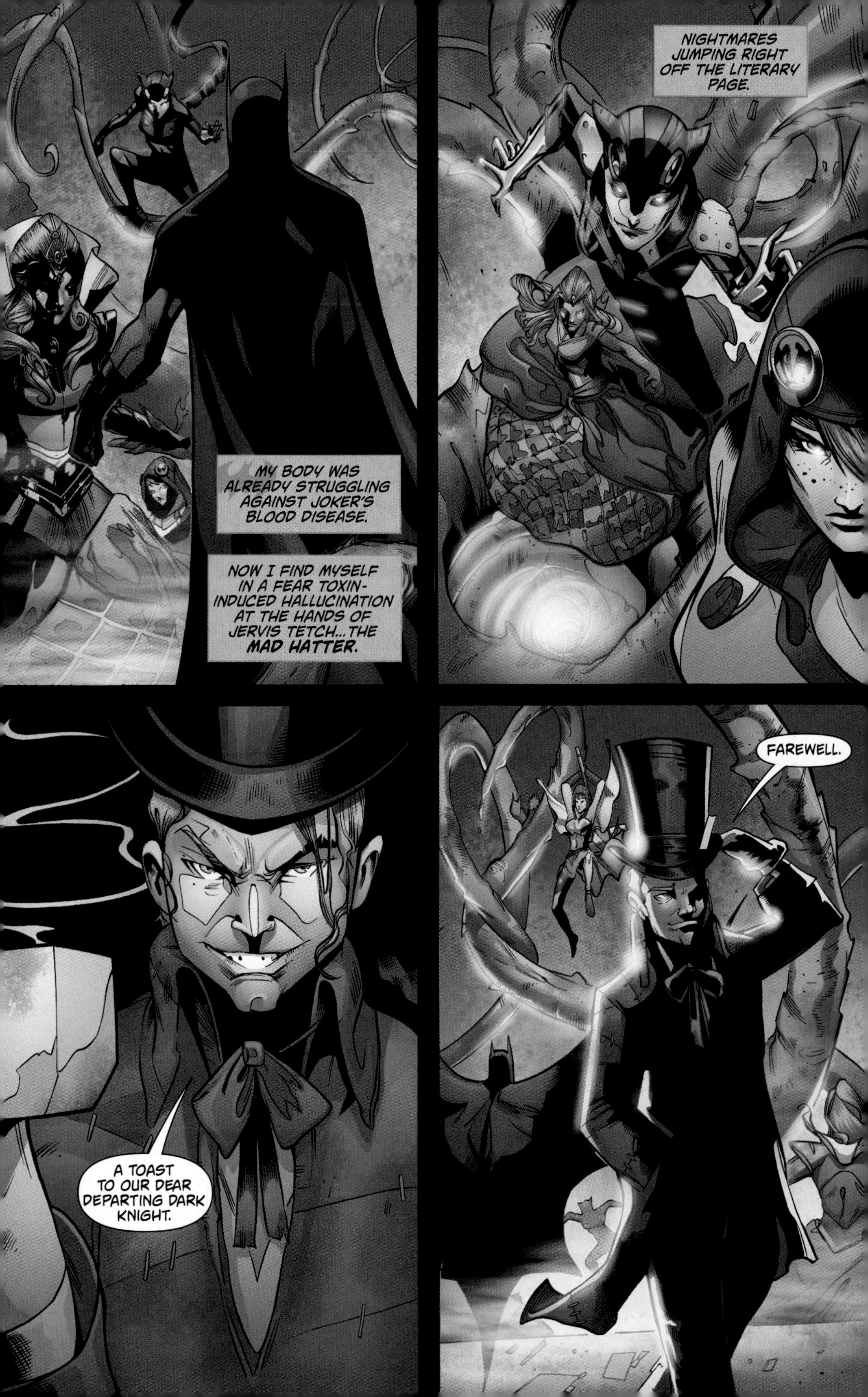
MY BODY WAS ALREADY STRUGGLING AGAINST JOKER'S BLOOD DISEASE.
NOW I FIND MYSELF IN A FEAR TOXIN-INDUCED HALLUCINATION AT THE HANDS OF JERVIS TETCH...THE MAD HATTER.
NIGHTMARES JUMPING RIGHT OFF THE LITERARY PAGE.
A TOAST TO OUR DEAR DEPARTING DARK KNIGHT.
FAREWELL.

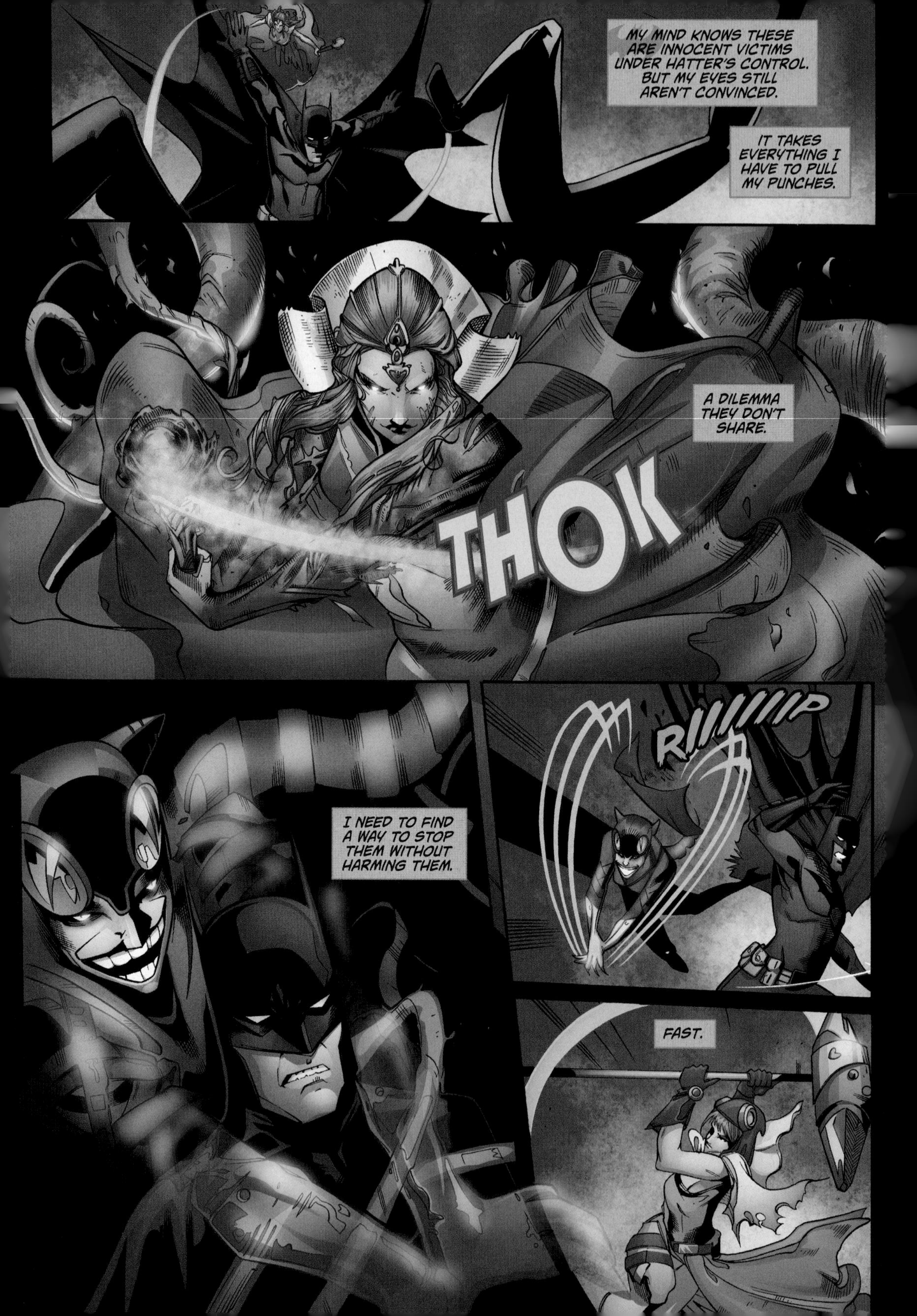
MY MIND KNOWS THESE ARE INNOCENT VICTIMS UNDER HATTER'S CONTROL. BUT MY EYES STILL AREN'T CONVINCED.
IT TAKES EVERYTHING I HAVE TO PULL MY PUNCHES.
A DILEMMA THEY DON'T SHARE.
THOK
I NEED TO FIND A WAY TO STOP THEM WITHOUT HARMING THEM.
RIIIIIIP
FAST.

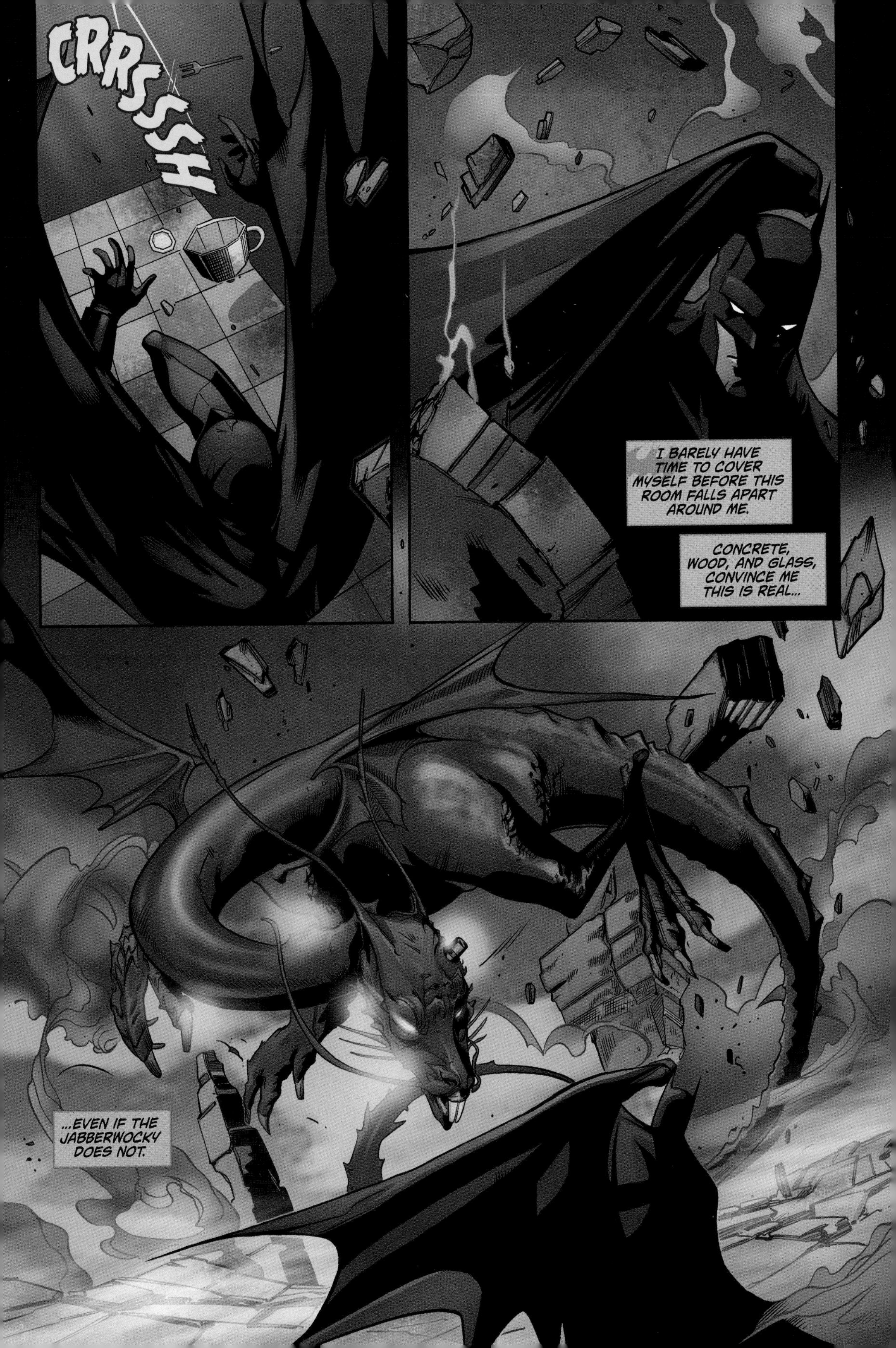
CRRSSSH
I BARELY HAVE TIME TO COVER MYSELF BEFORE THIS ROOM FALLS APART AROUND ME.
CONCRETE, WOOD, AND GLASS, CONVINCE ME THIS IS REAL...
...EVEN IF THE JABBERWOCKY DOES NOT.

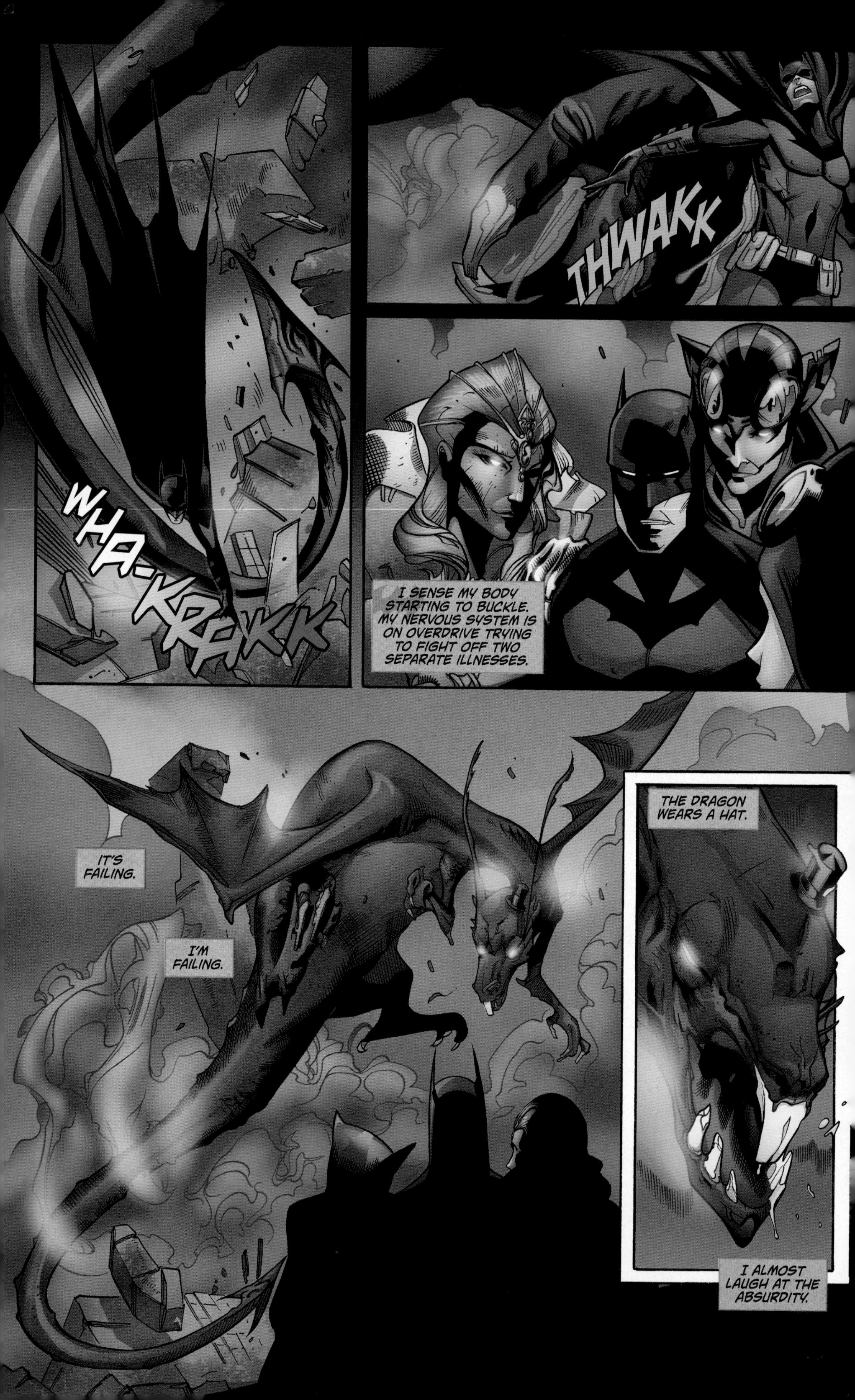
WHA-KRAKK
THWAKK
I SENSE MY BODY STARTING TO BUCKLE. MY NERVOUS SYSTEM IS ON OVERDRIVE TRYING TO FIGHT OFF TWO SEPARATE ILLNESSES.
IT'S FAILING.
I'M FAILING.
THE DRAGON WEARS A HAT.
I ALMOST LAUGH AT THE ABSURDITY.

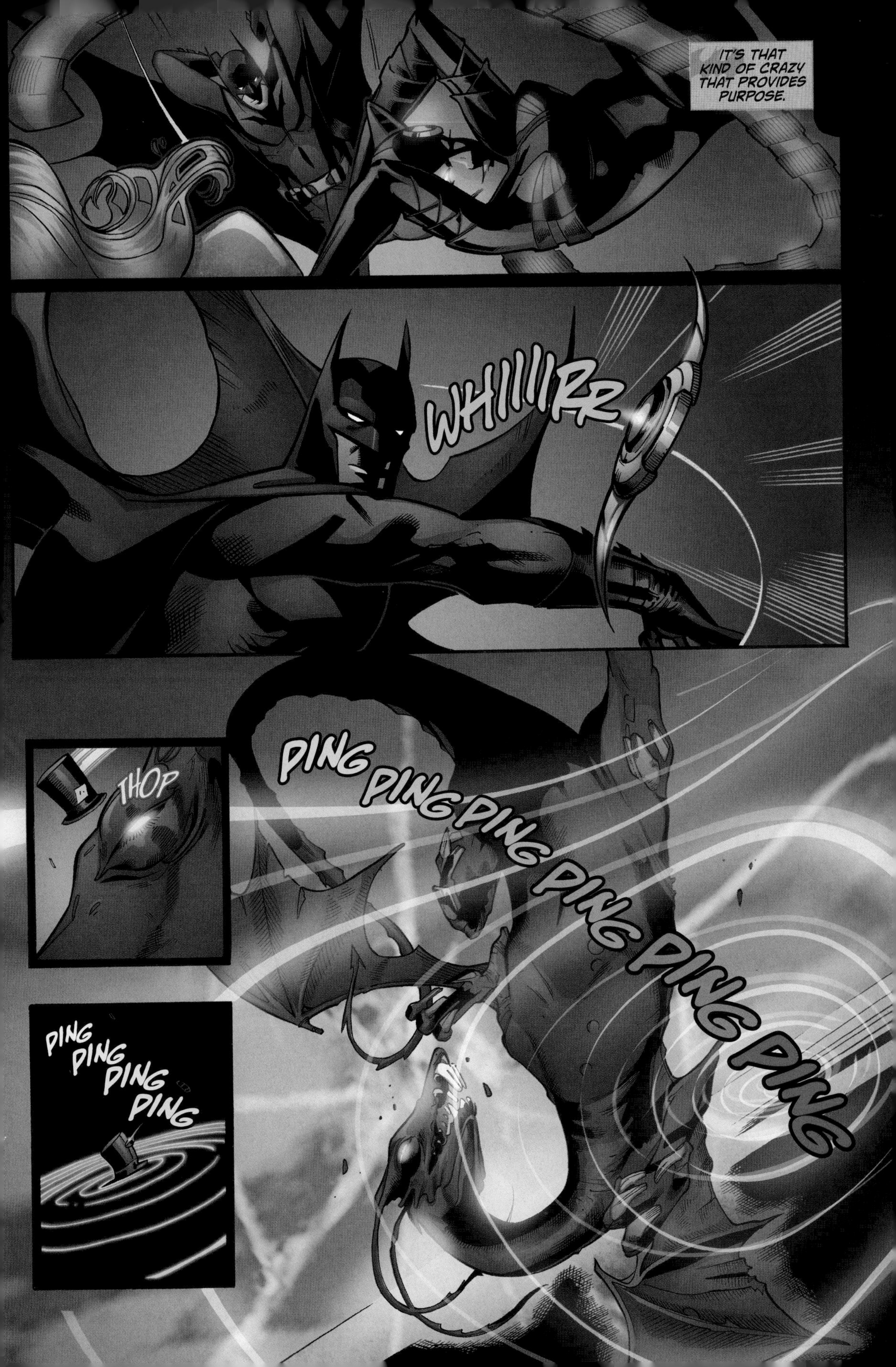
IT'S THAT KIND OF CRAZY THAT PROVIDES PURPOSE.
WHIIIIRR
THOP
PING PING PING PING PING PING PING
PING PING PING PING

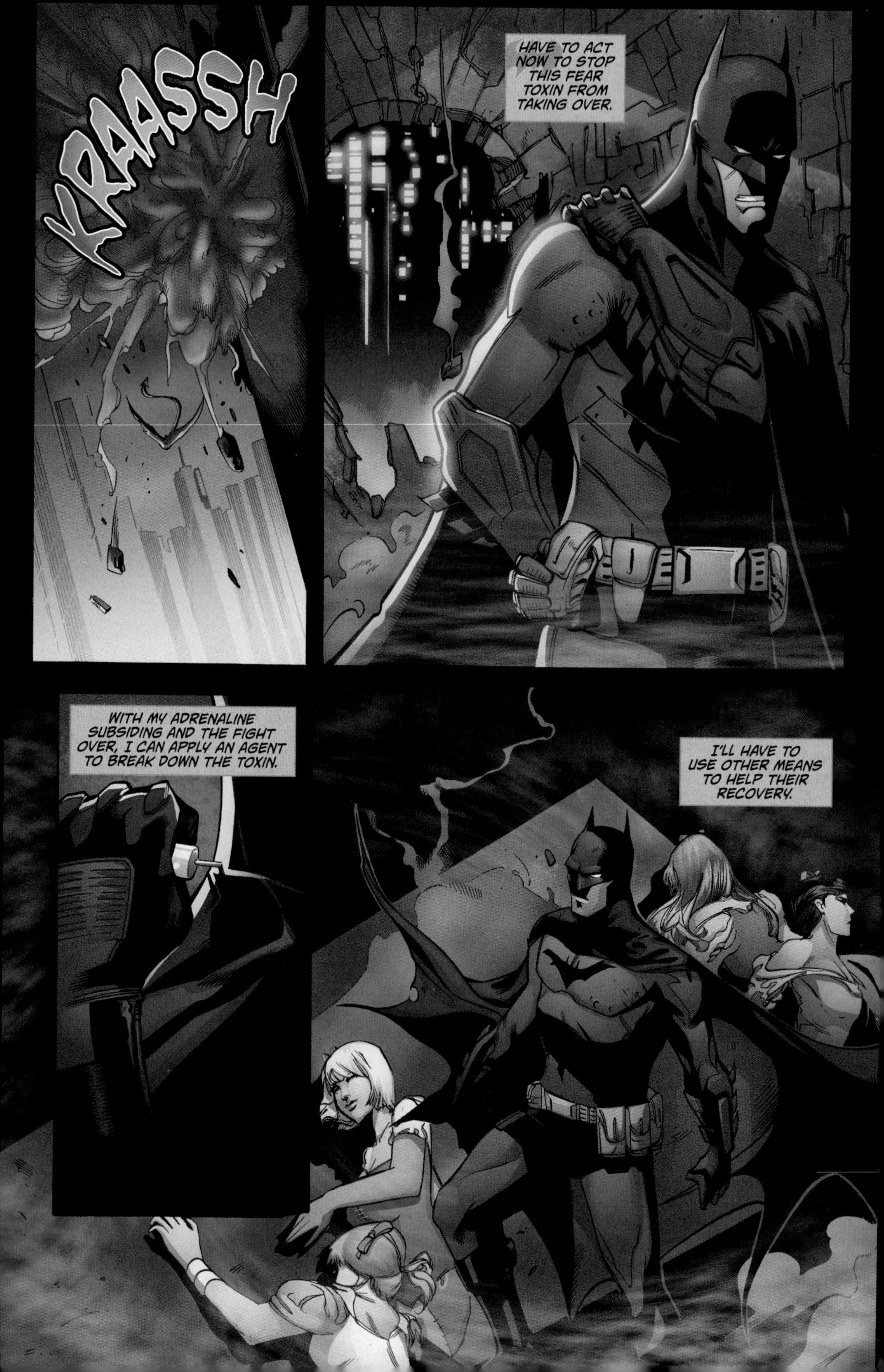
KRAASSH
HAVE TO ACT NOW TO STOP THIS FEAR TOXIN FROM TAKING OVER.
WITH MY ADRENALINE SUBSIDING AND THE FIGHT OVER, I CAN APPLY AN AGENT TO BREAK DOWN THE TOXIN.
I'LL HAVE TO USE OTHER MEANS TO HELP THEIR RECOVERY.

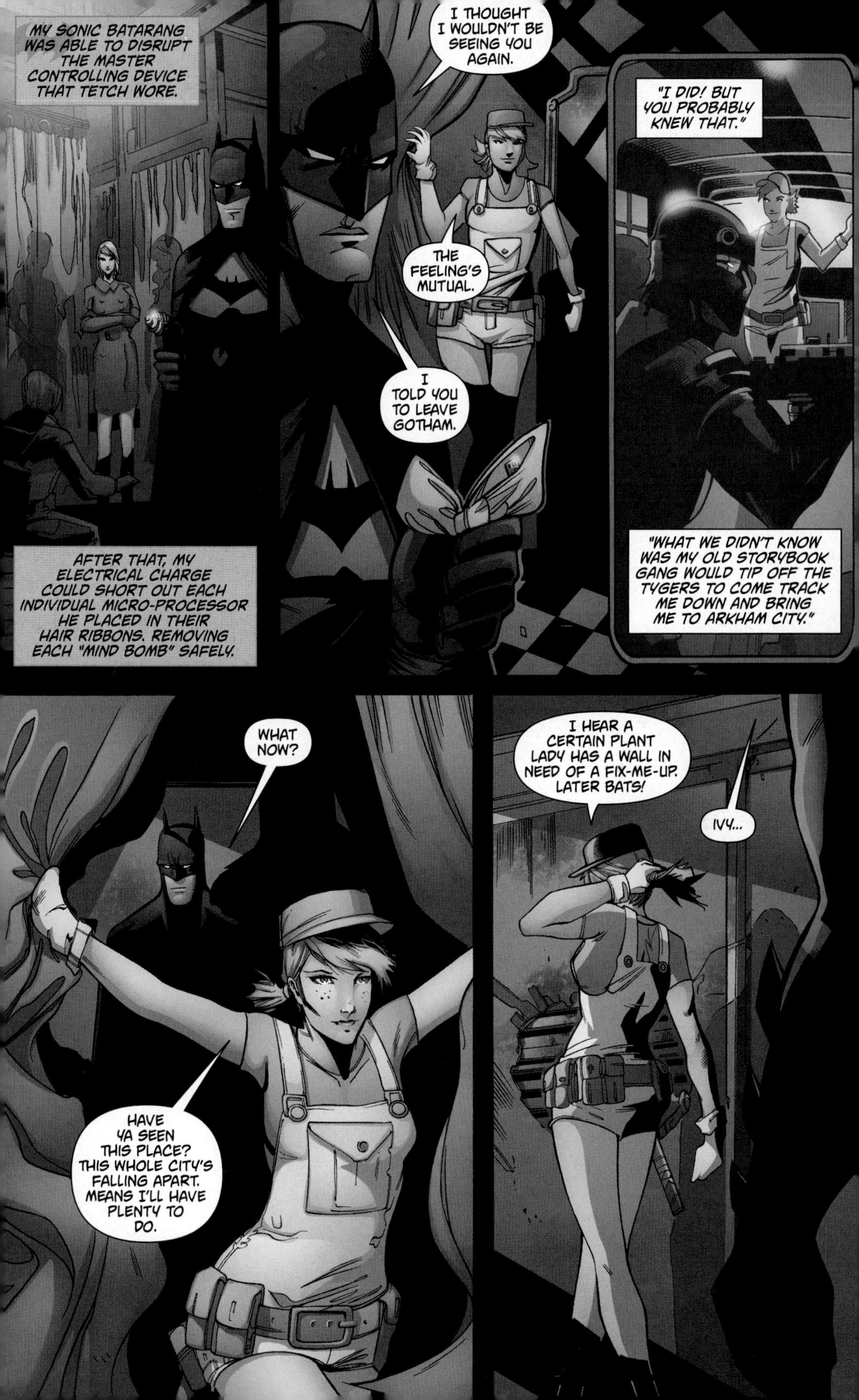
MY SONIC BATARANG WAS ABLE TO DISRUPT THE MASTER CONTROLLING DEVICE THAT TETCH WORE.
AFTER THAT, MY ELECTRICAL CHARGE COULD SHORT OUT EACH INDIVIDUAL MICRO-PROCESSOR HE PLACED IN THEIR HAIR RIBBONS. REMOVING EACH "MIND BOMB" SAFELY.
I THOUGHT I WOULDN'T BE SEEING YOU AGAIN.
THE FEELING'S MUTUAL.
I TOLD YOU TO LEAVE GOTHAM.
"I DID! BUT YOU PROBABLY KNEW THAT."
"WHAT WE DIDN'T KNOW WAS MY OLD STORYBOOK GANG WOULD TIP OFF THE TYGERS TO COME TRACK ME DOWN AND BRING ME TO ARKHAM CITY."
WHAT NOW?
HAVE YA SEEN THIS PLACE? THIS WHOLE CITY'S FALLING APART. MEANS I'LL HAVE PLENTY TO DO.
I HEAR A CERTAIN PLANT LADY HAS A WALL IN NEED OF A FIX-ME-UP. LATER BATS!
IVY...

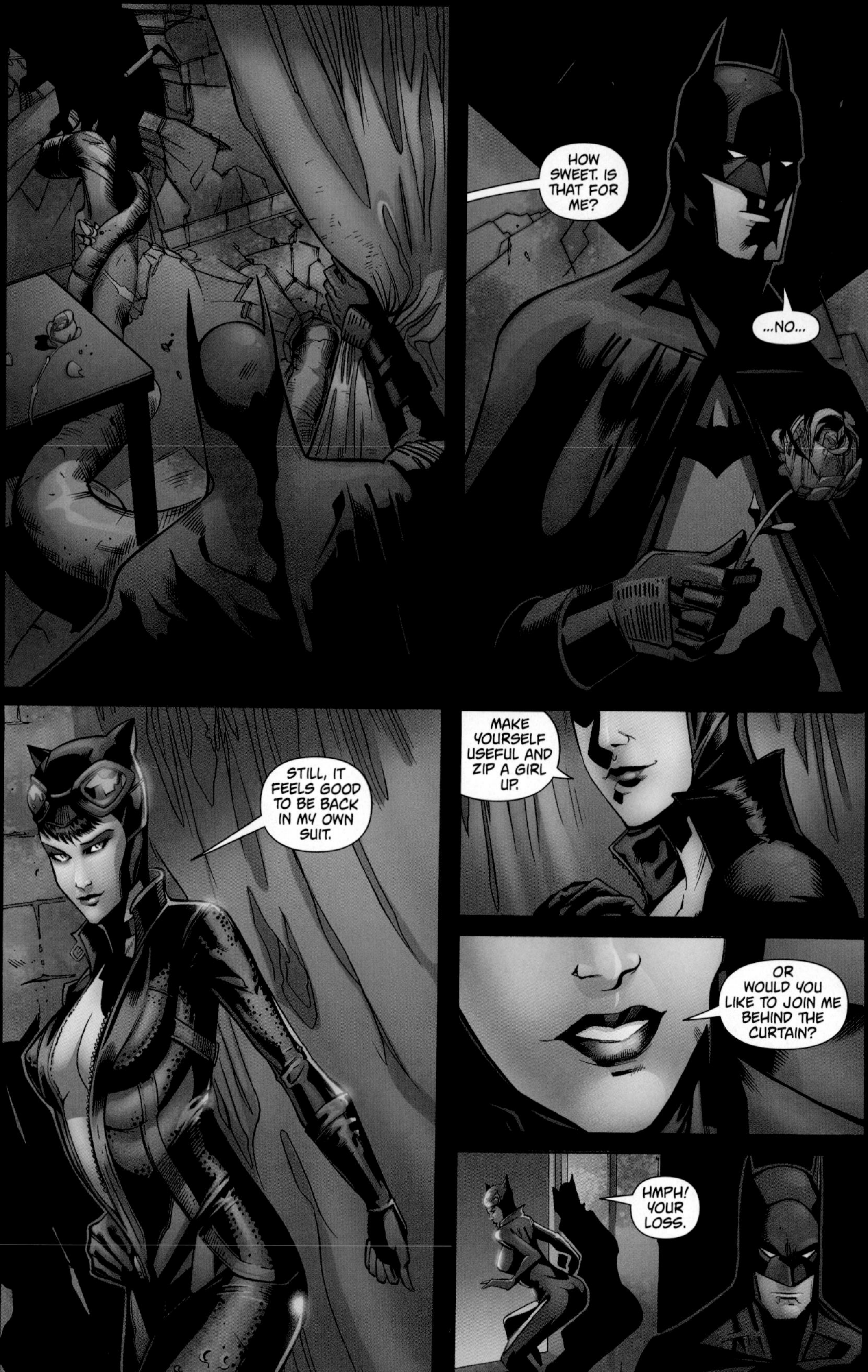
HOW SWEET. IS THAT FOR ME?
...NO...
STILL, IT FEELS GOOD TO BE BACK IN MY OWN SUIT.
MAKE YOURSELF USEFUL AND ZIP A GIRL UP.
OR WOULD YOU LIKE TO JOIN ME BEHIND THE CURTAIN?
HMPH! YOUR LOSS.

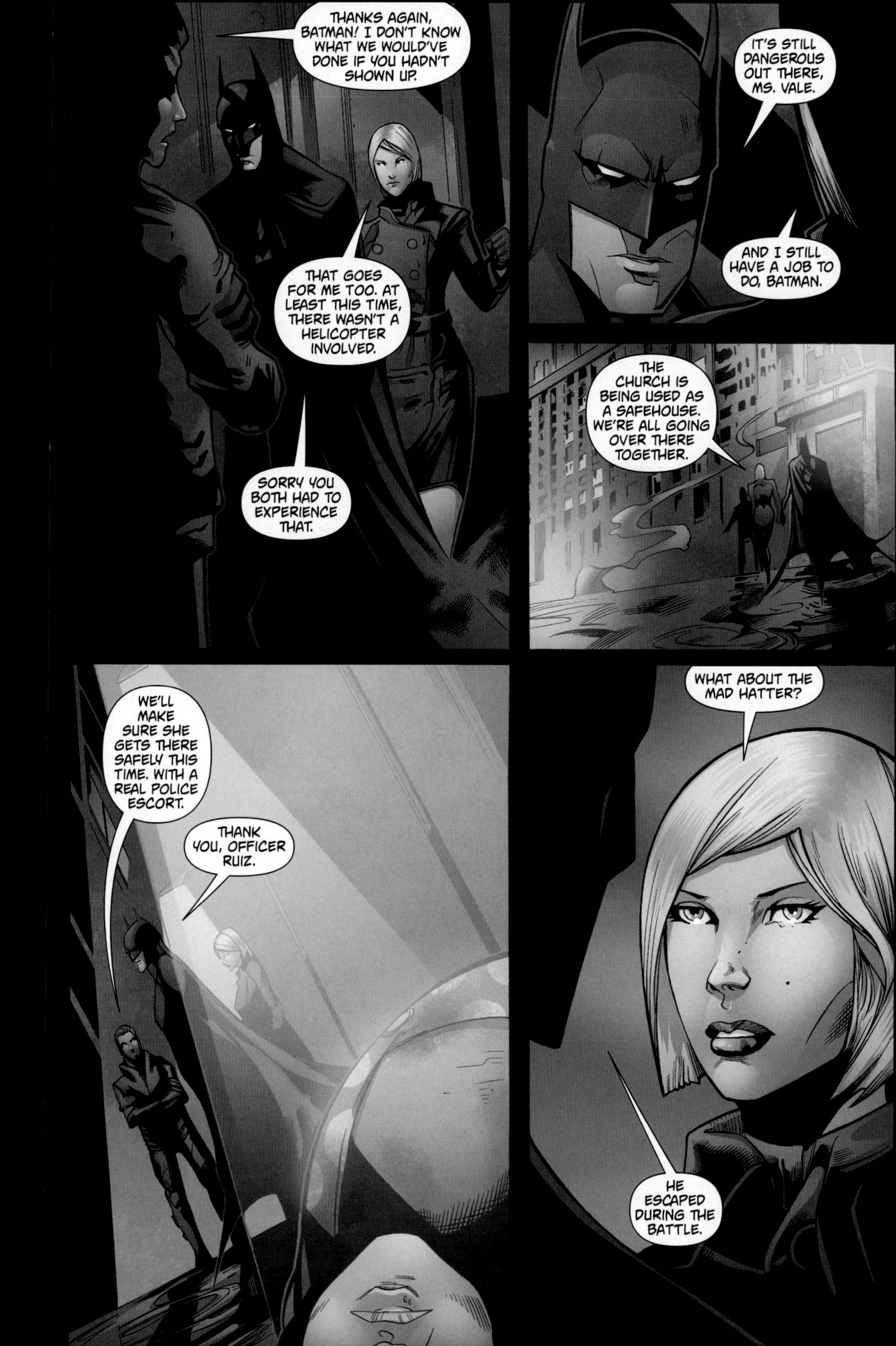
THANKS AGAIN, BATMAN! I DON'T KNOW WHAT WE WOULD'VE DONE IF YOU HADN'T SHOWN UP.
THAT GOES FOR ME TOO. AT LEAST THIS TIME, THERE WASN'T A HELICOPTER INVOLVED.
SORRY YOU BOTH HAD TO EXPERIENCE THAT.
IT'S STILL DANGEROUS OUT THERE, MS. VALE.
AND I STILL HAVE A JOB TO DO, BATMAN.
THE CHURCH IS BEING USED AS A SAFEHOUSE. WE'RE ALL GOING OVER THERE TOGETHER.
WE'LL MAKE SURE SHE GETS THERE SAFELY THIS TIME. WITH A REAL POLICE ESCORT.
THANK YOU, OFFICER RUIZ.
WHAT ABOUT THE MAD HATTER?
HE ESCAPED DURING THE BATTLE.

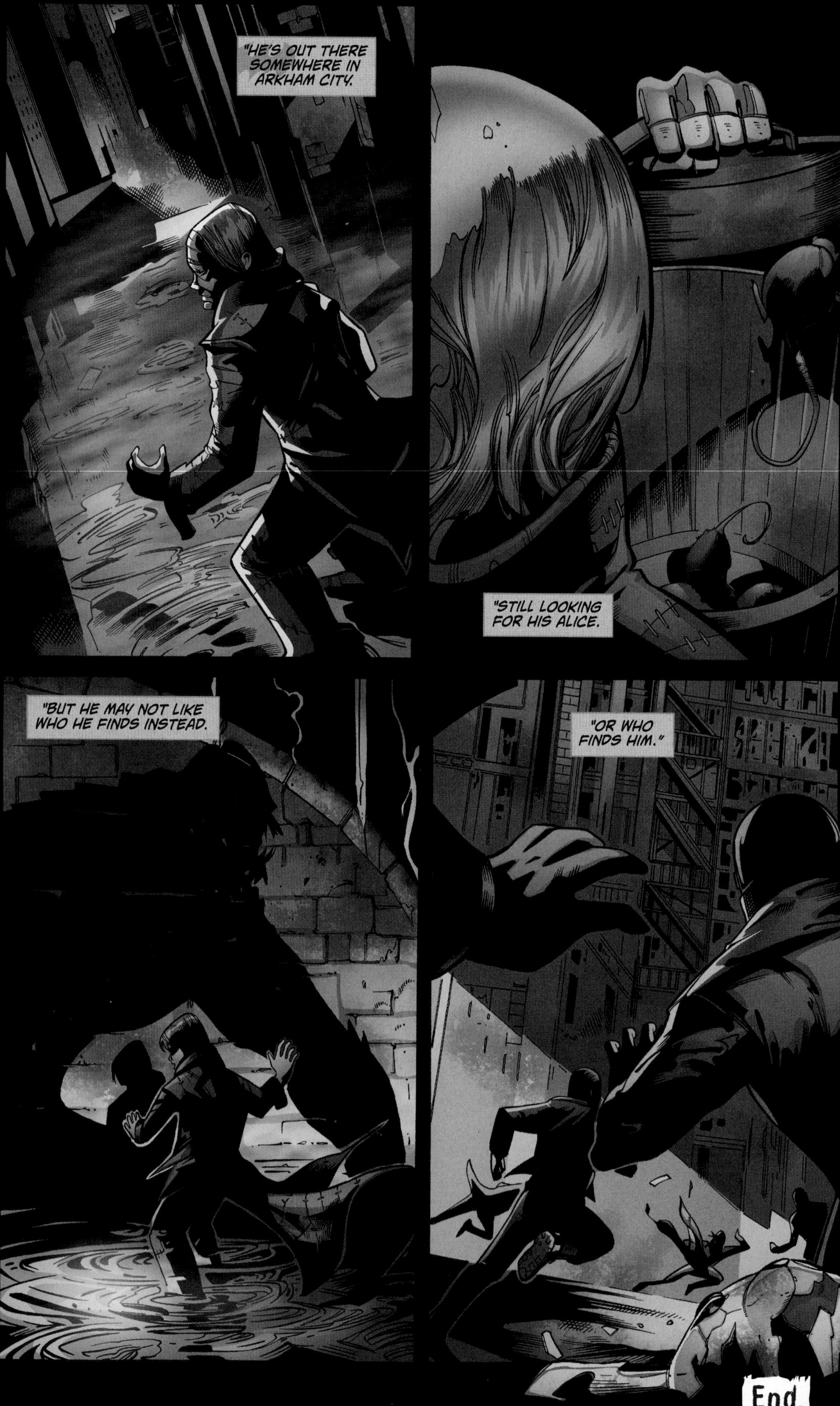
"HE'S OUT THERE SOMEWHERE IN ARKHAM CITY.
"STILL LOOKING FOR HIS ALICE.
"BUT HE MAY NOT LIKE WHO HE FINDS INSTEAD.
"OR WHO FINDS HIM."
End.

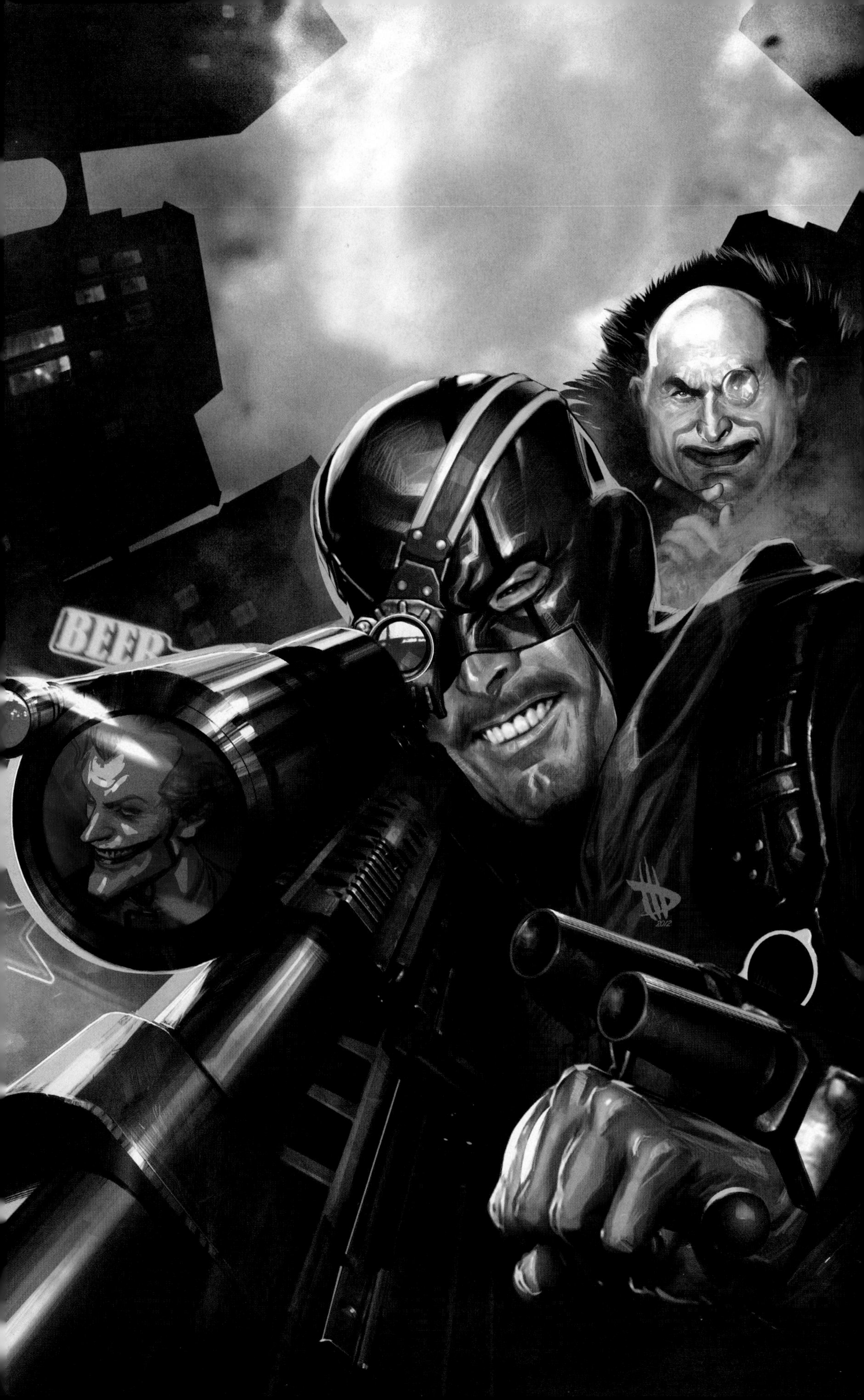
BEER
2012

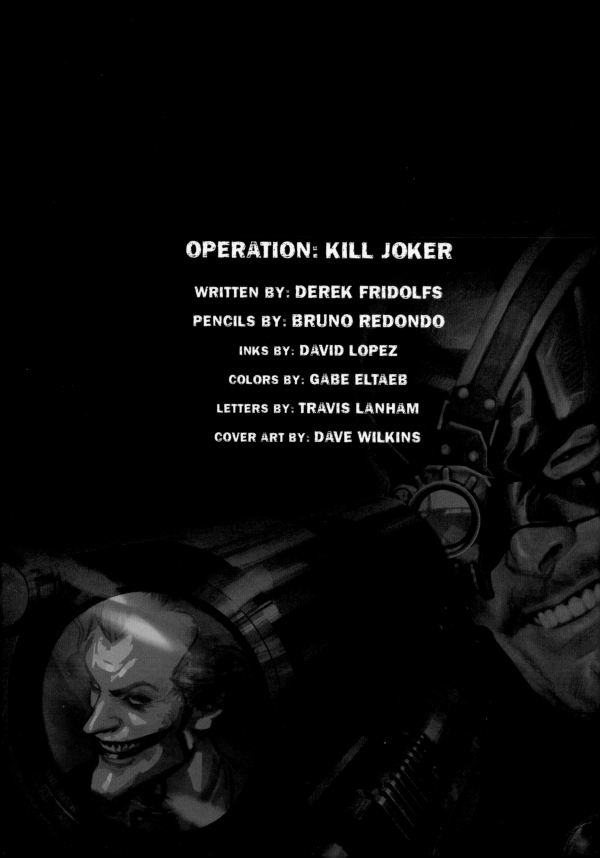

OPERATION: KILL JOKER

WRITTEN BY: DEREK FRIDOLFS

PENCILS BY: BRUNO REDONDO

INKS BY: DAVID LOPEZ

COLORS BY: GABE ELTAEB

LETTERS BY: TRAVIS LANHAM

COVER ART BY: DAVE WILKINS

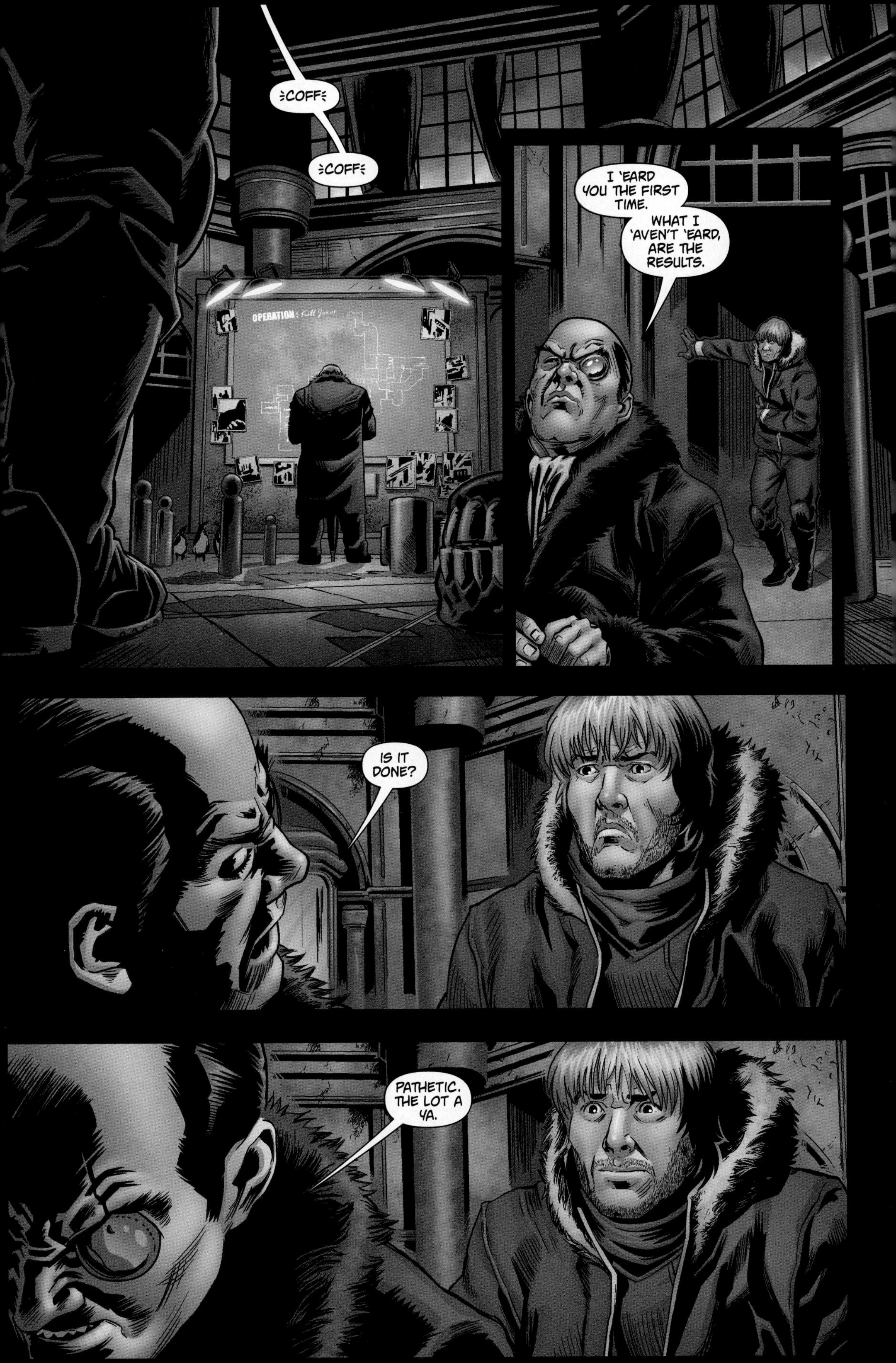
COFF
COFF
OPERATION: Kill Joker
I 'EARD YOU THE FIRST TIME.
WHAT I 'AVEN'T 'EARD, ARE THE RESULTS.
IS IT DONE?
PATHETIC. THE LOT A YA.

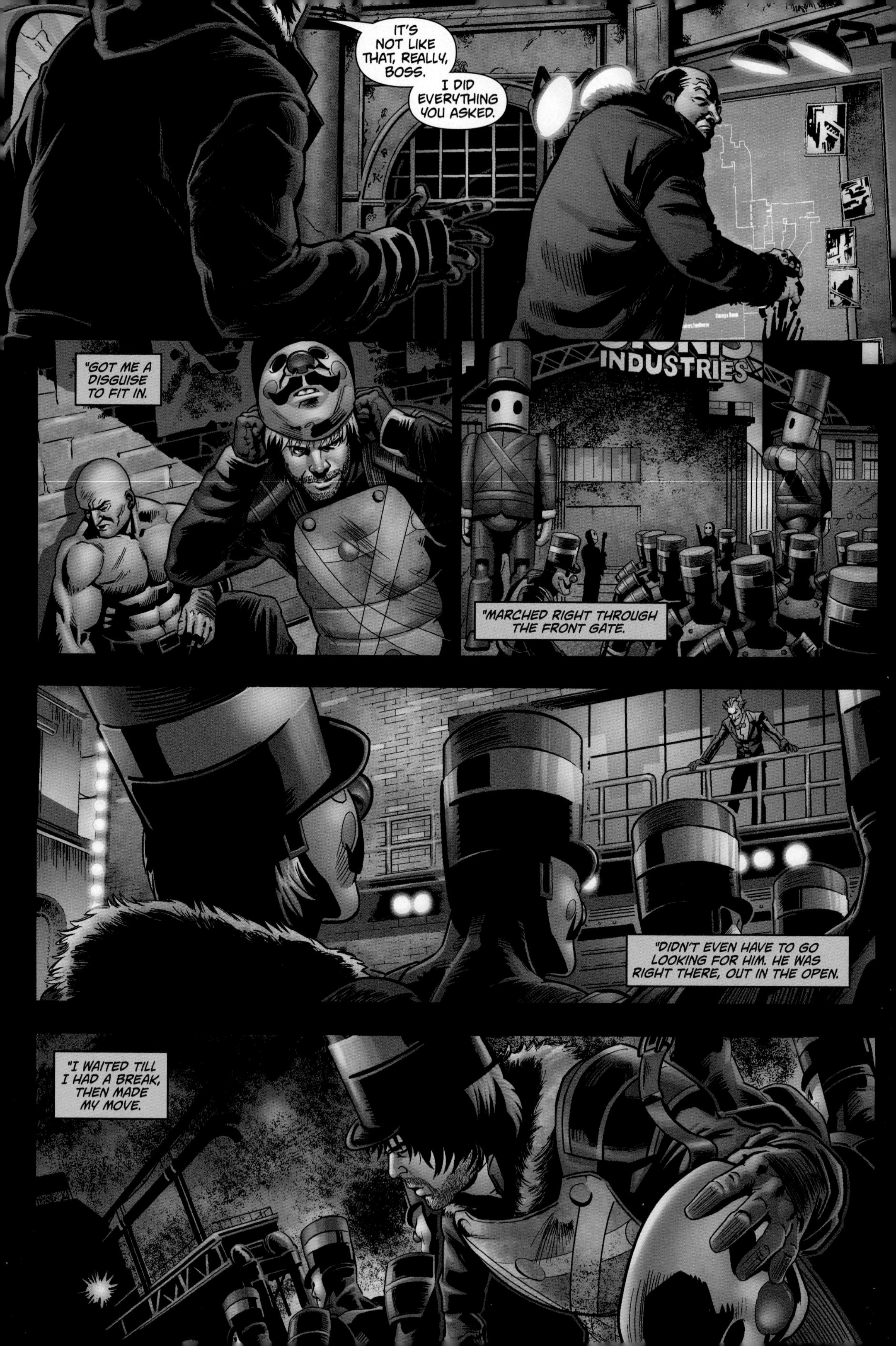
IT'S NOT LIKE THAT, REALLY, BOSS.
I DID EVERYTHING YOU ASKED.
"GOT ME A DISGUISE TO FIT IN.
INDUSTRIES
"MARCHED RIGHT THROUGH THE FRONT GATE.
"DIDN'T EVEN HAVE TO GO LOOKING FOR HIM. HE WAS RIGHT THERE, OUT IN THE OPEN.
"I WAITED TILL I HAD A BREAK, THEN MADE MY MOVE.

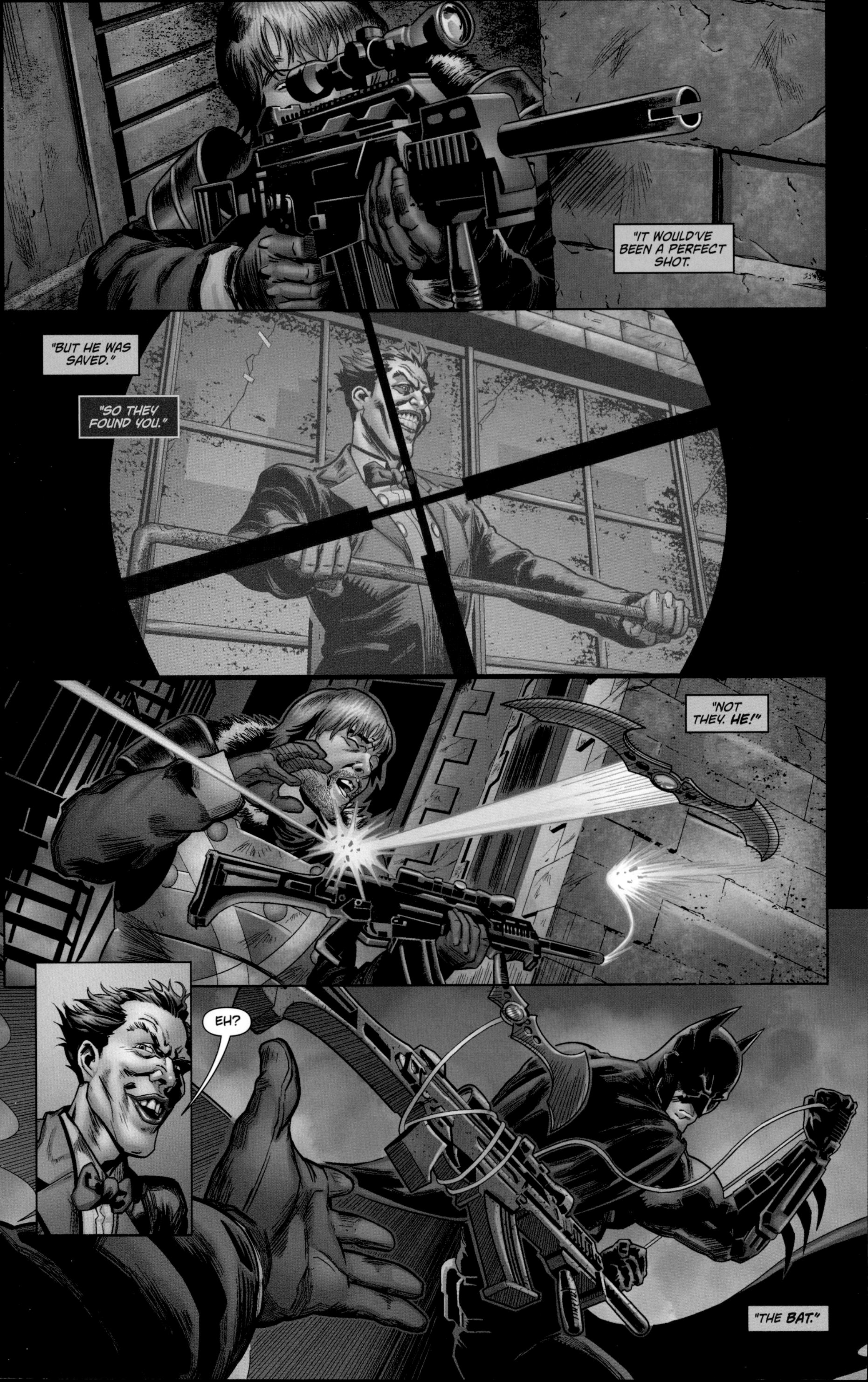
"IT WOULD'VE BEEN A PERFECT SHOT.
"BUT HE WAS SAVED."
"SO THEY FOUND YOU."
"NOT THEY. HE!"
EH?
"THE BAT."

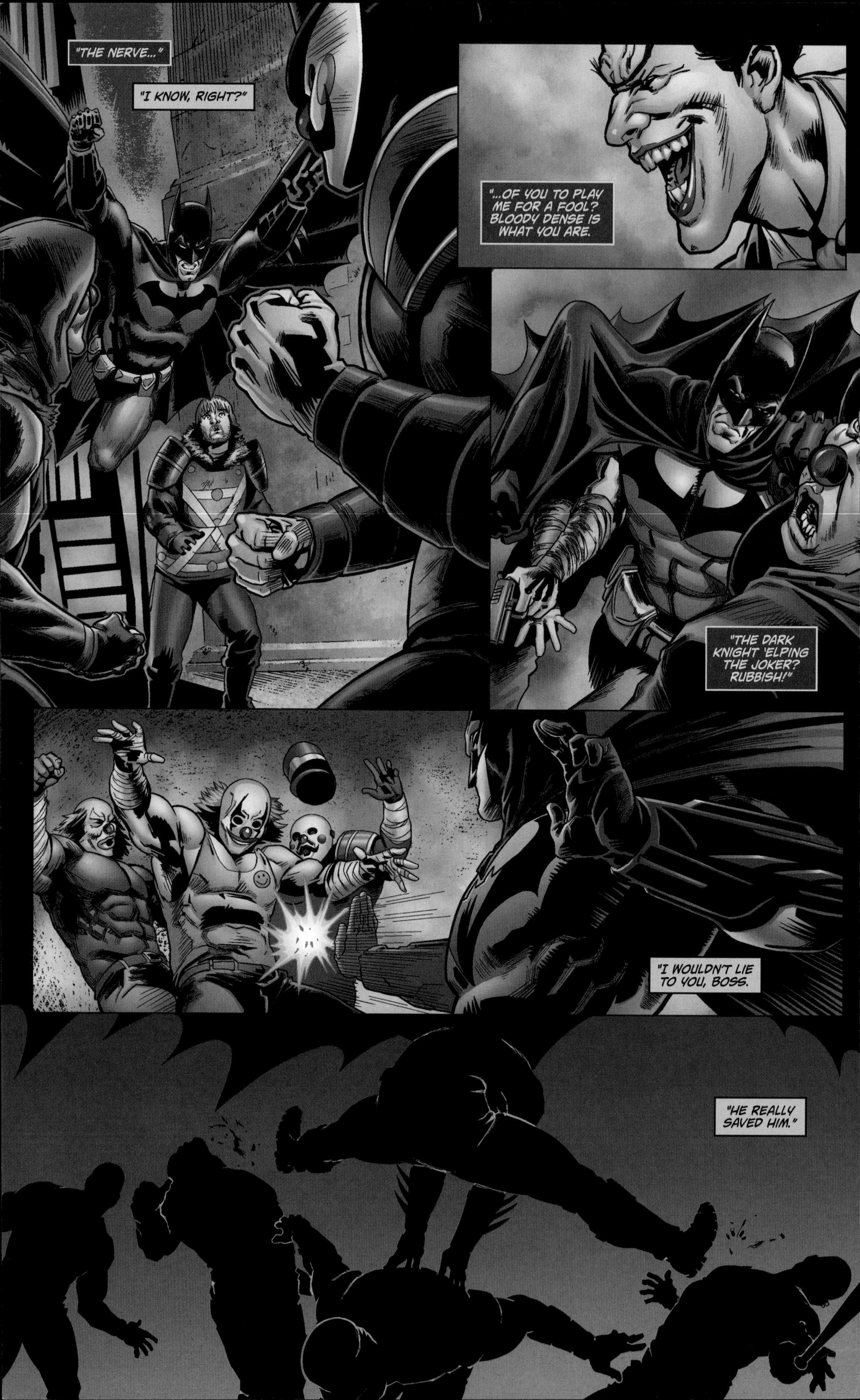
"THE NERVE..."
"I KNOW, RIGHT?"
"...OF YOU TO PLAY ME FOR A FOOL? BLOODY DENSE IS WHAT YOU ARE.
"THE DARK KNIGHT 'ELPING THE JOKER? RUBBISH!"
"I WOULDN'T LIE TO YOU, BOSS.
"HE REALLY SAVED HIM."

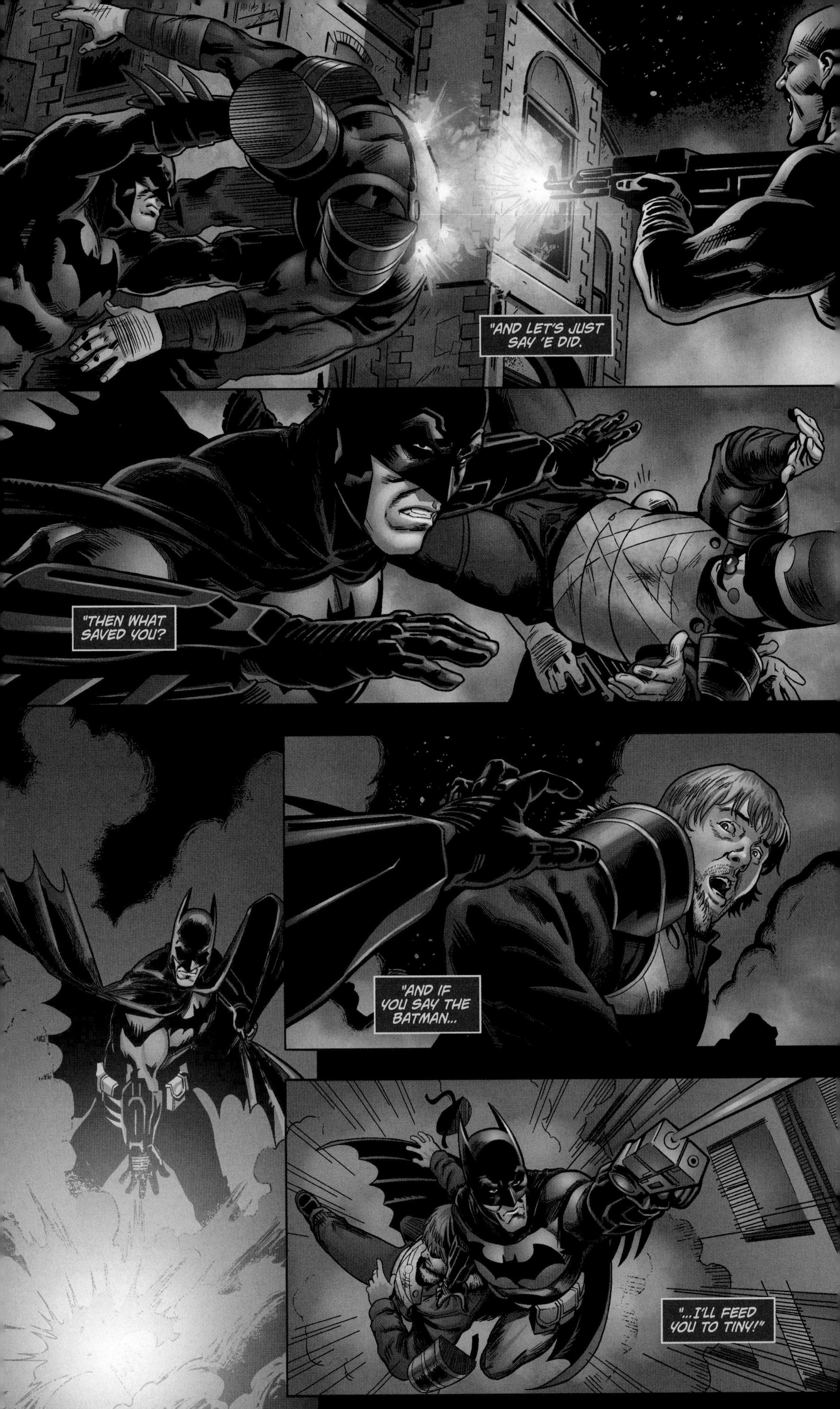
"AND LET'S JUST SAY 'E DID.
"THEN WHAT SAVED YOU?
"AND IF YOU SAY THE BATMAN...
"...I'LL FEED YOU TO TINY!"

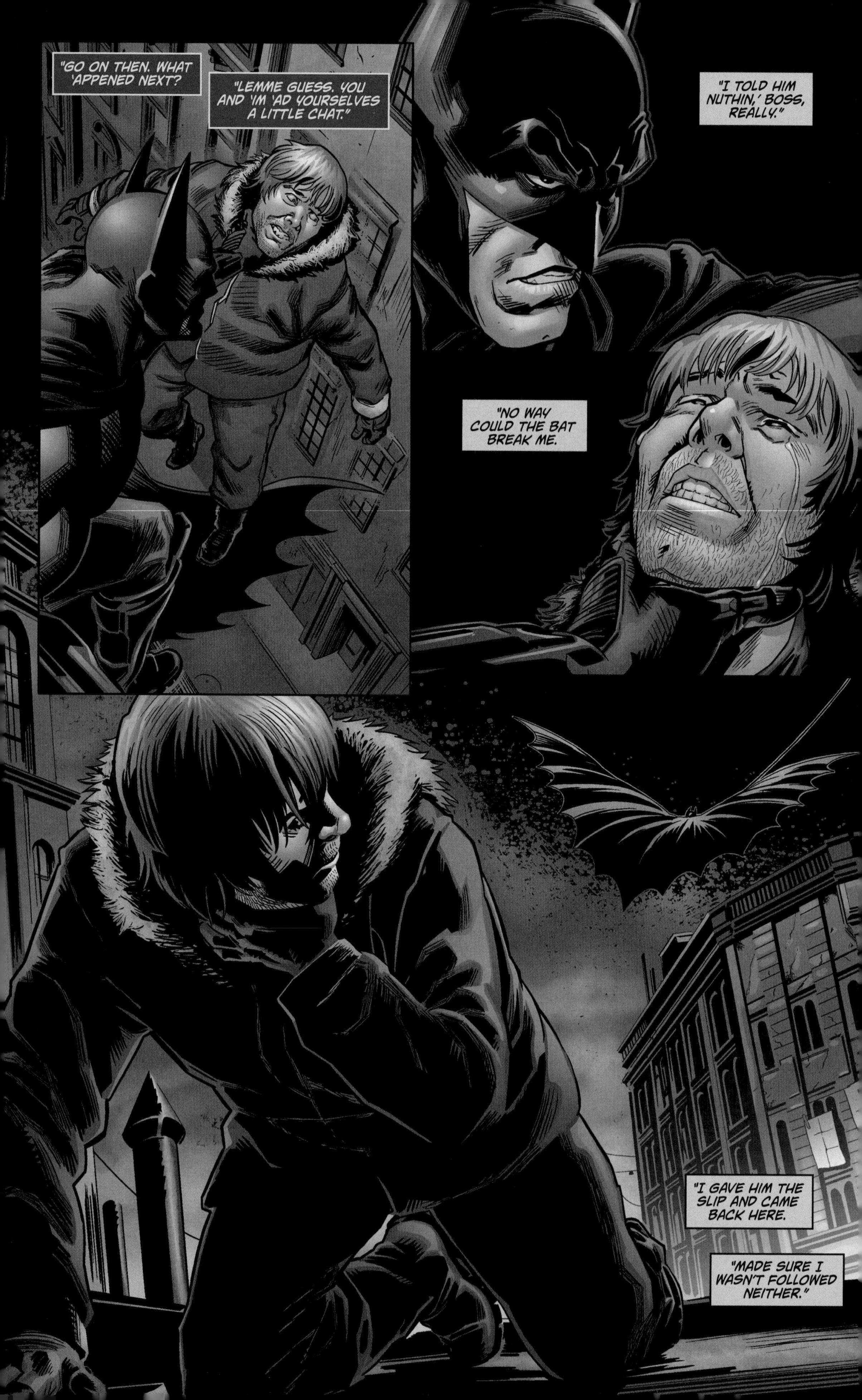
"GO ON THEN. WHAT 'APPENED NEXT?
"LEMME GUESS. YOU AND 'IM 'AD YOURSELVES A LITTLE CHAT."
"I TOLD HIM NUTHIN,' BOSS, REALLY."
"NO WAY COULD THE BAT BREAK ME.
"I GAVE HIM THE SLIP AND CAME BACK HERE.
"MADE SURE I WASN'T FOLLOWED NEITHER."

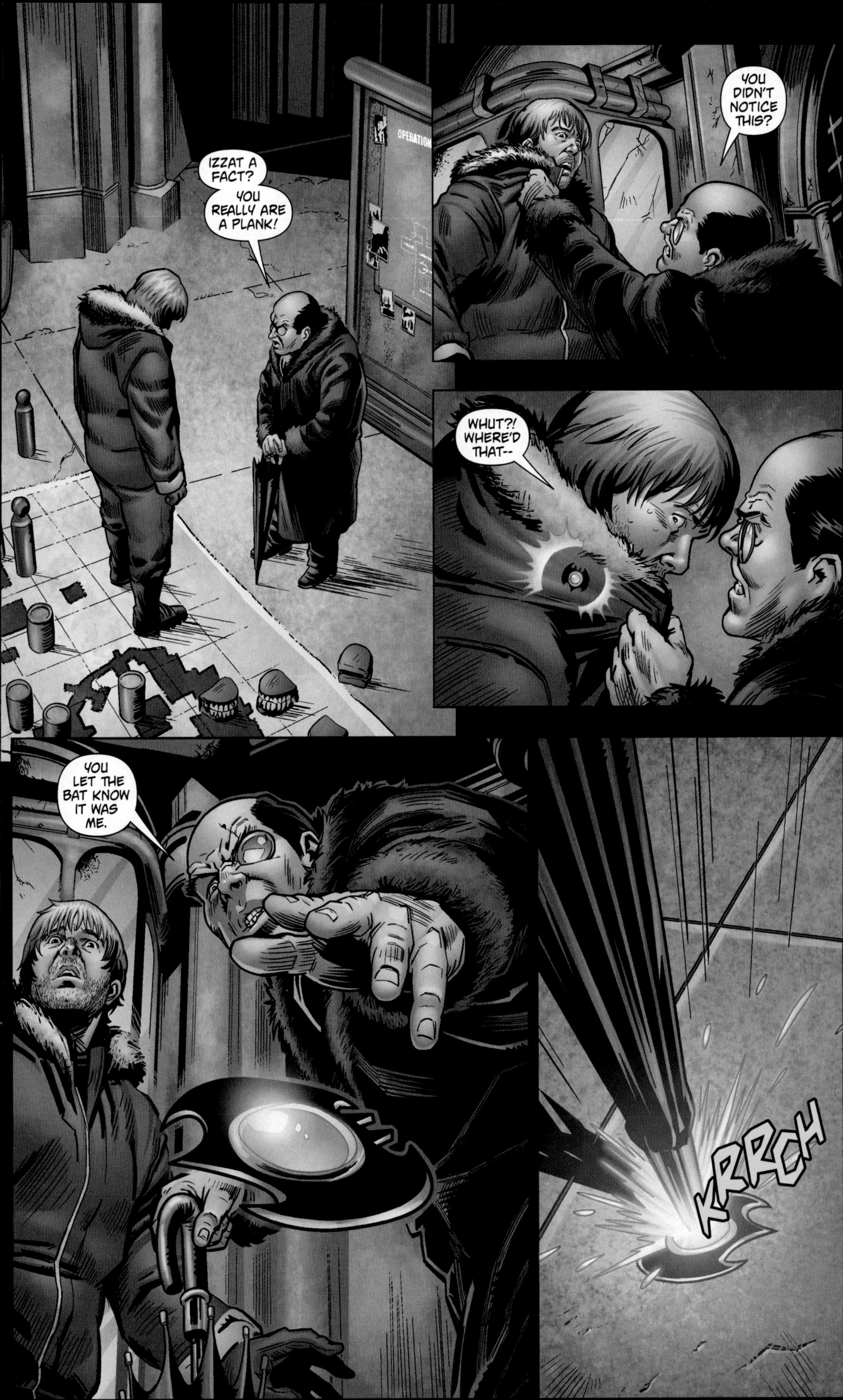
OPERATION
IZZAT A FACT?
YOU REALLY ARE A PLANK!
YOU DIDN'T NOTICE THIS?
WHUT?! WHERE'D THAT--
YOU LET THE BAT KNOW IT WAS ME.
KRRCH

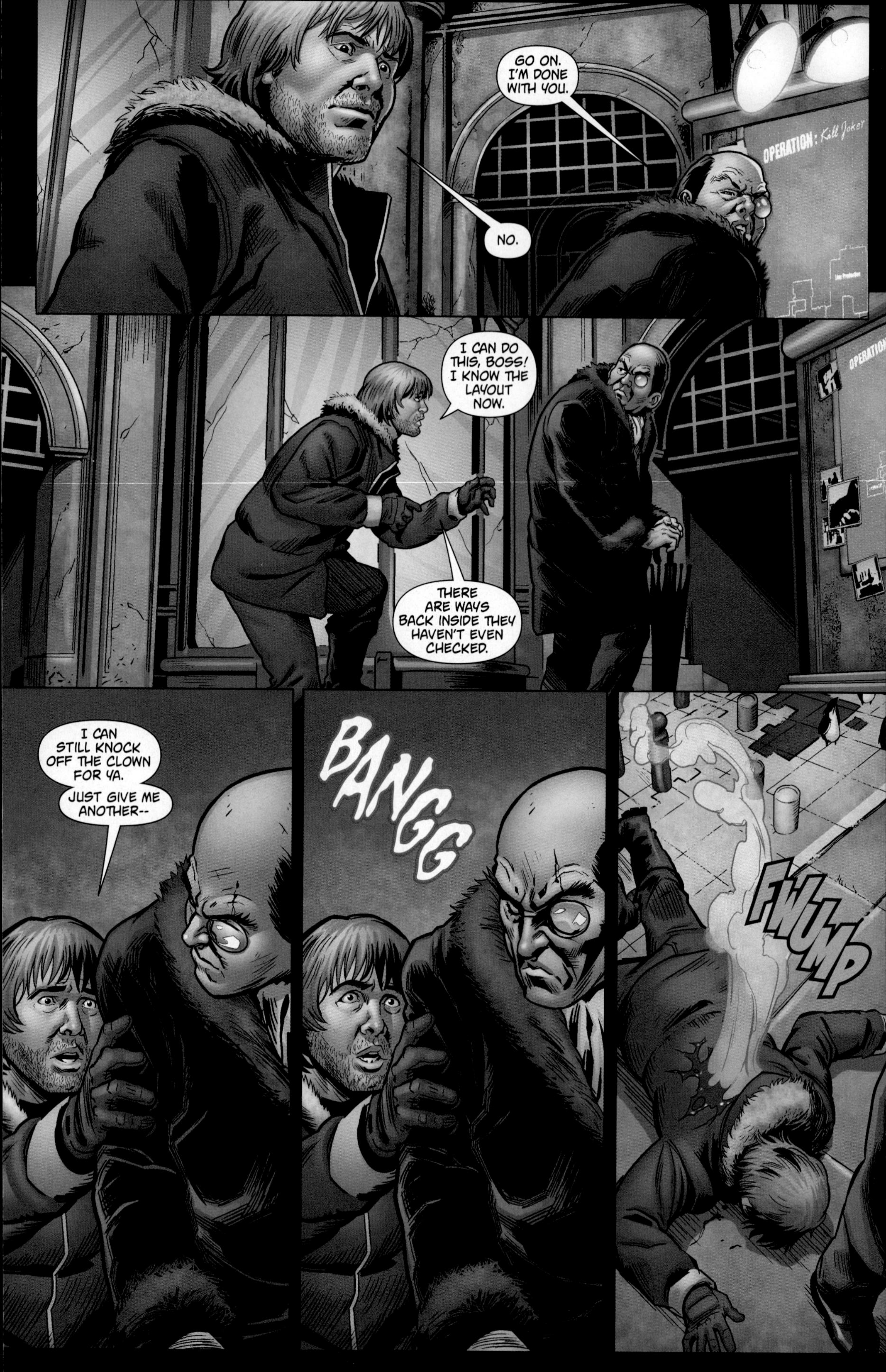
GO ON. I'M DONE WITH YOU.
NO.
OPERATION: Kill Joker
I CAN DO THIS, BOSS! I KNOW THE LAYOUT NOW.
THERE ARE WAYS BACK INSIDE THEY HAVEN'T EVEN CHECKED.
I CAN STILL KNOCK OFF THE CLOWN FOR YA.
JUST GIVE ME ANOTHER--
BANGG
FWUMP

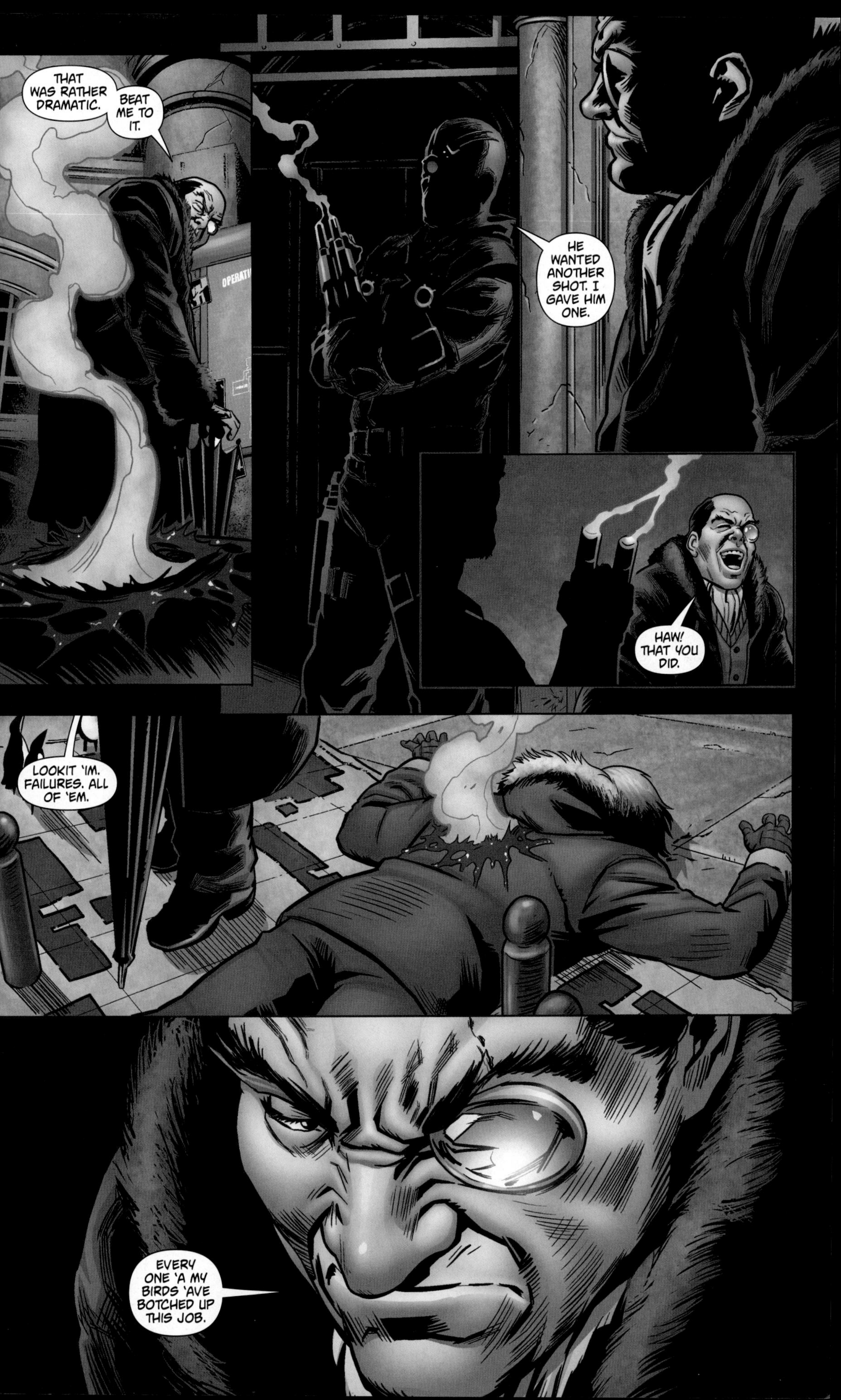
THAT WAS RATHER DRAMATIC.
BEAT ME TO IT.
HE WANTED ANOTHER SHOT. I GAVE HIM ONE.
HAW! THAT YOU DID.
LOOKIT 'IM. FAILURES. ALL OF 'EM.
EVERY ONE 'A MY BIRDS 'AVE BOTCHED UP THIS JOB.

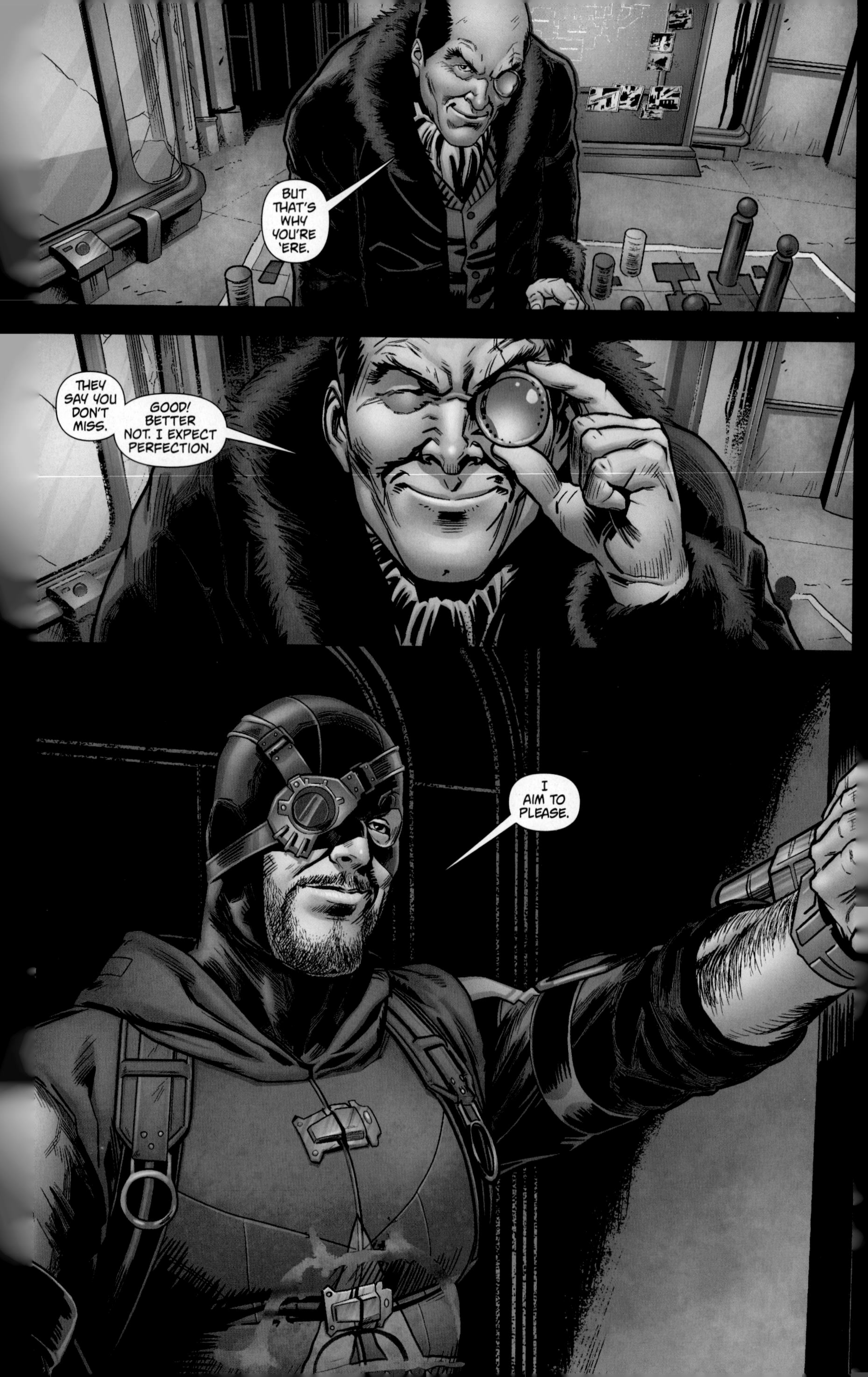
BUT THAT'S WHY YOU'RE 'ERE.
THEY SAY YOU DON'T MISS.
GOOD! BETTER NOT. I EXPECT PERFECTION.
I AIM TO PLEASE.

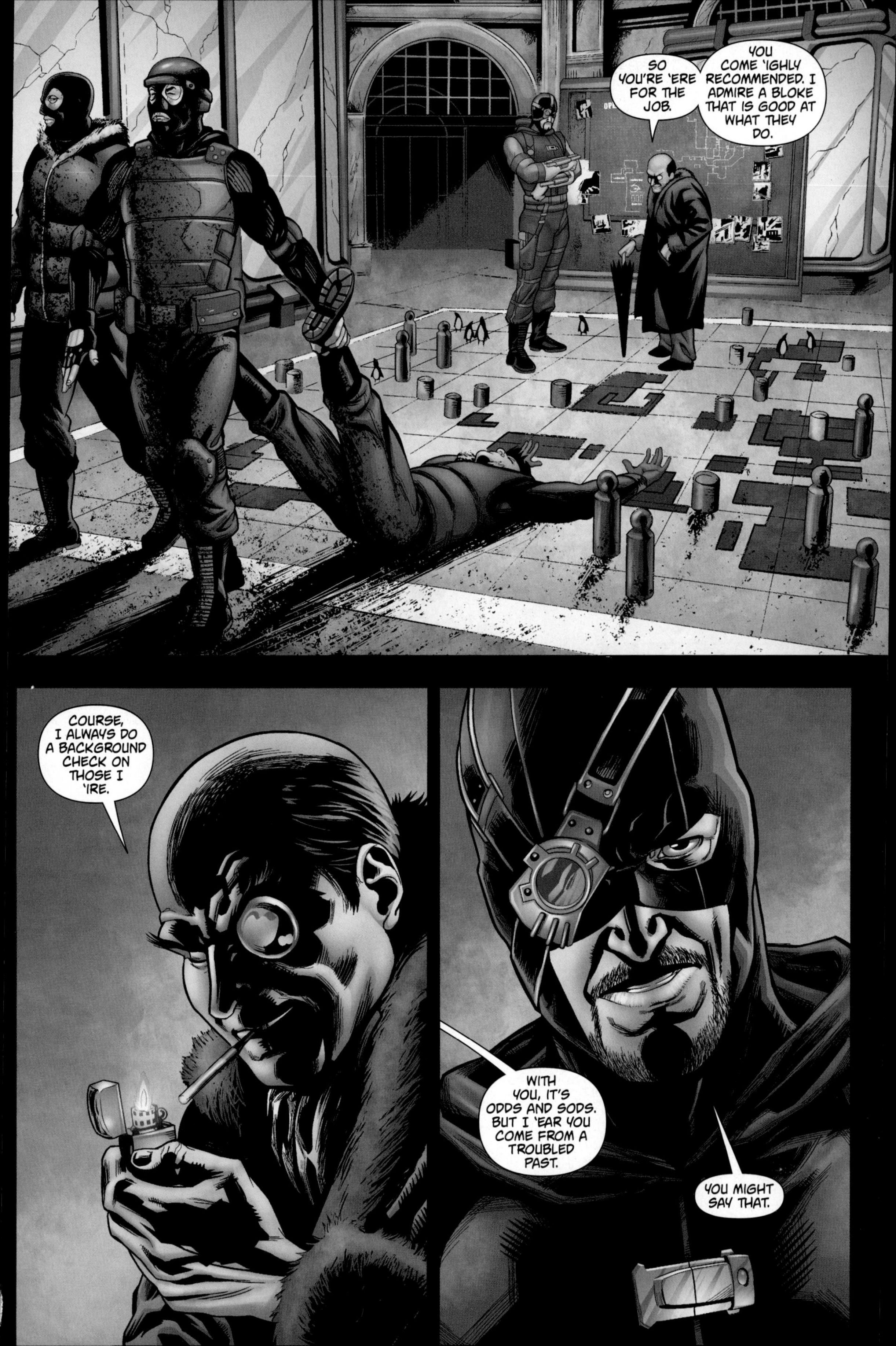
SO YOU'RE 'ERE FOR THE JOB.
YOU COME 'IGHLY RECOMMENDED. I ADMIRE A BLOKE THAT IS GOOD AT WHAT THEY DO.
COURSE, I ALWAYS DO A BACKGROUND CHECK ON THOSE I 'IRE.
WITH YOU, IT'S ODDS AND SODS. BUT I 'EAR YOU COME FROM A TROUBLED PAST.
YOU MIGHT SAY THAT.

"PRETTY NORMAL HOME LIFE. BROTHER I LOVED. MOTHER THAT LOVED ME.

"FATHER... NOT SO MUCH."

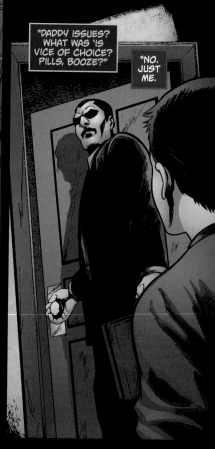

"DADDY ISSUES? WHAT WAS 'IS VICE OF CHOICE? PILLS, BOOZE?"

"NO. JUST ME.

"ACTUALLY, IT COULD HAVE BEEN ANY OF US

"ONE MINUTE, WE COULD ALL BE HAVING FUN TOGETHER.

"BUT IF IT STOPPED BEING ABOUT HIM, THAT'S WHEN IT GOT BAD.

"FOR ALL OF US."

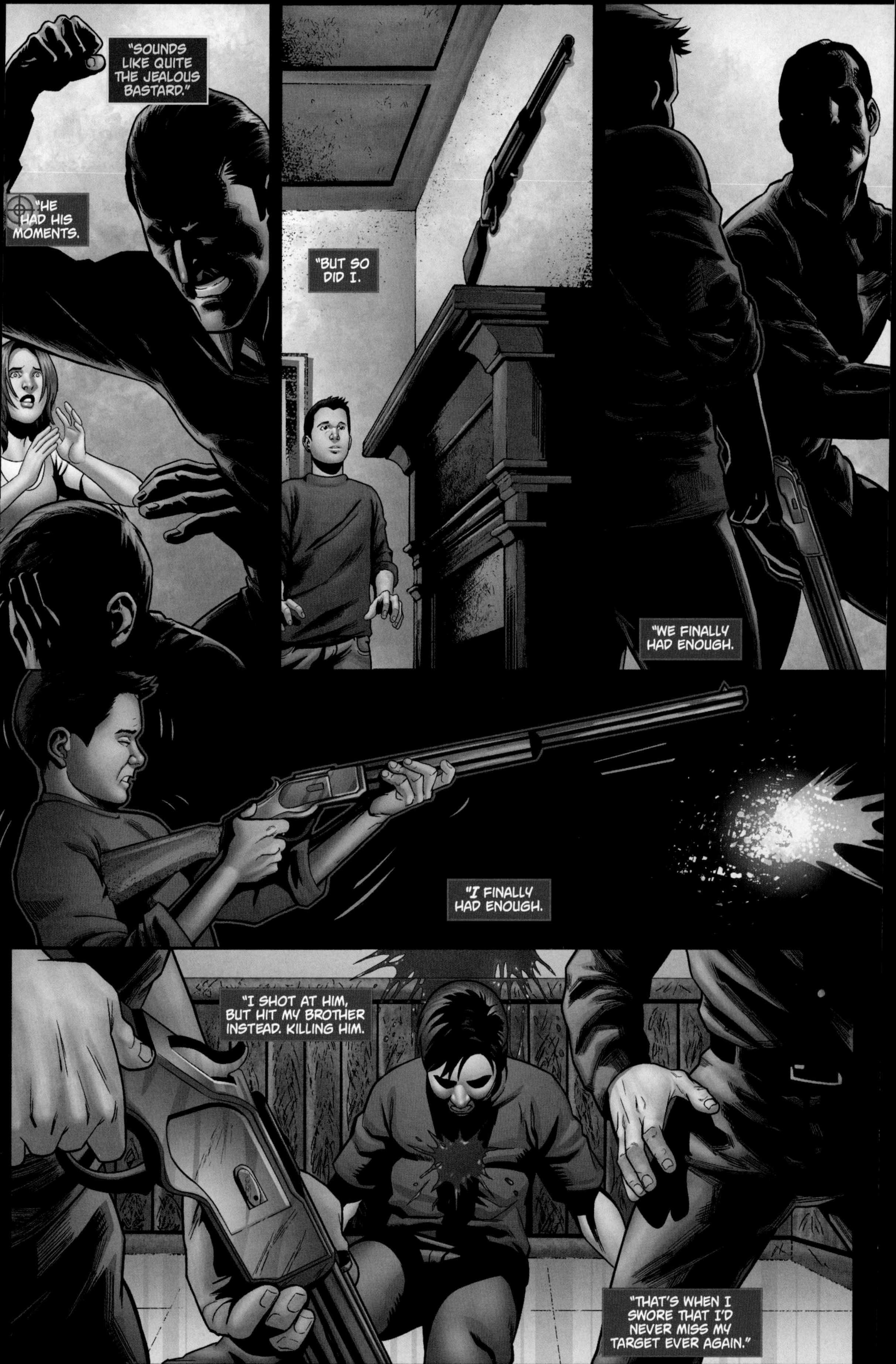
"SOUNDS LIKE QUITE THE JEALOUS BASTARD."
"HE HAD HIS MOMENTS.
"BUT SO DID I.
"WE FINALLY HAD ENOUGH.
"I FINALLY HAD ENOUGH.
"I SHOT AT HIM, BUT HIT MY BROTHER INSTEAD. KILLING HIM.
"THAT'S WHEN I SWORE THAT I'D NEVER MISS MY TARGET EVER AGAIN."

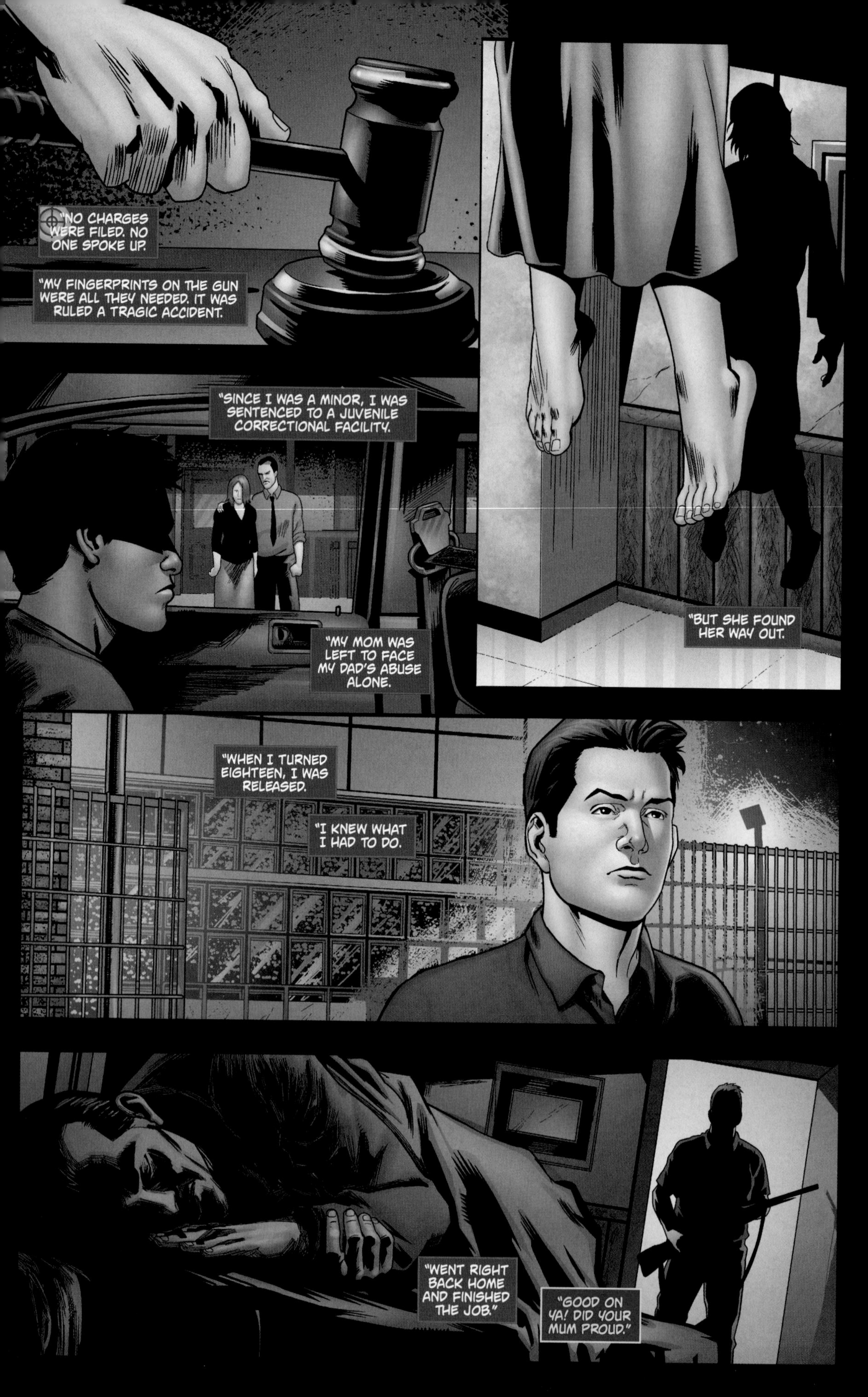
"NO CHARGES WERE FILED. NO ONE SPOKE UP.
"MY FINGERPRINTS ON THE GUN WERE ALL THEY NEEDED. IT WAS RULED A TRAGIC ACCIDENT.
"SINCE I WAS A MINOR, I WAS SENTENCED TO A JUVENILE CORRECTIONAL FACILITY.
"MY MOM WAS LEFT TO FACE MY DAD'S ABUSE ALONE.
"BUT SHE FOUND HER WAY OUT.
"WHEN I TURNED EIGHTEEN, I WAS RELEASED.
"I KNEW WHAT I HAD TO DO.
"WENT RIGHT BACK HOME AND FINISHED THE JOB."
"GOOD ON YA! DID YOUR MUM PROUD."

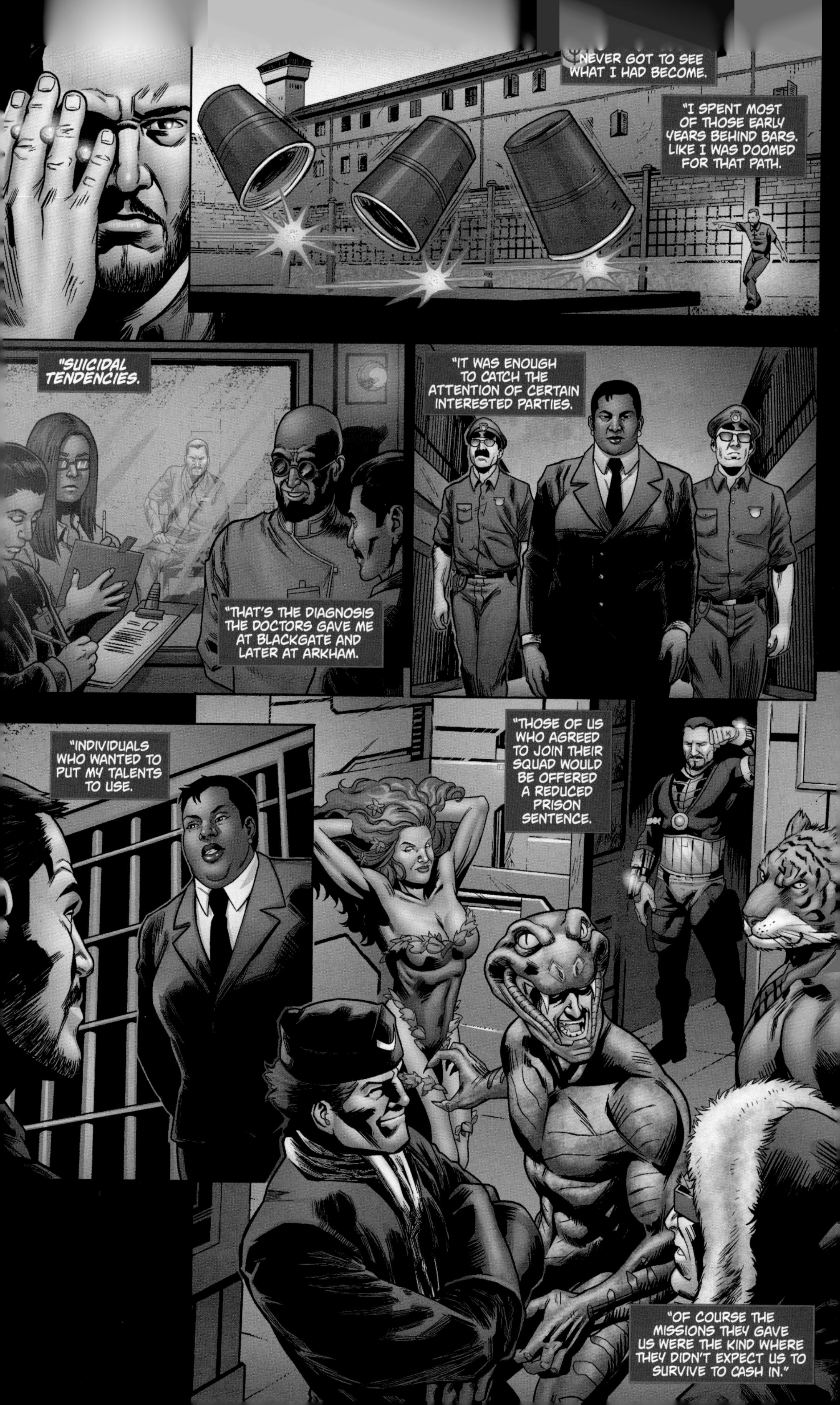
NEVER GOT TO SEE WHAT I HAD BECOME.
"I SPENT MOST OF THOSE EARLY YEARS BEHIND BARS. LIKE I WAS DOOMED FOR THAT PATH.
"SUICIDAL TENDENCIES.
"THAT'S THE DIAGNOSIS THE DOCTORS GAVE ME AT BLACKGATE AND LATER AT ARKHAM.
"IT WAS ENOUGH TO CATCH THE ATTENTION OF CERTAIN INTERESTED PARTIES.
"INDIVIDUALS WHO WANTED TO PUT MY TALENTS TO USE.
"THOSE OF US WHO AGREED TO JOIN THEIR SQUAD WOULD BE OFFERED A REDUCED PRISON SENTENCE.
"OF COURSE THE MISSIONS THEY GAVE US WERE THE KIND WHERE THEY DIDN'T EXPECT US TO SURVIVE TO CASH IN."

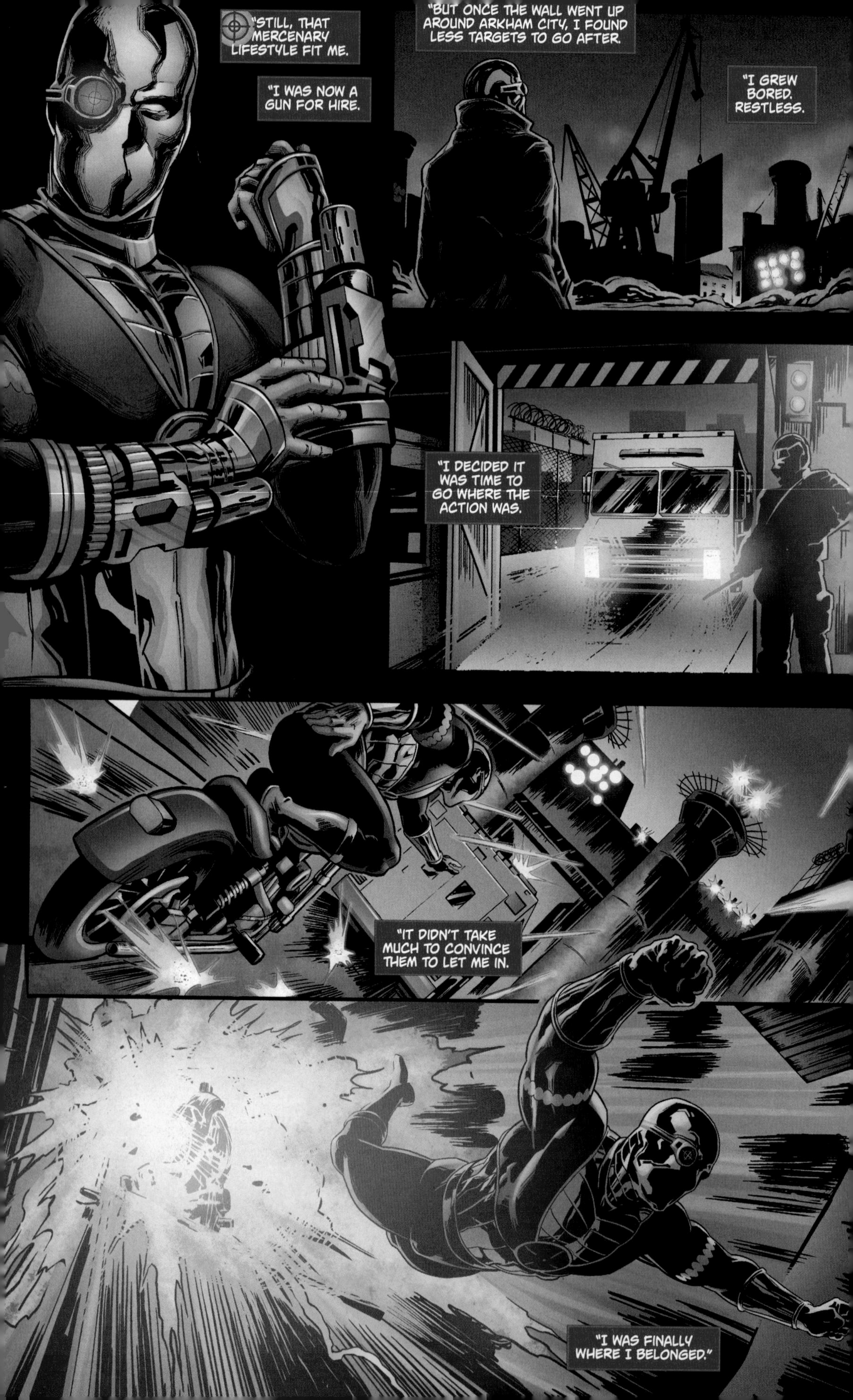
"STILL, THAT MERCENARY LIFESTYLE FIT ME.
"I WAS NOW A GUN FOR HIRE.
"BUT ONCE THE WALL WENT UP AROUND ARKHAM CITY, I FOUND LESS TARGETS TO GO AFTER.
"I GREW BORED. RESTLESS.
"I DECIDED IT WAS TIME TO GO WHERE THE ACTION WAS.
"IT DIDN'T TAKE MUCH TO CONVINCE THEM TO LET ME IN.
"I WAS FINALLY WHERE I BELONGED."

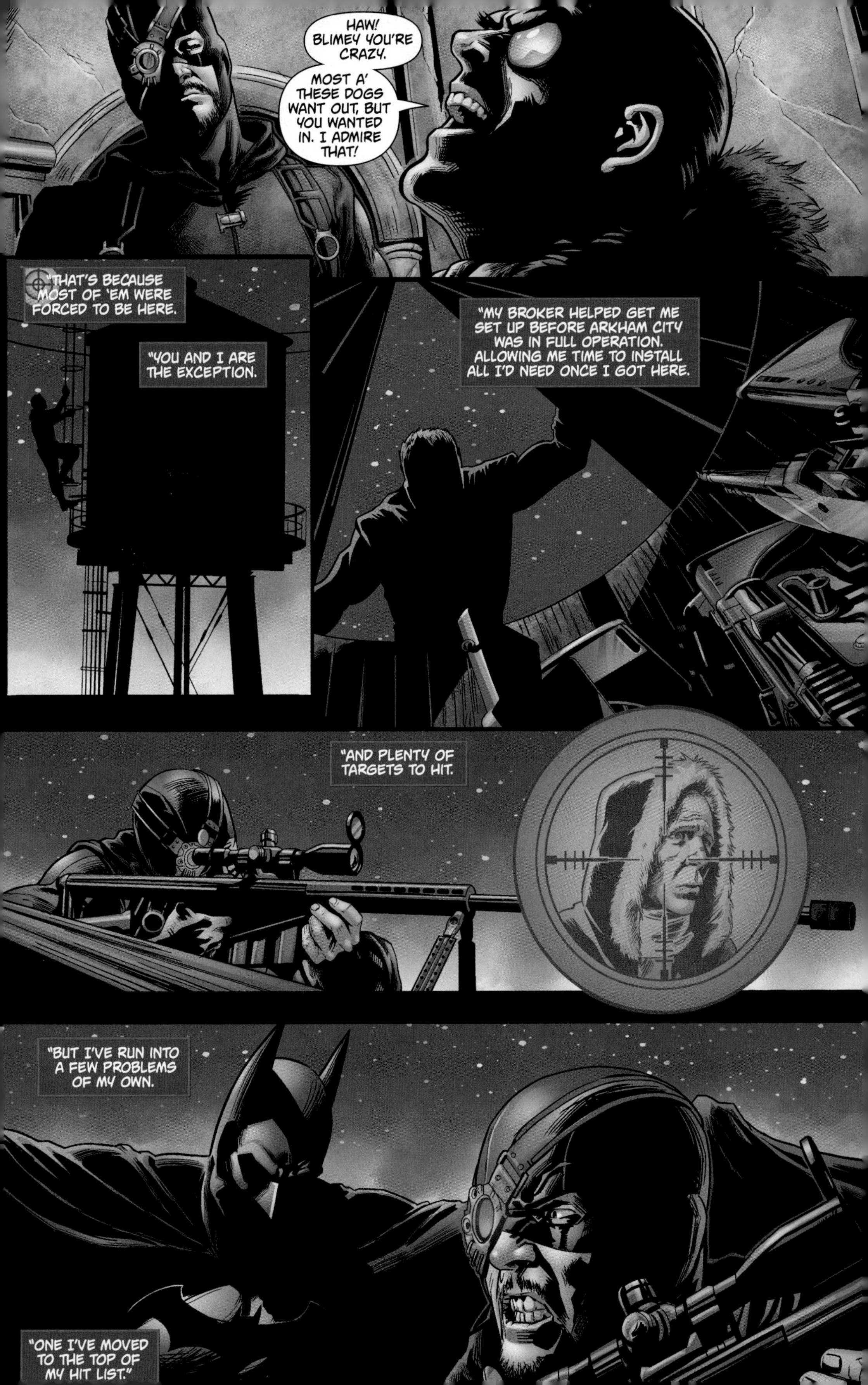
HAW! BLIMEY YOU'RE CRAZY.
MOST A' THESE DOGS WANT OUT, BUT YOU WANTED IN. I ADMIRE THAT!
"THAT'S BECAUSE MOST OF 'EM WERE FORCED TO BE HERE.
"YOU AND I ARE THE EXCEPTION.
"MY BROKER HELPED GET ME SET UP BEFORE ARKHAM CITY WAS IN FULL OPERATION. ALLOWING ME TIME TO INSTALL ALL I'D NEED ONCE I GOT HERE.
"AND PLENTY OF TARGETS TO HIT.
"BUT I'VE RUN INTO A FEW PROBLEMS OF MY OWN.
"ONE I'VE MOVED TO THE TOP OF MY HIT LIST."

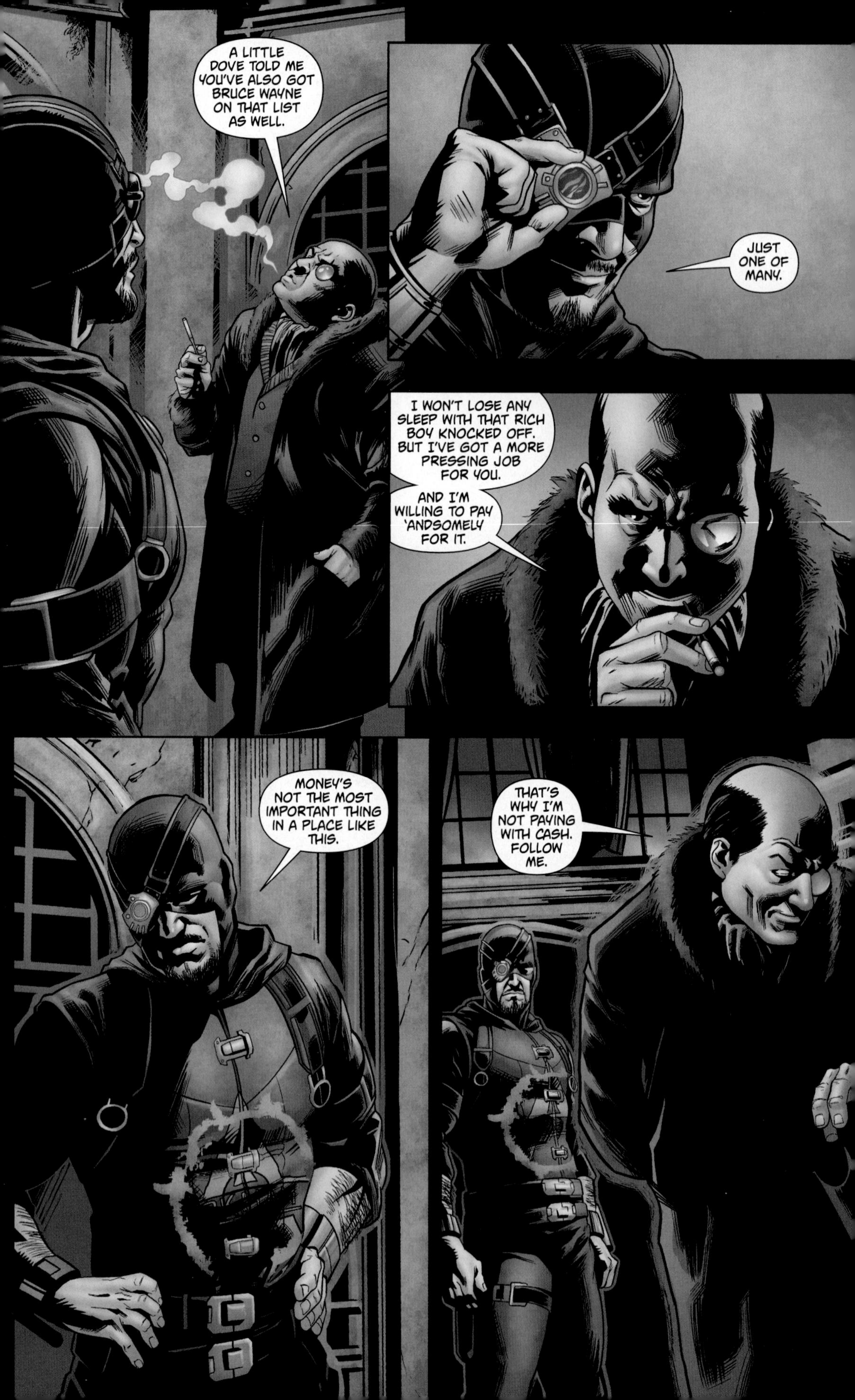
A LITTLE DOVE TOLD ME YOU'VE ALSO GOT BRUCE WAYNE ON THAT LIST AS WELL.
JUST ONE OF MANY.
I WON'T LOSE ANY SLEEP WITH THAT RICH BOY KNOCKED OFF. BUT I'VE GOT A MORE PRESSING JOB FOR YOU.
AND I'M WILLING TO PAY 'ANDSOMELY FOR IT.
MONEY'S NOT THE MOST IMPORTANT THING IN A PLACE LIKE THIS.
THAT'S WHY I'M NOT PAYING WITH CASH. FOLLOW ME.

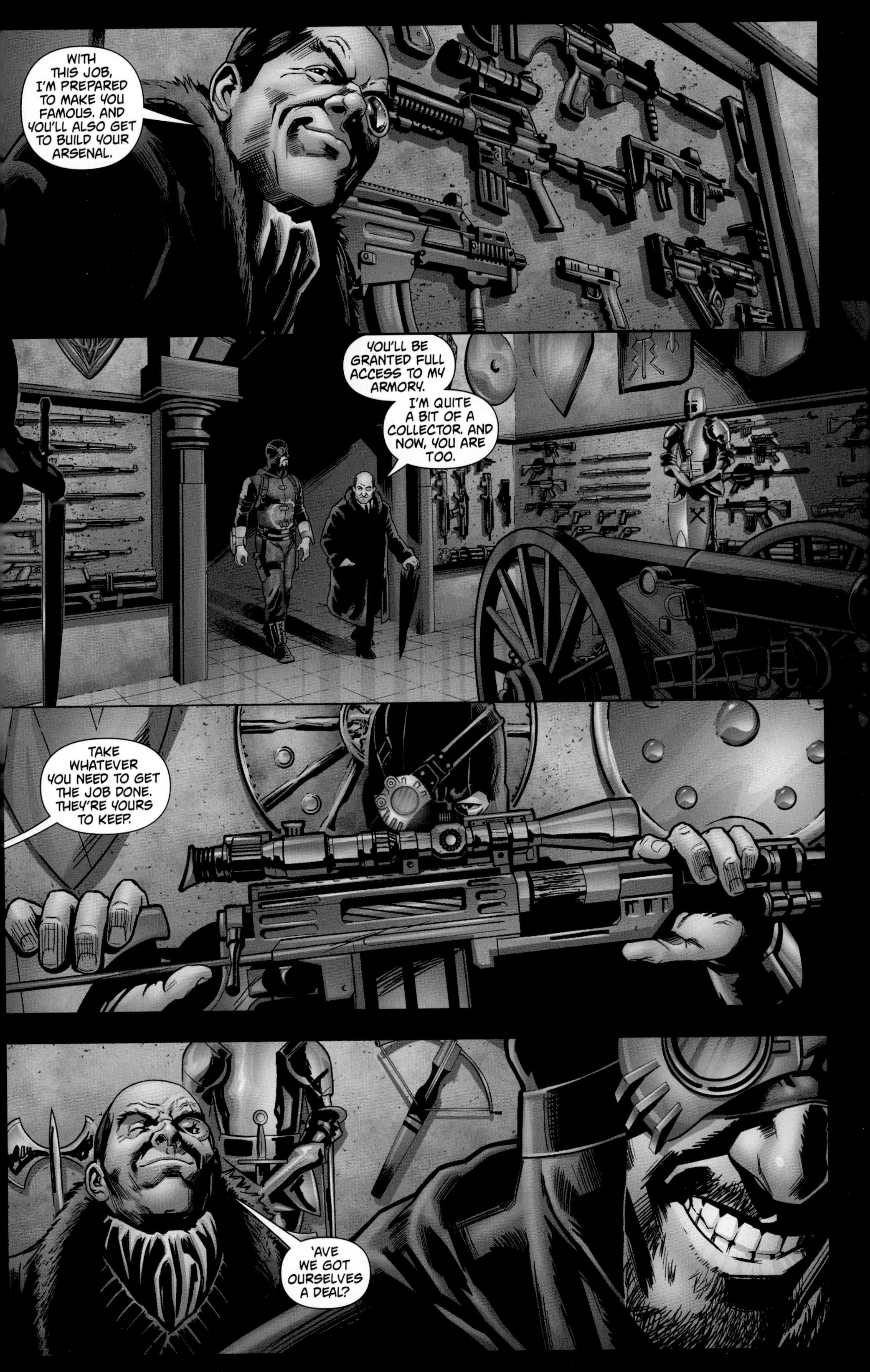
WITH THIS JOB, I'M PREPARED TO MAKE YOU FAMOUS. AND YOU'LL ALSO GET TO BUILD YOUR ARSENAL.
YOU'LL BE GRANTED FULL ACCESS TO MY ARMORY.
I'M QUITE A BIT OF A COLLECTOR. AND NOW, YOU ARE TOO.
TAKE WHATEVER YOU NEED TO GET THE JOB DONE. THEY'RE YOURS TO KEEP.
'AVE WE GOT OURSELVES A DEAL?

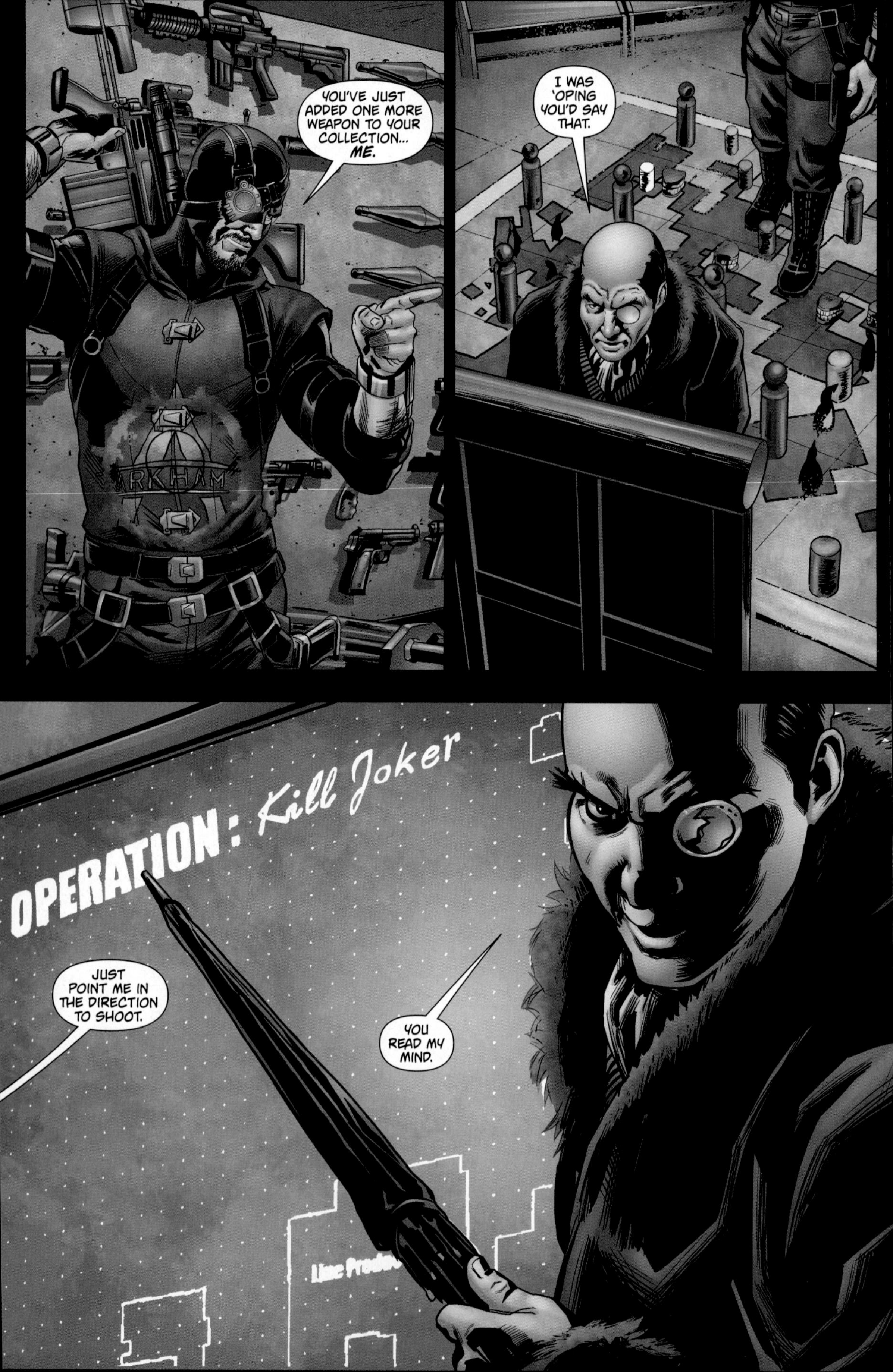
YOU'VE JUST ADDED ONE MORE WEAPON TO YOUR COLLECTION... ME.
I WAS 'OPING YOU'D SAY THAT.
OPERATION : Kill Joker
JUST POINT ME IN THE DIRECTION TO SHOOT.
YOU READ MY MIND.

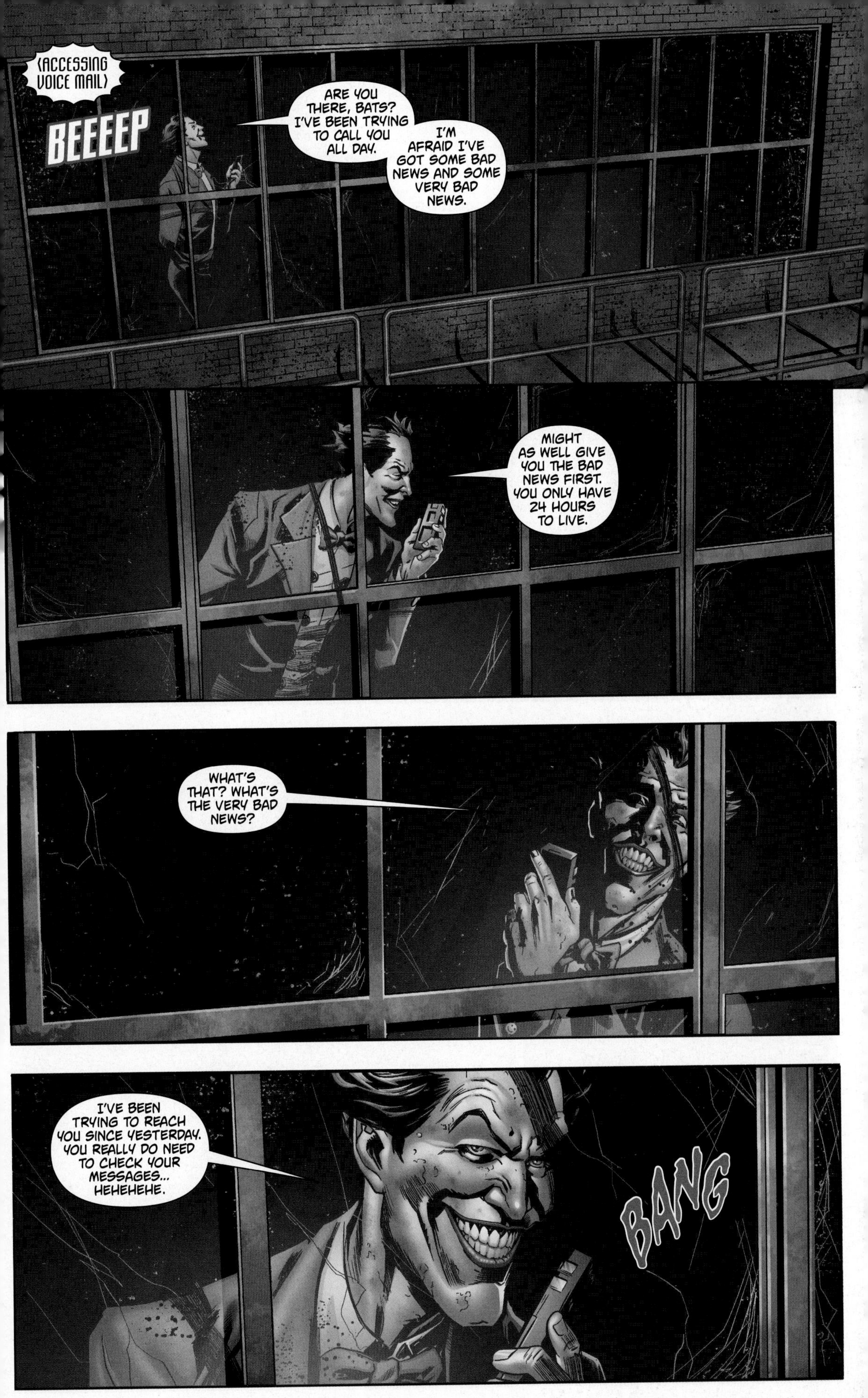
(ACCESSING VOICE MAIL)
BEEEEP
ARE YOU THERE, BATS? I'VE BEEN TRYING TO CALL YOU ALL DAY.
I'M AFRAID I'VE GOT SOME BAD NEWS AND SOME VERY BAD NEWS.
MIGHT AS WELL GIVE YOU THE BAD NEWS FIRST. YOU ONLY HAVE 24 HOURS TO LIVE.
WHAT'S THAT? WHAT'S THE VERY BAD NEWS?
I'VE BEEN TRYING TO REACH YOU SINCE YESTERDAY. YOU REALLY DO NEED TO CHECK YOUR MESSAGES... HEHEHEHE.
BANG

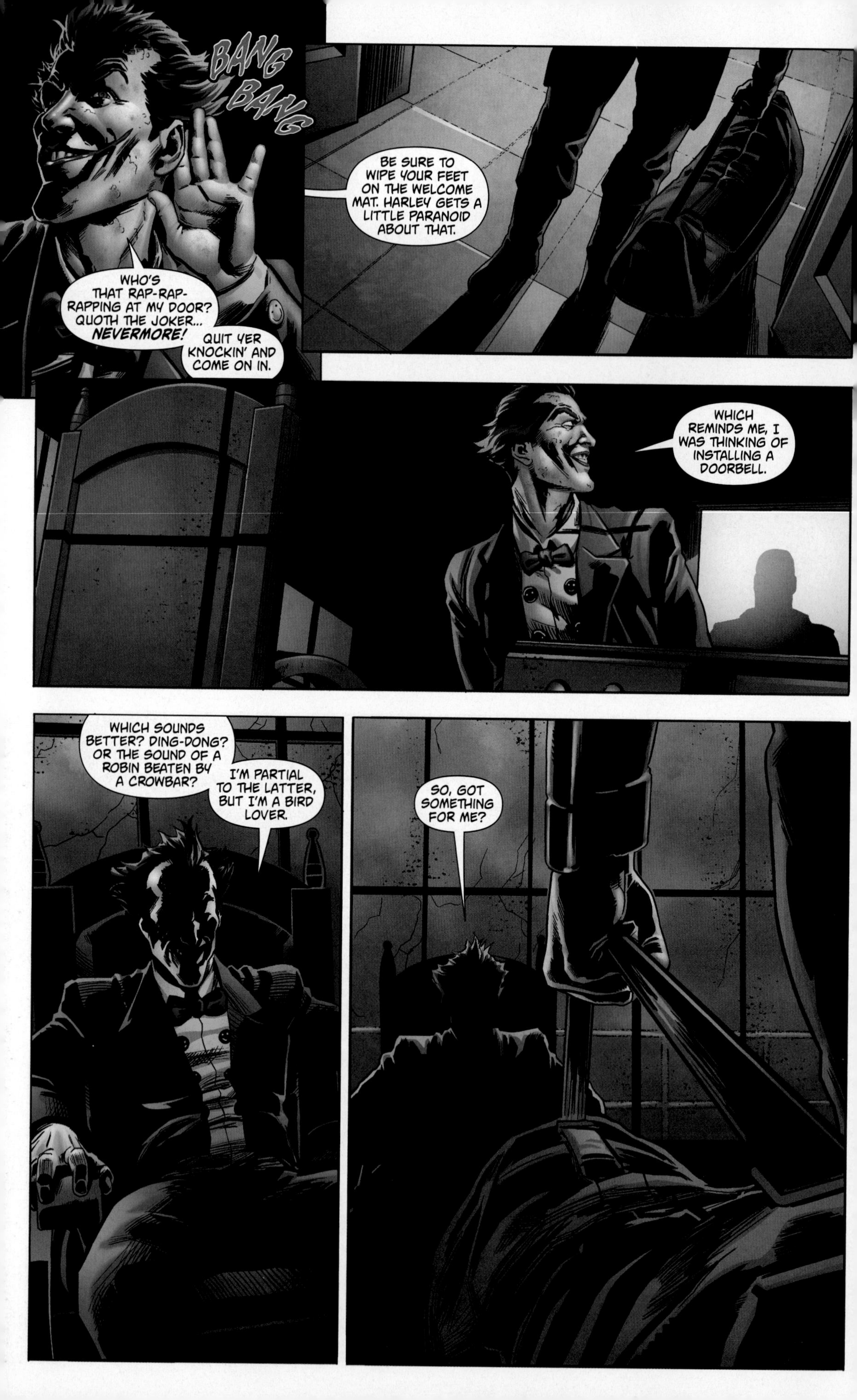
BANG
BANG
WHO'S THAT RAP-RAP-RAPPING AT MY DOOR? QUOTH THE JOKER... NEVERMORE!
QUIT YER KNOCKIN' AND COME ON IN.
BE SURE TO WIPE YOUR FEET ON THE WELCOME MAT. HARLEY GETS A LITTLE PARANOID ABOUT THAT.
WHICH REMINDS ME, I WAS THINKING OF INSTALLING A DOORBELL.
WHICH SOUNDS BETTER? DING-DONG? OR THE SOUND OF A ROBIN BEATEN BY A CROWBAR?
I'M PARTIAL TO THE LATTER, BUT I'M A BIRD LOVER.
SO, GOT SOMETHING FOR ME?

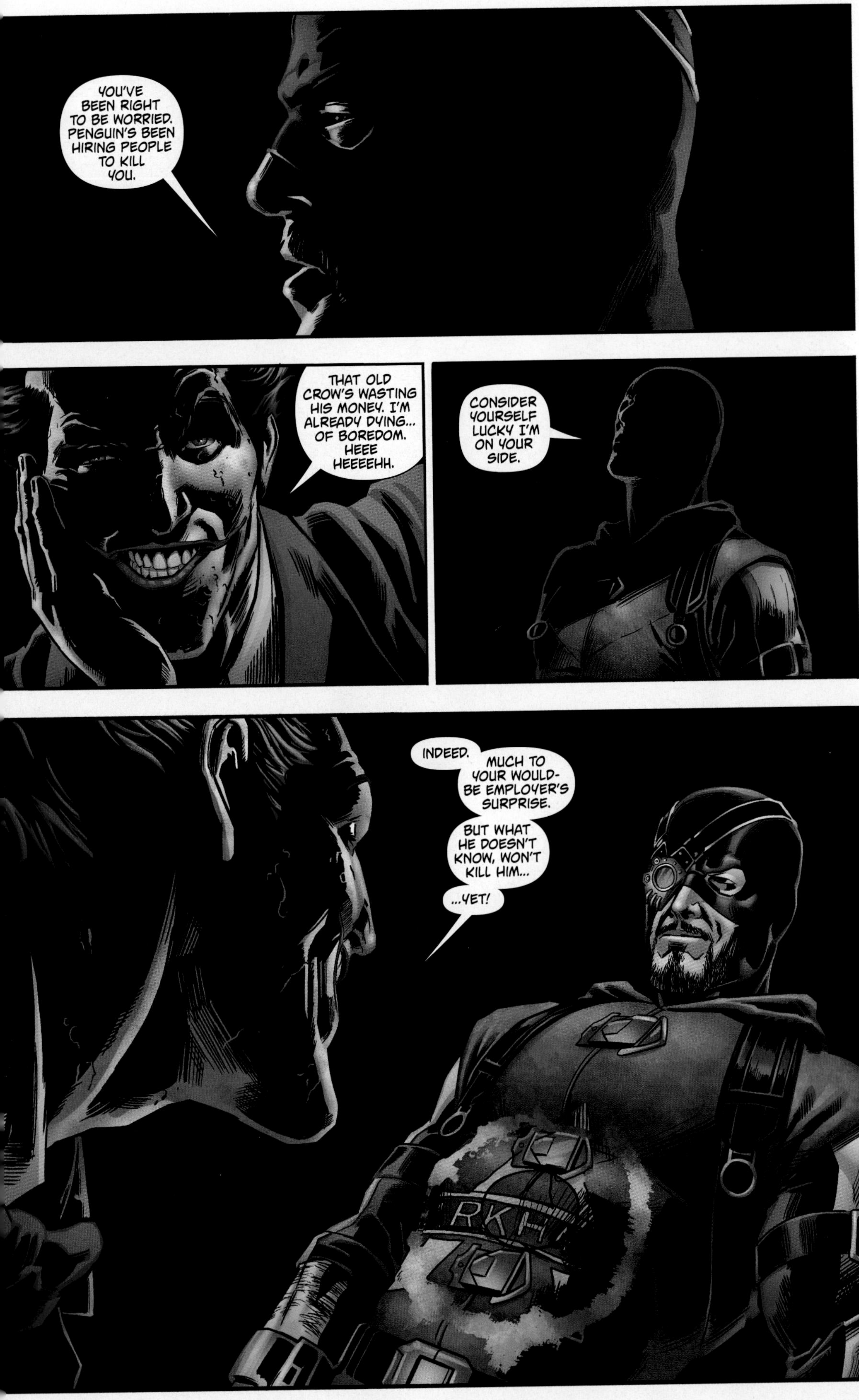
YOU'VE BEEN RIGHT TO BE WORRIED. PENGUIN'S BEEN HIRING PEOPLE TO KILL YOU.
THAT OLD CROW'S WASTING HIS MONEY. I'M ALREADY DYING... OF BOREDOM. HEEE HEEEEHH.
CONSIDER YOURSELF LUCKY I'M ON YOUR SIDE.
INDEED.
MUCH TO YOUR WOULD-BE EMPLOYER'S SURPRISE.
BUT WHAT HE DOESN'T KNOW, WON'T KILL HIM...
...YET!
RKH

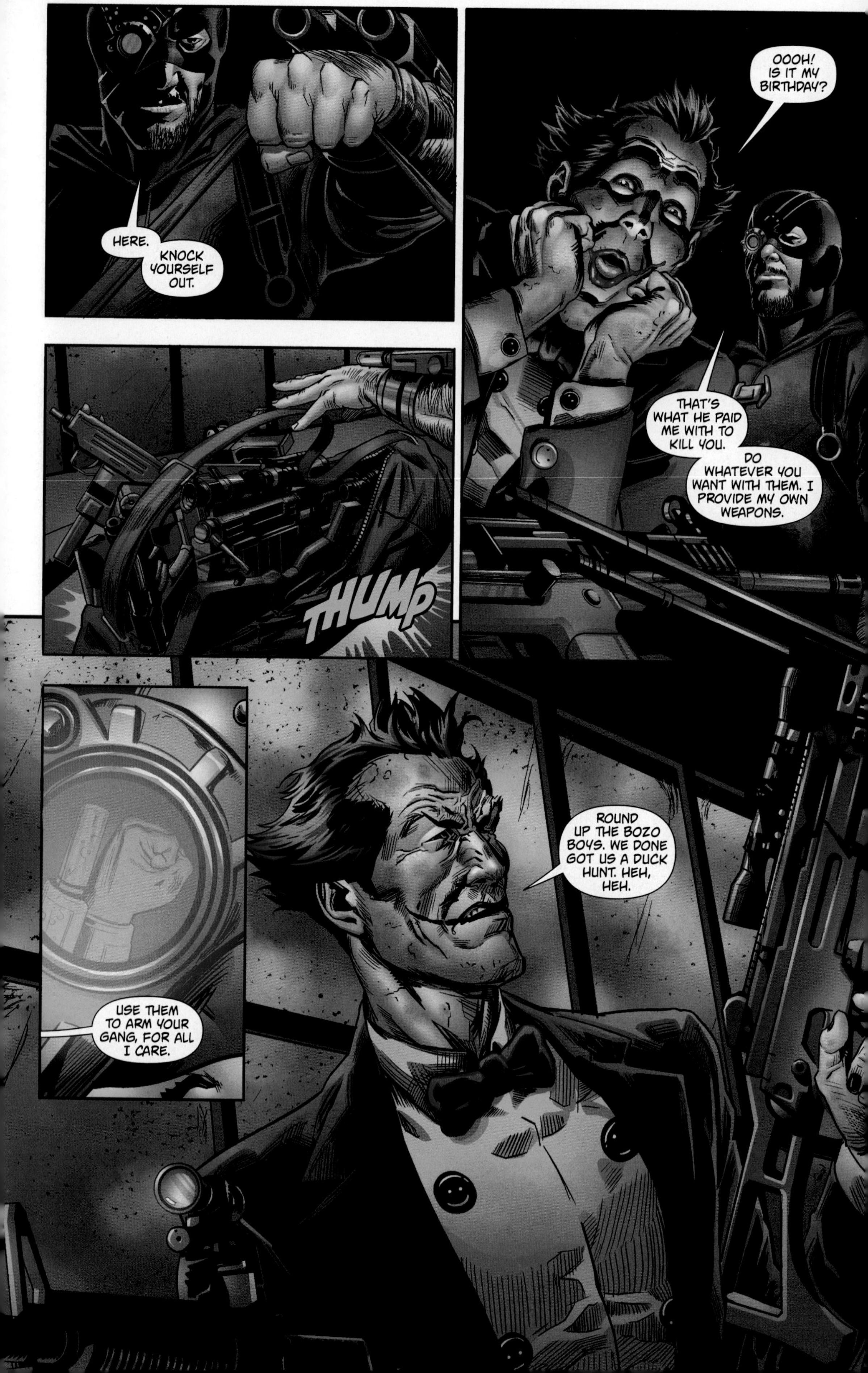
HERE.
KNOCK YOURSELF OUT.
OOOH! IS IT MY BIRTHDAY?
THUMP
THAT'S WHAT HE PAID ME WITH TO KILL YOU.
DO WHATEVER YOU WANT WITH THEM. I PROVIDE MY OWN WEAPONS.
USE THEM TO ARM YOUR GANG, FOR ALL I CARE.
ROUND UP THE BOZO BOYS. WE DONE GOT US A DUCK HUNT. HEH, HEH.

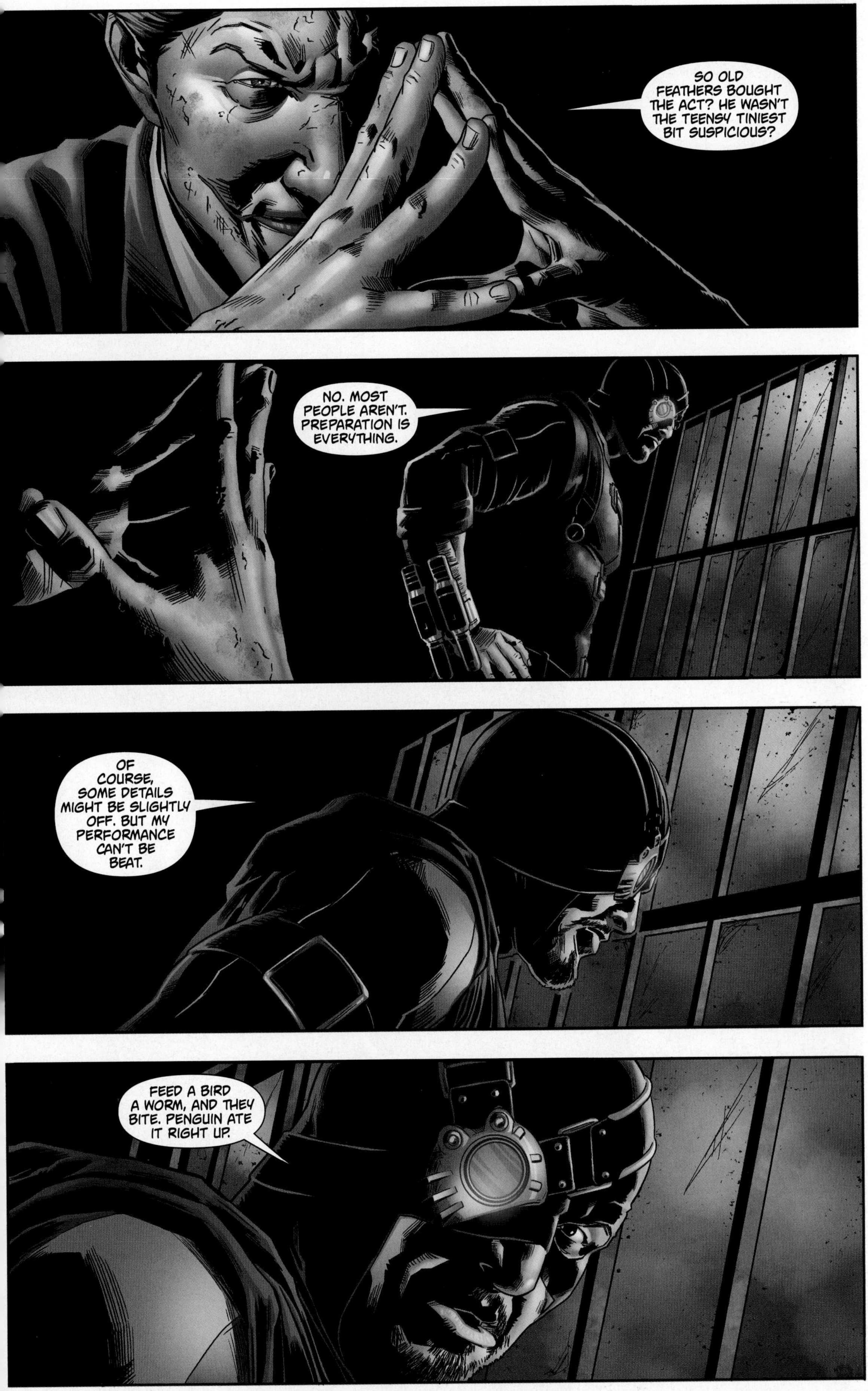
SO OLD FEATHERS BOUGHT THE ACT? HE WASN'T THE TEENSY TINIEST BIT SUSPICIOUS?
NO. MOST PEOPLE AREN'T. PREPARATION IS EVERYTHING.
OF COURSE, SOME DETAILS MIGHT BE SLIGHTLY OFF. BUT MY PERFORMANCE CAN'T BE BEAT.
FEED A BIRD A WORM, AND THEY BITE. PENGUIN ATE IT RIGHT UP.

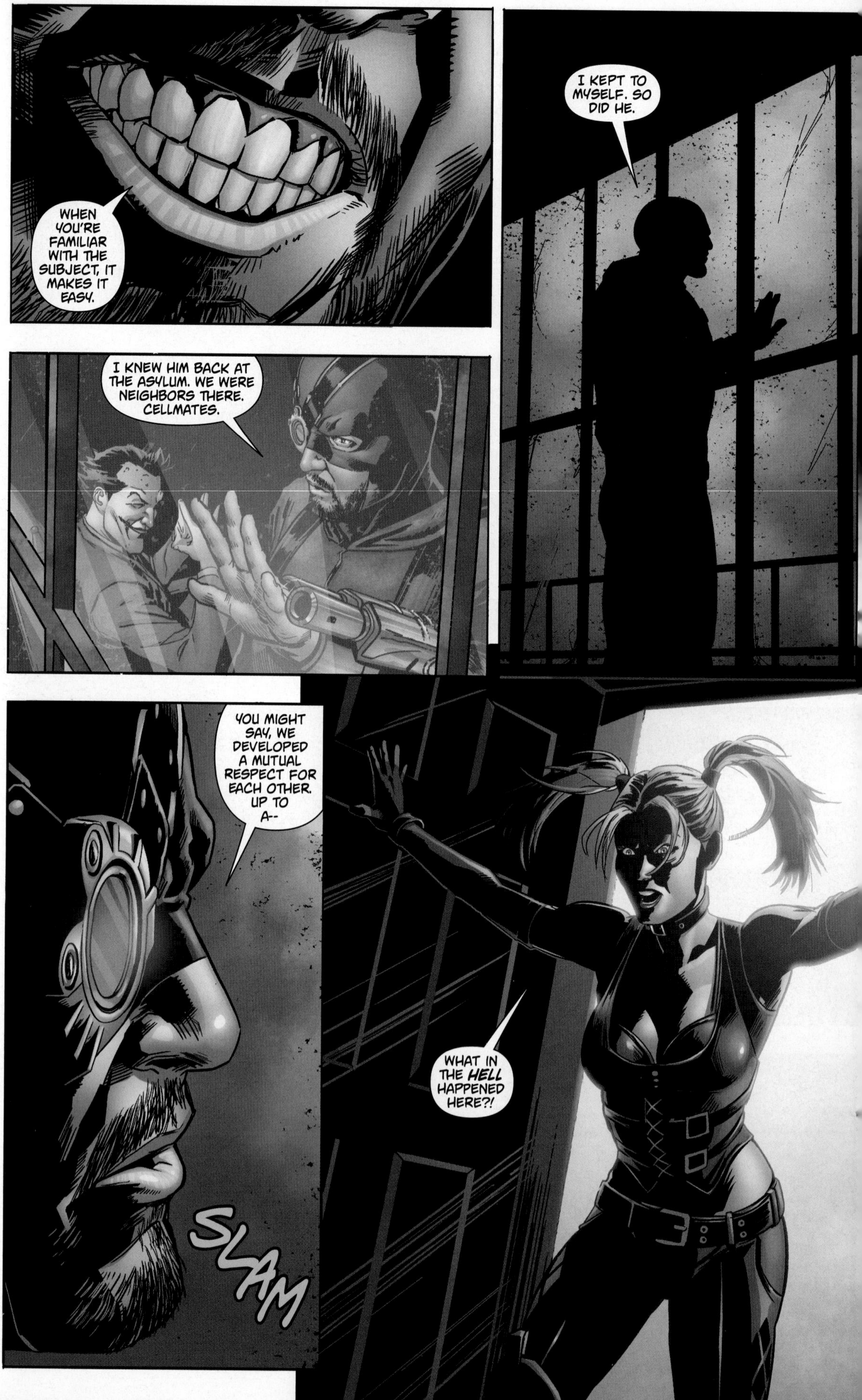
WHEN YOU'RE FAMILIAR WITH THE SUBJECT, IT MAKES IT EASY.
I KEPT TO MYSELF. SO DID HE.
I KNEW HIM BACK AT THE ASYLUM. WE WERE NEIGHBORS THERE. CELLMATES.
YOU MIGHT SAY, WE DEVELOPED A MUTUAL RESPECT FOR EACH OTHER. UP TO A--
SLAM
WHAT IN THE *HELL* HAPPENED HERE?!

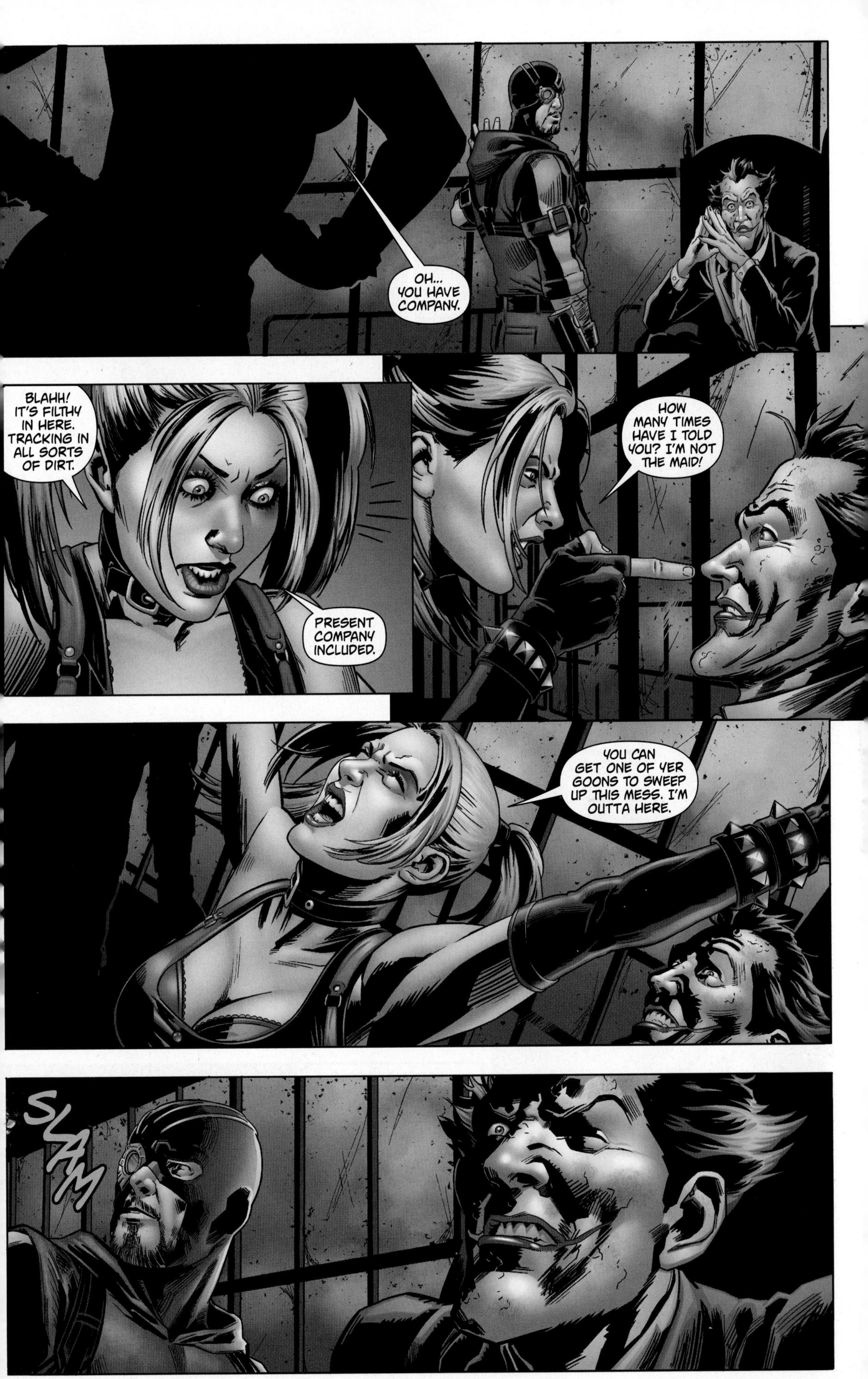
OH... YOU HAVE COMPANY.
BLAHH! IT'S FILTHY IN HERE. TRACKING IN ALL SORTS OF DIRT.
PRESENT COMPANY INCLUDED.
HOW MANY TIMES HAVE I TOLD YOU? I'M NOT THE MAID!
YOU CAN GET ONE OF YER GOONS TO SWEEP UP THIS MESS. I'M OUTTA HERE.
SLAM

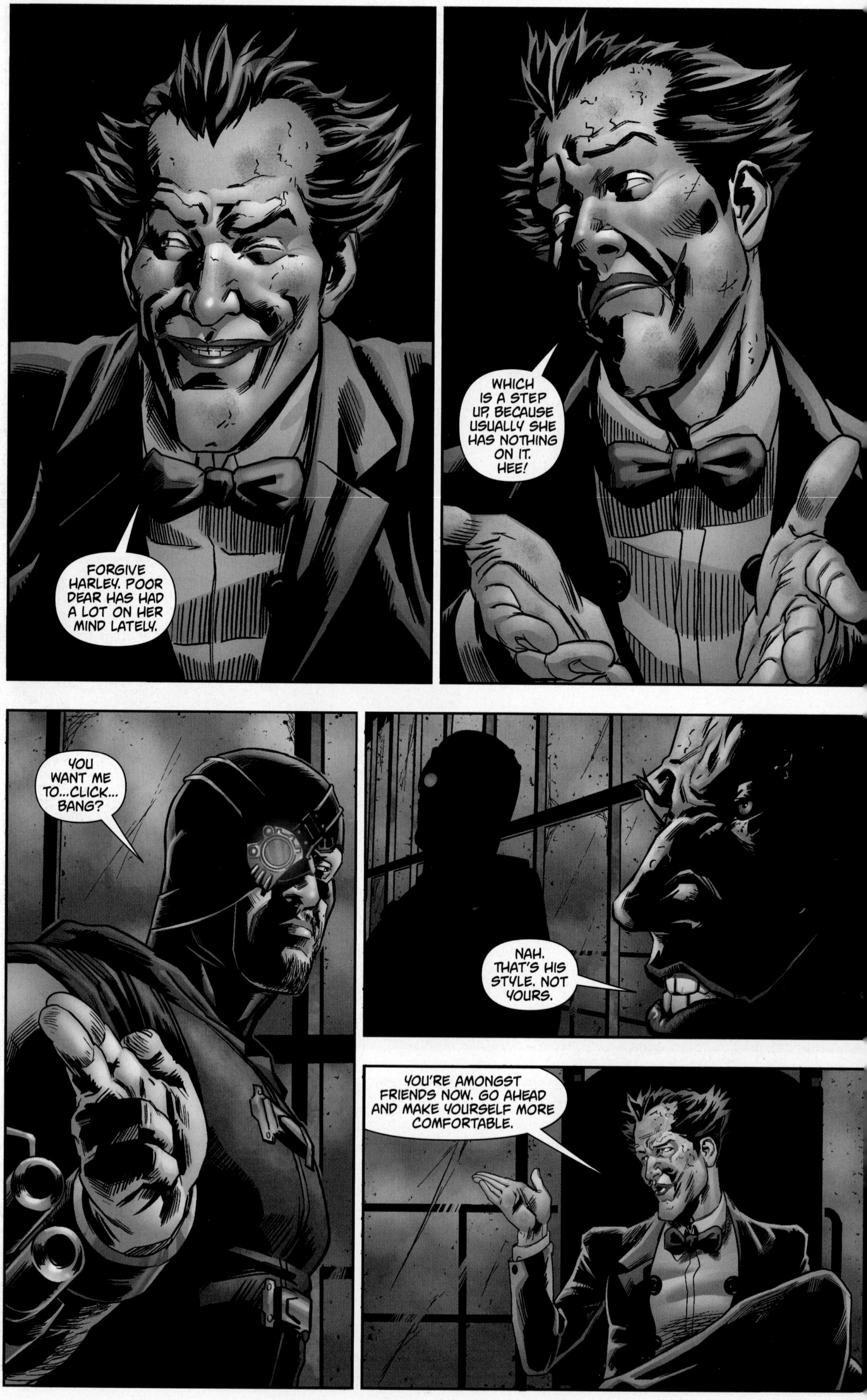
FORGIVE HARLEY. POOR DEAR HAS HAD A LOT ON HER MIND LATELY.
WHICH IS A STEP UP, BECAUSE USUALLY SHE HAS NOTHING ON IT. HEE!
YOU WANT ME TO...CLICK... BANG?
NAH. THAT'S HIS STYLE. NOT YOURS.
YOU'RE AMONGST FRIENDS NOW. GO AHEAD AND MAKE YOURSELF MORE COMFORTABLE.

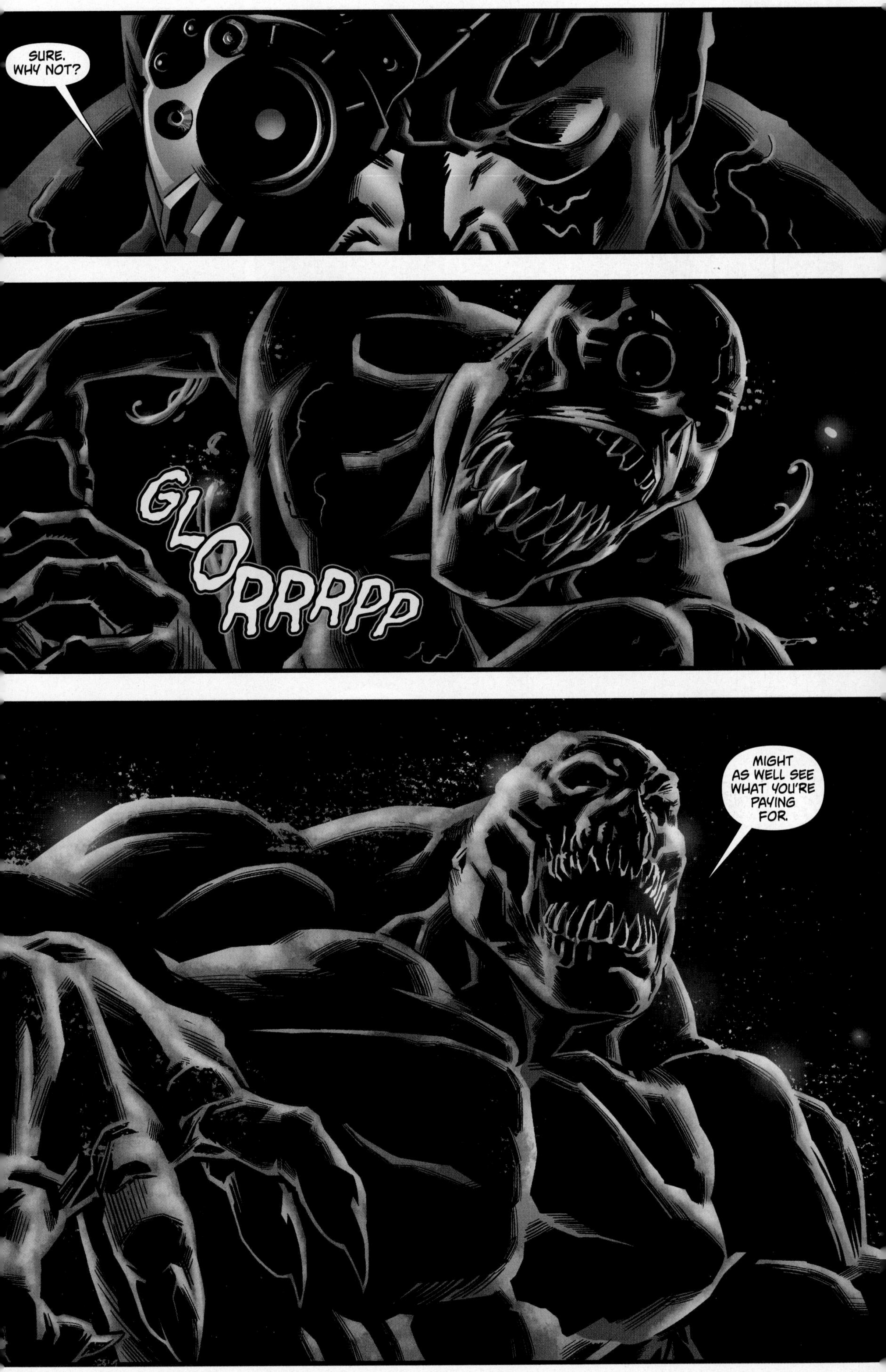
SURE. WHY NOT?
GLORRRPP
MIGHT AS WELL SEE WHAT YOU'RE PAYING FOR.

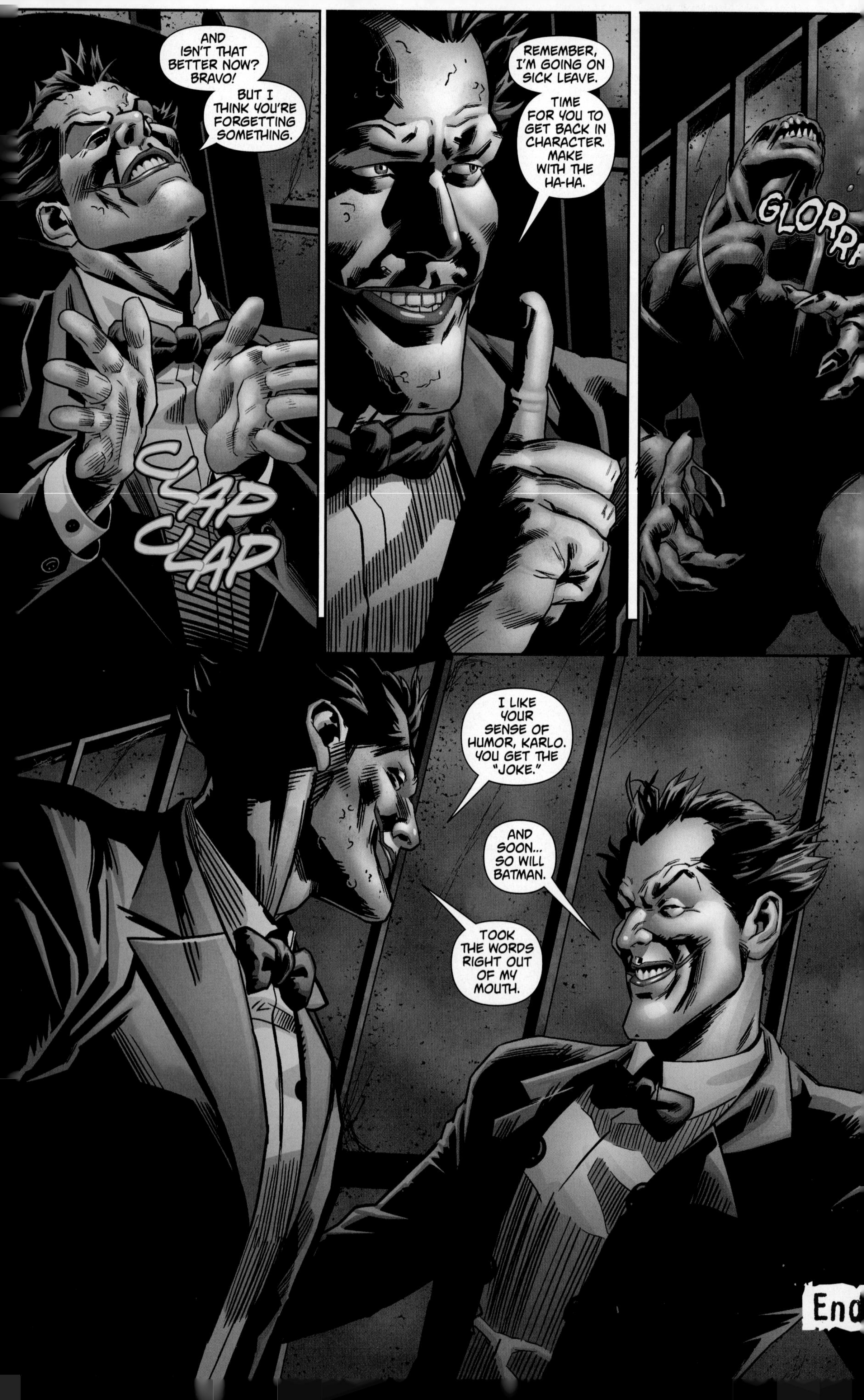
AND ISN'T THAT BETTER NOW? BRAVO!
BUT I THINK YOU'RE FORGETTING SOMETHING.
CLAP CLAP
REMEMBER, I'M GOING ON SICK LEAVE.
TIME FOR YOU TO GET BACK IN CHARACTER. MAKE WITH THE HA-HA.
GLORR
I LIKE YOUR SENSE OF HUMOR, KARLO. YOU GET THE "JOKE."
AND SOON... SO WILL BATMAN.
TOOK THE WORDS RIGHT OUT OF MY MOUTH.
End

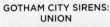

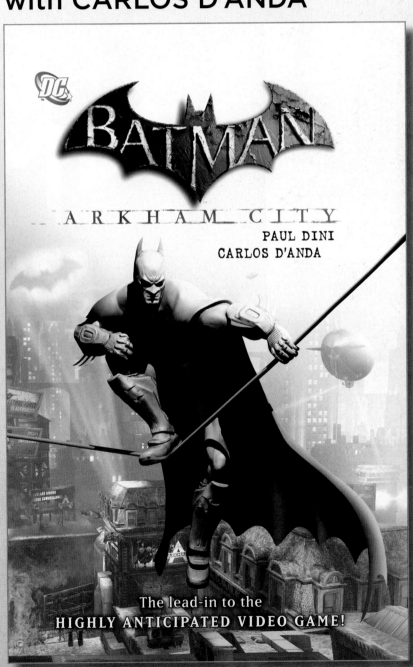

"A stunning debut. This is definitely in the top rank of the revamp."
—THE ONION / AV CLUB

"Snyder and Capullo reach new heights of collaboration here, with Capullo making inspired storytelling choices that add additional layers to Snyder's narration and dialog."
—VANITY FAIR

START AT THE BEGINNING!

BATMAN VOLUME 1: THE COURT OF OWLS

BATMAN & ROBIN VOLUME 1: BORN TO KILL

BATMAN: DETECTIVE COMICS VOLUME 1: FACES OF DEATH

BATMAN: THE DARK KNIGHT VOLUME 1: KNIGHT TERRORS

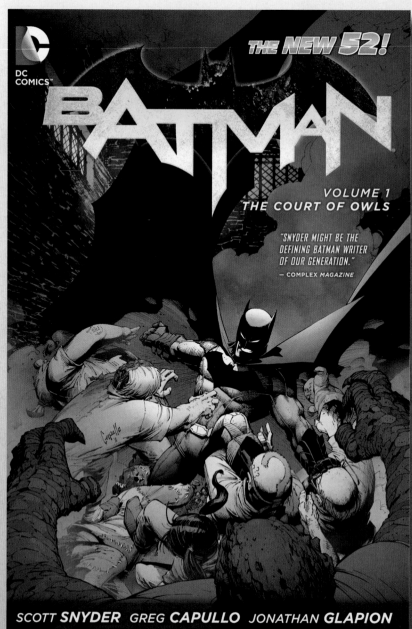

DC COMICS™

START AT THE BEGINNING!

NIGHTWING VOLUME 1: TRAPS AND TRAPEZES

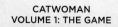

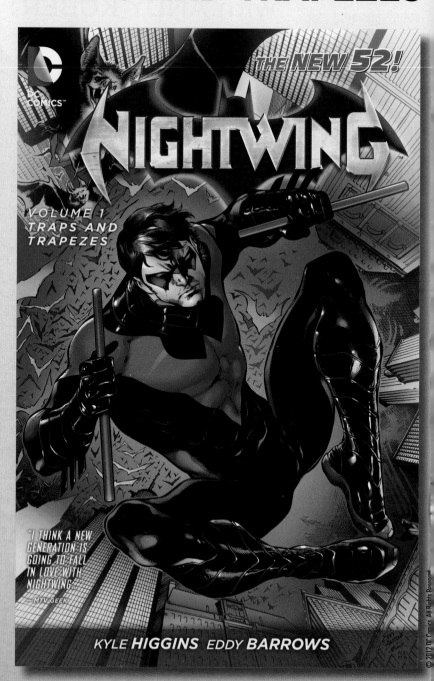

KYLE **HIGGINS** EDDY **BARROWS**